25 00

THE RULE OF SAINT BENEDICT
A DOCTRINAL AND SPIRITUAL COMMENTARY

CISTERCIAN STUDIES SERIES: NUMBER FIFTY–FOUR

THE RULE OF SAINT BENEDICT
A Doctrinal and Spiritual Commentary

by
Adalbert de Vogüé
Monk of La Pierre-qui-vire

Translated by
John Baptist Hasbrouck
Monk of Our Lady of Guadalupe Abbey

Cistercian Publications
Kalamazoo, Michigan
1983

Translated from the French original,
La Règle de saint Benoît, VII,
Commentaire doctrinal et spirituel
(Paris: Les éditions du Cerf, 1977)

Library of Congress Cataloging in Publication Data
Vogüé, Adalbert de.
   The Rule of Saint Benedict, a doctrinal and spiritual commentary.

   (Cistercian studies series; 54)
   Translation of: La règle de saint Benoît, commentaire doctrinal et spirituel, originally
published as v. 7 of La règle de saint Benoît. Paris: Editions du Cerf, 1971–
   Bibliography: p. 331
   Includes indexes.
   1. Benedict, Saint, Abbot of Monte Cassino. Regula. 2. Monasticism and religious
orders—Rules. I. Benedict, Saint, Abbot of Monte Cassino. Regula. French & Latin. Vogüé.
I. Title. II. Series.
   BX3004.Z5V6313   1983   255'.106   82-9738
   ISBN 0-87907-854-5

TABLE OF CONTENTS

vi   *Contents*

INTRODUCTION

THIS VOLUME is at one and the same time the last of a long series and an independent, self-sufficient work. Begun some twenty years ago, our research into the Benedictine Rule was concentrated at first on eighteen chapters which specifically treat the monastic community and its leader, the abbot.[1] In this first work, we made both a critical investigation into and a doctrinal reflection on each chapter or section of the Rule. This twofold effort was made possible by the limited scope of the texts chosen. But when we undertook a general commentary on the Rule, we were obliged to give up this simultaneous, two-level exegesis. The critical problem posed by contrasting/confronting Benedict and the Master was of such breadth that we were forced to devote ourselves entirely to that. Postponing until later, then, the doctrinal commentary which was the real purpose of our efforts, we wrote an historical and critical commentary in three volumes, attaching them to the edition of the Rule in the series Sources Chrétiennes.[2]

It has been only since finishing this lengthy seven year task that we have been able to take up again work on the text from a loftier perspective and to prepare the present volume of spiritual commentary. In it we have picked up one of the two threads which ran throughout *Community and Abbot.* For all that, we repeat, the present work is no simple continuation of the other. Unlike 'the historical and critical commentary' which leaves aside the eighteen chapters already studied in *Community and Abbot,* this 'doctrinal and spiritual commentary' encompasses the entire Rule, including the sections commented upon in our first work. Then, too, in referring frequently to the previous work, what is here appears as a relatively self-contained and complete whole.

As in our previous volumes, we have not limited ourselves to comment-

1

ing on the text chapter by chapter. However, a glance at the table of contents will show the reader that we have followed Benedict's ordering closely. By means of certain regroupings, his Prologue and seventy-three chapters are studied in twenty-two sections of very varied length. Sometimes one chapter of the Rule is the object of an entire section, sometimes several neighboring or connected chapters are commented upon together.[3] Some chapters do not appear in the titles of our sections or in the table which shows these titles, either because we have spoken about them abundantly in several places—such is the case for the admirable treatise on Lent [4]—or because they are lesser chapters which we cite in passing here or there.[5] An index of references will let the reader find the mention of these texts apparently omitted by our commentary. However, they are very few.

What do 'doctrinal and spiritual' mean? First of all, it is a matter of confronting the Rule with its inspiration, Scripture. Since all patristic thought is situated at the intersection of human experience and reflection upon the Bible, the first task of the interpreter is to set forth clearly the scriptural texts which form the web, and to examine how they attract and repel each other, complete and correct each other in the mind of the author. These scriptural sources are more or less manifest. Aside from formal citations and transparent allusions, he must be attentive to simple reminiscences and to the slightest echoes, doubtless scarcely conscious but none the less significant for all that. Sometimes the Bibical root is no longer apparent in the abridgement that the Benedictine Rule is, and it is only in a text of the Master, completely omitted or too abridged by Benedict, that it can be discovered.[6] In certain cases the Master himself does not reveal his scriptural source at first glance, but a further investigation will discover it in the spiritual and institutional tradition on which he depends.[7]

Nothing is more enlightening that this search for the word of God underlying monastic maxims and observances. More than once it reveals the continuous chain that binds our Rule, through the writings of the Fathers, to the teaching of the New and Old Testament. In other cases the influence of Scripture is not exercised through a literary tradition but directly, with Benedict drawing on the treasure of the sacred books quite independently. But no matter how he approaches scripture, Benedict's interpretation is rarely enclosed within the exact limits of the inspired text.

His fidelity is not without liberty, and his dependence goes beyond the limits of the text. While monasticism bases itself upon Scripture, it makes its own building rise to another level. The interpreter should first discern the scriptural base, and then—and this is not the least interesting part of his work—he should recognize this different level on which is located the monastic storey built upon it.

In other words, he should measure exactly the distance between the sacred text and what the Rule drew from it. Not that the modern exegete has to criticize this use which the ancients made of Scripture, from the point of view of his own Biblical science. It is only a question of confronting the monastic interpretation with the obvious sense of the inspired text, as it could have appeared—and sometimes did appear in fact—to the author's contemporaries, when it was not read under the influence of some particular preoccupation.

Sometimes a vestige of secular wisdom is perceived amid these traces of the Bible, but most often the author's mind seems possessed only with thoughts coming from Revelation. In order to understand his language, we must search for its references, first of all, if not exclusively, in the concepts and institutions of the Christian faith: Church and sacraments, Scripture and tradition, teaching authority and hierarchy, divine word and grace, virginal consecration and martyrdom. The analogies of this monasticism with those of the pagan Orient, in which there is so much interest these days, should not let the author's unconditional adherence to the Church of Christ be forgotten.

This primordial consideration of the relation of the Rule to the Bible implies, as we have just seen, a constant attention to the texts of the Fathers and of previous monks, in which is deployed, and sometimes unveiled, the scriptural vein which runs through our text. Benedict's work is inseparable from all this literature. Since it is in large part composed of extracts and summaries of an earlier Rule, it can only be understood in reference to it, and that is why the present commentary will be as much concerned with the Master as with Benedict. In addition, Benedict's sobriety obliges us to search in different places for the explanations which he does not give. This search is aroused and guided by Benedict himself, whose last chapter contains its well-known recommendations, and therefore the search bears naturally in the direction of Basil, Cassian, Augustine, the Rules and Lives of the

Fathers. More than once it brings us face to face not only with instructive parallels but with exact models which have inspired the Rule.

As necessary as the investigation of the Fathers' writings is to see the premises from which Benedict starts, to see what he means and where he is leading us, this investigation is still more necessary inasmuch as our times and culture are more remote from theirs. For lack of knowing this context of patristic thought and primitive monasticism, we are liable to inject our familiar notions into his text and to reduce his discourse to our present-day mental categories.

This harm is felt especially in monastic circles. The monk is dedicated to hearing the Rule frequently, to venerating it and drawing from it a spiritual nourishment for his own life, and so he is particularly exposed to making Benedict his contemporary rather than making himself Benedict's contemporary. The loss that results is not confined to the realm of knowledge. The monastic vocation itself suffers, for what we hear thus is less the provocative and fertilizing message of the Fathers than the echo of our own discourse as modern men.

Also, the discrepancy between present-day monasticism and the Rule will be strongly emphasized in this commentary. By so doing we wish to act not only as a historian but as a monk. While leaving to novice-masters and abbots the care of bringing the two terms together, we shall often place them in contrast. Our aim is not at all to invite the monks of today to estrange themselves from what remains their Rule, but to suggest to them—and to ourselves as well—the effort that must be furnished if we will to be faithful to it.

The fact that the author of this commentary feels himself personally engaged in regard to the text studied, and that in his commentary he thinks of other monks in the same situation, this fact may inspire fears for the scientific quality of his work. Let the reader judge if such conditions have harmed the objectivity. For ourselves, on the contrary, we feel the benefit of a personal relation to that object which incites us to scrutinize it with more energy and penetration. It is not a handicap for the interpreter but a piece of good fortune that he belongs to an institution which claims the Rule today as well as yesterday, and which gives a certain experience, limited but real, of observing it. In order to profit from this advantage without yielding to the temptations of reductionism mentioned above, it suffices that familiarity with the text be accompanied by the resolution, both scientific and religious, to perceive its voice and its demands, even when these latter call in question our usual ideas, when they jar our sensibilities and throw our habits into disarray.

It will be said that such a preoccupation pertains rather to the man of science than to the practical man who is dedicated to living with his time, and who therefore shares its conceptions and follows its norms. Does not the contemporary Church, the mother of the monks of today, impose on us a group of judgments and deportments, a vision of the natural and supernatural order, and an interpretation of the Gospel which are opposed on more than one point to what the Rule teaches, commands or implies? By laying one's finger on these points of opposition, by insisting on the distance which separates us from Benedict and his milieu, does not one lead the reader to the conclusion that Benedict's Rule is unsuitable to our present situation and should therefore be abandoned? The current illusion which makes Benedict seem close to us, has its advantages. To dissipate it is no doubt to perform a work of truth, but one risks estranging the sons from the Father and so making more difficult the 'accommodation' of his heritage to our times, as the recent Council desired.[8]

This problem which arises in almost identical terms in every study of 'Christian sources', is finally that of the relation between the Church of today and the Church of the Fathers, indeed between the two states of humanity to which these two Churches belong. A person might think that the flow of history always draws us further away from the patristic sources. It would be not only a constraining law but a beneficial one as well, the law of progress. For our part, we do not believe that Christian life and thought progress any more—in the qualitative sense of the word—than do the other higher expressions of the human spirit, such as art for example. The theology and spirituality of our time, with their riches and their weaknesses, their values and their limits, show here an advance and there a retreat, so that they make, of course, a quite different figure as a whole, but not a more completed one than that of such and such an epoch in the past. This synthesis which is in perpetual revision, can always integrate new elements rediscovered by the study of preceding syntheses, as it has already done. The drift away from the sources is not a necessity. A recuperation of certain values of the past is possible.

History attests in regard to monastic life what the experience even of our times reveals in other domains. Revivals of monastic life have constantly engendered returns to the primitive observance and ideal. The Benedictine Rule has not been for Western monasticism merely its original legislation, far in the rear, from which one would always move further away. It has remained the ideal which solicits good wills, the reproach which disturbs slothfulness, the program of reforms by which generous communities came close to it again. 'They drank from this spiritual rock which followed them'.[9] This strange image of Israel on pilgrimage, evoked by Saint Paul following a Jewish tradition, expresses quite well what the Rule, like Scripture, has been for monasticism on its journey through history, namely, a spring of water always close, to which it was enough to put out one's hand in order to drink.

The objection will be made that our situation is too far distant from that of the sixth century to allow us to ask anything but inspiration from a document of that epoch. The institutions and observances of the Rule must be renounced for good. We must therefore take the spirit and abandon the letter. The line to follow would be determined by answering the question: 'What would Benedict do today?'

As will be seen, our commentary scarcely enters into this problematic. To us it makes no sense to ask what Benedict would do today. That this man lived in the Italy of the sixth century is not an accident from which we may abstract, and his reincarnation in the twentieth century can be the object of merely chimerical speculations. The only reality we possess is the Rule such as we know it, together with the related documents which allow us to grasp it. This text is a given, which we can take or leave according to whether or not we feel ourselves concerned about its message. If we choose to expose ourselves to its influence, this influence will operate in the exact measure that we can conform ourselves to what it prescribes. Since it is a matter of a rule of life, fidelity to the spirit does not go without a certain observance of the letter.[10] The way of true renewal can only be, we think, that of a literalism that is intelligent, prudent and enlightened by spiritual discernment. Our hope in offering this modest work to our brothers is to serve such a renewal.

NOTES TO THE INTRODUCTION

1. *La Communauté et l'Abbé dans la Règle de saint Benoît* (Paris, 1961). E.T. by Charles Philippi and Ethel Rae Perkins, *Community and Abbot in the Rule of St Benedict*, CS 5/1 (1979)

and CS 5/2 (1983). As the second of these english volumes had not appeared when the present book went to press, we have omitted references to it in the footnotes.

2. *La Règle de saint Benoît*, t. I–II by A. de Vogüé and J. Neufville, *Introduction, Texte, Traduction, Concordance*, Sources chrétiennes 181–182 (Paris, 1971); t. III by J. Neufville, *Instruments pour l'étude de la tradition manuscrite*, Sources chrétiennes 183 (Paris, 1971); t. IV–VI by A. de Vogüé, *Commentaire historique et critique*, Sources chrétiennes 184–186 (Paris, 1971). We shall refer to these volumes only by their number in our edition (t. IV, V, VI).

3. Certain sections overlap so that the same chapter is sometimes considered several times from different points of view.

4. RB 49.

5. Thus RB 50 and 51.

6. Some samples are given in our article 'Per ducatum evangelii. La Règle de Saint Benoît et l'Évangile', *Coll. Cist.* 35 (1973), p. 186–198 (see p. 192–194).

7. Such is the case for the prayer of the hours (*art. cit.* pp. 194–5). The theory of the habit could be added (commentary on RB 55).

8. According to the very title of the Decree '*De accommodata renovatione vitae religiosae (Perfectae caritatis)*'.

9. 1 Co 10,4.

10. We have explained our position on this subject in several articles. See "Notre situation de moines et de moniales au XXe siècle", in *Coll. Cist.* 33 (1971), p. 171–178; "Sub regula vel abbate. Étude sur la signification théologique des règles monastiques anciennes" in *Coll. Cist.* 33 (1971), p. 209–241, specially p. 234–241 (E.T. in *Rule and Life*, Basil Pennington editor, Cistercian Publications, Spencer, Massachusetts (1971), p. 21–63); "Moines aujourd'hui?", in *Benedictina* 19 (1972), p. 227–238 (E.T. in Downside Review, vol. 92, no. 307, (April 1974), 109–119); *La Règle de saint Benoît, Séminaire pour maîtresses des novices cisterciennes*, (Laval, 1972), p. 142–180, specially, p. 142–143. See also the article quoted above (n. 6), specially p. 186–188.

Chapter I

THE MONASTERY AND THE CHURCH
(RB PROLOGUE)

S URVEYING THE LONG PROLOGUE prefixed to his Rule by Benedict, the modern reader gets a surprise. Because this is legislation intended for monks wishing to be perfect disciples of Christ, he would expect to see it introduced by something of a distinctly christian coloring. Yet we must admit that this christian character does not manifest itself with all the evidence we might wish. Christ is named here and there, certainly, notably at the choice places at beginning and end.[1] Certainly, too, the Gospel is mentioned several times,[2] and the words of the Apostles are reproduced, implicitly or explicitly.[3] But these New Testament references are less numerous and less apparent than the Old Testament ones. Anyone seeking the leading thread will soon see that this closely woven web of scriptural texts has for its warp two passages from the psalms (Ps 33:12–16 and Ps 14:1–5). The principal design of the author from the beginning of his text to its end is manifestly to introduce these quotations from the psalms, to present them, to gloss them, to connect them to each other, and to draw a conclusion from them. There is, therefore, at the center of our Prologue a double borrowing from the Old Testament, not to mention the many citations or occasional reminiscences of the psalter, the wisdom books and the prophets.[4] This predominance of the pre-christian is astonishing. Should christian monks base their obedience to Christ chiefly on the Old Testament?

Put like this, the question calls for a double response, which is furnished by an examination of Benedict's literary sources. If we wish to understand his Prologue, we must keep in mind that this section is, in essence, a simple extract from the Rule of the Master. The Master's rule is as a whole three times longer than the benedictine, and it begins with a vast four-part introduction (Prologue, *Thema* or parable of the spring, a commentary on the Lord's Prayer, a commentary on the psalms) which is also about three times longer than our Prologue. The benedictine redaction seems subject, therefore, from its beginning to one major imperative: to reduce the Master's text by two thirds. This result has been gained in the simplest possible way. In a few lines Benedict sums up the first three introductions of the Master,[5] and then reproduces almost without change the last part of the introduction, that is, the commentary on the psalms.[6]

Why he chose this fourth piece in preference to the preceding three we shall see further on. What is important at present is to understand how a christian Rule can begin with a Prologue in which the Old Testament predominates. The reason for this paradox should now be obvious. The benedictine Prologue is only a fragment of a long introduction in which the New Testament had indeed held the preponderant place which belongs to it in all christian legislation. Before commenting on the psalms, the Master had already commented, at much greater length, on the Our Father.[7] This commentary on the Lord's Prayer was itself only a sequel to the parable on the spring, in which the appeal to baptism and the monastic life resounded through the words of Christ in Matthew's Gospel: 'Come to me, all you that labor . . . for my yoke is sweet and my burden light'.[8]

The commentary on the psalms takes on its full meaning only if we reposition it after the two segments centred on the Gospel. Then we see that its only aim is to complete the evocation of baptism and the explanation of the Lord's Prayer. We scrutinize the words of the psalmist in the light of christian revelation preceived both in the rites of the liturgy and in the texts of the New Testament. The evangelical touches in the commentary on the psalms which seemed at first to be secondary regain their primordial importance in this light. By means of them the Master and Benedict draw from the psalms a program of life which is specifically christian.[9]

This first answer can be completed by another consideration which concerns the literary genre of the introductions to both rules. The Master, followed by Benedict, evidently chose a genre that is veiled, poetic, and full of images. Rather than going straight to the realities under discussion and calling them by name, he preferred to suggest them by figures, to speak of them with ambiguous words, and to proceed by allusions and by detours.

This playful manner appears in each of his introductory segments. The Master's Prologue, which has the proposal of the Rule as its purpose, does not pronounce its name (*regula*) until the end, after having led the reader for a long time in a sort of sacred fog in which this modest writing tends to get confused with Holy Scripture. The *Thema* which follows presents itself at first as a 'parable' and indeed answers to this name by its allegorical character. In it sinful humanity is represented by a caravan of exhausted travellers, the Gospel by a voice ringing out unexpectedly, and baptism by a spring discovered to the right of the road. And although it deals with entry into the monastery from that point on, the Master restrains himself from writing the name quickly. It is only after a long explanation of the Lord's Prayer and the psalms, in which the monastic life is everywhere envisaged but barely suggested, that he decides, in the act of concluding, to release the word *monasterium*.[10]

This decision to communicate by hints accounts partially for the phenomenon we are considering here. It would have been easy, no doubt too easy by our author's taste, to have given immediately the foundations of the monastic life as they can be found in the Gospel and the writings of the apostles. To so direct a presentation, the Master preferred a roundabout way, as was his habit. To tell the truth, neither time nor place were lacking to him. Since he was preparing to write the longest monastic rule that christian antiquity has bequeathed to us, he needed feel no pressure to declare the fundamental maxims of the New Testament in their proper terms. The later parts of his work would do this, each in its turn and at leisure. For this introduction to the matter, he wished rather to awaken the attention, to stimulate the curiosity, and to excite the appetite by suggesting christian realities by Old Testament words.

Thus we can explain the fact that the fourth and last introductory segment in which the Master intends 'to treat the works of our service'[11] and to propose a definition of the monastery, returns to the Old Testament after the parable of baptism and the explanation of the Lord's Prayer. This return is all the more singular at first sight in that it is accompanied by a correlative decline in regard to spiritual realities themselves. After the Lord's Prayer has proclaimed us sons of God, the commentary on the psalms seems to treat us as servants.[12] But this double regression to the Old Testament and to a servile condition is easily understood in the perspective of the game we have just discovered. Let us not seek here a

logical or an historical order. The author is only choosing to employ a
pedagogical procedure familiar to the Fathers,[13] that of recognizing christian reality in the shadows and figures of the Old Law.

Moreover, it is possible that the Master in this process was complying
with certain rites of the baptismal catechesis. The presentation of the *Our
Father* either before or after baptism, was usual in christian initation, and
the presentation of the psalms, though rarer, to be sure, is nevertheless attested by several documents. In commenting on the psalms after the
Lord's Prayer, the Master was perhaps conforming to a liturgical *ordo* in
force in his own Church or in that of the place from which came the literary sources on which he drew.[14] This would explain the curious passage
from the New Testament to the Old which we observe in him. The order
would be one of decreasing urgency. First of all, the prayer of Christ must
be expounded to the neophytes; then some psalms are explained to them.

But this liturgical substratum, far from contradicting our inductions
about the game the Master is playing, confirms them. Here again he is
playing games. Everything leads us to believe that the long baptismal
homily which is developed in the three sections of the *Thema* is a simple
fiction.[15] In reality, it is not delivered or set in writing for the newly baptized. In vain does the Master present baptism as a quite recent event and
lead the hearers directly from the baptismal fonts to the door of the monastery: this presentation surely corresponds to no concrete situation.
Thus the scriptural game we have just analyzed would have as its counterpart a literary game, and the apparent return to the Old Testament would
tend only to complete the imaginary evocation of a sermon addressed to
neophytes.

We see then the source of the Old Testament presentation of the last
segment of the Master's introduction. But why did Benedict treat it in a
privileged way, almost completely reproducing it, unlike the three preceding pieces? The reason is doubtless that the commentary on the psalms
contains the principal phrase to which the whole of the Master's discourse
was leading: 'We must therefore establish a school of the Lord's
service'.[16] It is not, as we shall see, that Benedict was particularly interested in this definition of the monastery as 'a school of the Lord's service'.
He is fairly indifferent to the term *scola*. But he could not avoid seeing that
these words were the climax of his predecessor's whole introduction, the
essential sentence which had to be preserved at all costs. And since this

final phrase was closely united with the whole commentary on the psalms, Benedict chose to reproduce this commentary integrally, at the price of summarizing the three first segments in a few lines.

We can see a proof that this was indeed the genesis of his decision by the addition he inserts just after the words 'We must therefore establish a school of the Lord's service'. At that point he interrupts the Master's phrase to insert a long gloss on its first member. He says that in this school which he is going to establish, he hopes to impose nothing painful, nothing overwhelming; yet there will perhaps be some observances that are a little strict; a person should then not run away; but take courage! Only the beginning of the road is narrow; afterward love expands the heart and we advance with pleasure, running. . . . It makes no difference that this optimistic gloss harmonizes ill with the end of the Master's phrase, where the reader passes on to the austere prospect of continual sharing in the sufferings of Christ by persevering in the monastery until death. What interests us here is that Benedict underlines with an insistent commentary the proposition in which the Master mentions 'the school of the Lord's service'. Nothing shows more clearly the importance which Benedict attached to that sentence. Surely for him, as for the Master, it is the key phrase of the whole section and the reason he thought he should recopy the piece from end to end.

The presentation of the monastery as 'the school of the Lord's service' therefore demands our full attention. What does this formula mean? To understand it we must again go beyond the overly narrow limits of the text copied by Benedict, back to the earlier parts of the Master's introduction. Our definition is rooted in his *Thema*. The foundation of the school we are dealing with here is a response to the appeal which Christ made in the parable of the spring, saying: 'Put yourself in my school' (*Discite a me*).[17]

This antecedent is so important for the understanding of our text that we must examine it carefully. The parable of the spring, as we said, represents the human race as a caravan in a piteous state. The crushing burden of sin overwhelms these thirsty men, who travel in this world on the road of exile, with no destination but death. But then they see a spring of fresh water and a voice invites them: 'Come to me, all you that labor and are burdened, and I will refresh you'.[18] When they have laid down their

burden and have drunk for a long time, the voice speaks again: 'Take up
my yoke upon you, and put yourself in my school, for I am meek and
humble of heart, and you shall find rest for your souls. For my yoke is
easy and my burden light'.[19] Then these men decide to abandon for good
the burden of their sins and the road of this world, in order to know only
the voice of the Lord, the law of Christ.

The meaning of the allegory is transparent. It treats a total conversion
from sin to God which is brought about in two stages. First, man approaches Christ and receives baptism; then he decides to enter the Lord's
school and to persevere in it without turning back. Baptismal regeneration and entrance into the Lord's service, these two acts answer two successive appeals of Christ, which our author distinguishes in the same
logion of the Gospel (Mt 11: 28–30): 'Come to me . . . and I will refresh
you'. In these first words the Master sees an invitation to baptism, in
which the man will be 'refreshed' and 'recreated' by divine grace. 'Take
my yoke upon you and learn of me . . . and you shall find rest for your
souls'. This second phrase, according to the Master, is an appeal to leave
the world and enter the monastery.

This analysis of the Gospel text has important implications which deserve to be set forth one by one. In the first place, we see that monastic life
appears as an immediate prolongation of baptism. In the text of Matthew,
the second appeal of Christ is inseparable from the first. Like the first, it is
addressed to all human beings overwhelmed by the weight of their faults.
It states the urgency and universality of the monastic vocation. In the eyes
of our author there is no baptized person who is not called. This explains
the severity he shows in more than one passage of his Rule to those who
do not answer this appeal and who remain in the world.[20] Even here he
abandons these 'negligent ones' to the 'weight of their faults'.[21]

These words 'fault' (*delictum*) and 'sin' (*peccatum*) deserve the greatest
attention. They designate the common enemy against which the baptistry
and the monastery form a solid front. To receive baptism is already to renounce sin, at least intentionally. Monastic life will only be the actuation
of this intention. It consists in 'not returning' after baptismal regeneration
to the 'burden of sin', once it has been laid aside. 'We have renounced'
. . . 'let us renounce'. The renunciation declared one day in baptism is
confirmed in the continuous effective renunciation of monastic conversion.[22] For the man who is crushed by the consciousness of his faults, the

law of Christ obtains an unspeakable 'relief', a marvellous impression of 'lightness'. This passage from guilt to innocence, from a sinful conscience to justice and holiness, will have its end in the perfect 'repose' of eternity.[23]

It will be noticed that this interpretation of the evangelical *logion* differs from the meaning we are accustomed to see in it. According to the exegesis common today and already well represented in patristic times, Christ here aims at 'the burden of the Law and the pharisaic observances which made it heavier still'.[24] For the Master, on the contrary, this insupportable burden is sins committed either in 'the ignorance of the law' and 'with a knowledge [of the latter] which knows nothing of baptism'.[25] Other patristic authors, in great numbers, similarly understand 'the weariness' relieved by Christ not as the jewish and pharisaic observances, but as the torments and servitudes of sin.[26] Such an interpretation probably came spontaneously to the mind of christian pastors for whom the relation of their flocks to the jewish law was no longer a problem, while the struggle against sin remained a permanent preoccupation.

This way of understanding Christ's *logion* in Matthew's Gospel makes it possible to reconcile it with another text of the same evangelist which seems at first sight to contradict it. In the Sermon on the Mount Jesus presents his doctrine as the 'narrow way' where only a small number have the courage to enter, while the greater part follow the 'broad way' which leads to perdition. This text is used by the Master in his Prologue, where it constitutes the only scriptural reference, [27] if we except the string of citations at the end about the word *'regula'* (rule). The *logion* of the two ways (Mt 7:13–14) is therefore for the Prologue roughly the equivalent of what the *logion* of the two burdens (Mt 11: 28–30) is for the Thema, namely, the basic scriptural text which supports the whole discourse. But in appearance at least, the two pericopes are scarcely in agreement. The first affirms that it is difficult to follow Christ, while the second says that this is an easy thing. One limits the disciples to a small number of courageous persons; the other extends an unlimited invitation to 'all who labor and are burdened'.

This superficial antinomy between the 'narrowness' of the way and the 'lightness' of the burden resolves itself, if we with our author understand the second, not as the easiness of a rule that does not demand much, but of the interior liberation and relief procured by purity. Objectively the way is narrow, certainly, and Christ's demands are formidable, but the deliverance from sin which is bought at this price gains the soul quiet, ease, and relief. The perspective opened by the Master is not very different from the views that Benedict was to expound in the final addition to his Prologue, when he spoke of the way of salvation, whose beginning seems narrow but whose sequel is only enthusiasm, love, and inexpressible sweetness.

Heaviness and lightness. For the Master, the evangelical contrast refers, not to the heavier or lighter character of the obligations imposed by the Old and New Law, but to the weight of sin in contrast to the sanctifying power of the grace of Christ and his precepts. This interpretation is valid for the whole pericope, but has also a precise application which distinguishes between the appeal to baptism, signified by the first phrase, and the later vocation to the school of Christ, perceived in the following phrases. The chronological succession thus established is not without analogy with that discovered by the Master in the pauline enumeration of the charisms. There Paul lists *first* the prophets—meaning those of the Old Testament—*then* the apostles of Christ, and *finally* the teachers or pastors of the Church.[28] In both places the Master read in a sacred text a *history* whose different elements are concomitant to our eyes.

Do other examples exist in patristic literature of such a dichotomy in the *logion* of Mt 11? At any rate, such a dichotomy is not found in the Master's predecessor, Basil. In his rule, Basil understood the text as a call to the separated life of 'Christians' entirely consecrated to the Lord, but it is the whole pericope which he understood in this sense, and especially the words, 'Come to me, all of you' in the first phrase.[29] Similarly, Chrysostom did not separate the two parts of the *logion*, but perceived in it a single and unique appeal of Christ, which is, according to him, the vocation to baptism.[30] It is possible therefore that the Master's thought, here as elsewhere, is quite personal and individual. The theology of the monastic life and its ties to baptism are not a theme to which christian antiquity gave much attention, at least in the West. The sketch our author traces is only more interesting for that reason.

These remarks on the Master's *Thema* have prepared us to understand the definition of the monastery as a 'school of the Lord's service'; to that we must now return. This project of 'establishing a school of the Lord's service' should be connected with Christ's words in Matthew's Gospel 'Put yourself in my school', even if the latin verb of this last phrase (*discite,* learn) does not suggest the connection with the same force as does this translation. Whatever may be the varied connotations of the word '*scola*', which we shall examine shortly, this word in the final phrase of the commentary on the psalms undoubtedly aims at Christ's teaching. The author continues: 'We must never depart from him, we must persevere in his teaching even until death'. The decision which concludes the commentary on the psalms, and with it the whole of the Master's introduction, bears indeed upon the establishment of a 'school' in which one will 'learn' from Christ in person how he must be served. It is impossible not to understand these expressions as a reminder of the Lord's invitation in the parable of the spring: '*Discite a me*, Learn of me'.

As a synonym of *monasterium*, which figures in the following phrase, the word *scola* makes the monastery the chief place where Christ teaches. The use of this term *scola* is laden with meaning. First of all, by means of it the monastery is connected to a word of the Gospel. Although neither the word *monasterium* nor even the idea of a monastery is found anywhere in the New Testament, indeed in the whole of Scripture, recourse to the word *scola* amounts to basing this new type of society on the word of God by making it seem like a response to the words of Christ, 'Learn of me'.

By this bias the Master succeeds in finding for all of monastic society a scriptural reference analogous to that which offers itself spontaneously for its leader, the abbot. The Master will say at the beginning of his second chapter that the title *abbas* refers the abbot to Christ himself, to whom the Holy Spirit makes us say: 'Abba, Father'.[31] In the same way, just when he is going to pronounce the word *monasterium* for the first time, our author carefully has it preceded by an equivalent term, *scola*, which evokes Christ, the master of divine wisdom. Thus the *logion* of Mt 11 plays in the *Thema* the same role the pauline saying (Rm 8) plays in the directory for the abbot. Each text serves to certify the christian character of the monastic institution by giving it a scriptural name and guarantee.

A second effect of the definition of the monastery as *scola* is to connect monastic life intimately with baptism. The analysis of the *Thema* has shown us that 'to enroll oneself at the school' of the Lord is possible only after having been 'remade' by him,[32] and reciprocally this 'recreation' worked by baptism has an adequate and lasting effect only on him who leaves the world and puts himself wholeheartedly in the school of Christ. These are two equally necessary phases of the renunciation of sin, as we have seen. But these two moments should also be seen in their positive aspect. Monastic life then appears as the natural development of the being who is 'renewed' by baptism and as the normal existence of the 'risen'.[33] It tends to conform the sons of God to him whose image they bear from their 'rebirth',[34] and whom they dare henceforth to call 'Father'.[35] Consequently it consists in submitting to the divine law, and more precisely to the 'Christian law', the Lord's commandments.[36] In addition, since our reparation has been obtained by the cross of Christ [37], we can complete it only by sharing in his passion. Only the sharing of his sufferings will make us co-heirs of his glory.[38]

The reader will have recognized in these last expressions the phrase which serves to close both the presentation of the monastery as a *scola* and the whole commentary on the psalms. That this sentence appears already in nearly the same terms in the baptismal context of the commentary on the invocation 'Our Father',[39] is a fact which shows the absolute identification established in the Master's thought between the monastic state and the quality of sons of God received at baptism. After God has 'restored to us the grace of adoption', the divine voice does not cease to 'invite us also to the kingdom of heaven'.[40] Baptismal grace tends therefore to the 'paradise' beyond,[41] and it is also to this eschatological kingdom that those who assemble in the monastery-school hear themselves invited, according to the commentary on the psalms.[42]

This sort of convertibility between monasticism and Christianity explains the at first sight astonishing simplicity and indetermination of the long invitation to monastic life which forms the last part of the *Thema*. In order to move his reader along towards his monastic 'school', the Master finds nothing to offer him but the prospect of the eternal 'life' and 'repose' which are proposed to every Christian.[43] Like every person who achieves salvation, the monk will be a 'dweller in the divine tabernacle',[44] and nothing more. To achieve this, he has nothing to do but to 'fulfil the duties incumbent on such a dweller', whoever he may be, namely 'to do good, to avoid evil', to observe the moral precepts and prohibitions which God in the Old and New Testament addresses generally to every creature.

The *scola* of the monastery therefore plays in the Master's thought a mediating role between the baptismal spring and the fulfilment of the kingdom. It allows passage from one to the other. After having been 're-created' by the sacrament, one must 'place oneself in the school' of Christ in order to arrive at the ultimate 'repose' which he has promised. This necessity of passing through the monastery-school is illustrated, in the Master's language, by the contrast of two series of expressions, both of which describe the Christian's condition in terms of sonship. At the end of the parable of the spring the neophytes proclaim that they '*already* have as mother the christian law', and '*already* have as father the Lord' who calls them,[45] for they reject the earthly maternity of Eve and the sinful paternity of Adam, and as they begin the Lord's Prayer they repeat that 'we have *already* found a mother in the Church and a father in the Lord who is in heaven'—which implies the abandonment of our father and mother according to the flesh.[46] But soon the phrase 'not yet' will reply to this triple use of 'already'. In the last part of the first chapter, a piece of great doctrinal importance where the homiletic tone and meditative vein of the introductions appear again, we read that obedience to a religious superior—a bishop or an abbot— is imposed on 'all those who *still* have folly for their mother'.[47] This is as much as to say that Christians reborn by baptism,for whom our author is opening his monastery-school, are *still not yet* the sons of wisdom. They have 'received'this wisdom of God at baptism, as is expressly said in the parable of the spring,[48] but for all that it has not properly speaking, become their mother.

Thus the Christian or the monk—it is all one—is in a dubious position. Already the son of God, of the Church, and of the christian law, he remains nevertheless a son of folly, incapable of directing himself and subject to the fatal illusions of his self-will. The exact purpose of the monastery is to procure for him the sure direction which he cannot do without, while awaiting the day when alone he will perhaps be able to keep himself from sin, with the help of God.[49]

Thus we are led to recognize a third implication of the word *scola*. This concept does not only set monasticism in relation with the Gospel and with baptism; it also establishes a relationship between the monastery and the Church. As we have just seen, the Church is the 'mother' who brings us to birth in the life of grace at holy baptism, after we have heard the Lord's first appeal, 'Come to me'. The monastery is 'the school where we serve the Lord', in accordance with his second appeal: 'Enroll yourself in my school'. Thus the '*scola*' supposes the '*ecclesia*', and brings its life-giving work to completion.

Yet the relation of the two institutions is not only one of succession in time, or, if you will, of cause and effect, but also one of analogy in structure and operation. Like the Church, the monastic school is essentially constitued by the presence and action of a pastor, or, as the Master loves to call him, of a 'teacher', who represents Christ and has as his mission the direction of souls in His name. Also, although it comes after the *ecclesia* logically and chronologically, the *scola monasterii* can be assimilated to it and set parallel with it. That is what comes to light in the last part of the Master's first chapter, a crucial passage whose importance we have already noted. Having to present the abbot, the superior of the monastery, the Master puts him alongside the bishop among the 'teachers' of whom Saint Paul speaks. These teachers succeed the prophets of the Old Testament and the apostles of the New, and 'rule the Churches and the schools of Christ by their command and their teaching'.[50] Later, at the beginning of chapter eleven our author takes up this parallel again and develops it fully. The abbot and his provosts are in the monastery while the bishop, his priests, deacons, and clerics are in the Church. These two societies run parallel to each other in the category of 'God's houses' where the Lord governs his household by means of men he can trust, whom he sets over their fellow-servants.[51]

The *scola* is therefore the extension of the *ecclesia*, being both beyond it and similar to it. This situation, which is already apparent when we examine simply the texts of the Master, becomes clearer still if we compare these passages with those in which Augustine describes the Church itself as the school of Christ. Augustine readily represents the Church by this image, taking either the upper school of the philosopher or the elementary school of the grammarian[52] as the term of the comparison.[53] In the light of this comparison we can say that the definition of the monastery as a school does not make it an institution radically different from the Church. Rather it makes it appear as the point where one of the constitutive aspects of the Church appears most clearly. The Church itself is a school where the Lord dispenses his doctrine. In its turn, the monastery is the pre-eminent place of Christ's teaching. Under this aspect the monastic *scola* appears again in the line of the Church, extending it and bringing its attributes to their perfection.

At this point we cannot evade a crucial question: is this monastic 'school' a part of the Church, or is it distinguished from it? The Master's expressions we have analyzed thus far give the impression that the two societies are certainly analogous and connected,but when all is said and done,outside each other. Whether we regard them as two successive moments in the same work or as two institutions of the same type, it is not clear that the monastery is *in* the Church. The same sentiment is felt when we see the Master having direct recourse to Scripture for the foundation of the monastic institution as for the Church itself. According to him, the *scola* of the monks has its proper foundation in the words of the Gospel 'Learn of me', just as baptism and the motherhood of the Church have theirs in the preceding words, 'Come to me'. Similarly abbots seem to enjoy the charism of 'teacher' by the same title as bishops, and the most solemn words of Christ to his apostles are applied equally to both. All this seems to make the monastery and the Church two independent entities of the same rank, equally rooted in the soil of revelation.

Must we conclude that the definition of the monastery as *scola* tends to exaggerate its importance and its independence in regard to the *ecclesia*? One fact prevents us from drawing such a conclusion too quickly. If the abbot, the keystone of the monastic school, is indeed likened by the Master to the bishop, our author nonetheless maintains that the new abbot is invested by a liturgical act whose essential rite is the bishop's prayer.[54] It is the bishops who 'ordain' the abbots. However much they may be 'teachers', abbots do not constitute an order perfectly symmetrical to the teaching-authority of the Church and independent of it. Only the episcopate inherits the apostolic succession in direct line. The hierarchy of the monasteries is grafted on that of the Church at each generation. This crucial fact indicates a real subordination of the *scola* to the *ecclesia*. From the latter the monastic school receives not only its pupils, the baptized, but also its master, the abbot.

Having said that, let us recognize that the Master's attitude towards the Church is not without ambiguity. Does not giving the monastery the name of 'school of Christ' and distinguishing it as such from the Church, insinuate that the Church is not fulfilling adequately its function as a school? We remember the severe judgment the Master makes, at least implicitly, on christian life in the world. Is not this 'broad way', this 'way of the world' in which people remain subject to sin, the way of the throng of the baptized and of their pastor, in other words, the way of the Church? In following this line of thought we come to ask if, in the Master's eyes, the bishops can still play the role of 'teacher' in which their ministry con-

sists, once the catechesis preparatory to baptism is over. The question is
surely indiscreet and exaggerated, and our author would doubtless not
have let it be asked of him, but is seems difficult to avoid in a system like
his.

Such, moreover, is the reef of every generous system of thought which
takes as its starting point the demands of evangelical perfection and rigorously infers from them the marks of the Church. If the Master has not
removed this danger from his path entirely, still he has not run upon it
fatally. In his introduction, whose poetic character must not be forgotten,
he seems to demand entry into the monastery quickly after baptism, but
this way of slighting the secular Church remains wholly implicit. When
he has the occasion to explain himself in chapters one and eleven, he admits the existence of an *ecclesia* in the world, parallel to his own monastic
scola and of the same divine authority, indeed of superior rank, as the rite
of abbatial ordination shows.

In the face of this serene recognition of ecclesiastical fact and law[55], it
seems fair not to interpret too strictly the passages of the Rule which appear to leave almost no place for christian life in the world. No doubt the
Master would have subscribed to the reflections suggested to us a little
while ago by the texts in which Augustine calls the Church the 'school of
Christ'. If the monastery defines itself thus, it is not because it has an
exclusive right to this title, or because it owes this quality only to itself.
Rather, it holds its nature as a school from the Church and shares it with
her. In the monastery, *ecclesia mater* develops and shows to the highest degree one of her essential attributes; the power to educate souls according
to the teaching of Christ and to lead them to salvation. The monastery is
therefore a 'school' only in the Church, by the Church, and for the Church.

Finally, these relations of the monastery with the Church cast light on
the fundamentally communitarian character of monasticism, as the Master conceives it. If the monk leaves secular society and the Church which
dwells there, he does so to find a still closer fellowship in the monastic
scola. Modelled on the *ecclesia* this *scola* puts him under the authority of
another 'teacher', the abbot, who together with his provosts will exercise
on him a much deeper and more extensive hold than that of the ecclesiastical hierarchy. The Master has resolutely set himself in a cenobitic perspective by presenting monastic professions as entry into 'the school of
the Lord's service', responding to the words of Christ, 'Put yourself in my

school'. The solitary life is licit only for someone who has fully assimilated the common teaching of the school. Following Cassian, the Master was shortly to declare that there is no legitimate *anachoresis* except that which is the fruit of long experience in the cenobium. Every true anchorite remains a cenobite by reason of his basic formation.

We have just spoken of Cassian. For him the monastery was also a school, but in a different sense than that of the Master, namely a school which prepares for solitude.[56] Thus the cenobitic *schola* appears either as a higher institution, seen in relation to the Church, or on the contrary as an elementary school, seen from the point of view of eremitism.[57]

The notion of school therefore puts the monastery in relation with solitude as well as with the *ecclesia*. Let us even note that it is this notion which makes it possible to conceive of cenobitism as open to the solitary life, as we find in our Rules. If the Master and Benedict, following Cassian, recognize the legitimacy of *anachoresis* this is precisely because they represent cenobitic society as an educative enterprise rather than as a community of brothers living together a life which has value in and for itself. If they, like other monastic legislators, had taken as their model the primitive Church, where the multitude of believers had but one heart and one soul,[58] they would scarcely have allowed an exodus to the desert which might seem to assail this communion in charity. There is scarcely any place for eremitism when the union of hearts appears as the supreme value. On the contrary, nothing prevents one from leaving a school, if it is certain that one has exhausted its educative resources and can lead a more difficult combat in the wilderness.

What we have said above about the communitarian character of the monastic life according to the Master should therefore have some nuances added to it. The Christian community, either ecclesiastical or monastic, appears in the Master as an educative institution, where the relationship of disciples to master means almost everything and the relations of the disciples to one another means almost nothing. The aim of this institution is to lead to eternal life each of the persons entrusted to it. There is scarcely any building here below of a house of brothers where it is 'good and pleasant to dwell together'.

In this regard, the Master's and Benedict's entry into their matter differs singularly from that of Basil, Augustine, and the Four Fathers. With these authors, the establishment of the brotherly community was the first

step or one of the very first steps. As soon as Basil had shown the necessity of separating oneself from the world in order to observe the divine
commandments, he demonstrated at length that the common life is no
less necessary for those who wish to serve God; and this demonstration
ends with the words 'Behold how good and how pleasant' of psalm 132
and the picture of the ideal community of the first believers.[59] Augustine
went to work more quickly. Right away he proposed the principle of
brotherly communion, which he also invoked by two scriptural images,
one from the Old Testament and the other from the New: 'the unanimous dwelling in one house' of which psalm 67 speaks; and the primitive
Church where union of hearts was shown by the common pooling of
goods. The Four Fathers have the same starting point. In view of the great
numbers of those who aspired to the perfect life and the impossibility of
living alone in the desert, they invoked the authority of Scripture,
which, in their opinion recommends the common life. If Serapion, their
spokesman did not then think of the first chapters of Acts, he did cite,
one after the other, the two psalm verses used by Basil and Augustine.[60]
This 'joy of brothers dwelling together' and this 'unanimity of those
who dwell in the same house', were therefore a kind of commonplace
for the authors of the first rules.

We should expect to find these scriptural quotations or others like them
at the beginning of the Master's and Benedict's work. Nothing of the sort!
Instead of affirming immediately the fact and value of the common life,
our authors begin by addressing an individual, a postulant whom they
urge to embrace the regular life if he wishes to assure his salvation. It is
true that their exhortation soon passes from 'you' in the second person
singular to 'we' but this plural form aims rather at a sum of individual vocations than at a true community, willed for itself and envisaged as such.
Proof of this is the frequent return to the singular which strews the
commentary on the psalms, often by reason of the text cited. For instance, the Lord seeking his workman, cries out in psalm 33: 'Who is the
man who desires life?' If the hearer answers, 'I do', the Lord answers,
'Keep your tongue from evil . . . turn away from evil and do good'. Further on, when psalm 14 asks, 'Lord, who shall dwell in your tabernacle?',
the answer again is a program of good works in the singular, concluded by
the Gospel *logion*, also in the singular, about the man who built upon
rock. Obviously this segment deals with personal salvation from one end

to the other, even if the preacher's 'we' presents this exhortation to individuals in collective form.

Let us remark also that in his earlier commentary on the Lord's Prayer, and especially at the beginning of it, the Master was often inspired by Cyprian's work entitled 'On the Lord's Prayer', but he did not think it good to repeat what the great African bishop had said about the plural form of the text.[61] For Cyprian it was significant that Christ makes us say: 'Our Father . . . Give us . . . Forgive us . . . Lead us not . . . Deliver us . . . '. The Christian never prays only for himself. By divine will his prayer always considers the whole body of Christ.

It is surely not by chance that this remark of Cyprian's never got into the Master's commentary. Our author was absorbed by his preoccupation with individual salvation, and could not give much attention to the communitarian dimension of christian prayer and life. If he firmly resolved to insert the neophyte and the new monk into a social framework, it was less to make him experience the riches and joys of a brotherly communion than to subject him to a sure guide, an authentic 'teacher'. His monastic society was less a community than a school, and the school's biblical foundation was found, not in the sweet words of the psalmist about the unanimity and joy of dwelling together or in the example of concord given by the Church of Jerusalem, but simply in the saying of Christ: 'Enter my school, learn of me'.

What we have just said shows well enough the importance and richness of the concept of *scola*. By means of it monasticism is connected with the Gospel, monastic life with baptism, and the monastery with the Church. We have not yet exhausted the implications of this word, however. Till now we have constantly taken *scola* in the sense obvious to a modern reader, the school. We were invited to do so by the context of the commentary on the psalms, where the decision to found the *scola* manifestly corresponded to the words 'Learn of me' in the parable of the spring, just as the sequel of the phrase spoke of Christ's 'teaching authority' and of his 'doctrine'.

But the school context which directs us clearly towards the most ordinary sense of *scola* should not make us overlook the other meanings of the word. In antiquity a *scola* could refer to a place set apart for some professional fellowship or to this association itself and its activities.[62] More especially, the term often designated a body of soldiers or civil functionaries, servants of the state and the prince. Perhaps this meaning was present to the Master's mind here when he spoke of the *dominici scola servitii*, of a *scola* for the Lord's *service*. In certain passages at the end of his Rule, the idea of public service is undeniably associated with the use of the word *scola*. In the course of the long homily addressed to the lay postulant the Master twice enunciates the great maxim on patience which governs all monastic life: 'He who wishes to serve in the *scola* must bear everything for the Lord'.[63] We knew already from the end of the commentary on the psalms and from the end of the first chapter that the monastery is the Lord's *scola*. But the expression we meet here, *militare scolae* (to serve in the *scola*), is new and interesting. It means that the activity exercised in this *scola* is a service, indeed a public service (*militare*), like that of the soldier or civil servant.

The connection of the two terms re-appears in the same discourse when the Master declares that 'with Christianity fully at peace, we serve (*militamus*) in the *scola* of the monastery, under the command of the abbot, by means of the trials and mortifications inflicted on our wills'.[64] No doubt here our author was thinking of real armed service. Three chapters earlier he had already put the postulant on guard against the temptations that might induce him to 'leave the service of the holy *scola* in order to return to the world and there serve (*militaturus*) his own will'.[65]

These texts at the end of the Rule throw light on what the Master meant by *dominici scola servitii* in his introduction. What the word *servitii* had made us suspect is confirmed strikingly. For our author, *servitium* was equivalent to *militia*,[66] and this latter term, which evokes military or civil service is ordinarily associated with the term *scola*. The definition given in the commentary on the psalms has therefore a double meaning. In the first place *scola* there designates a scholastic establishment, as the words *magisterium* (teaching authority) and *doctrina* (teaching) used soon afterwards show. But the word also connotes a corps of soldiers or civil servants, suggested by *servitium* (service).

The ambiguity presented here by *scola* crops up again where we consider the uses of the word throughout the Rule. In the last part of the first chapter the school sense predominates as at present, but without perhaps altogether excluding the other meaning, if we judge by the expression *imperio vel doctrina* (1.83: by command and teaching), *claudant et doceant* (1.84:

we will ~~establish~~ establi[sh] a school of the Lord's service, the curriculum of which will be the scriptures and the great teachers of Christ's church.

they enclose and they teach). The first term of each of these expressions suggests that the 'teachers' of the *scola*, like those of the Church, are not only instructors but also leaders and pastors. On the other hand, at the end of the Rule it is instead the military sense which predominates. But if the *scola* is associated with *militare* in the four passages we have quoted, another passage resolutely takes up again the metaphor of the school ('master . . . disciples . . . art'), [67] and yet another, which speaks of 'learning' and 'correcting vices', seems to refer to the same model. [68] Of the two last phrases which speak of *scola*, one is of uncertain hue, [69] but the other combines both images in a most suggestive way. He who enters the *scola monasterii* is there called successively *discipulus* and *miles*, 'pupil' and 'soldier'. [70]

The 'school of the Lord's service' is therefore a complex metaphor which makes the monastery appear both as a teaching establishment and as a corps of soldiers or civil servants. We have said enough about the first, but we should discover the implications of the second. What is there to say about the monastery as a corps of special troops or of civil officials?

Let us notice first that the image is not as profane as it seems at first sight. Although the expression *in scola . . . militare* can be applied to any category of public agents, [71] it is also found in Pope Gregory's writings referring to agents of the Roman Church called its 'defenders', [72] and parallel texts show that it might be used also for a properly ecclesiastical order such as that of the subdeacons. [73] When we know how inclined the Master was to connect monastic institutions with those of the Church, [74] Gregory's language, doubtlessly that of more than one roman cleric of the sixth century, helps us understand the Master's phrase *militare scolae*. The monks form a *scola*, a special category in the midst of the Church, a little like the defenders, the notaries, and the subdeacons. The Master says as much in referring to a liturgical particularity: the monastery is *quasi in peculiari servitio Dei*, that is, devoted to a particular service of God, distinct from the general and common service rendered by the *ecclesia*. [75]

Thus the word *scola*, taken in the military and administrative sense, delineates quite nicely the relationship of the monastery to the Church as the kinship of a part to the whole and, more exactly, of a chosen part to the mass of people, of an active elite to the whole nation. All the subjects of an empire or a kingdom serve the sovereign, and all the members of the Church serve the Lord, but certain persons perform this service by reason of an outstanding and exclusive title. Like the soldiers and functionaries in the state, the monks, together with clergy[76] and other ecclesiastical agents, fulfill a sort of public function in the midst of the christian people. They are enrolled in the service of God, withdrawn from every other occupation; and they give themselves wholly to serve God, and to do the will of the king, the Lord Christ.

Besides throwing light on the relationship between Church and monastery, the use of *scola* in this new sense has the advantage of enriching the image of monastic life in two important ways. Making the monastery a mere 'school' suggests that the monks do scarcely more than 'learn'. Even if the teaching received seems often of the sort that we today call 'professional' or 'technical', judging by the terms used by the Master—think of the metaphor of the 'holy art' [77]—, the monastic life appears under a rather passive aspect as an exclusively didactic thing. The second meaning of *scola* allows us to round out this too limited presentation. Thanks to it, the monk no longer appears only as a pupil or an apprentice, but also as a soldier or servant of the sovereign, for whose sake obedience and action are more called for than are learning and imitation. This more virile picture of monastic life better suits the adult status of most monks.

The service of the public agent and especially the soldier, moreover, is not lived without struggle, weariness, and dangers. Thus *militare* suggests not only action, but also pain and suffering. This element of endurance is not absent from passages where the Master speaks of the *scola*. The phrase of the commentary on the psalms which presents the monastery as 'the school of the Lord's service', ends, we remembered, by mentioning the passion of Christ, in which we must share patiently if we are to have a part in his kingdom. Similarly at the end of the Rule, the Master repeats to the postulant that 'he must bear everything for the Lord, if he wishes to serve in his *scola*'.[78] In the same passage he mentions 'the trials and mortifications of the will' to be endured by those who serve in the *scola* of the monastery.[79]

This theme of patience, which gives rise to the well-known developments in the chapters on obedience and humility[80], has therefore a relationship with the definition of the monastery as a *scola*. Thus the image proves astonishingly rich. It suggests in turn the docility of the pupil and the obedience of the soldier, activity and endurance. Correlatively, it allows the person of Christ to be invoked under three complementary as-

pects: the master who teaches, the leader who commands, and the re-
deemer on the cross.

If this is the meaning of the formula *dominici scola servitii* in the Master,
we have still to examine what Benedict did with it. We have seen that he
perceived its importance, because he kept it, together with the whole
commentary on the psalms which it climaxed, and he even added some
personal remarks which enhance its value. But the word *scola* never appears again in the benedictine Rule, and the parallel *scola-ecclesia* at the end
of the Master's first chapter he totally omitted. Benedict seems to have
taken no interest in this theory. Only the first phrase in which the *scola* is
presented matters to him, because this passage obviously constitutes the
reason and purpose of the Master's whole introduction.

However little Benedict cared to exploit the definition of the monastery as a *scola*, its significance seems not to have been foreign to him.
Doubtless the word *discipulus*, which often recurs in the first chapters of
the Master, is avoided more than once by the benedictine redaction,[81] but
this appearance of disaffection is compensated for by some autonomous
uses of the word,[82] and in any event it applies to only one aspect of the
scola, that of the 'school'. In the first phrase of the Prologue, composed
freely on a canvas provided by the Master and Pseudo-Basil, we find the
expression *praecepta magistri* (precepts of the Master), and this touch of
the school is more remarkable because neither of the two sources furnished it to Benedict.[83] By beginning this way, our author seems to announce the final words of his Prologue, in which following the Master, he
will speak of the 'teaching authority' of Christ and of his 'doctrine'.[84]

Furthermore, the rest of the benedictine exordium presents monastic
life as a 'laborious obedience', making reparation for the 'lazy disobedience' of sin, and again, as a 'renunciation of self-will in order to serve the
Lord Christ, the true king, with the most powerful and glorious arms of
obedience'. Such an insistence on obedience is indeed in line with 'the
Lord's service', for which the *scola* is soon to be established, inasmuch as
here Benedict uses the verb *militare* (to serve), whose connection with
scola in the other Rule we have seen. Surely this project of 'serving (*militare*) Christ the Lord' is in perfect harmony with the Master's concepts,
even if, in fact, Benedict seems to have borrowed the terms from Pseudo-
Basil.[85]

We recognize therefore in the first lines of the Rule the two components of the Master's *scola*: the school-element discreetly suggested by the
words 'the precepts of the Master' in the first phrase, and the military aspect which unfolds in the explicit formulas of the second phrase. Even the
note of pain and of patience can be guessed here, for Benedict speaks of
painful, laborious obedience (*oboedientiae labor*).

But it is especially in his final addition that he seems to have been
preoccupied with this painful aspect of the 'school of the Lord's service'.
He was invited to it by the Master's austere conclusion: 'to persevere until
death . . . to share in the passion of Christ by patience'. This perspective
of endless suffering here below visibly disturbed Benedict. By his addition
he introduced into it a series of comforting touches, the chief of which is
the promise of the expansion of the heart through love, and a sweet running in the way of God's commandments once the initial tightness of the
narrow way has been passed. The monk's earthly life therefore is not a
continual agony. Before the heavenly kingdom, it knows a certain happiness which Benedict even qualifies as 'ineffable'.

Optimism, care to encourage the weak,[86] interest in spiritual progress
here below,[87] an augustinian sense of the role of love in this
progress,[88]—many aspects deserve being picked out of this remarkable
passage. But especially should we measure its impact on the notion of 'the
school of the Lord's service'. Indeed, the only purpose of these lines is to
brighten the sombre atmosphere in which the Master had wrapped his
scola.

To this end Benedict declares, first of all, that he hopes to establish
'nothing harsh, nothing burdensome' (*nihil asperum, nihil grave*). In these
words we recognize with certainty an echo of the Gospel *logion* in which
Jesus promises that his yoke will be sweet and his burden light. Augustine
had already used the same terms (*aspera et gravia*) to designate the trials of
the christian life, apparently in contrast to Christ's promises.[89]

When pushed to the limits, Benedict remembered the great text of
Matthew, chapter eleven, which furnished his predecessor with the outline of the parable of the spring. But his use of it differs from the Master's.
Whereas the Master saw in 'heaviness' the effect of sin and in 'lightness'
the state of a purified conscience, Benedict thought of the exterior
'weight' of observances, which he wanted to make as 'light' as possible,
that is to say, objectively easy in themselves. His spontaneous interpre-

tation of the Gospel text is thus in line with modern exegesis, already present in more than one patristic commentary, as we have said; the 'burden' that Jesus lightens is not that of sin, but of the Law. It follows that the monastic rule should be made 'sweet' and 'light', like the yoke and burden of Christ, that is, like the Gospel itself. In this way Benedict made a first correction (based on the *logion* of Matthew) in the perspective of 'sharing in the passion of Christ' which, itself entirely scriptural, was the only thing the Master presented to the recruits of his *scola*.

This first retouching, however, called for another. Clearly, the monastic rule has its asperities and its weight. To account for this undeniable aspect, Benedict does not have recourse only to rational explanations, such as 'reasons of equity, the amendment of vices and the preservation of charity'. A scriptural image occurred to him, the narrow way (Mt 7). This new reference to the Gospel was to temper hopes for ease generated by the *logion* about the light burden. Like the yoke of Christ, the Rule should have 'nothing harsh, nothing burdensome', but as the way of salvation, it may be a little 'strict'. [90]

A simple change of biblical vocabulary allowed for the re-introduction of the austere reality which seemed excluded. But we should not fail to ask ourselves about the seriousness and validity of this procedure. Are we not in the midst of verbal illusions, playing with images and words? Does one text of the Gospel contradict another?

Before seeing how Benedict resolved the antinomy, let us note that the same contradiction is found in his predecessor. As we remember, the Master first presented his Rule as the code of the narrow way (Prologue), but later he issued an invitation to take Christ's yoke and his light burden (Thema, parable of the spring). The two evangelical images succeeded each other, but at some distance, without any effort to coordinate or reconcile them. Yet they harmonized in a rather natural way, because the Master placed the 'weight' and the 'lightness' not in the objective demands of a more or less severe law, but in the conscience of man, either enslaved to sin or set free from it. The way was narrow indeed because of its harsh demands, but at the same time the burden was light because the weight of guilt was eliminated.

Benedict in turn combined the two evangelical texts, and this time indiscriminately in the same passage. To reconcile them—and he had to do so—he did not have at his disposal the interpretation of Matthew chapter eleven that the Master had given himself. This time the 'lightness of the burden' is applied fair and square to the demands of the law. In this case it really is opposed to the 'narrowness of the way' presented in Matthew chapter seven, which signifies the difficulty of the law. Benedict also searched for reconciliation by means of an audacious exegesis of this second text; for it he used a versicle of Psalm 118: 'I have run the way of your commandments, for you have enlarged my heart'. According to him, the way of salvation is narrow only at its beginning; afterwards 'as a result of love the heart enlarges, and we run the way of God's commandments with unspeakable sweetness'.[91]

Thus grace and divine love [92] intervene as we advance in the monastic life, and lessen the initial impression of severity. The observance still remains objectively what it is, but the heart within is changed. In other words, Benedict relativized the concept of the 'narrow way', drawing attention to the subjectivity of the man who follows it. The opposition between the 'narrow way' and the 'sweet yoke' is not suppressed for all that, but this way of interiorizing the problem makes it lose its sharpness. 'Narrowness' and 'breadth', difficulty and ease are measured less by the objective tenor of the *ascesis* imposed than by the inmost dispositions of the ascetic. These latter improve with time and by virtue of the *ascesis* itself, until one experiences something more than the 'easiness' and the 'lightness' announced by Jesus, namely a 'sweetness' that cannot be expressed because it proceeds from 'love'.

Thus a verse of the psalms suggested to Benedict the solution which reconciled two contrary affirmations of the Gospel.[93] It is a subjective solution, a solution by love which Augustine had already pointed out in a homily on Matthew eleven. It is love, he said, either the love of concupiscence or the love of charity, which makes sweet and light to men the pains they impose on themselves.[94] And charity, added Benedict, maintains and expands itself by means of these same pains. Love requires austerity at first, then growing by means of it, makes it lovable.

The final addition of the benedictine Prologue recalls then, in a suggestive way, the first pieces of the Master's introduction, omitted by Benedict. The Master cited first, in his Prologue, the *logion* of the two ways and then, in his Thema, that of the light burden. Benedict proceeded in inverse order. First he protested his desire to impose nothing 'burdensome', but then he recognized the necessity of a little 'strictness'. But this route was imposed on him by the new context in which he confronted these two aspects, the end of the Master's commentary on the psalms. The Master presented the 'school of the Lord's service' as an unending patience in sharing Christ's sufferings. In the face of this dolorous perspective Benedict reacted by recalling that Christ's yoke is sweet and his burden light. And although he had to concede quickly that the way of salvation is narrow, the hope of an interior expansion returned him to his optimistic proposal.

This whole note therefore is an amendment to the sombre project of the *scola* laid down by the Master. The 'Lord's service' will not be uniformly hard and painful. It will include restrictions, to be sure, but love will transform them into sweetness. And Christ does not reserve consolation for us only in his kingdom; even now he is for us both a lovable master and a companion in suffering.

Thus Benedict notably completed and corrected the picture of the *scola* sketched by the Master. He did it by recourse to three passages of Scripture, two of which figured in the Master himself before his commentary on the psalms. Was Benedict conscious of using Gospel texts already used by his predecessor? In any case, his addition seems less like an innovation than the concentration in a few lines of a scriptural substance lying scattered in the first pieces of the other Rule. And since the words of Christ in the parable of the spring, 'Learn of me', announced and called for the opening of the *scola* which would be settled upon at the end of the commentary on the psalms, we can say that recalling this word of Christ well suited the moment when Benedict reproduced the decree instituting the school.

Even more, Benedict cast new light by connecting the two ends of the Thema. The *logion* of Matthew eleven is not only the remote, and easily forgotten, source of the school here established. This Gospel text enters into immediate contact, indeed into open conflict, with the project of the *scola* raised up by it. From this confrontation is born a problem, and its solution in turn engenders a deepening and a progression. If the benedictine addition is inserted awkwardly in the Master's text,[95] this literary clumsiness seems generously compensated for by the doctrinal enrichment, at least when one is fortunate enough to possess the canvas on which Benedict worked and to be able thus to discern the progress of his thought together with the stages of his redaction.

Yet the Rule of the Master not only allows us to understand and appre-

ciate the conclusion of the benedictine Prologue; it proves equally indispensable in throwing light on the definition of the monastery as the
'school of the Lord's service'. Without it, we must admit, we would be
ignorant of the scriptural root of this formula—the words of the Gospel
'Learn of me'—as well as of the connection between monastic life and
baptism,[96] and between the monastery and the Church. What is more,
we would scarcely be able to guess the military resonances of the word
scola.[97] In sum, almost the whole doctrinal substance of this essential
phrase would escape us. We see of what riches Benedict deprived himself
by abridging the work of the Master, beginning with his introduction. Of
this introduction his Prologue indeed kept the most important word,
which comes at the end, but it is stripped of the context which reveals its
meaning. In spite of the fine original passages at beginning and end, Benedict's introduction remains essentially a simple extract, a mutilated composition.

When we have restored to Benedict's definition the fullness of its meaning and significance, thanks to the Master, we can ask ourselves what it
means for us today. Let us confess that at first sight it disappoints our
expectations. Avid as we are for fraternal communion and charity, we
experience some surprise at not finding these values explicitly proposed as
the principal element of a rule for the common life. Just as the way in
which Augustine, Basil, and the Four Fathers began their work seems
proper to us, so the ways of the Master and of Benedict leave us perplexed
and unsatisfied. In spite of the plural which predominates in their introductions, we feel that their appeal is addressed more to the individual than
to the group, and that this was viewed as a necessary means rather than as
a good in itself.

On the other hand, if their invitation to listen to the word of God
touches us by its biblical resonances, it seems to us too general to be the
foundation for the particular kind of life they are proposing. What Christian with an eye on eternal life cannot, and should not, enroll himself in
Christ's school, whether he is in the world or in the cloister? This question is the more pressing because entry into this school implies leaving the
world, and therefore a restriction of charity's sphere, a break with human
society, if not with the Church herself, and this raises a problem.

Finally, we do not see clearly the benefit to be derived from an institution conceived chiefly as a teaching establishment. What has this school to teach us? With what superior knowledge are its masters provided that they can teach us all our lives long? The Gospel is simple, clear, ready for being lived wherever one is, and it seems that a person will progress better in the knowledge of Christ by living it simply and intensely in the concrete condition where he is.

This sketch of our objections as moderns, to which each reader can easily make his own additions, does not really call for a reply. Rather than devising a section refuting objections, which would convince no one, we would do better to substitute the astonished, respectful attention of a person confronted with a way of thinking which in part remains alien to him. We do not have to banish this voice coming to us from ancient monasticism with the noise of our familiar themes, nor do we have to force it into unison with them, but rather let its original, irreplaceable sound resonate in us in its purity.

What the Master and Benedict make us understand is, first of all, that Christianity is a serious thing. The christian law has a moral and ascetic content which is not encompassed at the first glance; its spiritual demands are far-reaching. To receive this teaching in its fullness and to put it into practice requires nothing less than a life wholly consecrated to the task. Indeed, the divine message finds man far from God, and the ideal which it proposes can only be obtained at the price of a deep-seated conversion and an amendment of life that is difficult to bring to a successful conclusion. The whole attention of the faithful man is required at every instant of his life, if he is to succeed in God's service. This demands both the direction of qualified masters, capable of helping a man see clearly and reform himself, and an appropriate framework to life which makes it possible for him to attend continually to God and to his will. On this last point the Master and Benedict only repeat Basil. Their *scola* is but the realization of the project outlined by the second Question of the basilian Rule, a place where the Christian can work continually, without obstacle or distraction, at the great work of fulfilling the divine commandments.[98]

The second fundamental postulate of his spirituality is that such a program required separation from the world. 'No man, being a soldier to God (*militans Deo*), entangles himself with secular businesses'.[99] Our Rules translate this pauline axiom further on by the maxim 'To become a stranger to the world's ways'.[100] But it applies from the present moment on, since the *scola* of the Master and Benedict aims precisely at the service of God, the 'soldiering' for Christ. The Greek etymology of the term suggests the same. The *scola* originally meant freedom from business, leisure. The school of the philosopher and the corps of special troops confirm this primitive meaning, each in its own way. In the *scola* one was freed from the cares of ordinary life, withdrawn from the affairs of the world, and occupied solely with a superior and disinterested object, whether it was the service of the prince or the search for wisdom. For the Master and for Benedict, as for all the monastic legislators, there is no doubt that the service of Christ and attention to his word made legitimate and even demanded an analogous liberation, and they found the formal recommendation of it in the Gospel.[101]

This remark leads us to another important observation. Our authors considered their monastery, separated from the world, as a simple consequence of the teachings of Christ and his apostles. In no way was monasticism to their eyes a universal religious phenomenon, originally independent of Christianity, which Christianity had assumed as best it could.[102] On the contrary, according to them, monastic conversion replies purely and simply to the Gospel; the monastery is connected only with the baptistery; the school of the Lord's service can be compared only with the Church.

Moreover, the Master habitually avoided the word *monachus* (monk), and he used *monasterium* for the first time only in a somewhat furtive way,[103] preceding it with the well-known paraphrase which explained and justified it, 'the school of the Lord's service'. Yet these scruples about terminology raise a suspicion: was the Master cognizant that the monastic vocabulary does not have its origin in Scripture? His reluctance to call things by their name might be an indication of some embarrassment. Our author, knowing that monasticism appeared, in fact, well after the New Testament and, as it were, on its margin, would have tried to have this alien origin forgotten as far as possible. The strictly christian references we have enumerated—the Gospel, baptism, the Church—would therefore be an overlay, a sort of camouflage.[104]

Without excluding the possibility that the Master may have been conscious of a certain distance in origins between monasticism and the Gospel, we should note nevertheless that the absence of the word *monachus* is an almost general fact in most ancient monastic rules. In this regard, the Master's behavior is like that of Caesarius, his contemporary.[105] Although the word *monasterium* was current with the Master, as already with Augustine and the Four Fathers,[106] we should not be astonished at seeing it introduced by our author in a relatively late and cautious way, at the end of the commentary on the psalms and after the well-known circumlocution. The term *regula* (rule), at the end of the Prologue, is the object of a similar presentation. For a long time the Master spoke only of *scriptura*, as if surrounding his work with a sacred halo,[107] and the biblical citations which he multiplied around the word *regula* tended manifestly to legitimatize this 'Rule' by attaching it to Scripture. The appearance and scriptural illustration of the word *abbas* (abbot) at the beginning of chapter two, shows the same thing.[108]

Rule, monastery, abbot: these three key-words of monastic language are therefore introduced with equal circumspection. But is it truly their monastic character which makes them be treated this way? We can ask ourselves this question when we see our author also using artifices to speak of a purely and simply christian reality like baptism.[109] The fact that he half-veils this in figures shows a bent towards mystery. The same proposal, as we have seen, is glimpsed in the commentary on the psalms where Old Testament texts are in the majority while the author is engaged in suggesting a program of life according to the Gospel.[110]

With this in mind, we can think that the Master's precautions in regard to monastic terminology proceed less from embarrassment or reticence than from a method of exposition and from literary taste. Instead of using these well-known words without reflection, as was commonly done in the short legislations before him, the Master treated himself to the luxury of introducing them in an artful manner. Thus he satisfied his imagination and his taste for play, while at the same time instructing his readers and making them feel the greatness of the monastic institutions. For him—and this is the point to remember—the Gospel alone is the guarantee of this greatness. Monasticism is simply a christian phenomenon, a reality of the Church.

We note also that the monastic theology of the Master and Benedict present a remarkable trait: Christ appears in it essentially as a superior and a leader. In the monastery *scola* he is both the master who teaches and the Lord who gives orders. In terms of family relations, he is represented ordinarily as a father.[111]

This way of conceiving Christ and the monks' relationship with him is connected with a concept of cenobitism that is chiefly vertical. In the *scola*, as we have said, the 'teacher' is almost everything; the relations of the disciples among themselves are of only secondary importance. The accent is not on the presence of Christ in the least of those who believe in him, according to the teaching of Matthew twenty-five,[112] nor on the pauline image of the body and the members,[113] but on the hierarchy by which Christ is represented among us as master, Lord, and father. This paternalism, to use a frightful modern word, is very clearly opposed to our fraternalism.

Finally, we are struck by the orientation of that society towards the next life. Its major and almost exclusive concern was indeed to prepare each of its members for the Last Judgment. It gave almost no thought to its own value as an earthly community. Even in regard to individuals, it dealt less with attaining spiritual perfection here below than with obtaining the reward of their labors in the future life.[114] In this matter, the perfectionist note added by Benedict to the end of his Prologue should not make us forget the whole eschatological perspective of the entire piece that he has recopied from the Master's Rule. Moreover, the hope of the *merces*, the heavenly reward, plays no less a role in the benedictine Rule than in its source. The gaze of these men was so fixed on eternity that it seems to us to have ignored somewhat the realities of time, even the supernatural ones. No doubt we are right to be more careful of them, but perhaps our expectation of the world to come is less ardent and less assured than was theirs.

NOTES TO CHAPTER 1

1. Prol 3 and 50. See also Prol 28. In Prol 13, quotation of Jn 12:35.
2. Prol 21 and 33.
3. Prol 31–32 and 37 (explicit); Prol 8 (*scriptura*); Prol 11 (Rev 2:7); Prol 21 and 50 (various reminiscences).
4. Prol 1,10,18,28,30,38.
5. Prol 1–4. The Master's Prologue and Thema have also left some important traces on Prol 46–49, as we shall see later.
6. Prol 5–50 = Ths 2–46.
7. Thp 1–81.

8. Th 1–25. Cf. Mt 11:28–30. In the Master's Prologue, which precedes the Thema, the New Testament is prominent. See Pr 13–14 quoting Mt 7:13–14. In addition to this central quotation, cf. Pr 23–25.

9. See *La Règle de S. Benoît*, IV, pp. 52–58.

10. Ths 46 = Prol 50.

11. Ths 1.

12. Transition from one to the other in Ths 2–4 = Prol 5–7. Besides this transition from the condition of sons to that of servants and from the New Testament to the Old, note the transition from prayer to action. If the Master here considers the Christian as a servant, it is because this image is more suitable than that of son when one wishes to speak of works to be done. Moreover, the commentary on the 'Our Father' was already filled with themes of action and of service. See t. IV, p. 38.

13. An idea dear to Augustine is that there is more interest and profit in discovering christian truths hidden under the veil of the Old Testament than in stating them directly and in specific terms. See for example *De doctrina christiana* II, 7–8.

14. See t. IV, p. 45, note 63.

15. See t. IV, pp. 48–49.

16. Ths 45 = Prol 45: *Constituenda est ergo nobis dominici scola servitii.*.

17. Th 14 (Mt 11:29).

18. Th 10 (Mt 11:28).

19. Th 14–15 (Mt 11:29–30).

20. See in particular RM 88. 14: for a postulant to re-enter the world is for him to be taken back by the devil into his city.

21. Th 22.

22. Th 17: *Non revertamus . . . ad sarcinas peccatorum*; Th 18 (*abrenuntiavimus*) and 21 (*renuntiemus*).

23. Does the divine 'rest' promised in Mt 11:29 (Th 14,20,23) mean the appeasement here below of the purified conscience? That would be in the line of an exegesis which sees the weight of guilt in the 'burden' removed by Christ. However, it seems that the Master is thinking rather of the 'rest upon the holy mountains' (Ths 19; cf. Ps 14:1), that is, eternal happiness. Thus the *logion* of Mt 11:28–30 would preach not only baptism and monastic conversion, but also the eschatological goal of the latter.

24. P. Benoît, 'L'Évangile selon S. Matthieu', *Bible de Jérusalem* [2], (Paris, 1953) p. 82, note *a*. It was already understood in this way by Ambrose, *Exp. Ev. sec. Luc.* III. 29; by Augustine, *Serm.* 70.3; by Hilary, *Com. Ev. Mat.* XII, 11, 13; and by Jerome, *Com. Ev. Mat.* II (PL 26:75d). However, Hilary and Jerome understood it also as the burden of sin (n. 26). For the same ambiguity in Cyril of Alexandria (fragments 149–151) and Theodore of Heraclea (fragments 81–83) see J. Reuss, *Matthäus-Kommentare aus der griechischen Kirche*, TU 61 (Berlin, 1957) pp. 79 and 201; Theodore of Mopsuestia, fragment 67 (p. 118) thought only of the Law.

25. Th 19; cf. Th 4: 'ignorance of good deeds'.

26. Besides Hilary and Jerome (note 24), see Basil, *Mor.* 44; Chrysostom, *Hom. Incompr.* 5. 605–616 (ed. Malingrey, SCh 28 bis; pp. 322–323), *Cat. Bapt.* 1. 28 (ed. Wenger, SCh 50; pp. 122–123), *Hom. Mat.* 38, 2–3, (PG 57: 431–432); Cyril of Jerusalem, *Cat. Bapt.* 1. 1; Augustine, *En. Ps.* 7, 16; 80, 9; 113 (I), 6; 139. 13, (cf. *Serm.* 69, 1); Cassian, *Conf.* 24,25,3–4; Eusebius Gall., *Hom.* 19, 2; Caesarius, *Serm.* 70,3; 107, 4; cf. Gregory, *Mor.* 30, 50.

27. Pr 13–14, quoting Mt 7: 13–14. The context speaks constantly of 'going' (Pr 3), and 'running' (Pr 16).

28. RM 1. 82, quoting 1 Co 12:28 (cf. Eph 4:11).

29. Basil, *Long Rules* 10, 1. The first edition of the Rules (Basil, *Reg.* 6) quotes only Mt 11:28.

30. Chrysostom, *Cat. Bapt.* 1. 26–33.

31. RM 2,2–3 = RB 2,2–3 (Rm 8:15). In the preceding page (RM 1, 82–92) which is an introduction to the *Qualis debeat esse abbas* (RM 2), the word *abbas* was not spoken, the abbot being presented as 'teacher', a scriptural term (note 28). This slowness in speaking of *abbas* recalls the last-minute appearance of the word *regula* at the end of the Prologue, and of *monasterium* at the end of the commentary on the psalms. Note, however, the presence of the word *abbas* in RM 1.2 = RB 1.2. We can ask whether the *De generibus monachorum* (RM 1.1–75 = RB 1.1–13), of which this premature mention of *abbas* is part, has not been inserted later.

32. Th 13: *recreaverat*; Th 17: *recreationem*. Cf. *reficiam* (Mt 11:28) in Th 10.

33. Th 12: *resurrectionem*; Thp 5: *resurgat*. Cf. Th 11: *renovati*.

34. Conformation of sons to the Father: Thp 12–14. 16 etc. Rebirth: Th 25 (*renativitate*); Thp 5 (*denuo renati per baptismum*).

35. Thp 2: *ausi sumus*; Thp 10: *audemus*. No doubt there is an echo here of the liturgical formula introducing the Lord's Prayer.

36. Th 23: *christianam legem*; Thp: *mandata mea* (Jn 15:10). See also the entire commentary on the third petition.

37. Thp 5 and 7.

38. Thp 11; Ths 46 = Prol 50.

39. See the preceding note. Cf. Thp 10: *baptismi*.

40. Thp 8. Cf. Th 20 and 23 (*requiem*); Ths 19 (*requiescet*).

41. Thp 6: *ut . . . illum redeat in paradisum generatio nostra per gratiam . . . .*

42. Ths 17: *ut mereamur eum qui nos vocavit in regnum suum videre.*.

43. Ths 11: *vitam* (Ps 33:13); Ths 19 *requiescet* (Ps 14:1).

44. Ths 39 (Ps 14:1).

45. Ths 23–24: *iam . . . iam*.

46. Thp 2: *iam*.

47. RM 1. 87: *omnes quibus adhuc insipientia mater est*.

48. Th 20 *sapientiam Dei accipientes*.

49. *Adhuc* (RM 1. 87) alludes perhaps to the distinction between cenobites and anchorites expressed earlier (RM 1. 1–5 = RB 1. 1–5; see however note 31). Of the anchorites the Master says *securi iam sine consolatione alterius* (RM 1.5 = RB 1.5). This new *iam* makes us think of those of Th 23–24 and Thp 2.

50. *Sub quorum imperio vel doctrina Christi regerentur ecclesiae et scolae.* RM 1. 83. Cf. Rm 14: 13–14.

51. RM 11, 5–14.

52. Augustine, *Serm.* 177.2: the *schola Christi* is the only one which teaches how to get rid of avarice, while the philosophers are content to censure it in words. Augustine, *De disc. christ.* 11–12. (PL 40: 675–676), speaks of fearing the rod of the Master (Christ), by remembering the punishments undergone in school as a child. The Church of Christ is a *schola* (*De disc. christ.* 1,9,15) where we learn to live well. Christ is its *magister*, who has his teaching-chair in heaven while the school itself is on earth (9 and 15; cf. *Serm.* 234.2: for the thief, the cross was the *schola* where Christ taught him from his elevated teaching-chair, that is, his own cross). See Augustine, *Serm.* 70.2 for the punishments inflicted on children in their *schola*.

53. Besides the two Sermons cited in the preceding note, see Augustine, *Serm.* 292.1: *Loquamur non tamquam magistri, sed tamquam ministri, non discipulis, sed condiscipulis, quia nec servis, sed conservis. Magister autem unus est nobis, cuius schola in terra est et cathedra in coelo.* On

this distinction between *cathedra* and *schola*, see *De disc. christ.* 9 and 15 (preceding note). Take notice of the passage from the school image (*discipulis . . . condiscipulis*) to the slave image (*servis . . . conservis*); the Master will do the same. See also *Serm.* 98.3. With Augustine, *De praed. sanct.* 13 (PL 44: 970), we find *schola* in the sense of a school where God teaches, but the text concerns the secret of hearts, not the Church.

54. RM 93. 26–29. See *La Règle du Maître*, t. I, pp. 111–114.

55. Other honorable mentions of the clergy occurs in RM 76, 83, 87.

56. Cassian, *Conf.* 3. 1.2; 18.16.15; 19.2.4; 19.11.1. The word is always used in the plural by Cassian.

57. Compare the two meanings of *schola* in Augustine (note 52).

58. Ac 4:32. This text is not cited by the Master or even by Benedict. Both indeed refer, at least implicitly, to the primitive Church (Ths 46 = Prol 50), but it is in regard to 'perseverance in teaching' (Ac 2:42); therefore it refers to the school aspect rather than to fraternal communion.

59. Basil, *Reg.* 3, quoting Ps 132:1–2 and Ac 2:44 as a conclusion. Reading Rufinus (*unanimorum*) it seems that Basil also thought of Ps 67:7, but nothing corresponds to this word in *Long Rules* 7.4, (PG 31: 933B). On the other hand, the greek text adds several explicit citations, in particular, Ac 4:32, following Ac 2:44.

60. Augustine, *Praec.* 1. 2–3, citing Ps 67:7, Ac 4:32 and 35. *Reg. IV Patr.* 1.5–9, citing Ps 132:1 and 67:7.

61. Cyprian, *De dom. or.* 8.

62. See B. Steidle, 'Dominici schola servitii' in *BM* 28 (1952) 396–406, and our note on Ths 45.

63. *Omnia debet pro Domino sustinere, qui eius cupit militare scholae.* RM 90. 12 and 46. As C. Mohrmann notes in *Études sur le Latin des chrétiens*, II, (Rome, 1961), 338, '*militia* and *militare . . .* in the time of the Empire . . . no longer meant exclusively military service, but they were applied also to the civil service, especially that of the subordinate employees of the imperial palace'.

64. RM 90, 29.

65. RM 87, 9.

66. In RM 87, 9, *militaturus* corresponds to *servitio*. Cf. RM 2.19 *servitii militiam* (genitive of identity), which becomes *servitutis militiam* in RB 2.20. In a passage unique to him, Benedict again unites, while distinguishing, the service of the master (*domino servitur*) and that of the king (*regi militatur*): see RB 61, 10. This last expression recalls Prol 3.

67. RM 92. 26–27.

68. RM 92. 29–32.

69. RM 90. 55. This passage which speaks of accomplishing the divine will, seems rather in the 'military' line (cf. 90. 29).

70. RM 92. 62–63.

71. See the text of the Council of Chalcedon quoted by Blaise, *Dictionnaire*, s.v. *schola*, #5: '*in schola devotissimorum magistrianorum militans*' (II. 3, Schwartz, p. 287, 14).

72. Gregory, *Reg.* 9.118 = *Ep.* 11.39: *in defensorum illum (Vitum) schola . . . militandum esse praevidimus.* Cf. *Reg.* 9.97 = *Ep.* 11,38: *ut officium defensoris accipias.*

73. Gregory, *Reg.* 8.16 = *Ep.* 8,14: parallel between the *schola notariorum atque subdiaconorum* and the defenders. In these texts does *schola* designate an abstract body, a simple category of persons without reference to a determinate place? In that case, there would be a notable difference with the *schola monasterii* of the Master, which seems to be conceived as a local entity, like the *ecclesia*.

74. See *La Règle du Maître*, t. I, p. 116 and de Vogüé, 'La Règle du Maître et la Lettre apocryphe de S. Jérôme sur le chant des psaumes', in *SM* 7 (1965) 366–367.

75. RM 28.46. More exactly, the Master here writes *ecclesiis*, in the plural, and *monasterio* in the singular. Does this last mean the whole group of monasteries, or does the Master wish to speak only of his own? Note that *schola* is always in the singular with him, except in RM 1. 83.

76. The monks are compared to clerics in RM 81. 6: the dress of one should be different from that of the other, *ut aliquid distet a clerico monachus*. This connection of the simple monk and the cleric should not be confused with the parallels established between the officers of the monastery (abbot, provosts) and the members of the clergy (RM 11. 5–14; 46. 3–7).

77. RM 92. 26–26: *scholae Dei ordinabitur magister, artem dominicam, quam ipse iam perfecte adinplet, Christi discipulis monstraturus.* Cf. RM 2. 52 and 3–6.

78. RM 90. 12 and 46.

79. RM 90. 29.

80. RM 7. 57–66; 10. 52–60 = RB 7. 35–43.

81. See t. IV, p. 339, note 183. It is only in RB 7 that *discipulus* is systematically avoided.

82. RB 3.6 (cf. RB 6.6 = RM 8.37); 36.10.

83. See t. IV, p. 75–87.

84. The question can be asked if *magistri* (Prol 1) does not represent Christ, at least in part. See t. IV, pp. 75–76.

85. Cf. RB 61.10: *uni regi militatur*, where Benedict remembers perhaps what he wrote in Prol 3 under the influence of Pseudo-Basil.

86. See t. IV, p. 94.

87. See t. I, pp. 65–66.

88. See t. IV, pp. 91–93.

89. Augustine, *Serm.* 70.2: the *aspera et gravia* (bis) borne by Saint Paul, contrasted with the *suave iugum* and the *levis sarcina* of Mt 11:30.

90. Prol 47: *restrictius*. Same confrontation of Mt 7 and 11 in Chrysostom, *Hom. Mat.* 38.2–3, (PG 57: 431–432: conciliation by generosity in the divine service); Augustine, *De op: mon.* 29.37 (conciliation by hope; this, together with generosity, is also invoked by Apollinarius of Laodicea, [67] in J. Reuss, 'Matthäus-Kommentare . . . ' TU 61, p. 19); Diadochus, *Cap.* 93 (the way is narrow at the beginning; later, good habit makes one find the burden light, and 'the soul runs with pleasure all the paths of the virtues'). Cf. Eusebius Gall., *Hom.* 4.5. More generally, the conciliation of Mt 11:30 with the many texts of Scripture speaking of the troubles of the just is a problem often studied by the Fathers. See Augustine, *Serm.* 70. 1–3, quoting notably 2 Tm 3:12 and Ps 16:4 (conciliation by the action of grace within and especially by love); *Serm.* 96.1 citing Ps 16:4 (conciliation by love). In *Serm.* 70. 3, Augustine perhaps alludes to Mt 7:14: *Et si angusta est [sarcina? via?] paucis eligentibus, facilis tamen omnibus diligentibus.* Cassian, *Conf.* 24.22–25, quotes Ps 16:4 and 2 Tm 3:12 (conciliation by absolute renunciation). See also Caesarius, *Serm.* 159. 1 (conciliation by charity); 236.5 (grace and habit).

91. Free translation. In fact, *dilectionis* is attached to *dulcedine*, and this latter can be attached either to *curritur*, or (more probably) to *dilatato*. Cf. Ps 118:32, whose conciliation with Mt 7:14 was often attempted by the Fathers (see t. IV, 90–92). According to Eusebius Gall., *Hom.* 4.5 a person makes the burden 'light' by entering the narrow way *cuius finis in latitudinem beatitudinis introducit*.

92. The role of grace, about which Benedict says nothing (cf. t. IV, p. 92), is implied by the *dilatasti (tu, Deus)* of the psalm.

93. This solution consists of subjectivizing Mt 7:14, just as the Master subjectivized Mt 11:28–30.

94. Augustine, *Serm.* 70.3 and 96.1. See above, note 90.

95. See t. IV, pp. 71–72: Prol 50 (= Ths 46) makes a strange sequel to Prol 46–49. Light is thrown on this state of things when we consider the Benedictine addition as a corrective, perhaps first written in the margin, to the Master's last phrase.

96. There is indeed an allusion to Baptism in Ths 2 = Prol 5, but it is seen clearly only in the light of the Thema and the commentary on the Our Father.

97. Not knowing the RM, C. Mohrmann, *Etudes sur le Latin des chrétiens*, II, pp. 339–340, denies that *scola* can mean 'a corps of troops' or even 'organization' in Benedict. Besides the two texts of Cassian which she quotes, account must be taken of other monastic uses of *scola* which I have pointed out in *La Règle du Maître*, t. I, p. 116, note 1. In these texts of Faustus of Riez and the *Passio Eugeniae*, *schola* means the preparation for the hermit's life no more than it does with the Master or Benedict.

98. See t. IV, pp. 306–308 for the relations of the first degree of humility with the basilian Rule. In addition, the *ars sancta* of our Rules (RM 3–6; RB 4) recalls Basil, *Reg.* 2, where the necessity of continual attention to the commandments of God is illustrated by the image of an artisan absorbed by his work (afterwards comes the recommendation of a society off by itself.)

99. 2 Tm 2:4.

100. RM 3.22 = RB 4.20.

101. See RM 87. 13–14 quoting Mt 19:21; RM 90. 65, quoting Mt 19:29; RM 91. 11–22 quoting 2 Tm 2:4, Mt 6:20–24, Mt 19:21–24, Lk 14:33, 1 Tm 6:9–10; RM 91. 38 quoting Lk 9:62; RM 91. 44, quoting Mt 19:21.

102. An idea current today, and indeed not without foundation. Cf. A. Heising, 'Benediktinisches Mönchtum und biblische Botschaft', in *Mönchtum - Ärgernis oder Botschaft?. Liturgie und Mönchtum, 34* (Maria Laach, 1968) 13–19, especially pp. 16–17; O. du Roy, *Moines aujourd'hui* (Paris, 1972) pp. 13 and 362; J. Leclercq, 'Le monachisme comme phénomène mondial' in *Le Supplément*, 107 (Nov. 1973) 461–478; 108 (Feb. 1974) 93–119.

103. Ths 46 = Prol 50.

104. Compare the effort of Cassian, *Inst.* 2.5 and *Conf.* 18.5 to connect cenobitism with the Acts of the Apostles.

105. See t. I, pp. 31–32. Caesarius does not use *monachus* in his masculine Rule.

106. Only the '*Regula*' of Basil takes no notice of this word.

107. See t. IV, pp. 30–31.

108. Account must be taken of the premature mention in RM 1.2 = RB 1.2 (see note 31 above).

109. See the Thema (parable of the spring).

110. See note 9 above.

111. Cf. A. de Vogüé, 'La paternité du Christ dans la Règle de saint Benoît et la Règle du Maître', in *VS* 46 (1964) 55–67. However, we are 'co-heirs' of Christ, and therefore his brothers, according to Thp 11 and Ths 46 (in this latter passage, *coheredes* is changed to *consortes* by Prol 50).

112. This scene of the last judgment (Mt 25:31–46) is scarcely evoked except in RM 3.15–16 = RB 4. 15–16; RM 70. 3 (cf. RB 36. 2–3), to which Benedict adds RB 53. 1.

113. See *La Règle du Maître*, t. I, p. 117, note 2. Allusion to 'members' in RB 34.5, to 'body' in RB 61. 6.

114. Account must be taken of the ideal of the 'spiritual brother' sketched by the Master (*La Règle du Maître*, t. I, pp. 102–107) and Benedict's notes on spiritual progress here below (cf. t. I, pp. 65–66).

Chapter II

COMMON LIFE AND SOLITARY LIFE
(RB 1)

T HE READING OF THIS FIRST CHAPTER engenders two contrary impressions.[1] Certain readers are chiefly sensitive to the praise for
anchorites which follows the definition of the cenobites. This second paragraph seems to them of great importance to the understanding of
cenobitism itself; for beyond it a more difficult and sublime career opens
up, for which the common life is the necessary preparation.

Others, on the contrary, are struck chiefly by the decision with which
Benedict turns towards cenobitism at the end and fixes his choice on it.
This preference accorded the cenobites includes not only the avowed
'omission' of the two bad types, the sarabites and gyrovagues, but would
also appear to imply the rejection of eremitism, at least in the practical
order. After having duly saluted the anchorites in conformity to the literary tradition on which he depends, Benedict turned away from them to
give all his attention to the common life.

Benedict's attitude toward eremitism therefore gives rise to discussion.
His laudatory reference to it can be seen either as an insight of great
doctrinal bearing, or as a rather platonic homage disguising an exclusion.

Yet these two interpretations presuppose equally that the function of
the chapter is to introduce the cenobitic legislation which will make up
the whole of the Rule. In fact, it is thus that Benedict presents his first
chapter. He defines cenobites at the beginning, and declares at the end
that he is going 'to undertake the organization of this most valiant kind' of
monk: *ad coenobitarum fortissimum genus disponendum, adiuvante Domino,
veniamus.* Then he passes quickly to the chief moving force of cenobitic

society, the abbot. The other kinds are thus described only in order to characterize communitarian monastic life more exactly. The whole chapter seems like a preamble where the cenobites are defined and situated in the general framework of monasticism before being organized methodically throughout the Rule. Thus although this chapter 'On the Kinds of Monks' counts as the first chapter, it is instead, following the Prologue, a second introduction to the whole Rule.

Before any analysis of the doctrinal content of this text, it would doubtless be good to examine the literary function which Benedict seems to assign to it. For that, it is indispensable to have recourse to the first chapter of the Rule of the Master, on which that of our Rule closely depends. We know indeed that Benedict first literally reproduced the Master's account on the first three kinds of monks, abridging only the third; then he summarized in one simple phrase the Master's interminable satire on gyrovagues, and finally re-expressed in two concluding phrases the condemnation of bad monks and his proposal to deal with cenobites,[2] saying nothing more.

In passing from the Master to Benedict, the chapter has therefore undergone three modifications of unequal importance. First, the section on sarabites has been shortened a little. Then, the description of the gyrovagues has been massively reduced; instead of having sixty-one verses, it has only two. Finally, the long conclusion of the chapter in which the Master presented the abbot-teacher (Rm 1, 76–92) has simply been omitted.

This last modification is surely the most notable and the most laden with consequences. Indeed it removes what was in the Master's eyes the very reason for the whole chapter. In the Master this chapter aimed only to introduce the one 'On the Abbot'. Its real object was not to describe the various kinds of monks, or even to situate cenobitism among them or give it a definition, but to present the 'teacher' of the monastic *scola*, that is, the abbot.[3]

This major importance of the final presentation on the teacher becomes apparent as soon as we compare our chapter with the introduction preceding it in the Master. We find here the same manner of composition as in the *Thema*. This latter, it will be remembered, has as its sole aim the presentation of the monastery-school, and it arrived at this goal only in its last phrase, after a score of pages dedicated to the evocation of baptism, the explanation of the Lord's Prayer, and the commentary on two passages of the psalter.

The Master adopts here the same slow, sinuous, nonchalant method. In order to lead his readers to the meeting with the abbot-teacher, he takes a detour which goes through the description of the different kinds of monks according to Cassian's *Conference* 18, and then through the satire on the fourth kind, named 'gyrovagues', on which he expatiates with a particular complacency.[4] Only after having emptied his arsenal of sarcasm does he decide to 'return to the rule of the cenobites',[5] and engages in an exhortation of the same kind as in the *Thema*, in the course of which he affirms the necessity of submitting to a 'teacher'.

This conclusion is indeed much more ample, both in absolute value and in relation to the whole which it concludes, than was the simple phrase presenting the monastery-school at the end of the *Thema*. Nevertheless it fulfills an analogous function. In both of them the key-text is placed at the end, and everything preceding it is only literature. At the beginning of his chapter 'On the kinds of monks', the Master could have put a notice like an exergue to the Thema: 'I shall open my mouth in parables'.

This structural analogy of Chapter I and the *Thema* is also verified by three traits they have in common. First, each piece uses a literary source which is different in each case, but clearly characterized. That of the chapter 'On the Kinds of Monks' can be pointed out with precision; it is Cassian's *Conference* 18, attributed to Abba Piamun. That of the *Thema* remains unknown to us in spite of certain reminiscences of Cyprian and certain family traits with the Pseudo-Chrysostom and Augustine. Still there is no doubt that the Master had before him a more or less precise clerical model when he first evoked baptism and then commented on the Our Father and the psalms. Thus the successive grand phantasies of the *Thema* and 'On the Kinds of Monks' both rest on literary borrowings. Both of them are not only a game, but also an imitation of someone. Only the prototype is different: like a bishop in his episcopal chair in one case, and like Abba Piamun in the other. In the first case the model is simply ecclesiastical, in the second it is specifically monastic.

A second common trait is the passage from the general to the particular which takes place between the initial phantasy and the conclusion. In one case we pass from the Church to the monastery, in the other from monasticism to cenobitism. In each case the reader is placed at the outset before a vast assembly and at the end the better part is chosen.

However—and this is the third common trait—this final choice is not made without preparation. The chosen part is not merely unveiled at the end; but was also announced at the beginning. The foundation of the monastery-school, decreed at the end of the commentary on the psalms, answers to the words of Christ 'Learn of me', which ring out in the parable of the spring. In the same way the 'return to the rule of the cenobites', decided upon at the end of Chapter One, echoes the first notice in the Chapter 'On the Kinds of Monks' , and the appeal to submit oneself to a superior, which fills this last page, corresponds to the mention of the abbot in the initial definition of cenobitism. 'To be under the power of one superior' takes up and develops the words 'serving under an abbot'.[6]

In both cases, the Master at the beginning of his preparatory piece sows a seed which will sprout and produce its fruit at the end. The only difference is that the *Thema* avoids pronouncing the proper word (*monasterium*) until its last phrase, whereas Chapter One speaks of the *abbas* from the beginning[7]. Perhaps in this regard the chapter 'On the Kind of Monks' is less well-composed than the *Thema*, but except for that difference the two pieces present an obvious structural likeness. By all the evidence the same author composed both of them, following the same method whether consciously or unconsciously.

This analysis of the Master's Chapter One allows us to measure the gravity of the amputation inflicted on it by Benedict. By suppressing the final exhortation he has removed the end towards which the whole discourse moved. Only the treatment 'On the Kind of Monks' remains, that is, the preparatory piece with its chief elements: the notice about the cenobites, the first mention of the abbot, and the concluding phrase effecting the return to the cenobites. Since these elements no longer support the final segment, we are tempted to see them only as teething-stones now unused, or the foundations of a ruined edifice. Yet when we consider the new edifice, the Benedictine Rule, we can still recognize a function and meaning in them, but the function and meaning have been profoundly renewed.

First of all, in Benedict's short chapter the account about the cenobites takes on a different significance than it has in the Master's forest. Now its purpose seems to be to give a solemn definition to the cenobites, before proceeding to 'organize' it, chapter by chapter, throughout the whole Rule. It is no longer a simple landmark, the first mention of the abbot, heralding his formal presentation, but is rather the frontispiece of the entire Rule.

This function seems all the more important since *abbas* has ceased to be, in Benedict, the only new element in the definition of cenobites. *Regula* (rule) figures in it, for this word had no place in the summary Benedict made of the Master's Prologue at the beginning of his own Prologue. Thus the initial account in the chapter 'On the Kinds of Monks' states for the first time the two constitutive principles of cenobitism. This doubling heightens still more its striking effect. Everything contributes to make it a magnificent threshold to the Rule.

The mention of the abbot, which was the essence of this phrase for the Master, also takes on a new significance with Benedict. The words 'under an abbot' no longer announce the phrase 'under the power of a superior' as in the Master's conclusion, but rather, in a more remote and less evident way, Chapter Two itself.

Again, the concluding phrase in Benedict's chapter—'Let us go on to organize the valiant kind, the cenobites'—no longer has the same function as its homologue in the other Rule.[8] With the Master, it was a '*return* to the rule of cenobites'. With Benedict, we '*go on* to organize' them. Instead of marking the transition from the preparatory piece to the exhortation, from the excursus to the continuation of the text, the phrase announces a proposition presented as a new element. 'Up to now', it seems to say, 'we have not yet entered into our subject. Everything before was only an introduction. Now we are going to organize our *coenobium*.'

A break has thus been established between the chapter 'On the Kinds of Monks' and the rest of the Rule. The chapter seems a preamble to the presentation, no longer merely of the teacher, but of the entire Rule. As a result a new meaning is attached to the whole description of the different kinds of monks. The chapter 'On the Kinds of Monks' seems less like a literary game than a serious deliberation—an impression strengthened by the insistent condemnation and formal exclusion of the bad kinds pronounced by Benedict before 'going on to organize the cenobites'.[9]

The omission of the Master's final section has therefore changed the character of the chapter 'On the Kinds of Monks'. With the Master it was a simple prelude, but it becomes the whole chapter with Benedict. A new title, reduced to 'On the Kinds of Monks' proclaims this reduction of the content of the chapter and the change of object which results from it.[10]

Furthermore, we should note that in thus abridging, Benedict is applying a procedure opposite to that which he used in the Prologue. There, it will be remembered, the last part was kept. Here, on the contrary, it is suppressed. Since the Master in both cases has placed his essential affirmations in the last part, it seems that Benedict's abridgement was happy in the first case, and unhappy in the second. The presentation of the monastery-school continues to exist at the end of the Benedictine Prologue, but that of the abbot-teacher has disappeared from the end of the first chapter.

What could have been the motives for this unnatural abridgement? To speak of inadvertence and awkwardness would be more to state a fact than to explain it. Once the decision was taken to abridge, according to the general purpose of the Benedictine redaction,[11] the treatment 'On the Kinds of Monks' was recommended both by its prestigious source—the Conference of Abba Piamun—and by the mention made of it in the Master's title. On the other hand, the title did not clearly point out the final exhortation, and still less the theory of the abbot-teacher.[12] Moreover, the assimilation of abbots to bishops was not perhaps to everyone's taste.

These are some reasons which could have lead to keeping the part 'On the Kinds of Monks' and omitting the Master's last section. But if it is difficult for us to perceive them, we are scarcely better placed to answer another question: in what measure was Benedict acting consciously and deliberately when he made his first chapter a sort of general introduction to his Rule? Was this presentation chosen for itself, or did it result more or less involuntarily from the constraints of abridgement and from poorly known motives which made the first part preferable to the second?

Seen in relation to its source, Benedict's chapter is therefore less easy to interpret than it seems when considered in isolation. It is difficult to rely upon the aspect of a general introduction to the Rule presented by the chapter, because of uncertainty about Benedict's intentions and the meaning of his abridgement. In any case, this appearance cannot make us forget the different and much more modest function that the chapter 'On the Kinds of Monks' fulfils in the other Rule. In order to be fruitful, our commentary must work especially at discovering the Master's thought. This offers more consistency than Benedict's secondary redaction and problematic intentions.

Before considering the Master's chapter for itself, let us try in its light to appreciate the two opposed interpretations of the Benedictine text which we mentioned at the beginning. The first, as we said, insists on the doctrinal significance of the paragraph on the hermits, and in fact, this is remarkable—as we shall soon see. But this paragraph had not at all the same material importance with the Master as with Benedict. Instead of being about the same length as the two following accounts, it was notably shorter than the description of the sarabites and almost negligible in comparison with the enormous satire on the gyrovagues. The account of the anchorites cuts a very small figure in the great collection of the Master's Chapter One, which includes moreover the long final section on the abbot-teacher.[13]. The prominence it has in Benedict is therefore a mere effect of abridgement, if not an optical illusion.

The opposite interpretation, which sees the Benedictine chapter as a choice of cenobitic life matched by the polite exclusion of eremitism, seems no less problematic when we examine the Rule of the Master, where the concluding phrase 'On the Kind of Monks' says merely that we are going 'to return to the rule of cenobites'. This 'return' to the subject lets us understand that the whole treatment 'On the Kind of Monks' was only an excursus and a game. What is more, it seems that the Master had no thought here of making a choice between the two kinds of respectable monks. The Rule that he writes was a rule for cenobites from the beginning, as he implicitly admits in this phrase.

Moreover, the same observation can be made about the corresponding phrase in Benedict. The words 'Therefore . . . let us go on to organize the valiant breed of cenobites' makes us think of those at the end of the Prologue: 'Therefore we must establish a school of the Lord's service'.[14] Just as then the foundation of the monastery-school was decided upon, so now the organization of cenobitism is decided upon. The decree promulgated at the end of the Prologue is therefore here renewed. Only the vocabulary is modified to conform with the contribution of the chapter 'On the Kinds of Monks'. We knew by the Prologue only that the monastery to be founded was to be a 'school'; now we know in addition that it will gather 'cenobites serving under a rule and an abbot'. With that difference the second conclusion repeats the first. It is less a matter of making a choice—that was made already—than of reaffirming in new terms a plan already decided upon long before.

Let us now examine the Master's chapter 'On the Kinds of Monks' to try to appreciate its significance. Above all we should be reconciled to this capital fact: the entire piece is only a prelude to the presentation of the abbot-teacher. The amplitude of his preamble may surprise us, for it is four times longer than the text it must introduce. Yet the Thema also was but the interminable preparation for the presentation of the monastery-school. The thematic relationship between the introduction and the piece introduced is as loose in one case as in the other. The chapter 'On the Kinds of Monks' no more lets us guess the theory of the abbot-teacher than the Thema seems to promise a definition of the monastery-school. If the two objects are indeed well announced at the beginning of the respective sections, this announcement is only perceptible retrospectively or to an alert ear. The reader who has not been forewarned feels himself carried away by a huge flood of words towards an unknown destination. What is more, he risks not even grasping that this whole discourse is only a game.

Secondly, the chapter 'On the Kinds of Monks' constitutes an evident borrowing from Cassian. As such, it announces the chapter on humility which will follow very closely, it too being a passage of the same author. The great spiritual section of the Rule, or the *actus militiae cordis* (treatment of the heart's service),[15] is thus opened and closed with a piece inspired by Cassian. To the exposition of Abba Piamun (*Conference* 18) corresponds that of Abba Pinufius (*Institutes* 4,39).

This inclusion proclaims the decided adherence of the Master to the monastic doctrine of the author of the *Conferences*, who held eremitism to be a fully legitimate way, even superior to the common life. In this he parts company from Basil who did not admit the solitary life at all.[16] On the other hand, the Coptic *Lives* of Pachomius put eremitism far below the *Koinonia*, without proscribing it.[17] The Master then, in appropriating this page of *Conference* 18, chose a presentation of monasticism not universally admitted in ancient monasticism. We cannot be surprised that he did not make the doctrine of the Coptic *Lives* upon the superiority of the common life his own, for doubtless he had never heard of it. On the other hand, he seems to have known the Basilian Rule.[18] Nothing therefore prevented him from reproducing the condemnation Basil passed against the solitary life. This circumstance gives a certain weight to the eulogy of anchorites which we read in our Chapter One. In spite of Basil, the Master felt no embarrassment, that is the least we can say, about extolling with Cassian their manner of life.

His attitude is more remarkable in that his contemporaries themselves were not unanimous on this subject.[19] Soon after him, while Benedict was recopying his first chapter without reserve, Eugippius seems to have felt a certain uneasiness. Not only does the florilegium E* place the conclusion of the *Thema* after the Master's first chapter, as if to neutralize the idea of passing from the common life to solitude by inviting the monk to 'persevere in the monastery even to death',[20] but the same collection ends with the third Question of Basil, a formal condemnation of the solitary life, and by a fragment from Jerome, carefully chopped so as to ratify this sentence.[21] Not a single one of the other cenobitic rules, from the beginnings to the middle of the seventh century, envisages cenobites passing over to eremitism.[22] It is therefore notably original of the Master, owing in part to the exceptional length of his Rule, to have mentioned this eventuality, even if he did it only in close dependence on Cassian and very briefly.

Such an acceptance of the solitary life, at least in theory, is a doctrinal trait very significant in a legislator so smitten with a wholly ecclesiastical conception of monasticism. As we have said, only the definition of the monastery as a 'school' could allow such openness towards eremitism. This latter goes along with a certain effacement of the values of fraternal communion which characterizes both the Rule of the Master and the descriptions of Egyptian cenobitism traced by Cassian and Jerome.[23]

In this regard we note that the Master has not profited by a suggestion which he found in his immediate source, *Conference* 18 of Cassian. When the Abba Piamun retraces the origins of cenobitism there, he discovers its first attestation in the picture of the primitive Church at the beginning of the Acts of the Apostles. And he recalls the 'one heart and one soul', the disappropriation and the community of goods, the distribution of what was necessary to each one according to his needs.[24] It will be remembered that these are the key phrases cited by Basil, Augustine, and the Four Fathers at the beginning of their respective rules,[25] defining immediately the perspective of the communion upon which they were entering. These texts do not play the same role in the Egyptian cenobitism described by Cassian, but they are nonetheless cited by him, in *Conference* 18, as proof of the apostolic origin of monasticism in its cenobitic form.[26]

When the Master drew up his Chapter One according to Cassian, he had an occasion for reproducing these citations of Acts, which are not found even once in the rest of the Rule. But he did not do so. This omission can certainly be explained by the briefness of his summary of *Conference* 18, in which he neglects notably what concerns the historical origin of each kind of monk. But this brevity did not prevent him from making a clear allusion to Ananias and Sapphira, the ancestors of the sarabites who 'lie to God'.[27] If he did not think of making the slightest allusion of this sort to the first Christians as models for the cenobites, the reason seems to be that the model of the primitive Church as a communion of hearts signified by a sharing of goods was outside his vision of cenobitism.[28]

As curious as it may be, this lack should not make us forget the positive fact associated with it, that is, the Master's recognition of the legitimacy of eremitism, beyond the common life. Since this schema of the relation of the two lives is a simple borrowing from Cassian, it is important to know if this latter was its inventor, as has been suggested recently,[29] or only one of its theorists and propagators. For that, we need only question the author to whom Cassian was indebted for his exposition on the different kinds of monks as much as, and no doubt more than, he was to Abba Piamun. In his letter to Eustochium, which is the certain source of *Conference* 18,[30] Jerome states summarily but in all clearness the fact which Cassian attests here and in many other passages of his work:[31] the anchorites, says Jerome, 'go forth from the cenobia'.[32] In its generality the affirmation seems to leave no room for exception.

Thus, as early as 384, or some forty years before Cassian began to write, a Latin observer held as an obvious fact that every Egyptian anchorite received his first formation in a cenobium. In 404, halfway between Jerome and Cassian, Sulpicius Severus gathered the same information from a traveller returning from Egypt.[33] These two witnesses leave no doubt as to the significance of Cassian's assertions in this matter. When the author of the *Institutes* and the *Conferences* presents eremitic withdrawal as a sublime way of life for which one should prepare oneself in the cenobium, he is expressing not a purely personal idea based on his own experience, but the common doctrine and practice of a whole milieu.

The same can be said for the effacement of communitarian values in the cenobitism described by Cassian. Rightly has J. Leroy pointed out that Book IV of the *Institutes* presents the education of the young monk and the whole cenobitic life as a search for individual perfection in which only the spiritual master, 'the senior' or 'abbot', seems called to play a positive role.[34] But this wholly vertical presentation which foretells the Master's 'school', is not, as has been recently thought,[35] the fruit of Cassian's ignorance and presumption which, because he did not know true Egyptian cenobitism—meaning the Pachomian congregation—caused him to try to pass off as such a way of life belonging only to the semi-eremitical milieux of Lower Egypt. We have only to re-read the description of the cenobites made by Jerome in his letter to Eustochium to verify the same lack of attention to fraternal relations[36] and the same almost exclusive interest in the educative work of the superiors.[37] On this point again Cassian's testimony is fully confirmed by that of his predecessor.

But let us return to the relationship between cenobitism and eremitism. One is conceived by the Master as a pitched battle in which the monk struggles against the devil, shoulder to shoulder with his brothers in arms; the other is a singlehanded combat. The first is thought easier, the second more dangerous. A monk must begin therefore with the first in order to harden himself little by little for war and so make himself capable, eventually, of the second. The warrior theme reproduces Abba Piamun's presentation, except for one variant which we shall study later. According to Piamun, the cenobite is the object of the insidious attacks of a hidden enemy, while the anchorite confronts the same adversary face to face.[38] For the Master and for Cassian, cenobitism and eremitism are the two successive phases of one progressive struggle.

This way of making the superiority of eremitism consist in the more difficult effort it requires[39] had appeared already in Jerome's Letter to Eustochium. The only feature of the anchorite's way of life reported by Jerome was the extreme frugality of their regime: 'when they leave the cenobia, they take with them to the desert nothing but bread and salt'.[40] But a little earlier the same author had noted the menu of the cenobites: bread, dry vegetables, green vegetables, and the seasoning of salt and oil.[41] The comparison of the two regimes makes clear the increased austerity of the anchorites' diet. It is understandable that Jerome then extolled 'their *ascesis* and manner of life, which is in the flesh but not of the flesh'.[42] The anchorites deprive themselves of the normal supports of existence, as regards both human companionship and nourishment. They walk far in advance of the cenobites in the way of renunciation.

Thus the relations of the cenobium and the solitary life are envisaged in the perspective of combat or of abnegation. If the solitary life is superior to the common life, this is because the monk there has a more dangerous combat and imposes on himself more costly restrictions. Nothing shows better the thoroughly ascetic ideal of this Egyptian monasticism, which continues through Jerome and Cassian to our two rules.

Alongside this summary perspective of struggle and renunciation, common to all the authors mentioned, we find in Cassian a more complex and elaborate view which uses the concepts of action and contemplation. Contemplation is the aim of the anchorite,[43] and it supposes the active life —meaning *praktikè* or *ascesis*—which the monk ought to have led to perfection in the cenobium.[44] This theme of life in society as preparation for the retired life of the contemplative had been well presented in Philo[45] and already applied by him to the two forms of Jewish monasticism of his time,[46] but it did not pass from Abba Piamun's *Conference* to our two rules. The Master was no more interested in it than he was in the New Testament origin of cenobitism indicated by the same Piamun, namely the primitive community of Acts.[47] Furthermore, our author neglects the scriptural model not only for cenobites, but also for anchorites. Cassian developed Jerome's indications,[48] and abundantly illustrated the 'second kind of monks' with examples and biblical testimonies.[49] Nothing of all that passed over to the Master.

Our two rules then describe the praiseworthy monks—the cenobites and hermits—with neither reference to Scripture nor trace of hellenic terminology. This silence is the more remarkable because the abbot at the end of the chapter will be presented as a 'teacher' linked with the Pauline enumeration of charisms, with the evident preoccupation of giving the abbatial office a scriptural base and an historical tradition reaching back to the apostles. The more the Master develops the presentation of the three fundamental realities which form the object of his introductions—the rule, the monastery, and the abbot—the more he simplifies the theory of the kinds of monks bequeathed him by Cassian. This contrast makes very evident the subsidiary role of the chapter 'On the Kinds of Monks', which is a simple prelude to the theory of the abbot-teacher.

However little interested the Master seems to have been in describing anchorites, he has still added quite a personal touch. We have already observed that he modified the opposition established by Cassian between the *sly* warfare undergone by cenobites and the *open* struggle faced by anchorites. With the Master, the first ones fight *as a body* while the latter engage in *single* combat. The interest of this modification lies in its insistence on the advantages of the common life. 'The help of many, the battle line of brothers, the consolation of another'—these expressions tell of the precious help which the cenobite receives from his brothers, a value which Cassian completely ignored.[50] Perhaps the Master remembered here the recommendation of the exercises common to the christian community which Leo addressed to the faithful of Rome in announcing the Ember days to them.[51] The Master remained quite far from this ecclesiastical theme—for Leo, the intermittent efforts of the entire Church are more efficacious than those of individuals habitually left to themselves—but he would at least draw from it his positive appreciation of brotherly help and collective combat.

Whether the Master owed these emphases to Leo or drew them from his own resources, in any case he goes beyond Cassian's concepts, but without departing from Cassian's underlying intention. What the whole of Abba Piamun's exposition tended to demonstrate was the grandeur of cenobitism, the only mode of monastic life going back to the apostles and furnishing indispensable formation for the solitary life. Even in its praise of anchorites *Conference* 18 was intended as a recommendation of the cenobium.

We can say the same for the chapter 'On the Kinds of Monks' of our two rules. Like their source, this section only aims at establishing the primordial necessity of the common life. The celebration of the anchorites is itself, after all, only an element of this demonstration. Not that there is room to suspect its sincerity, but if our authors admit with Cassian that the anchorite is great and admirable, this is precisely because they see in him a perfect cenobite, capable of doing without cenobitic discipline after having fulfilled it to perfection.

Perhaps the chief interest of this account of anchorites is that it places mercilessly before us an embarrassing fact; the Master's cenobitism, like

Cassian's, regards the common life as a means and not as an end. We made this remark when commenting on the definition of the monastery as a school. We verify it again here. The most important thing in the cenobium does not seem to be the fraternal union in itself, but the struggle against the common enemy. When a member of the 'battle line of brothers' becomes capable of fighting alone, the monks admire his assurance and let him display his skill in solitude, with the help of God. Doubtless the Master gives cenobitism a more communitarian aspect by the Leonine touches of which we have spoken, but this community is a community of action, turned towards a well-defined goal and one exterior to itself, so to speak. We would dare call it an open cenobitism, both because it can empty out into a further eremitical stage and because, far from taking itself as an end point, it is ordered to a purification of consciences which is each person's business.

Thoroughly ascetic and individualist, such a concept supposes that the monk takes very seriously 'the struggle against the vices of the flesh and of thoughts'. Monasticism, under its two valid forms, pursues this enterprise methodically. It has a task to accomplish which it holds as sovereignly important and absorbing. It is not by chance that the paragraph on hermits ends with the warlike formula we have just cited. The same formula is found equivalently at the end of the chapter on the abbot and on humility.[52] It expresses therefore a constant thought, a definite design. The purification of man, the elimination of 'vice'—that is indeed the great business of monastic life.

Thus the account about anchorites throws a very keen light on cenobitism itself. And since the recommendation of cenobitism is the underlying intention of the whole piece, we would do well, in concluding, to examine carefully the small opening phrase which defines cenobitism. We have stated elsewhere what this definition owes to, and what it adds to, that of Abba Piamun.[53] But these relations of the phrase with its source in Cassian should not make us neglect its function within the Rule itself.

In this regard, the definition of cenobites ('. . . who live in monasteries, serving under a rule and an abbot') is a wonderful summary. First of all, in the adjective (*monasteriale*) it turns to profit the term 'monastery' (*monasterium*) which has just appeared for the first time in the conclusion of the commentary on the psalms.[54] The second term, the participle 'serving' (*militans*) makes us think of one of the meanings of *scola*, a body of troops, and thus recalls again the end of the preceding section. The words 'under a rule' look still further back, in referring the reader, at least in the Master, to the presentation of the Rule which terminates his Prologue. The final phrase 'and an abbot' draws our attention ahead, towards the presentation of the abbot-teacher at the end of the Master's Chapter One and towards the directory for the abbot in both rules.

Although the principal purpose of this opening formula is no doubt to announce by its phrase 'under an abbot' the concluding phrase of the chapter, 'under the power of one superior', it also possesses the privilege of mentioning together the three great realities which the Master wishes to present separately in his three successive introductions: the Rule, the monastery-school, and the abbot. Such a meeting has not taken place by accident, especially since the word 'rule' was absent from the source of the phrase, Cassian. We witness here a remarkable effort at synthesis which succeeds in striking a nice concise formula.

At first sight, the sequence of the three terms seems different from the order the Master followed in his expositions, for the word 'rule' here does not precede the monastery-school but follows it. Yet in reality, the position of *monasteriale* (= 'those who live in monasteries') as 'the common factor' commanding both the phrases 'under a rule' and 'under an abbot', corresponds well to that of the monastery-school (end of the *Thema*) between 'rule' (end of the Prologue) and 'abbot-teacher' (end of Chapter One). Just as it is materially in the center of the ample triptych of introductions, the monastery is logically central in this short synthetic formula, being flanked by the two principles of authority which rule it.

This is an admirable constitutional formula—the Rule and the abbot, —that is, the law and the leader, the authority of the letter and that of the living person. If one is placed before the other, this is perhaps because the laws of composition oblige the author to speak of the 'rule' before anything else. Is not the work itself the first thing to be presented at the beginning of a work? But when we see that the Master in the rest of his Rule habitually mentions the Rule first and then the abbot,[55] we ask ourselves whether this order does not imply some sort of priority of law to person.

In fact, the Rule of the Master claims to trace for the abbot not only the directing lines of his government, but a regime which he and his community must follow even in details.[56]

This predominance of the written law over the person of the leader, of the dead letter over life may seem suffocating, and for want of any express declaration, Benedict's manner of legislating lets us think that he judged it so as well.[57] Yet the Master's formula has the merit of recalling that an abbot is nothing without a rule, written or unwritten, to underlie his authority and direct its exercise. If the abbot holds the place of Christ in the monastery, the Rule plays there a role analogous to that of Scripture in the Church.[58] It flows from the word of God, and constitutes, on an equal footing with the abbot, a mode of the divine presence and action in the midst of the monks.

NOTES TO CHAPTER 2

1. See *La Communauté et l'Abbé*, p. 61, note 3 (E.T. p. 47, n. 27).

2. See *Ibid.*, p. 49–51 and 68–77 (E.T. p. 38–40 and p. 52–59), as well as the notes to our edition of RB (t. I, pp. 436–440). There is a special study of the two last notices and Benedict's conclusion in our article 'Le *De generibus monachorum* du Maître et de Benoît. Sa source. Son auteur', in *RBS* II, pp. 1–24.

3. It is true that RM 1. T does not mention the abbot-teacher. But the last part of this title (*actus et vita monachorum in coenobiis*) denotes probably the presentation of this person in RM 1. 76–92 (see *La Règle du Maître*, t. I, p. 448). On this problematic title, see t. IV, p. 69, n. 120.

4. The long text of this satire (mss P* and A*) is indeed authentic, as we have shown in the articles 'S. Benoît en son temps', in *RBS* I, pp. 178–179, and 'Le *De generibus monachorum* du Maître', in *RBS* II, pp. 12–18.

5. RM 1. 75. For the meaning of this phrase, see *La Règle du Maître*, t. I, pp. 191–195.

6. Compare RM 1.2 (= RB 1.2) and RM 1.87.

7. This fact is all the more surprising since the conclusion of the chapter (RM 1.76–92) will avoid pronouncing this name, replacing it with 'doctor'. On this subject, see the preceding chapter, notes 31 and 108.

8. Compare RM 1.75 (*revertamur*) and RB 1.13 (*veniamus*).

9. On this global condemnation of RB 1. 12 framed by *per omnia deteriores sarabaitis* (1.11) and *His ergo omissis* (1.13), see the article 'Le *De generibus*', in RBS II, pp. 15–16. The mention '*adiuvante Domino*' in the final phrase (RB 1.13) produces moreover the same effect, reinforcing the impression of being present at a serious decision. It is lacking in the Master.

10. Already the Master's Table of chapters (RM Cap 1) gave *De quatuor generibus monachorum*. See above, note 3.

11. The abridgement here is very radical (close to 6/7; see t. I, pp. 201–203), perhaps in prevision of the two following chapters (RB 2–3) where Benedict, by way of exception, will be a little longer than the Master.

12. See above, note 3.
13. Cf. *La Communauté et l'Abbé*, p. 62, n. 1 (E.T. p. 48, n. 28).
14. Compare Prol 45 and 1.13. The idea of obligation in *constituenda est* is absent from *ad . . . disponendum*, but this latter is joined to the jussive *veniamus* and makes one decision with it.
15. RM 10. 123. Cf. RM 11.1: *actus iustitiae*.
16. Basil, *Reg.* 3.
17. L. Th. Lefort, *Les Vies coptes de S. Pachôme*, (Louvain, 1943) pp. 176–178 (Bo 105); 267–269 (S⁵ 120–122). Cf. p. 106, 8–13 (Bo 35). Yet Pachomius venerates Antony: *ibid.* p. 268, 30–32 (S⁵ 120). However Antony's opinion on the relative value of the two lives, as S⁵ presents it, is not confirmed by the Apophthegmata relative to the saint. Two of them (no. 21 and 29; PG 65: 81d and 85a) are even severe towards the cenobites. But whatever Antony's sentiment on cenobitism, the account in S⁵ is at the very least a witness of the Pachomians' opinion on the subject. [Cross reference has not been made to the English translations of the *Lives* (*Pachomian Koinonia I*— Kalamazoo, 1980) because both Lefort and Veilleux cite by paragraph number - 3.].
18. See t. IV, pp. 306–308 (correct *La Communauté et l'Abbé*, p. 63, n. 2; E.T. p. 49, n. 30).
19. At least in the West. In the Palestinian milieu, as reflected in the Lives of Cyril of Scythopolis, the solitary life seems to enjoy the highest esteem. The normal preparation for it is in a cenobium.
20. See t. IV, p. 67.
21. See our articles 'Nouveaux aperçus sur une règle monastique due VIe siècle', in *RAM* 41 (1965) pp. 51–52, and 'La Règle d'Eugippe retrouvée?', in *RAM* 47 (1971) p. 240.
22. The Reg. IV Patr. 1,2 (E only) mentions the two kinds of life, but to effect the opposite movement, from eremitism to cenobitism. It treats moreover of a group of monks, not of individual cases.
23. Jerome, *Ep.* 22. 35; Cassian, *Inst.* 4 (in particular 4. 40) and *Conf.* 18–19 (in particular 19. 6. 6; 19. 8. 3).
24. Cassian, *Conf.* 18. 5. 1, citing Ac 4:32; 2:45; 4:34–35.
25. See above, Prologue, nn. 59–60.
26. Cf. *Inst.* 2. 5. 1.
27. RM 1.7 (= RB 1.7), alluding to Ac 5:4. See our Corrigenda to t. II, p. 912, and our article 'Le *De generibus*', in *RBS* 2, p. 5.
28. See above, Prologue, n. 58, and *La Règle du Maître*, t. I, p. 117, n. 1.
29. J. Leroy, 'Le cénobitisme chez Cassien', in *RAM* 43 (1967) p. 158: 'His doctrine on the relations of cenobitism and eremitism could well be only a discreet, and quite normal, justification of his personal attitude'.
30. As a good number of literary points of contact show. Compare Jerome, *Ep.* 22. 34–36 and Cassian *Conf.* 18. 4–7.
31. See Cassian, *Inst.* 5. 4. 1; 5. 36. 1; 8. 18. 1, and *Conf.* 3. 1. 2; 5. 12. 3; 18, *Praef.*., 2 (Provence); 18. 6. 1–2; 18. 8; 18. 16. 15; 19. 2. 2–4; 19. 3. 1; 19. 10–11; 20. 1. 2.
32. Jerome, *Ep.* 22. 36. 1: *de coenobiis exeuntes*. Cf. *Ep.* 125. 9: *de ludo monasteriorum . . . egredi*. See also Jerome, *De obedientia*; CC 78: 554–555. The end of this homily (lines 77–102) treats of solitaries living at some distance from the cenobium from which they went forth (cf. lines 79–80: *In coenobio vixisti: placuit tibi ut maneres in decimo miliario?*) Jerome does not mention as Sulpicius Severus does (see the following note), the necessity of obtaining the authorization of the 'father', but he notes that the latter sometimes obliges a proud young solitary to visit the cenobium.
33. Sulpicius Severus, *Dial.* 1.10–11. Severus adds several important features: the abbot's

permission is required for a cenobite to pass over to eremitism; the latter remains subject to his abbot's surveillance; a marvellous event which had just happened to a hermit living six miles from there aroused a general desire among cenobites of the monastery visited to pass over to solitude.

34. J. Leroy, 'Le cénobitisme chez Cassien', *RAM* 43, 147–148, citing in particular Cassian, *Inst.* 4. 40.

35. A. Veilleux, *La Liturgie dans le cénobitisme pachômien au IVe siècle*, Studia Anselmiana 57, (Rome, 1968) pp. 152–153. Cf. A. de Vogüé, 'Les Pièces latines du dossier pachômien. Remarques sur quelques publications récentes', in *RHE* 67 (1972) pp. 26–67, in particular pp. 62–66.

36. Jerome, *Ep.* 22, 35. About the only thing one can cite in regard to fraternal relations is the evening conference in the houses, when the dean exhorts his men to admire the good examples given by the brothers (¶4), which scarcely corresponds with the counsels of Cassian, *Inst.* 4. 40 (see above, note 34).

37. See *La Communauté et l'Abbé*, p. 53; (E.T. p. 41). The same almost exclusive stress on obedience is found in Sulpicius Severus, *Dial.* 1.10–11 and 17–19.

38. Cassian, *Conf.* 18. 6. 2. Cf. Evagrius, *Pract.* 5: 'The demons fight openly against the solitaries, but they arm the more careless of the brethren against the cenobites, or those who practice virtue in the company of others' (translation by F. E. Bamberger in CS 4, p. 16). This struggle with men is much less harsh, according to Evagrius, than close combat with demons.

39. This theme of difficulty as the source of merit can, moreover, be used in the opposite sense to put the *ascesis* of the cleric in the world above that of the monk in solitude. See *La Communauté et l'Abbé*, p. 334, n. 2.

40. Jerome, *Ep.* 22. 36. 1: *excepto pane et sale amplius ad deserta nil perferunt.* Augustine, *De mor. eccl.* I. 66 goes further still: *pane solo . . . et aqua contenti.* Sulpicius Severus, *Dial.* 1. 10. 2 is more vague: *panis vel quilibet cibus alius,* but in what follows he speaks only of bread. Cf. Cassian, *Conf.* 2. 19: one pound of bread, neither more nor less: 19. 4. 2. Other foods are used only for visiting strangers, it seems (*Conf.* 19. 6. 3: cf. 8. 1).

41. Jerome, *Ep.* 22. 35. 4: *vivitur pane, leguminibus et olere, quae sale et oleo condiuntur.*

42. Jerome, *Ep.* 22, 36. 3: *horum laborem et conversationem in carne, non carnis.*

43. Cassian, *Conf.* 18. 6. 1; 19. 8. 4. Cf. *Conf.* 1. 8–15; 9. 2. 1.

44. Cassian, *Conf.* 18. 4. 2: *prius in coenobiis instituti iamque in actuali conversatione perfecti solitudinis elegere secreta.* Cf. *Conf.* 1. *Praef.* 4–5.

45. Philo, *De fuga* 36–37: 'It is fine to struggle to the end of the active life before approaching the contemplative life, a way of preparing for a more perfect combat' (translated from E. Starobinsky-Safran (Paris, 1970) p. 125; *De praemiis,* 51, etc. See A. Guillaumont, 'Philon et les origines du monachisme', in *Philon d'Alexandrie, Actes du colloque national de Lyon* (Paris, 1967) pp. 361-373, in particular pp. 363-365.

46. Philo, *De vita cont.*, 1.

47. Cassian, *Conf.* 18. 5. 1. See above, note 24.

48. Jerome, *Ep.* 22. 36. 1–2.

49. Cassian, *Conf.* 18. 6. 2–4. To John the Baptist, the only one mentioned by Jerome, Cassian adds Elijah, Elisha and the persecuted prophets (Heb. 11:37). Jerome cites only Lam. 3:27–31; to this text, shortened however (Lam 3:27–28), Cassian adds a series of citations from Job and the Psalms. Unlike the cenobites, the anchorites are not connected with their scriptural prototypes by an uninterrupted historical chain. Since they began with Paul and Antony, their manner of life is a kind of christian resurgence of the life of the prophets and the Baptist.

50. See above, notes 23 and 34.
51. Leo, *Serm.* 89. 2. Cf. *Serm.* 18. 2; 88. 3–4. See note on RM 1. 4–5.
52. RM 2. 40 = RB 2. 40; *a vitiis emendatus*; RM 10. 91 = RB 7. 70: *mundum a vitiis et peccatis*.
53. See *La Communauté et l'Abbé*, pp. 59–61 (E.T. pp. 45–47), and the article 'Sub regula vel abbate . . . ', pp. 210–215. (E.T. *Rule and Life. An Interdisciplinary Symposium*, CS 12, ed. M. Basil Pennington [Cistercian Publications, Spencer, Massachusetts 1971] pp. 21–29).
54. Ths 46 = Prol 50.
55. See the article 'Sub regula vel abbate', p. 211, n. 7 (E.T. p. 24, n. 7).
56. Cf. *La Règle du Maître*, t. I, pp. 120–121.
57. See t. I, pp. 55–57.
58. See the article 'Sub regula vel abbate', pp. 217–221 and 228–230 (E.T. pp. 31–37 and 45–48).

Chapter III

THE COMMUNITY AND THE ABBOT

(RB 2-3 & 64)

ALTHOUGH CHAPTERS Two and Three are distinct in Benedict, they form a unit in the Master, and that is why we treat them here. It is true that at first sight the Master himself seems to make the abbatial directory a complete whole followed by a paragraph on the council which is clearly distinguishable and looks like an appendix. If we look more closely, however, more than one trait connects this annex with the body of the treatise.[1] The Master had reasons for bringing together in one chapter these two apparently heterogeneous elements. For him the council of brothers is concerned directly, indeed exclusively, with the abbot's charge. Since the abbot has to make every decision, he must provide himself with everyone's insights when it comes to temporal administration.

Benedict, for his part, does nothing to loosen the bonds uniting the council to the abbot. Although he treats the two questions in separate chapters, this superficial dissociation is accompanied in Chapter Three by a reinforcement of the abbot's prerogatives in relation to the council of brothers, and by a redoubled attention to the abbot's duties in this area.

We shall join to these two chapters, so closely connected, the chapter on the abbot's ordination (RB 64). Both in Benedict and in the Master, it is connected to the treatise on the abbot and council not only by an evident thematic relationship, but also by literary references and verbal reminiscences.[2] By uniting these three chapters we shall be able to take quite a wide synthetic view of the relationships between the community and the abbot.

'What sort of man should the abbot be?' This is the first question which our authors pose. Nothing takes precedence over the abbot in their description of cenobitism, which they have just located on the map of the monastic world. The primordial place which they thus recognize in the abbatial office contrasts with the last place which Augustine assigns it in his directory for a superior.[3] What came first in the Augustinian Rule was the union of hearts and the community of goods, of which our rules say nothing at the outset. The two perspectives are thus clearly distinct: on one side, Augustine's communion, and on the other, the Master's and Benedict's school. And this school, as is right, has nothing more important than its teacher, the abbot.

A similar contrast is observed between our authors and Basil, who also addresses the superiors only rather late.[4] On the other hand, the Master's and Benedict's procedure reminds us of Horsiesius in his *Liber*. This document, which comes closer to the literary genre of our rules at their outset than does any other Pachomian document, begins like them with admonitions to the superiors. It is only after having traversed all the degrees of the cenobitic hierarchy from the heads of the monastery to the house assistants that Horsiesius comes to the simple brothers, whose first duty is obedience.[5] References to 'our Father' (Pachomius) precede and accompany each step of this review of the hierarchy.[6] The superiors are constantly invited to imitate their founder and respect his instructions. This long directory for superiors suggests both by its tenor and by its place the capital importance attributed to authority-figures in the Pachomian congregation. It falls to them, as 'members of Pachomius'[7] and 'fathers' in their turn after him,[8] to continue his work of education and salvation.

This primordial role of the Father and his collaborators is also found in the other cenobitic milieux of Egypt described by Jerome, Sulpicius Severus, and Cassian.[9] All these witnesses of monastic Egypt insist equally on the vigor of the hierarchical framework. Taking account of local variations,[10] we can therefore speak of a common Egyptian tradition in this matter. Our rules belong to this tradition. Through Cassian they are connected in essentials with this Egyptian cenobitism, of which Pachomianism is for us the most ancient, the most prestigious, and the least poorly known, example.

In repeating thus what we have already advanced in our first works,[11] we are not ignorant that attempts have been made in the meantime to establish a radical break between Pachomius and Cassian.[12] According to them, the two men represent milieux that were completely different and without communication. On the point before us, their concepts are basically opposed: Upper Egypt and Lower Egypt, cenobitism and semi-eremitism. On one side is the spirit of service and effacement of the humble, good Pachomius, who wanted only to be a center of communion for his brothers; and on the other, the figure of the spiritual father of the eremitical milieux, similar to the master of the urban catechetical school, which Cassian illegitimately transposed into a 'cenobitic' framework of his own invention. This image, moreover penetrates even the Pachomian congregation itself, but only after Pachomius and through the fault of his successors. Cassian bequeathed it to Western monasticism, so marked by his influence, and it is found again in the abbot of the Master and Benedict.

We have examined these theses elsewhere.[13] Here we need only say that the works in question attribute to Pachomius an aspect more in conformity with certain aspirations of our day than to the witness of the Pachomian documents themselves. Certainly people are right in stressing Pachomius' ideal of fraternal communion, the model of the primitive Church by which he was inspired, the preference he gives to cenobitism over the solitary life—all these being traits which distinguish his work more or less clearly from other cenobitic concepts, Cassian's, in particular. But the Pachomian congregation was second to none of the other forms of Egyptian cenobitism in regard to the recognized importance of the Father and the hierarchy. As the former disciple and son of the anchorite Palamon, Pachomius was indeed the Father of the *Koinonia*. This spiritual paternity, extended to his collaborators and transmitted to his successors, establishes a profound analogy between his congregation and the rest of monasticism in Egypt, both cenobitic and semi-eremitical.

In addition, this sense of paternity was expressed among Pachomians, as with Cassian, by a very real assimilation of the cenobitic hierarchy to that of the Church. Here, as we shall see, is a new point of contact between this tradition and that of the Master and Benedict.

The first phrase of our chapter draws attention to the title *abbas*, from which the Master and Benedict draw a program of life for the abbot. According to them, this name indicates the function of the 'vicar' of Christ, who is himself our *abba pater* in the Holy Spirit, as Saint Paul testifies (Rm

8:15). The abbot bears one of Christ's names and appears as his representative. Such is the point of departure and the leitmotiv of the exhortation
which follows: that the abbot's teaching and the example of his life should
reproduce faithfully those of the Lord whom he represents. He should
have constantly in his mind the account he will have to render to him
who entrusted the flock to him.

Our authors thus answer their initial question: 'What sort of man
should the abbot be?' But for us it is less important to follow them in the
details of their answer than to examine the principle from which they
draw all these conclusions. What interests us especially is the question:
'What is an abbot?'. Our authors see in him the 'representative of Christ
in the monastery'. What does that mean?

The formula seems like a summary of the doctrine expounded by the
Master in several places, but almost no trace of it remains in Benedict.
These passages, the first and most important of which immediately precedes our chapter,[14] can be summed up as follows: The abbot is a layman,
exercising a function analogous to that of the bishop and belonging like
the latter to the category of 'teachers', that is, ministers placed by Christ
at the head of his Church in the last times, after the prophets of the Old
Testament and the apostles, whom they legitimately succeed.[15] Yet the
Church properly speaking is ruled by the bishop, while the abbot governs
only a 'school of Christ' or monastery. Just as the bishop is helped by
priests, deacons, and clerics, so the abbot is helped by 'provosts'. These
two hierarchies, ecclesiastical and monastic, can avail themselves equally
of the words addressed by Christ to the apostles and to their successors:
'Feed my sheep. . . . Behold I am with you until the end of the world. . . .
He who hears you, hears me'[16]

To enter upon his function, the abbot is first designated by his predecessor when he sees himself nearing death. The criterion of this designation is
the perfect observance of the law of God and of the monastery's rule, or,
if you will, perfect conformity to the example given by the former abbot.
In the case of the abbot's sudden death, the abbot of another monastery,
named by the bishop, is charged with designating the new superior, according to the same criterion as before. As soon as he is designated, the
one chosen is 'ordained' by the bishop of the place after his name has been
inscribed on the diptychs of the monastery, in a ceremony that consists essentially in two prayers by the pontiff.

This ordination rite throws light upon the Master's whole teaching about the abbot. It shows that our author, while likening the abbot to the bishop, recognizes a certain subordination of the one to the other. The abbot is a 'teacher' and a successor of the apostles like the bishop, but he holds this quality from the bishop himself. The monastic hierarchy is not linked directly to Christ, but is grafted at each generation upon the unique hierarchy instituted by the Lord, that of the Church.

It might seem that the abbatial ordination as it is described at the end of the Rule brings a very late and quite external corrective to the solemn declarations at the beginning, where the Master seemed to put the two hierarchies on a level of equality pure and simple. But although these first declarations make no mention of the rite of ordination,[17] the first chapter presents the relationship between *ecclesia* and *scola* in terms which imply that the latter depends on the former. For the Master, the monastic 'school' is an institution distinct from the secular Church, but it is part of the great Church of all places and all times.[18] The name *ecclesia*, borne by both 'churches', suggests that the monastery is not simply independent of, and of the same rank as, the local Church. The local Church, representing the universal Church here and now, has a certain pre-eminence over the monastery. It envelopes it, while leaving it autonomous.

The Master is only conforming to the common thought and practice of his time in regard to the abbatial blessing and the relations of the monastery with the Church. The 'ordination' of the abbot by the bishop was in the sixth century an indispensable rite assuring each monastery its legitimate government.[19] A series of conciliar and papal decisions recognized this government's full authority in its domain,[20] excepting the ecclesiastical hierarchy's right of correction in a case of disorder. Even the designation of the new abbot by the former resembles that of the new bishop by his predecessor, a system officially in force at Rome from Symmachus to Felix IV, that is, during the very time of the Master.[21]

Because the Master was basically ecclesiastical in his principles, norms, and models, he did not think that the abbots receive their investiture directly from God, as though they were charismatics. It would be inexact to speak of 'charism' in this regard, since they are designated—at least in the Master's monasteries—only after being recognized as better than all others and chosen by God himself. In fact, the criterion of the divine choice is simply the perfect conduct of the subject, the fruit of his persevering efforts throughout the contest in virtue set up by the former abbot. It is more a matter of good works than of gifts, of human liberty than of grace. If the abbot has a charism, a term the Master never uses, it must be a pastoral charism which he receives, like the bishops, by a quasi-sacramental rite. Therefore he is not invested by the direct action of the Holy Spirit, but by means of an hierarchical ordination, which, like the election itself, is considered the work of God.[22]

The assimilation of monastic superiors to those of the Church does not constitute a novelty either. In the ecclesiastical documents of the sixth century we find abbots joined with bishops,[23] and this coupling implies a certain parity between the two offices. In monastic tradition the parallel in question is constantly supposed by the application to abbots of New Testament texts concerning the hierarchy of the People of God. Basil and Jerome invoke the words 'He who hears you, hears me' to demand obedience be paid to the heads of the monasteries.[24] Horsiesius sees in the heads of the houses pastors to whom are addressed the words of Christ to Peter, 'Feed my sheep'[25] He claims for the superiors of cenobia the same obedience which the Epistle to the Hebrews demands for those of the Churches.[26] He reminds them that they will have to render an account for the entire flock 'over which the Holy Spirit has placed them as bishops, so that the Church of God may be fed'.[27] These references and other like it[28] attest that the third superior of the Pachomian congregation conceived the congregation as a quasi-Church in which the superiors played a role analogous to that of the clergy in the Church. Similarly, Cassian represents the *seniores* of Egyptian monasticism as a sort of *magisterium* watching to safeguard an ascetic and spiritual tradition going back to the apostles.[29]

The Master therefore is not innovating in making the abbot the vicar of Christ in the monastery and the homologue of the bishop. His chief originality lies in explicitating and systematizing thoughts which had remained till then more latent than formulated, more lived than reflected upon. The concept of 'teacher', the successor of the apostles, helps him thus integrate the abbatial office into the christian hierarchy, alongside the episcopate. This theory, drawn from a debatable reading of 1 Corinthians 12:28 is reinforced by another scriptural reference (Rm 8:15) which gives him the very name of *abbas*. These two Biblical arguments are new, it seems, but the idea they illustrate is not. In formulating it, the

Master is only giving precise form to what had been commonly thought for two centuries.

The abbot therefore is the successor of the apostles as 'teacher' (*doctor*), and the representative of Christ as *abbas*. These two aspects of his charge are scarcely different, for apostles and doctors are nothing but the Lord's emissaries. We can therefore consider the inaugural definition of Chapter Two as an equivalent of the final declaration of Chapter One. The latter is connected with the definition of the monastery as 'school';[30] Christ's *scola* should have its *doctor* who holds the place of the one and only Master. The inaugural definition of Chapter Two is based on contemporary religious terminology; it was the custom to call the superior of the monastery *abbas*. Our author does not consider the monastic origin of this title. He was not concerned with the use made of it by the monks of Egypt and elsewhere,[31] but went straight to the New Testament and referred it immediately to Christ. Thus *abbas* does not mean anything different from *doctor*. The two notions have different foundations, but the same import. Both indicate an authority emanating from Christ.

It makes little difference therefore that Benedict in abridging the Master's work left aside the end of the first chapter.[32] In reproducing the beginning of the second chapter he kept the complete substance of his predecessor's teaching in a concise way. The repetition of this formula at the other end of the Rule shows that it did not continue by chance to exist with him. There, Benedict writing for himself prescribes that the abbot is called *domnus* and *abbas*, 'because he appears as the representative of Christ' and 'for the honor and love of Christ'.[33] The principle which laid the foundation for the exhortation addressed to the abbot in Chapter Two, becomes here a rule of conduct for the brothers. Benedict thus shows that he has made his own and taken to heart the Master's reflexion on the title and function of the abbot.

To the question 'What is an abbot?' then Benedict gives substantially the same answer as the Master. More personal is his response to the question 'How should the abbot behave?' This time instead of abridging, he prolongs. Not only is his Chapter Two a little more developed, all in all, than the Master's, but a second wholly original, abbatial directory, treats the matter again in Chapter Sixty-four.

We need not go into detail here about these two texts on which we have commented at length elsewhere.[34] It is enough to note that Benedict's personal contribution denotes not only the extreme interest he brought to the question of the abbot in general, but also a particular solicitude for the consideration which the superior should have for the different characters of his subjects. This theme was not absent from the Master's directory,[35] but Benedict repeats it in his with a remarkable insistence. The three suppressions and three additions which he makes in Chapter Two almost all tend to weaken the principle of equality dear to the Master,[36] and to recommend diversity of treatments according to persons,[37] and he renews this recommendation in his second directory, referring back to the first.[38]

This feeling for, and respect of, persons is generally one of Benedict's distinctive traits in comparison to the Master,[39] but it is particularly interesting that he makes it a special duty of the abbot. In this way he replies to one of the chief criticisms addressed in our days to authority as it seems to have been exercised traditionally in the religious life. Superiors are much reproached for having ignored the graces and personal needs of their subjects, who are sacrificed to collective interests and to an inhuman concept of obedience.[40] These complaints seem motivated in large part by an aspiration for a new statute concerning the religious superior, who would henceforth be placed 'in the center of the community and in no way above it'.[41]

We scarcely need say that this new image of authority is alien to our rules and the efforts made recently to find it in primitive Pachomianism have turned out to be quite vain.[42] But if the abbot of the monastic tradition is decidedly above the community, this fact, which can in no way be changed, does not prevent an extreme sensibility on the part of the legislator—as we see in Benedict—to the needs and weaknesses of individuals, a sensibility which he seeks in every way to communicate to the abbot. In this way the Benedictine Rule offers a permanent remedy to what seems to be one of the chief causes of the present uneasiness.

The chapter on the council (RB 3) proves interesting in that it places the abbot before the community and clearly defines their relationship. Without expatiating again on this treatise of Benedict and its source (RM 2.41–51),[43] we will only underline two important facts. First, Benedict's insistence on the rights and duties of the abbot. The rights are not substantially different from what they were in the Master, as has been thought recently,[44] but they are pointed out with an increased precision, which shows a preoccupation with preserving them. Still more clearly than the Master, Benedict reserves every decision to the abbot, the brothers being called only to express their opinion. The abbot is also entirely in charge of the procedure; the convocation of the council, the determination of the order of the day, the exposition of the question, all depend on him.

The abbot's duties are also traced out by Benedict with a new vigor. They no longer consist only, as they did with the Master, of surrounding himself with everyone's advice, as if that was enough to guarantee a good decision. The abbot is invited beyond this to 'dispose all things with foresight and justice', and to 'do all things in the fear of God and respect for the rule', pondering divine judgment. These recommendations show a new sense of the superior's fallibility. Yet from this, Benedict does not conclude to the necessity of limiting his powers and sharing his authority. On the contrary, as we have said, the abbot's rights are instead reinforced. Therefore it seems that Benedict accords him full powers, not with a naive confidence, but with full knowledge and the conviction that, all things considered, things would not go better if they were ordered differently.

The second important point is the obligation laid on all, brothers and abbot, to follow the Rule.[45] The Master made only a veiled allusion to the Rule.[46] With Benedict it appears as the supreme norm which should absolutely dominate every consultation of the monks and every decision of the superior. Doubtless this recourse to the Rule is related to the difficulties of the moment which we have just glimpsed, namely, that the law should both sustain the authority of the leader, and contain it. But the reminder has a permanent significance. At all times and especially in periods of universal decline, the community and the abbot have no better safeguard than a religious respect for an untouchable rule. An abbot is nothing without a rule.

To conclude, Chapter Sixty-four sets before us again the community and its superior. This time, it concerns the abbatial election. The mode of designation advocated by Benedict may seem more democratic than that of the Master. In fact, it constitutes a return to the normal after an exceptional regime. As we have said, the Master was doubtless inspired by the example of the Roman See during the first three decades of the century when he entrusted the designation of his successor to the abbot. In returning to the ancient and general norm, that of election by his subjects, Benedict in his turn followed the example of Rome, where the traditional method was re-established, at least in principle, after 530.

The indications of the Rule are curiously imprecise and unsatisfying when compared with our modern electoral techniques. What appears clearly is that Benedict was very little concerned with the form. Only the result counted for him. To obtain this result, an abbot who is 'worthy', any means seemed good to him. And the 'worthiness' of the one elected does not result mechanically from a vote, but is measured by an objective criterion, the law of God.[47] No majority, no unanimity can prevail against the imprescriptible rights of the Rule.

Thus we are led back to the Rule, to this 'abridgment of all the doctrine of the Gospel, of all the teachings of the Holy Fathers, and of all the counsels of perfection'.[48] The Master made its perfect observance the mark of the suitability of the future abbot.[49] In different words and another juridical framework, Benedict's thought is scarcely different. Not only does he, like his predecessor, recommend to the newly elect 'above all, to keep in all its points the present Rule',[50] but he has the same exclusive concern as the Master for the spiritual value of the new abbot, of his capacity to teach the regular life by example and by word.[51] Our two legislators say not a word about knowledge of the world and of men, of intellectual and practical talents, of charm, of suppleness and sensibility to the taste of the day, for their look is fixed upon a point transcending every human horizon: holiness according to the Gospel.

NOTES TO CHAPTER 3

1. See A. du Vogüé, 'L'abbé et son conseil. Cohérence du chapitre second du Maître', in *RBS* 2-3, pp. 7-13.

2. See A. de Vogüé, "Semper cogitet quia rationem redditurus est" (RB 2.34 and 64.7). Benoît, le Maître, Augustin et l'Épitre aux Hebreux' in *Benedictina* 23 (1976) pp. 1-7.

3. Augustine, *Praec.* 7,3.

4. Compare Basil, *Reg.* 15 (superior) and 3 (community).

5. Compare Horsiesius, *Liber* 7–18 (superiors) and 19 (obedience). The first six chapters are a sort of introduction which makes us think of those of our rules.

6. Horsiesius, *Liber* 5,9,10,11,12,13,16.

7. L. Th. Lefort, *Les Vie coptes*, p. 231, 17 (Bo 208) and 272, 29 (S⁵ 125).

8. Horsiesius, *Liber* 19 (p. 121, 2 and 9). Cf. *Liber* 15 (p. 118,7).

9. See Jerome, *Ep.* 22. 35; Sulpicius Severus, *Dial.* 1.10.1 and 1.17.6 – 19.6; Cassian, *Conf.* 18.4.2 etc. (cf. *Inst.* 4.8–10, etc. where the role of educator is played by the *senior* or dean, the delegate of the abbot).

10. The 'houses' of Pachomius do not correspond exactly to the 'tens' of Jerome and Cassian.

11. See *La Communauté et l'Abbé*, pp. 25, 135–136, 511–512, 533–534, etc. (E.T. p. 21, 107–108.

12. A. Veilleux, 'La théologie de l'abbatiat et ses implications liturgiques' in *VSS* 86 (Sept. 1968) pp. 351–393. Cf. A. Veilleux, *La Liturgie*, pp. 171–181; F. Ruppert, *Das pachomianische Mönchtum und die Anfänge klösterlichen Gehorsams* (Münsterschwarzach, 1971) p. 201, n. 316, and p. 400, n. 94.

13. A. de Vogüé, 'Saint Pachôme et son oeuvre d'après plusieurs études récentes', in *RHE* 69 (1974) pp. 245–253. Cf. 'Les pièces latines du dossier pachômien', in *RHE* 67 (1972) pp. 26–27, especially pp. 54–56 and 62–66.

14. RM 1. 82–92. See also RM 11. 5–14; 14. 13–15. Cf. RM 83. 9; 89. 18–20; 93. 4–5.

15. See RM 1. 82, citing 1 Co 12:28 with a characteristic inversion. Cf. *La Règle du Maître*, t. I, pp. 110–111.

16. RM 1. 85–86 (Jn 21:17, Mt 28:20); 1. 89 (Lk 10:16).

17. Cf. A. Veilleux, *La théologie*, p. 373.

18. Compare RM 1.82 (*Ecclesiae suae . . . Dominus*) and 83 (*Christi . . . ecclesiae et scholae*).

19. See t. I, pp. 116–117 (to note 58, add Pelagius I, *Ep.* 42); *La Règle du Maître*, p. 120, n. 1 (Justinian).

20. See *La Communauté et l'Abbé*, p. 403, n. 1; p. 414, n. 1. Cf. p. 343, n. 3.

21. See our 'Scholies sur la RM', in *RAM* 44 (1968) pp. 154–155. [Translator's note: Symmachus 498–514; Felix IV 526–530].

22. Cf. RM 93. 1–2.

23. Caesarius, *Serm.* 1; ed. Morin p. 18, 5. Cf. *Serm.* 136, 1; Morin, p. 536, 3 (*in ecclesiis et in monasteriis*).

24. Basil, *Reg.* 70; Jerome, *De obedientia*; CC 78: 552, 12.

25. Horsiesius, *Liber* 17 (Jn 21:15–16).

26. *Liber* 19 (Heb 13:17).

27. *Liber* 40 (Ac 20:28).

28. In particular *Liber* 11 (1 Tm 6:20).

29. Cassian, *Inst.* 1.2.2–4; 2.1–6. See A. de Vogüé, 'Monachisme et Église dans la pensée de Cassien', in *Théologie de la vie monastique* (Paris, 1961) pp. 213–240.

30. RM Ths 45 (cf. Th 14, citing Mt 11:29).

31. Let us note only that RM 1.2 (*abbate*) corresponds to Cassian, *Conf.* 18. 4. 2 (*senioris*; cf. *Conf.* 18. 7. 4: *abbatis*). Therefore, the term makes its appearance in the Master in dependence on the Egyptian tradition.

32. Cf. A. Veilleux, *La théologie*, pp. 374–375. Moreover, *scola* occurs in RB Prol 45, and *doctor* in RB 5,6.

33. RB 63.13. Cf. RB 63.14 (*dignus sit*) referring to RB 2.1.

34. See *La Communauté et l'Abbé*, pp. 78–186 and 367–387 (E.T. p. 65–144).

35. RM 2.12 and 25 (= RB 2. 12 and 25).

36. Benedict omits RM 2.21 and 30–31.
37. See RB 2. 18–19; 2. 27–29; 2. 31–32.
38. RB 64. 14 (cf. RB 2. 26–29 and 32).
39. See t. I, p. 36 and 57–60; *La Communauté et l'Abbé*, pp. 484–503 and 521–524.
40. See as an example J. M. R. Tillard, 'Autorité et vie religieuse', in *NRT* 88 (1966) pp. 786–806, especially pp. 796–798 and 802–804.
41. J. Tillard, 'Autorité', p. 793; A. Veilleux, *La théologie*, pp. 383–386.
42. See the article 'Saint Pachôme', cited above, n. 13.
43. See *La Communauté et l'Abbé*, pp. 187–206 (E.T. p. 161–173).
44. See in RBS II, p. 13*–18*, our review of M.P. Blecker, 'Roman Law and Consilium in the Regula Magistri and the Rule of St. Benedict', in *Speculum* 47 (1972) pp. 1–28.
45. RB 3.7–11.
46. RM 2.48: this *sententia monasterii* is called *sententia regulae* in RM 16.61.
47. RB 64. 1: *secundum timorem Dei*.
48. Bossuet, 'Panégyrique de S. Benoît' (1665), in *Oeuvres oratoires*, ed. J. Lebarcq, t. IV (Paris, n.d.), p. 630.
49. RM 92.8; 93. 51.75; 94. 7.8.10.
50. RB 64.20; Cf. RM 93.15.
51. RB 64.2: *vitae merito et sapientiae doctrina* (cf. 64.9).

Chapter IV

THE MAXIMS OF THE SPIRITUAL ART

(RB 4)

THIS CATALOGUE of the 'instruments of good works' is without doubt the most unexpected part of the Rule. At first glance it astonishes the reader by its unusual make-up—a list of maxims— and by its lack of connection with the surrounding treastises. Upon further examination the reader is disappointed to find in this succession of little phrases little or no order. Moreover, if it is a program of good works to accomplish with an eye to eternal life, one would expect a different choice. Why is the important side by side with the secondary; 'To love God and the neighbor' with 'Not to love laughter'; the solemn commandments of the decalogue with 'Not to be a great eater' or 'Not to be sleepy'? A list of seventy-four maxims is either too many or too few. Why not an infinity of others, neither more nor less useful? Finally, this collection of maxims astonishes us by its indecisive coloring, its uncertain relationship with monastic reality. To whom and of what is the author speaking? To seculars who are married and exposed 'to committing adultery', or to monks who have made a vow 'to obey their abbot'?

Almost all these diverse questions find at least partial answer in the Rule of the Master, whose Chapters Three to Six contain the same matter under a slightly different title (*ars sancta*) and with some variants. The literary genre of these maxims seems much less unusual when we have read in the Master such various sections as the mysterious parable of the spring, the commentary on the Lord's prayer in the form of a sermon, the picturesque satire on gyrovagues, and the majestic presentation of the doctors. The reader who has become used to changes of scenery discovers this new stage setting without astonishment.

The relationships of this treatise to those around it are more or less clearly indicated by the Master. The most apparent is its link with what immediately precedes it, that is, the directory for the abbot and its appendix on the council of the brothers. The *ars sancta* presents itself as a program for the conduct and teaching of the abbot.[1] Following this teaching by example and by word becomes as well a program for the abbot's disciples, a norm for the whole community. From this springs the 'we' of the conclusion, which is found again in Benedict: at the end of the chapter brothers and abbots appear together, undifferentiated, before God's judgement. The author has thus passed from the abbot alone to the abbot joined by the brothers, before speaking almost exclusively to the brothers in the following chapters.

More remotely, our treatise is also attached to the Master's introductions, to great trilogy of the *Thema*. In particular it recalls those little moral instructions, the sections of psalms cited and commented upon in the third part (our Prologue). What Psalms 33 and 14 indicated summarily—the conditions to fulfil in order 'to have life' and 'to dwell within the tabernacle'—the present chapter develops and makes precise, multiplying the precepts to be observed here below and extolling the beatitude promised to those who keep them. In their details, a good number of these precepts recall the formulas of the *Thema*, such as the golden rule of the Sermon on the Mount[2] or the double invitation, drawn from Galatians 5:16–17, 'not to accomplish the desires of the flesh' and 'to hate self-will'.[3] Just as the *Thema* ended with the presentation of the monastery where one must persevere until death, so the last word of the *ars sancta* is to recommend the monastery, considered as the 'workshop' where good works are produced by means of perseverance.[4]

In the other direction, our chapter looks forward to the trilogy of monastic virtues which will be the subject of the following treatises. Obedience, taciturnity, humility: these three words are pronounced with increasing vigor as the reader advances in the *ars sancta*. The catalogue of good works, the only part kept by Benedict, speaks expressly only of obedience,[5] while taciturnity and humility are evoked under other names.[6] Also, the three sister virtues are scarcely discernible because they are mentioned separately and without order. On the contrary, the following chapter of the Master speaks in proper terms of *humilitas, oboedientia, taciturnitas*. The three virtues are now reunited, and they appear prominently right after the three theological virtues and the first fruits of the Spirit.[7] The progression is affirmed again in the list of vices of Chapter Five. This time, the trilogy is put at the beginning: *superbia, inoboedientia, multiloquium*. Thus little by little the Master draws the reader's attention to the three cardinal virtues of the cenobite, which are going to be analyzed in the following treatises. The *ars sancta* functions as a vestibule for them.

Our catalogue also plays this preparatory role by anticipating many series of themes which will be extensively developed in the degrees of humility. The most striking of these is the announcement of the ideas basic to the first degree: meditation on the last ends, faith attentive to God's scrutiny, watchfulness over present conduct with an eye to the last judgment, rejection of evil thoughts, repression of idle words.[8] The sequence of the *ars*, by which the monk passes from 'the desires of the flesh' and from 'self-will' to obedience to the abbot, prefigures exactly the sequence of degrees one to three.[9] But before sketching so clearly and so consecutively the first degrees, the Master had inserted an outline of the fourth degree, with its scriptural illustration already partly recognizable.[10] Even the fifth can be guessed at in the maxim on the 'evil thoughts which come into one's heart',[11] while the condemnation of laughter, together with pointless words, makes us think of degrees ten and eleven.[12] In short, almost half the ladder of humility is already here, more or less clearly, in the maxims of the *ars sancta*. One of the purposes of this chapter is to present for the first time, in the form of detached pieces, a certain number of spiritual principles with which the reader will become familiar by following the ample organic expositions of the chapter 'On Humility'.

A last trait completes the connection between the two treatises. Both of them end, at least in the Master, with a long description of paradise in which certain details are even repeated word for word.[13] Benedict has almost effaced this likeness, both by reducing the Master's first description to a simple apophatic evocation,[14] and especially by supressing the second one completely. But even with him the ladder of humility tends visibly towards heaven,[15] and this goal mingles with that of the instruments. In other words, the art and the ladder are two equivalent metaphors, both expressing the effort towards eternal life, conceived as a 'retribution' and a 'recompense'.[16]

The 'instruments of good works' therefore are more related to the surrounding treatises than they might seem to be. The deliberate design which has placed the chapter at this place in the Rule is recognizable as well in the ordering of its maxims.

The two great commandments of the Old Law and of the Gospel come first, followed by six articles of the decalogue—five of them in the form in which they are cited by Jesus himself—and the golden rule as stated by the Book of Tobias and the Sermon on the Mount (RB 4,1–9).

After this exordium, which gathers together the most precious part of the two testaments. we pass from Christ's teaching to his person, mentioned for the first time. 'To follow Christ' demands that one 'renounce oneself', that is, 'one chastizes the body', notably by fasting and mortification of the taste. The counterpart of these restrictions on food will be generosity towards one's neighbor, who is to be fed, clothed, and helped in his various needs, in accordance with the words which Christ will pronounce at the last judgment, according to Matthew 25:31–46 (RB 4,10–19).

The twofold movement of renunciation and attachment to Christ which began this section is repeated at the beginning of the next. This time, the express object of renunciation is the 'things of this world', and attachment takes the form of a preference over every other thing.[17] Just as the preceding section quickly turned toward the neighbor and prescribed serving him by doing him good, so this section too passes quickly to relations with the other, intending to banish anger, falsity, hatred, oaths, and lying. Mortification of the irascible appetite succeeds that of the concupiscible, and the words of the Sermon on the Mount (Mt 5:22ff.) succeed those of the scene of the last judgment. The same passage from the Sermon on the Mount, bolstered by other New Testament reminiscences,[18] also inspires non-resistance to evil, the bearing of injuries, love of enemies, words of blessing in reply to curses, and patience in persecution (RB 4,20–33).

According to the parallel constituted by the fourth degree of humility we might also attach the maxim on hope (RB 4,41) to this section. But already in the Master's text this is separated from the group by a series of short negative maxims, each showing a fault to be avoided, beginning with pride and drunkenness, doubtless harkening back to a list in the pastoral epistles[19] (RB 4,34–40).

After this interruption, the invitation to hope seems the reply to the trials of the persecuted, evoked above. This hope has God for its object. Leaving aside the relations with the neighbor which have predominated so far, the thought henceforth moves in the field of immediate relations with God. This attention to God begins with the recognition of his action in us: from him comes all the good we do, from ourselves all the bad (RB 4,41–43).

By this theological appraisal of himself, the monk approaches a consideration of human destiny and the last things: judgment, hell, and eternal life, of which death is the entrance. This final meeting with God arouses fear, vehement desire, daily anxiety, sentiments which in their turn engender man's continual vigilance over his acts, in the certainty of being everywhere under divine scrutiny. He smashes his evil thoughts against Christ. He keeps himself from every evil word, avoiding much speaking, saying vain or funny things, and laughing much or noisily (RB 4, 44–54).

For disorderly human words is substituted converse with God: the monk listens to holy readings and replies to them by frequent prayers in which he confesses to God his past sins, which he must avoid in the future (RB 4,55–58).

By this demand for amendment the monk returns to the struggle against the evil which has remained in his evil thoughts and words. Now he attacks the desires of the flesh and self-will, that is, the double principle of evil actions denounced by the Epistle to the Galatians.[20] This power of evil will be held in check by obedience to the abbot (RB 4,59–61).

While noting in this regard the discrepancy which may exist between the abbot's directives and his conduct, Benedict seems to introduce the following maxim which contrasts real holiness and apparent holiness.[21] The same insistence on authenticity is seen in the invitation to 'carry out daily God's precepts in acts' (RB 4,62–63).

Then by means of the 'love of chastity' the list returns to fraternal relations which have been left aside for a long time. This last section prolongs in a way the series which was supported by the Sermon on the Mount, which will be cited again towards the end. Hatred is condemned, as is jealousy, and envy, and contentiousness, as well as haughtiness, the root of all these evils.[22] In a positive sense, Benedict points out the reciprocal sentiments proper to the seniors and juniors. Prayer for enemies, according to Matthew 5:44, and reconciliation before the end of day (Eph 4:26) crown these recommendations (RB 4,64–73).

To conclude the whole catalogue, Benedict invites the monk never to despair of the mercy of God (RB 4,74). This God-centered conclusion echoes the midpoint maxim on hope, as well as the great commandment at the beginning.

Such is the ordering of this list of 'instruments', which Benedict has taken from the Master without much change.[23] It shows evidence of more reflection that it seems to do. The first section, which is entirely scriptural, seems to have furnished the model which inspires the following two sections. In brief, the author first proposes the love of God, and then passes to the love of neighbor, whose manifestations are given in detail in a long series of articles. From section to section the two themes develop in a certain order. 'To love God' becomes 'to follow Christ' and 'to prefer nothing to the love of Christ', both these latter maxims being preceded by a demand for renunciation, first of self, then of the world.[24] Love of neighbor is verified first in the great prohibitions of the decalogue and the golden rule, then in works of mercy, and finally in patience under contradictions and goodness towards enemies.

Beyond the list of seven faults to be avoided (RB 4,34–40), one of whose chief aims seems to be to break the formal monotony of the verbal phrases, the thought of God becomes dominant, and almost exclusive. In this second section the alternation of God and neighbor is found again, but the proportions are reversed: a long intimate conversation with the Lord precedes a few maxims concerning love of the brothers. In short, everywhere solicitude for God comes first. The sequence of the two great commandments has served as the matrix for the entire list.[25]

This primacy of God is also seen again at the level of the implicit references. Almost everywhere Scripture is cited first. It is the exclusive mistress of the first section, and it informs the following ones, where the divine word more than once furnishes the beginning and the thread of the argument.

What has just been said about the place and ordering of the catalogue already gives at least a partial reply to another question we asked about the choice of maxims. As we now see, this choice is partly guided by the intention of preparing a methodical exposition of asceticism which will be developed in the first degrees of humility. In addition, attention to Scripture often influences the choice.

Even where these two motives are not directly operating, a deliberate thought is nonetheless present, and according to it what seems to us of small importance may appear very important. Thus in the Master's eyes loud laughter and pleasantries are obviously not harmless, indeed healthy, if not necessary, things, as they seem to us. Their condemnation is repeated with insistence, and with even more severity, in the following chapters of Benedict and especially in those of the Master.[26] Texts of Scripture are cited in support, and to them are added considerations drawn from the example of Christ as emphasized by many authors anterior or contemporary.[27] In general, the monastic spirituality of antiquity is severe on this point.[28]

Although these maxims are surprising to us, they result from a firm doctrine and not from an ill-considered choice. The same can be said for 'Not to be a great eater' and 'not to be sleepy'.[29] These maxims put the finger on a distinctive trait of anthropology and ascetic doctrine to which we shall have to return, namely, the importance attached by the ancients to the mastery of the bodily appetites. Thus this catalogue plays for us, too, though in a different way, the role of admonition assigned it by the Master and Benedict. By presenting us with what seems a lightweight precept side by side with the gravest commandment, it draws our attention to the distance which separates our scale of values from theirs.

The last cause for surprise mentioned above was the indecisive and, in the end, scarcely monastic character of these maxims. In this regard recourse to the Master's text has a double effect: at first it accentuates our surprise, and then it dissipates it.

The *ars sancta* is still less monastic than Benedict's instruments. We find in it neither the 'spiritual *senior*' nor the 'ancients' nor the 'juniors'. Loans and alms figure among the works of mercy, and fidelity to promises among the acts of loyalty, as though the cenobite were capable of fulfilling such duties. 'To honor father and mother' figures in its place in the decalogue, and has not undergone the prudent correction that Benedict applies to it.

But this catalogue, so close to secular life, is explained in the Master in the light of many other passages in his work. We have already noted that the final mention of the monastery-workshop corresponds to that of the monastery-school which terminates the *Thema*. In both places the monastic reality scarcely appears until the last words. In both the *Thema* and the *ars* almost everything before the end is stated in terms that are deliberately general and vague, and pertain to the secular Christian as well as, if not better than, to the monk. The same character will reappear in the long ascetic exposition which opens the Master's chapter on taciturnity,[30] and in the long allocutions, inspired by the penitential discipline of the Church, which he puts on the lips of the abbot and the culprit in the chapters on excommunication.[31]

Therefore the neutral color of the present catalogue is not rare in the Rule of the Master. To limit ourselves to what Benedict keeps of it, the instruments of good works pertain to the same genre as the commentary on the psalms, from which he composed his Prologue. Just as the latter presupposes, as we have seen, a rite of baptismal catechesis, so the catalogue of instruments corresponds to the moral instructions which christian pastors since the apostolic age had given their neophytes. The beginning of the list, with a series of biblical precepts which was already found in the *Doctrina apostolorum* and the *Didachè*, is particularly significant in this regard.[32] No doubt the Master uses here, as in the Thema, some document originating in the secular churches. And this re-use or this imitation is not a mere literary game. It corresponds to a doctrinal intention: to put monastic doctrine in relationship with ecclesiastical preaching, and to base monasticism upon the foundations of christian tradition and Scripture.

This intention of taking root in the common ground of Christianity appears nowhere more clearly, as we have said, than in the first maxims. We must dwell on this fact, for here we find one of the most remarkable originalities of our rules and one of the poles of their teaching.

It is not that the Master and Benedict are the first among monks to emphasize the two great commandments. Both the Augustinian *Ordo monasterii* and the Rule of Basil begin with the love of God and love of neighbor, 'because these are the two commandments given us by priority', as the *Ordo* notes simply.[33] Basil explains at length that there is an express order to the Lord's commands, and nothing can be set before these two general, complementary precepts, inscribed by God in our hearts as well as in his law.[34] The double commandment, thus placed at the head of these two legislations, plays an even greater role in them than it does in our rules, where it begins only one special chapter. The importance of the theme cannot be exaggerated, especially in Basil, to whom separation from the world and cenobitism appeared as the demands of the love of God and of neighbor respectively. Thus the Basilian brotherhood draws its very form from the two commandments.

On the other hand, Cassian's spiritual theology makes no use of these two fundamental precepts. The three Gospel passages in which Christ decrees them together are never cited in his work.[35] The source of the phrase in Leviticus on the love of neighbor is not cited either,[36] and if that of Deuteronomy on the love of the Lord does figure once in the *Conferences*,[37] it does so only as an example of a biblical word whose literal meaning is perfectly clear and satisfying, without recourse to allegory. It is about the same for the two verses of the discourse after the Last Supper where Jesus promulgates his new commandment and makes its observance the sign by which all may recognize his disciples.[38] Cassian cites them, but only in passing and in a context which singularly reduces their importance. The 'new commandment' is evoked, along with other texts, only to show the necessity of humility.[39] The sign of Christ's true disciples appears only where it is called for by the subject treated: in the *Conference* on friendship.[40] But Cassian's great spiritual syntheses in *Conferences* One, Three, and Eleven, to cite only the chief ones, develop without recourse either to this commandment of mutual love or to that of the love of God.

However strange this may appear, it can be said therefore that Cassian's teaching ignores the two great commandments, especially in the combined form in which they are promulgated by the Lord in the synoptics. And this oversight is not the effect of chance. For Cassian could scarcely present love as the object of the *first* two commandments, if, following Evagrius, he makes charity the *term* to which the whole effort towards perfection tends. In this Evagrian perspective, suggested by certain famous texts of Saint Paul and Saint John, charity appears as the 'infallible' and 'perfect' virtue which eliminates every fault and casts out servile fear.[41] Love thus placed at the summit of the spiritual ascent is indeed confirmed as an amazing and sovereignly desirable good, but it is also remote and hard to approach. It is reserved for perfect men, victorious over every passion, for those who have passed beyond the condition of slave and mercenary and have arrived at the condition of a son. It is not right to propose it indiscriminately to everyone, as the logion of the two great commandments seems to do. This logion is therefore passed over in silence.

The Master and Benedict do not ignore this draught of Cassian's. Their chapter on humility is even derived from it. But while they place charity at the top of the ladder, they are not loath to speak of the love of God and of the neighbor at the beginning of their enumeration of good works.[42] In truth, these two ways of magnifying love are not opposed to each other, if only one avoids treating one of them as privileged and drawing the consequences too rigorously. That is what our authors do. Being less careful about coherence than Cassian and his predecessors were, they tranquilly juxtapose the presentation of *agapè* according to the Gospels and the sublime vision of this virtue elaborated by the Alexandrians on the basis of the epistles.[43]

The beginning of the *ars sancta* and the instruments of good works takes on a considerable interest therefore when we confront it with the fact that Cassian had neglected the double commandment of love. In relation to their principal source, our rules show an enfeeblement of the speculative design, but also an enlargement of the scriptural base on a point of the first importance. By proposing love from the beginning of their catalogue, they offer an image of it which completes and balances that of the chapter 'On Humility'. Charity is not only the goal of a long ascent, the sublime state in which one accomplishes the whole divine will 'without any effort, as though naturally', but also and especially the 'first' commandment which each Christian puts into practice as soon as he sets himself to work for God. Thus the whole monastic life, not excepting even its first steps, is completely enveloped in the love of God and of neighbor.

But the two great commandments are not the only things absent from Cassian's thought. It is the same for the precepts of the decalogue. Only once does he reproduce the list, and then it is to establish a point of history: even before the promulgation of the Mosaic law, the saints observed its principal articles.[44] Elsewhere he cites 'You shall not fornicate' alone, but only as an example of the different interpretations to which a word of Scripture can lend itself.[45] None of the four New Testament formulations of the decalogue are found in his work.[46]

When we note that the golden rule is also absent,[47] we can measure the distance separating Cassian from our two authors. Cassian does not even mention what they, following Scripture, put at the head of their spiritual art. The remark made earlier about the first two commandments can be extended to the whole group of the Lord's commandments enumerated at the beginning of our catalogue, namely, this introduction of the Master and Benedict fills a gap in Cassian's spirituality. Unlike him, our rules opportunely recall the paramount importance of the divine law.[48] It is not important that 'not to kill' or 'not to commit adultery' seems more or less pertinent to a rule for monks. What the authors want the monks to understand is that no other foundation can be laid than that laid by God himself. This whole introduction is a profession of faith and submission to the Gospel.

The conclusion at the other end of the chapter also calls for our attention, and for the same reason. The aim of the spiritual art is presented in terms of an eschatological 'recompense', indeed of a 'salary' (*merces*). Such a representation may seem mercenary, ungenerous, downright vulgar. Nonetheless it is profoundly evangelical. The Greek *misthos* and the Latin *merces* are key words in the gospels, especially in Matthew,[49] as well as in the Old Testament and the apostolic writings.[50] The Master and Benedict, following Scripture, often appeal to this hunger, this hope.[51] In the middle of their catalogue they make it a good work to be done,[52] and at the end they propose it as the great spring which moves one to practise the whole spiritual art.[53]

Again, this 'mercenary' perspective contrasts with a certain theory of Cassian which has set its mark on a famous page of our rules. Explicitly in the first *Conference* of Chaeremon and implicitly in the clothing discourse of Pinufius, Cassian relegates the desire for reward to the imperfect motives surpassed and rejected by pure love.[54] From the discourse of Pinufius this teaching passed to the Master and to Benedict: the ascent of humility leads to perfect charity, which formally excludes fear of punishment, but also tacitly, if examined closely, the hope of reward.[55] We know that this sublime ending has been corrected by the Master, who hastens to add to it a long description of paradise. But Benedict suppressed this last bit, so that his chapter 'On Humility' ends, as did Pinufius' exposition, with the celebration of disinterested love and complacence in virtue. The present conclusion of the 'instruments of good works' acquires thereby all the more interest. It shows that Benedict, like the Master, remains faithful to a more modest but basically biblical vision of the motives which drive the Christian and the monk to act well.[56]

NOTES TO CHAPTER 4

1. RM 2.51–52; 3, T. See t. IV, pp. 119–126.

2. RM 3.9 = RB 4.9; Thp 59.

3. RM 3.65–66 = RB 4. 59–60; Thp 27–28. See our commentary on Chapter 5 below, nn. 9–11. This correspondence between RM 3.65–66 and Thp 27–28 should be added to the table of our t. IV, p. 165. Correct therefore pp. 166–168 and 179: according to this correspondence with the Thema, the maxims of RM 3.65–66 seem to belong to the 'primitive catalogue'.

4. RM 6.1–2 = RB 4,78; Ths 45–46 = Prol 45–50.

5. RM 3.67 (*obœdientiam*) et RB 4.61 (*obœdire*). Cf. RM 3.76 (*obœdire*).

6. Silence: see RM 3.57–59 = RB 4.51–53; humility: RM 3.39 = RB 4.34.

7. RM 4.3.

8. RM 3.50–59 = RB 4.44–53; RM 10.10–22 = RB 7.10–18.

9. RM 3.65–67 = RB 4.59–61; RM 10.30–51 = RB 7. 19–34. Since the Thema already announces these maxims of the *ars sancta* (above, note 3), this latter seems like a relay station between the Thema and the ladder of humility.

10. RM 3.35–38 and 45 = RB 4.30–33 and 41; RM 10. 56–60 = RB 7.39–43. This fact was mentioned only in passing in *La Communauté et l'Abbé*, p. 259, n. 1 (E.T. p. 219, n. 93); *La Règle de saint Benoît*, t. IV, p. 147, n. 81 and pp. 154–155, nn. 107 and 109. The comparison of the texts suggests, here as elsewhere, that the redaction of RM 3, preceded that of RM 10. The citation of 1 Co 4:12 is better reproduced in RM 3, both in the order of the terms and the tenor (*sustinere*), and the word *magis* is understood better in RM 3.37, where it echoes the *e contrario* (1 Peter 3:9b), than in RM 10.60.

11. RM 3.56 = RB 4.50; RM 10.61 = RB 7.44. Since the image of Christ the rock against which one smashes thoughts is found already in Ths 24 = Prol 28, the *ars* again seems like a relay station between the Thema and the chapter 'On Humility' (cf. n. 9).

12. RM 3.59–60 = RB 4. 53–54; RM 10. 78–80 = RB 7. 59–60.

13. Compare RM 3. 82–94 and 10. 93–117.

14. RB 4. 76–77.

15. See RB 7. 5–8 = RM 10. 5–8. Cf. t. IV, pp. 332–333 and 340–341.

16. RM 3.82 = RB 4. 76 (*merces . . . recompensabitur*); RM 10. 92 (*retributionem*). See also RM 10. 56 = RB 7. 39 (*retributionis*).

17. Cf. 2 Tm 2:4; Mt 10:37. See t. IV, p. 141, n. 70.

18. 1 Peter 3:9; 1 Co 4:12.

19. Ti 1:7.

20. Gal 5:16–17. See above, notes 3 and 9.

21. This sequence is secondary, since RB 4. 61 b is an addition. But perhaps it is not fortuitous. The proximity of RB 4.62 could have suggested the preceding addition.

22. RB 4. 69 (*elationem fugere*) is unique to Benedict, who often adverts to this matter on his own (RB 28.2; 31.1; 38.2; 62.2).

23. On the Master's ordering, see t. IV, pp. 138–165 and 291–300 (a little corrected here). On that of Benedict, *ibid.*, 190–208.

24. In the same way, in RB 4. 59–61, renunciation of one's desires and wills precedes obedience.

25. It is also the first section (RB 4.1–9) which set the tone from the literary point of view: the style of the whole catalogue derives from it. However, the second person singular (*Diliges*) is habitually replaced with the infinitive, from the beginning and throughout. In this

regard, the Master's catalogue resembles the description of the will of God in Cyprian, *De dom. or.* 15, which also begins like RM 3 (*Voluntas autem Dei est* . . .). From this passage of Cyprian also comes RM 3.35 = RB 4.30.

26. RM 9.51 = RB 6.8; RM 10. 78–80 = RB 7.59–60; RM 11. 49–58 and 75–80; RM 92.24. In RM 5.9 loud laughter is one of the things which 'merit gehenna'.

27. Basil, *Reg.* 8 = *Long Rules* 17.1, followed by Chrysostom, *In Ep. ad Hebr., Hom.* 15,4; PG 63: 122 (addressed to *monazôn*), and by Ferreolus, *Reg.* 24. Cf. Basil *Reg.* 53 = *Short Rules* 31.

28. See I. Hausherr, *Penthos* (Rome, 1944) pp. 109–120. E.T. by Anselm Hufstader (Cistercian Publications, 1982).

29. *Non multum edacem:* see RM 16. 62–63 (cf. RB 31.1); 26.6. *Non somnolentum:* see RM 32, 15 (cf. RB 22. 8); 44.17; 69.7.

30. RM 8. 1–25.

31. RM 13–14.

32. See t. IV, p. 132, n. 42. Texts in synopsis in J. P. Audet 'La Didachè' (Paris, 1958) pp. 138–153.

33. *Ordo monasterii* 1, p. 148, 1–2 Verheijen.

34. Basil, *Reg.* 1–2 = *Long Rules* 1–6.

35. See the *Index scriptorum* of M. Petschenig in CSEL 17, pp. 391–409, at the following references: Mt 22:37–39; Mk 12:30–31; Lk 10:27.

36. Leviticus 19:18. Only the second part of the verse is cited in *Inst.* 8.15; *Conf.* 19. 14. 5. The phrase derived from it in Rm 13:8,10 is absent, as well as the citation of Rm 13:9; Gal 5:14.

37. *Conf.* 8. 4 citing Dt 6:5.

38. Jn 13:34–35. The repetitions of this commandment (Jn 15:12 and 17) are absent.

29. *Conf.* 15. 7. 3.

40. *Conf.* 16. 6. 5.

41. *Conf.* 11. 6. 1: *Caritas numquam cadit* (1 Co 13:8; on the other version of this text (*Caritas numquam excidit* or *excidet*), see the Prolegomena of M. Petschenig in CSEL 17, p. xc); *Inst.* 4. 39. 3 and *Conf.* 11. 12–13: *perfecta caritas* (1 Jn 4:18).

42. The same in RM 4. 1: *Fides, spes, caritas* (1 Co 13:13).

43. Benedict even introduces *pro Dei amore* in the third degree of humility (see *La Communauté et l'Abbé*, pp. 265 and 449–450: E.T. p. 233). The Master unites fear and charity in RM 3. 1.

44. *Conf.* 8.25.5 citing Ex 20:4,12–17, or Dt 5: 8,16–21.

45. *Conf.* 14.11.2, citing Ex 20:14 or Dt 5:18.

46. See the Index of M. Petschenig , at the references: Mt 19:18–19; Mk 10:19; Lk 18:20; Rm 13:9.

47. Mt 7:12; Tob 4:16.

48. On the law in Cassian, see A. de Vogüé, 'Sub regula vel abbate', in *Rule and Life*, CS 12, pp. 30–31 and *Collectanea Cist.* 33 (1971) pp. 216–217. To the references indicated (n. 31), add *Conf.* 17.30; 23. 4. 3.

49. See Mt 5:12,46; 6:1,2,5,16; 10:41–42; 20:8.

50. See 1 Co 3:8,14 and 9:17–18; 2 Jn 8; Rev 11:18 and 22:12.

51. See the concordance. The Master has *merces* some ten times in this theological sense. Benedict has it six times (unique to himself), a figure that is relatively high.

52. RM 3. 52 = RB 4. 46. The Benedictine redaction is insistent.

53. Similarly, the *Doctrina Apostolorum* 6. 4–5 ends by promising the 'crown' to those who accomplish 'every day' the preceding instructions. See J. P. Audet, *La Didachè*, p. 153.

54. *Conf.* 11.6–13; *Inst.* 4. 39. 3. See t. IV, pp. 351–352.

55. RM 10. 87–90 = RB 7.67–69. See t. IV, pp. 352–354.

56. Benedict concludes his second catalogue of maxims (RB 72.12; cf. 72.2) in the same way with the 'entry into eternal life'.

Chapter V

OBEDIENCE

(RB 5)

B ENEDICT'S CHAPTER 'ON OBEDIENCE', a simple abridgement of the
Master's Chapter Seven, has neglected none of the three constitutive parts of this long treatise. We find in it, first, a description of
immediate obedience,[1] then an evocation of the 'narrow way' of cenobitic
obedience according to the example of Christ,[2] and finally an enumeration
of the, especially interior, qualities which this obedience should present.[3]

Not the least merit of this abridgement is that it has preserved the two
great Gospel sayings which provide the deepest foundation for the Master's doctrine: 'He who hears you, hears me' (Luke 10:16) and 'I have not
come to do my own will, but the will of him who sent me' (John 6:38).
To obey Christ, and to obey like Christ: these two aspects of obedience,
which result from these two Gospel texts, were the object of our reflection in *Community and Abbot*.[4] But even if it is legitimate to distinguish
different types of obedience in this way and to study their interferences,
we must recognize that the Master and Benedict themselves do not make
this distinction. In RM the two words of Christ seem less like the bases of
different theories than successive layers of masonry in one and the same
piece of construction.

Here we would like to proceed differently. Instead of limiting ourselves
to a reflection on the scriptural sources of the chapter 'On Obedience', we
shall examine the preparations of this treatise in the Master's work so we
may reconstitute the progression of his thought on obedience. We shall
see thus that each of the two evangelical texts plays a decisive role in one
of the steps in this staircase.

The Master's doctrine on obedience is not contained in one chapter. However ample it may be, this chapter 'Of what sort should the disciples' obedience be' speaks, in conformity with its title, of almost nothing but the 'qualities' of obedience. It does not methodically treat its *foundations*. These have been laid already in two previous passages of the Rule[5] which Benedict did not reproduce: the commentary on the third petition of the Our Father,[6] and the final exhortation of the first chapter.[7]

The commentary on the words 'Thy will be done' stands out immediately because of its extraordinary length. No other petition of the Our Father is explained by the Master at such length, and his source, which is St Cyprian's commentary 'On the Lord's Prayer', was far from attributing the same unparalleled importance to these words. Obviously the Master was very particularly interested in the question of the divine will, for it offered him the first occasion for staking out a doctrine dear to him beyond all others: obedience.

Monastic obedience is addressed to God. 'To do his will' is its sole goal. Consequently, before any explicit presentation of the human superiors whom the monk obeys, the Master thought it good to establish at length and with solidity, the necessity of doing God's will, and therefore of renouncing one's own will. The whole commentary of the third petition will be used for that. Then, at the end of the first chapter, he will be able to deduce from this premise the duty of obeying the men by whom the Lord makes known to us his divine will.

For us to say to God 'Thy will be done' is to make a voluntary act and a choice. The first reality encountered by the Master in reflecting on these words is our free will. Indeed, to do the will of God is not automatic for so complex and divided a being as man. 'Thy will be done' is the cry of the spirit in us, but the flesh opposes the spirit, and the flesh dominates our soul, imposing on it harmful desires suggested by the devil. The divine will therefore can be accomplished only at the cost of voluntarily rooting out our self-will. The Master finds affirmation for the necessity of such a rooting out in a word of St Paul's, whose citation and interpretation doubtless came to him from the Basilian Rule: '*Ut non quaecumque vultis, illa faciatis*' ('Never do what you will').[8] 'Thy will be done' is therefore translated negatively as 'I shall not do what I will'.

Thus from the beginning, the will of God appears opposed to the spontaneous human will, the will of the soul enslaved to the flesh. In everything we should substitute the accomplishment of the divine will for that of 'self-will', in order to avoid being condemned on the day of judgment. This is the first foundation of monastic obedience. It is a matter of salvation, nothing less.

Before proceeding, we should note that this doctrine alludes to the famous duel of the flesh and the spirit as St Paul describes it at the end of the Epistle to the Galatians.[9] Between the flesh and the spirit the Master places the 'soul', according to the exegesis common since Origen. From the soul emanate these 'wills' which Paul invites us 'not to accomplish',[10] bad carnal wills which the Master conceives of as equivalent to the 'desires of the flesh' of which the Apostle had spoken.

Meditation on Galatians 5:16–17 is thus at the base of the pair whose importance in the eyes of the Master and of Benedict is well-known: the 'desires of the flesh' and 'self-will'. The Apostle had reproved these two sorts of tendencies in almost the same terms: '*et desideria carnis non perficietis . . . ut non quaecumque vultis illa faciatis*' (and you shall not fulfil the desires of the flesh . . . never do what you will). The Master and Benedict in their turn join the two in the same disapproval.[11] They are the common enemies of the will of God, and the purpose of monastic obedience is to fight and extirpate them.

'Self-will' is therefore a tendency to evil which comes from the flesh. But what flesh are we speaking about? Today when we read the Pauline passage, we perceive that the 'works of the flesh' are far from being all mere sensual passions. After lust, impurity, immodesty, Paul mentions idolatry, poisoning, enmity, rivalry, jealousy, and we conclude from this that the 'flesh' represents the collection of sinful tendencies to which the whole man, body and soul, is subject. We distinguish then the 'flesh' from the body, recognizing in the Pauline term the wider meaning of 'human nature' which it ordinarily has in the Bible.

The Master perceived the same thing, no doubt, but he drew a different conclusion from it. If the most varied faults are called by the Apostle '*opera carnis*' (works of the flesh), it is because the 'flesh'—meaning the body—is at the origin of every bad will. From this arises the axiom stated at the end of the Rule: 'Every self-will is carnal and comes from the body'.[12] Such an affirmation does not only suppose the equivalence already noted, of the self-will and the desires of the flesh; it also implies in its second part the identification of the 'flesh' with the body. Cyprian had already passed easily from one to the other in paraphrasing the Pauline text.[13] This identification did not entail for him a Manichaean repudiation of the body of flesh any more than it did for the Master. The body, formed by God, put on again by Christ and promised at the resurrection,[14] remains basically good, and the responsibility for the faults of which it is the instrument, lies with the soul which is its mistress.[15]

Bringing the words of the Our Father 'Thy will be done' into relation with the 'Never do what you will' of the Epistle to the Galatians has set against the divine will this human will which is contrary to God, that which the Master, following Basil and Cassian,[16] calls 'self-will'. The same opposition of the two wills, God's and man's, results from a series of Christ's statements, already gathered by Cyprian in his commentary on the third petition: 'I have not come to do my own will, but the will of him who sent me' (Jn 6:38); 'Father, if it be possible, let this cup pass from me; but not what I will but what you will' (Mt 26:39). By taking up and completing this series of texts,[17] the Master appeals to the Gospel to confirm what he has just discovered in the Apostle. The example of Christ shows better than anything the necessity of renouncing one's self-will to do God's will. And self-will appears again in the example of Christ in agony as the 'voice of the flesh' resisting the spirit.[18]

Moreover, an experimental consideration illustrates the law of renunciation of one's own judgment. Can a man see his own face? How then could he judge his own conscience? In the light of this comparison we see becoming more specific the obligation of submitting all our conduct *to another*.[19] But who is this 'other'? Although it is not yet time to say—we learn only in the final exhortation of the first chapter—we already catch a glimpse of the human 'teachers': the bishops and abbots to whom God entrusts the execution of His will. These human mediators of the divine will are also suggested a little further on, in the first explanation of the words *sicut in coelo et in terra* (on earth as it is in heaven)—'heaven' and 'earth' representing angels and men—when the Master speaks of the 'prophets' and 'apostles' by which divine orders accomplished on earth.[20]

These discreet anticipations are, however, less important here than is the fundamental thesis of obedience to the will of God and renunciation of our self-will. The Master returns to this thesis forcefully in concluding his commentary on the third petition. His second explanation of *sicut in coelo et in terra*—'heaven' and 'earth' representing Christ come from on

high, and our earthly body—leads him to cite John 6:38 again. Not to do
our will but the will of the Father, after Christ's example, in order to be
not condemned but crowned: this is the great lesson he draws from this
petition of the Lord's Prayer.[21]

The first foundation of the doctrine of obedience is therefore constituted by meditation on three texts or series of texts of the New Testament:
the prayer taught by Christ (Mt 6:10); the example he gave (Mt 26:39-42
and Jn 6:38); and the teaching of his apostle (Gal 5:16-17). The 'earth' on
which we ask that the divine will be accomplished is the 'carnal men' who
live on earth[22] or our body which is taken from the earth and must return
there.[23] And since we make it the object of a prayer, the accomplishment
of the divine will should not be automatic; a will opposed to the divine
will comes out of that 'earth'. The opposition appears clearly when the
only Son renounces his own will, which is precisely the will of the flesh,
to accomplish what his Father wills. Thus there is no 'Thy will be done'
which is not preceded by 'Not what I will'. This prior negative stage is
also proposed by Saint Paul: 'Do not what you will', and the context of
the Epistle to the Galatians shows again that this desire of the soul which
must be renounced is identified with the 'desire of the flesh' opposed to
that of the spirit. The pair 'heaven and earth' in the Lord's prayer corresponds therefore to the Pauline opposition of 'flesh' and 'spirit'.[24] The
three series of New Testament texts seem to blend perfectly with each
other. A single message results: in order to do the will of God, which is
both the aspiration of the spirit within us and the condition of our salvation, we must not do what we will; we must renounce the self-will which
springs from the depths of our flesh.

With this foundation laid, the Master can add something new which
appears at the end of the chapter 'On the Kinds of Monks'.[25] Even
though quite distant from the commentary on the third petition, this
passage is nonetheless a continuation of it, as is clearly indicated by a
reference back by which we are invited 'to do God's will, not our own,
because what the Lord commands us in the spirit to do is one thing, and
quite another is what the flesh, in our soul, impels us to commit'.[26]

Then follows a solemn presentation of the 'teachers' instituted by the
Lord (1 Co 12:28) in his Church, which comprises both the secular
'churches' and the monastic 'schools'. These 'teachers' and 'shepherds' of

our time, meaning the bishops and abbots, as the successors of the prophets and apostles, are affected by the injunctions and promises which Christ
addressed to Peter and the Twelve: 'Feed my sheep' (Jn 21:17); 'Teach
them to do whatever I have commanded you. Behold I am with you always, even to the end of the world' (Mt 28:20). To them also is applied
the Lord's word to his disciples: 'He who hears you, hears me and he who
despises you, despises me' (Lk 10:16).

Thus the phrase cited above: 'The Lord gives us commands *in the spirit*'
can be replaced with this one: 'The Lord gives us commands *by a teacher*'.[27]
The Master in this way has established the second point of his doctrine of
obedience. To obey God we must obey the man who represents him, the
'teacher', the abbot. And a new reminder is added to seal the cohesion of
this demonstration in two points: here as in the commentary on the third
petition, obedience is presented as the condition of our salvation on the
day of judgment. By doing what the teachers tell him, the monk eliminates all self-will, which would be condemned, and fills his life with the
divine will, for which he deserves glorification.[28]

'He who hears you, hears me'. This word of Christ's plays here a role
analogous to that of John 6:38 ('I have not come to do my own will, but
the will of him who sent me') in the preceding stage. The Lord shows us
whom to obey, after he has offered himself as a model of obedience. To
listen to the teachers is to listen to him, and he listens to his Father, as we
already know. Thus a chain of voluntary obediences connects the disciple
of the monastic *scola* with the God he seeks. On a later page the Master
will close one of these links of the chain by demanding of the abbot-
teacher a total conformity of his teachings to the law of the Lord.[29] Here,
where he is addressing the disciples, it is enough to quote the words of
Christ which lay the foundations of his vicars' authority.

The mission of these vicars is both to communicate the will of God and
to prevent the accomplishment of our self-will. In describing their task,
the Master did not forget what he established in his explanation of the
petition 'Thy will be done' and which he recalled at the beginning of this
concluding section of Chapter One: the divine will encounters in us opposition from the flesh, moved by the devil who dominates the soul.[30] Also,
the first benefit expected from the direction of superiors is 'that one learns
to ignore the way of self-will'.[31] The positive aspect—receiving 'the
Lord's orders' through them—is mentioned only afterwards.[32]

'The Lord gives us commands *in the spirit*. . . . The Lord gives us commands *by teacher.*' The substitution of one phrase by the other, in which consists the whole of this second step of the theory of obedience, may seem a blow to individual conscience, indeed to the conscience of regenerated man moved by the Holy Spirit. Without prejudice to the solid foundations of this doctrine, we should note that the Master is certainly not thinking that the teachers' intervention puts an end to liberty of spirit. His thought is the opposite: authority does not eliminate the spirit, but liberates it. The true adversary of the spirit is the flesh and the self-will which emanates from it. The 'teacher' comes to the help of the spirit by putting an end to the tyranny of carnal desire. The will of God to which the spirit aspires is presented and imposed by the teacher. In the Master's eyes no opposition exists between these two servants of the divine will, these two allies.

The two foundations of obedience appear in two segments widely separated. In spite of the references in the second to the first, one might doubt that the Master considered them as two articles of one and the same exposition, as we have just done. But our interpretation is fully confirmed by a passage in the *ars sancta* where the Master himself unites these two thoughts:'Not to fulfil the desires of the flesh. To hate one's own will. To be obedient to the admonitions of the Abbot'.[33]

Here denial of the desires of the flesh and of self-will, in the spirit of Galatians 5:16–17, is immediately followed by obedience to the abbot's instructions. Although the will of God is not mentioned, it is the subject from start to finish; the first two articles echo the explanation of 'Thy will be done', and the third the exhortation to obey the teachers.

The same transition from the divine will to that of human superiors is found again in the first three degrees of humility. The first, recapitulated by the second, preaches renunciation of self-will and of the desires of the flesh in order to do the will of God,[34] while the third proposes that the monk 'submit himself in all obedience to the abbot'.[35]

This passage reassures us of the legitimacy of the connection established above. Since, in the *ars sancta* and the ladder of humility, the Master himself associates the two themes materially, there is no doubt that he mentally connected the two widely-spaced passages in which he successively developed them. The explanation of the third petition of the Our Father

and the end of the chapter 'On the Kinds of Monks' are indeed the two
stages of one and the same presentation of obedience.

We might expect to find these two stages in the treatise 'On Obedience'
(RM 7). In fact, however, obedience to God and obedience to superiors
are not presented separately but are united,[36] and the two great gospel
citations, instead of forming the expected sequence (Jn 6:38 before Lk
10:16), occur in the reverse order.[37] These facts, surprising at first sight,
show clearly that the chapter 'On Obedience' is located *at the end* of the
logical road we have just followed. Once the Master has posited his two
premises singly and drawn the necessary conclusion, he can contemplate
as a whole the obedience practised by true monks in the cenobia. Description of the qualities of obedience and celebration of its virtues follow the
analysis of its elements and the methodical proof of its necessity.

The two major elements of the teaching are nonetheless present in this
treatise, though not clearly distinguised or arranged in good order. The
theme of the renunciation of self-will as correlative to the accomplishment of God's will gives rise to a new crop of citations which renew the
teaching of the commentary on the third petition. Only the citation of
John 6:38 has survived: 'I have not come to do my own will but the will
of him who sent me'. The Master makes only remote allusions to the
maxims of the Epistle to the Galatians condemning the desires of the flesh
and self-will.[38] To replace them he found a saying of Ecclesiasticus which
reproduces the two prohibitions: 'Go not after your lusts, but turn away
from your own will'.[39] Three other new *testimonia*, scriptural and other,
illustrate the same theme.[40] This scriptural apparatus has been chosen for
its image of the 'broad way', the gospel figure which serves here as a
framework for criticism of bad monks and their self-will.[41]

More interesting than this anthology on self-will are two allusions to
the Gospel which the Master introduces to illustrate the twofold movement of renunciation of self and obedience to the Lord commanding
through superiors. The first, which appears at the beginning of the chapter, is so discreet it can scarcely be seen. Yet it seems that in describing the
monks who 'immediately leave their things' (*relinquentes statim quae sua
sunt*) to 'follow the voice of him who commands them', the Master had in
mind the immediate obedience of the first disciples to Christ's appeal.[42]
Further on, anyway, our author very clearly evokes the 'self-abnegation'

Christ required of the disciples who want to 'follow him'.[43] The two underlying gospel texts present the same two-part structure: first, one 'abandons' or 'renounces', then one 'follows' Jesus. The first stage is a figure of the non-accomplishment of one's own will, and the second the accomplishment of God's will. Thus the Master discovers in the synoptics the double movement of renunciation and adherence formulated in John 6:38.[44] What Christ said of his relations with his Father in this last passage, he reproduced in his disciples' relations with him. We give him obedience in the image and as a prolongation of his own.

The second theme, that of the divine institution of human superiors, is represented not only by 'He who hears you, hears me', cited twice by the Master in places of honor at beginning and end, but also by a saying of the Psalmist: 'You have put men over our heads'.[45] This saying re-echoes, moreover, in the course of an original development on the heroic patience worthy of martyrs that the obedient must display. This description of patient obedience marks a progression in relation to the simple affirmation of the duty of obedience posed at the end of Chapter One. Here too the logion of the 'two ways' (Mt 7:13–14) makes its influence felt. Just as the image of the 'broad way' provoked the renewal of the scriptural illustration of the first theme, so the image of the 'narrow way' leads to a dramatization of the second: to submit to superiors is to set out on the road of trial, indeed of martyrdom.

With the chapter 'On Obedience' we have almost reached the end of the Master's reflections on obedience. Several later passages, notably the first four degrees of humility and the long sermon in Chapter Ninety to the postulant will return to this teaching,[46] but without adding new views. Only the scriptural illustration will be notably developed, especially in Chapter Ten. The most important of these new *testimonia* is, no doubt, Philippians 2:8: 'Christ became obedient unto death'.[47] On the other hand, the third petition of the Our Father ('Thy will be done'), not cited in the chapter 'On Obedience', reappears in Chapters Ten and Ninety,[48] as if to give us additional assurance that the explanation of this petition is indeed the point of departure for the theory of obedience.

When we consider the whole collection of texts in which this theory is deployed, we are struck by the importance our author gives it. If the chapter 'On Obedience' is the only one which treats it *ex professo*, the two methodical preparations for this treatise (Thp 24–53; 1.76–92) and two extensive reproductions of it (10.30–60; 90.3–62) leave no doubt of the extreme care which the Master brought to the establishment and inculcation of his doctrine on obedience.

This zeal should not astonish us. Obedience is necessarily at the heart of a monastic institution which defines itself as *scola dominici servitii* (school of the Lord's service). Whether we take this definition in the scholastic sense or the military sense, we are immediately confronted with the hierarchical relationship—of disciples to their Master, or of soldiers to their leader—which constitutes such a society.

The importance of obedience in the Master's eyes derives also from the relations of this virtue with the fundamental theme of *hearing*. Indeed, according to an etymology of which our author was quite conscious,[49] *obaudire* (to obey) is connected with *audire* (to hear). But 'to hear' is surely the key word of the Master's entire spiritual doctrine.[50] In the direct line of biblical tradition he represents God as a person who speaks to man and says that man must 'listen' if he wants to be saved. Not by chance do our two rules begin with an invitation to 'listen'.[51] 'To listen' in the full sense of the word means not only to hear and to understand, but also to acquiesce and to obey. Obedience to superiors, which is the proper object of the chapter 'On Obedience' and connected passages, derives its importance from being a privileged, irreplaceable mode of 'listening' to the word which saves.

Of the three major virtues to which the Master devotes long treatises, obedience is the first and in some ways the most important. Taciturnity, which follows it, owes a great deal of its importance to the hierarchical point of view from which it is considered. If the monk must be silent, this is precisely so he may 'listen' to the master.[52] Taciturnity thus represented as an attitude befitting a 'disciple' is much like obedience, which has visibly colored it.[53] Humility, which is more important than obedience in many ways,[54] never provoked the Master to such an effort of reflection and exposition.[55] Although sovereignly important in itself, humility—unlike obedience—does not pertain to the very essence of the cenobitic pact as our author conceives it.

The theory of obedience which we have just analyzed must be situated within the history of this doctrine. First, we should relate the Master to the two authors who seem to have inspired him directly, Cyprian and Basil. Cyprian furnished the Master with the matter for his commentary on the words 'Thy will be done'. To him therefore our author owes the rooting of his theory in the third petition of the Lord's Prayer, the appeal to the example of Christ (Mt 26:39 and Jn 6:38), the theme of the struggle between the spirit and the flesh, the latter being this 'earth' on which we ask that the Lord's will be done—in a word, the chief elements of his first exposition. At the outset Cyprian established a certain opposition between our will and the will of God. The Master set this opposition at the base of his system, stressing it heavily.[56]

Cyprian therefore set his mark on the first phase of the Master's reflection, but he does not seem to have influenced it in the following stage. Although in his correspondence he twice uses the words 'He who hears you, hears me' to defend episcopal authority,[57] these citations of Luke 10:16 are not set in relation with the doctrine of obedience to God proposed in the explanation of 'Thy will be done'.

Basil, together with Cyprian, seems to have influenced the first stage of the Master's doctrine by furnishing him with the citation and interpretation of Galatians 5:17d, united to the example of Christ in agony. These notations in the Basilian Rule (Q. 81) are located in the context of obedience to men, in the midst of a quasi-monastic community and in regard to morally indifferent actions such as learning to read and spending time in reading. That is, they pertain, if not by the tenor or the scriptural citations, at least by the application made of them, to the second stage of the Master's reflection, obedience to men. This obedience to human superiors is not yet proposed clearly in the Master's commentary on the Our Father, but only suggested in an allusive way and envisaged as the end to which the argument tends. By using Question 81 of Basil in the first part of his exposition, the Master has kept within the formal framework of obedience to God what Basil took to be obedience to men.[58]

This remark draws our attention to the different procedures of the two authors. Basil goes straight to the duty of submitting oneself to the brothers, seeing in this a lesson immediately deduced from Christ's example and the Apostle's teaching, but the Master proceeds more methodically. Before claiming obedience for superiors, he establishes the duty of obeying God, as Cyprian taught him. Certainly Basil was not ignorant of this primordial obligation, but he stated it at the beginning of his Rule (Q. 2), far away from these considerations on obedience to the brothers (Q. 81), which are hardly related to it.[59] The Master's originality, therefore, is to have both sharply distinguished and clearly united the accomplishment of the divine will and that of the superior's will, both of them articulated as two bits of one and the same theory of obedience.

An analogous observation can be made about the words 'He who hears you, hears me' (Lk 10:16). This word of Christ, from which the Master draws the duty of obeying the teachers, was not unknown to Basil, who cites it in his Question 70. Basil's application of it to obedience to the superior of the community[60] in regard to work is already fully in the line of the Master's thought.[61] But Basil felt no need to prove this application. We find in him no argument establishing the superior's right to avail himself of such a promise and to speak in the Lord's name. Here also the Master is innovating by prefacing his first citation of Luke 10:16 with a solemn presentation of the 'teachers' as the legitimate successors of the apostles in the task of teaching and governing.

To appreciate the originality of our Rule, we need only compare it, after Cyprian and Basil, with two other works which have contributed a great deal to the Master in other areas: the *Historia monachorum* and the monastic writings of Cassian. The *Historia* comments on the trials of obedience imposed by Anthony on his disciple Paul in terms which foretell the Master's commentary on the Our Father and his chapter 'On Obedience': 'not to obey one's own will . . . to renounce oneself [cf. Mt.16:24] and to abandon one's own will' according to the example of Christ proposed in John 6:38.[62] Certain resemblances even made Cuthbert Butler think that this passage of the *Historia* was a late interpolation inspired by the Benedictine Rule.[63] More probably, RM owes something to this text, and their other points of contact are explained by their common dependence on Cyprian.[64] Anyway, these analogies concern only a small number of points of the Master's doctrine. The author or translator of the *Historia* does not treat obedience to God separately any more than Basil did, nor does he take the passage from this to obedience to superiors.

Lastly, Cassian wrote much on the theme of monastic obedience. Book IV of the *Institutes*, which is filled with it, is however limited to describing the usages of the Egyptian cenobites in this regard (particularly their promptness in obeying, which the Master will remember) and to indicating their ascetic bearing. No theoretical justification is given; no reference is made to Scripture. Abba Joseph indeed quotes John 6:38 and Matthew 26:39, but to recommend that 'friends' obey each other mutually.[65] Elsewhere these two citations come to the support of properly cenobitic obedience, and Cassian forbids the 'doing of one's own will', with the help of other texts.[66] Elsewhere John 6:38 is matched with Philippians 2:8.[67] But in all these passages Cassian restricts himself to reproving self-will and proposing the example of the obedient Christ. No enlightenment is furnished on the opposition of the human will to the will of God. No distinction and no relation is established between this divine will and that of monastic superiors, whose authority remains without foundation.[68]

The Master's theory therefore remains unique. Although the scriptural material he uses is found scattered in various authors[69] and is almost complete in Basil,[70] the construction remains his alone. It is the fruit of an exercise in reflection and organization of which the literature of ancient monasticism offers no other example.

If the Master's teaching is clearly set off from that of the authors closest to him, it differs still more from recommendations to obedience found in other documents. Of these the most representative is, no doubt, the Augustinian Rule. In it obedience is not presented at the beginning, as in the Master, but towards the end.[71] The two short phrases dealing with it contain no quotation of Scripture, but the first seems to allude to several biblical texts. 'The superior should be obeyed as a father, with due respect, so that God is not offended in his person; even more should be the priest who bears responsibility for all of you . . . . By being more obedient, therefore, show mercy not only towards yourselves but also towards the superior whose higher rank among you exposes him to greater peril.'

The first words echo Hebrews 13:17 ('Obey your superiors'), as does the conclusion of the superior's directory later.[72] The superior (*praepositus*) is therefore conceived as one of those leaders of the christian community spoken of in the Epistle to the Hebrews, who are responsible before God for the souls over which they 'watch'.

But this ecclesiastical model has another image associated with it. The monk should obey the superior 'as a father, with due respect,' (*honore servato*). These words recall the fourth commandment of the decalogue: 'Honor your father'.[73] The honor given to parents, being prescribed by the divine law, redounds to God. Augustine makes it a religious duty: to fail in it would be 'to offend God'.[74] Already Saint Paul had seen in the 'obedience' of sons the concrete expression of this 'honor' demanded for parents by the Old Law.[75]

Leader of the community and father: such is the superior in Augustine. Obedience is owed to him under this double title, according to scripture. At first sight such an obedience does not differ much from that preached by the Master. Although the scriptural references are different, the 'superiors' of the Epistle to the Hebrews and Augustine correspond pretty much to the 'teachers' of the First Epistle to the Corinthians and the Master. Although the Master does not propose the family model directly, he does teach that *abba* means 'father' and that this paternity refers to Christ,[76] so that to despise the abbot is to offend Christ himself.[77]

In spite of these analogies, the two perspectives remain distinct. In the eyes of the Master, obedience is a matter of salvation for each 'disciple'. How to do the will of God and not at all one's own will, according to the example of Christ? This is the primordial problem, and its solution lies in obedience to the teachers. The only purpose of the monastery-school is to make it possible. Therefore it is spoken of at the outset.

For Augustine, on the contrary, the duty of obeying seems to result from the fact that the monks are gathered in a fraternal community. This community requires a leader, who holds the place of a father. Here, the primary element is the society. The society does not exist to secure the direction of a teacher; it is valid by itself and for itself, as a communion of hearts and a community of goods in charity. The superior is only an organ, necessary indeed and willed by God, but it is a necessity of means rather than of salvation, secondary and not primary.

Obedience is seen by the Master in a thoroughly individual perspective, even if it has as its obligatory framework a monastery-school, a quasi-church. Augustine's perspective is more deeply communitarian. It ignores the theme of the imitation of Christ and renunciation of self-will to do the will of God, and considers obedience from the point of view of the common life.[78]

'Obey your superiors. Obey your parents'. These New Testament recommendations caught the attention not only of Augustine. We find them, together or separate, in several ancient monastic authors. By a singular coincidence Horsiesius cites these same two texts in the passage of his *Liber* which addresses simple monks. After having exhorted each of the categories of superiors to their respective duties, the head of the *Koinonia* asks the subjects to obey them as their 'parents' and their 'superiors'.[79] Evagrius, in his turn, seems to think of the fourth commandment of the decalogue in a section of his Sentences to cenobites which treats the obedience and respect due 'the father'.[80] The same care for obedience to 'the father' is found in Jerome, who recalls the example of the sons of Noah before citing 'He who despises you, despises me'.[81]

Finally, the Rule of the Four Fathers makes Hebrews 13:17 the first of the *testimonia* to be cited in laying the foundation of obedience.[82] It is true that, unlike the Augustinian Rule, this very ancient document treats obedience at the beginning. But it is significant that the presentation of the superior and the obedience due him is preceded by an exordium which sets forth first of all the 'good and pleasant dwelling of the brothers all together', 'the dwelling together in the same house of those who have but one soul', in the words of the Psalmist.[83] In the line of Augustine, and this time in all clarity, obedience is presented as a demand of the common life: for all to be one, they must have a superior and must obey him. It makes little difference that afterwards the word of Christ is invoked: 'I have not come to do my own will'.[84] This subsidiary argument, which might lead to an ascetic type of obedience, does not prevent the social motivation from being first and clearly dominant.

We can therefore discern in these ancient texts two main lines of thought, and the various authors follow, more or less expressly, one or the other. The one we have just examined starts from the community constituted like the Church and the family; in it obedience to the superiors appears analogous to the obedience Christians give to their pastors and children to their parents. The other, which the Master set forth with an incomparable sharpness, starts from the twofold obligation to do the will of God and not to do one's own will. As the will of God is shown by the word of his ministers, the monk submits himself to them in the *scola* they direct. The aim is more ascetic[85] than communitarian, and the society appears, not at the beginning, but at the end.[86]

If the Master represents perfectly one of these lines of thought to the exclusion of the other, what about Benedict? By omitting the commentary on the Lord's prayer and the conclusion of Chapter One, Benedict lost the two pieces which most clearly characterize his predecessor's development. But what he has kept of the chapter 'On Obedience', together with the first four steps of humility, are enough to range him with the Master among those who attribute to obedience a primordial importance and a role that is chiefly ascetic, indeed salvific.

The same impression stands out at the beginning of the Prologue, where Benedict summarizes in a few lines the introductions of the other Rule. The word 'obedience' is pronounced there twice and contrasted with 'disobedience' and 'self-will'.[87] It would be difficult to make the theme of obedience more conspicuous in the exordium of a monastic rule. This virtue appears both as the road by which one returns to God and as the 'powerful and glorious weapon' of the soldier enrolling in Christ's service. A unique road and a unique weapon. Benedict doubtless was remembering the explanation of the third petition. But however imposing this piece was in the Master, he was far from setting obedience in such a position of prominence.

At the other end of his work Benedict resolutely returns to obedience. In pages which owe almost nothing to the Master but in which the influence of Basil is more than once felt, he submits absolutely everything to the control of the abbot,[88] demands obedience even in 'impossible' things,[89] and prescribes mutual obedience.[90] In regard to this last precept he presents obedience again as 'the way by which we go to God'.[91] Three times he makes it a matter of charity.[92]

The curtailments made at the beginning of the Rule have therefore deprived Benedict of a reasoned presentation of obedience and its foundations, but the prestige of this virtue is not in the least diminished with him. It can even be said that his principle of mutual obedience goes far beyond the limits foreseen by the Master. And this extension is not a simple practical matter. It shatters the Master's theory as well. With mutual obedience there is no longer a question of accomplishing the will of God transmitted hierarchically through superiors, but of cultivating obedience as a 'good' in itself,[93] whoever gives the order. Thus the ascetic and salvific value of obedience is exalted by Benedict to the highest degree. While he surpasses his predecessor's thought, he remains in the same line: obedience is for him less a demand of the common life than the great way offered to each person to renounce himself and to go to God.

Of the two lines of thought just traced, the thought of Augustine and other like-minded men is doubtless the less problematic for people today. In it authority and obedience have a functional significance, easy to justify by reason and easy to establish by Scripture, with their religious meaning, moreover, intact. On the other hand, the Master's perspective presents a good number of difficulties:[94] the severity of his condemnation of 'self-will'; the authoritarianism which substitutes the direction of the 'teacher' for the motions of the 'spirit'; and the insufficiency of some of his exegesis.[95]

We shall not seek to 'defend' the doctrine of our rules here, any more than we have elsewhere. Whatever the value of their theological presuppositions and scriptural interpretations, it seems to us that this doctrine has the merit of using several great images and maxims of the New Testament: the narrow way, the renunciation of oneself to follow Christ, the promptness of the first disciples in leaving all for him, the preference given to him over every other human affection, and above all, his own example. To make the monk's obedience an imitation of Christ Jesus 'obedient unto death' is to give it a mystical significance which adds singular value to it. Jesus' *fiat* in agony can be compared to the divine *fiat* of Genesis: what one created, the other redeemed and saved.[96] The doctrine of obedience, by having this word repeated and this decisive act reproduced, touches the very core of the redemptive drama.

The effect produced by the disobedience of one man has been annulled by the obedience of one man, says Saint Paul.[97] This contrast of the two Adams seems to have been present to Benedict's mind when he coined the equally general maxim in his Prologue: 'Return by the labor of obedience to him from whom you had departed by the sloth of disobedience'.[98] If nothing obliges us to identify Christ's obedience to his Father with the monk's obedience to his abbot, we should at least recognize that the latter is analogous to the former,[99] and finds in this analogy the most powerful of motives.

NOTES TO CHAPTER 5

1. RB 5.1–9. Cf. RM 7.1–21.
2. RB 5. 10–13. Cf. RM 7.22–66.

3. RB 5.14–19. Cf. RM 7.67–74.

4. See *La Communauté et l'Abbé*, pp. 266–288 (E.T. pp. 224–241).

5. See A. de Vogüé, 'La doctrine du Maître sur l'obéissance. Sa genèse', in *RHS* 50 (1974) 113–134.

6. Thp 24-53.

7. RM 1. 76–92.

8. Thp 27, citing Gal 5:17d. Cf. Basil, *Reg.* 81 (= *Short Rules* 96).

9. See Thp 28, paraphrase of Gal 5:16–17. Cf. Cyprian, *De dom. or.* 16, which paraphrases and cites Gal. 5:17 and 19–23.

10. On this exegesis see the article cited above, note 5, in RHS 50, pp. 117–119, notes 12–18. This pair (desires-wills) is found not only in Gal 5:16–17. It reappears in Eph 2:3, where *conversati sumus in desideriis carnis nostrae* is followed by *facientes voluntatem carnis et cogitationum.* This latter passage could only encourage those who understood Gal 5:17d as referring to a bad, carnal will. Perhaps it underlies RM 1.5 = RB 1.5 (*vitia carnis vel cogitationum*).

11. RM 3.65–66 = RB 4. 59–60; RM 10.12 and 30–36 = RB 7. 12 and 19–25.

12. RM 90.51. Cf. Cassian, *Conf.* 5.4.4: all the vices are 'carnal' (Gal 5:19–20).

13. Cyprian, *De dom. or.* 16, passes from *corpus . . . et spiritum* (Hartel, p. 278,10) to *carnem et spiritum* (p. 278,12).

14. See Thp 52 (cf. Gn 2:7); Thp 36 (*carnis indutae*); Pr 20 (resurrection).

15. RM 8.11 and 17–18; 14. 82–83. It is the flesh, not the body, which 'presses' the soul to do evil and enslaves it to its desires (RM 1.80–81; cf. Thp 28).

16. See *La Communauté et l'Abbé*, p. 225, note 1 (E.T. p. 193, n. 24). To the references indicated, add Cassian, *Conf.* 16.3.4: *voluntates proprias* (to 'mortify' after the 'expulsion of vices', in view of keeping the friendship). Suppress Basil, *Reg.* 81 and 181. The expression *idion thelema* occurs twice in Macarius, *Hom.* 4.5, and nine times in *Hom.* 5.6. See also *Hom.* 53.10 and 18 (ed. G. L. Marriott, *Macarii Anecdota. Seven Unpublished Homilies of Macarius* [Cambridge, Mass., 1918] pp. 33 and 37) Ep. Magna; ed. W. Jaeger, *Two Rediscovered Works of Ancient Christian Literature: Gregory of Nyssa and Macarius* (Leiden, 1959) pp. 238 and 296.

17. Thp 34–38 (Thp 39 adds Mt 26:42). Cf. Cyprian, *De dom. or.* 14. Same connection in Ch. Péguy, *Deuxième élégie XXX* (Paris, 1955) p. 388 ('Clio', first edition).

18. Thp 36: *vox timoris erat carnis indutae.* Perhaps the Master is alluding to Mt. 26:41: *Spiritus quidem promptus est, caro autem infirma.* Cf. Cyprian, *De dom. or* 14: *infirmitatem hominis quem gerebat ostendens.* The Master retains the *caro* of Mt. 26:41, while Cyprian had kept *infirma.* Ch. Péguy also felt that Christ in saying these words was referring to his own agony (pp. 384–388).

19. Thp 41–42: *ab alio iudicetur.*

20. Thp 46: *per prophetas et apostolos.*

21. Thp 48–53.

22. Thp 46: *in carnalibus hominibus.*

23. Thp 52 (Gn 2:7 and 3:19).

24. This correspondence, which is marked by Cyprian, is not pointed out by the Master.

25. RM 2. 76–92.

26. RM 1. 80.

27. RM 1. 88.

28. RM 1. 90–92.

29. RM 2. 3–4.

30. RM 1. 80–81; cf. Thp 26–28.

31. RM 1. 87.
32. RM 1. 88.
33. RM 3. 65–67. In RB 4. 59–61 the last 'instrument' becomes: *Praeceptis abbatis in omnibus oboedire*. The word *monitio* is avoided as it is in RB 2.5.
34. RM 10. 30–36 and 42–44 = RB 7. 19–25 and 31–33. Note the citation of Mt 6:10 in RM 10,31 = RB 7.20.
35. RM 10. 49 = RB 7.34.
36. The mentions of God and of the superiors alternate from one end of the chapter to the other.
37. See RM 7.6 (Lk 10:16) and 51 (Jn 6:38). However Lk 10:16 returns in RM 7.68 where it is better situated than in RM 7.6. Lk 10:16 forms a pair with Ps 17:45 (cf. RM 10.50–51) and seems subordinate to the psalm in the first case, but in the second it is chosen for itself.
38. See RM 7. 48–49: *desideriis suis et voluptatibus*, the first term being already found in RM 7.31 and 41, the second scarcely differing from *voluntatibus* (cf. RM 7.33 and 39).
39. *Post concupiscentias tuas non eas, et a voluntatibus tuis avertere*. Si 18:30, cited by RM 7.46.
40. Ps 13:1; Pr 16:25 (*viae*); *Acta Sebastiani* 14 (*iuxta introitum*), cited by RM 7.39,40,45.
41. Cf. the verbs of movement (*non eas . . . avertere*) of Si 18:30, as well as *viae* and *iuxta introitum* of the other two citations (see preceding note). Only Ps 13:1 remains without link to the theme.
42. RM 7.7–8 = RB 5.7K8. Cf. Mt 4:22. Already in RM 7.4 we find *in sequendo* corrected by RB 5.4 (*in faciendo*). See also RM 7.38.
43. RM 7.52. Cf. Mt 16:24, which will be cited formally by RM 90.10.
44. It is just after Jn 6:38 that the Master alludes to Mt 16:24 (RM 7.51–2).
45. RM 7.63–64, citing and paraphrasing Ps 65:12a.
46. See RM 10.30–60 = RB 7.19–43; RM 90. 3–59. See *La Communauté et l'Abbé*, pp. 207–245 (E.T. pp. 179–208).
47. RM 10.49 = RB 7.34.
48. RM 10.31 = RB 7.20; RM 90.54.
49. See t. IV, p. 262, notes 9–10.
50. See our article 'Expérience de Dieu et paternité spirituelle', in *L'Expérience de Dieu dans la vie monastique* (La Pierre-qui-vire, 1973) pp. 56–59.
51. Pr 1–2: *qui me obscultas . . . Deum te convenientem cognosce* (cf. Pr 8); Prol 1: *Obsculta*.
52. RM 8:37 = RB 6.6. Cf. RM 9 and RB 6.7.
53. See t. IV, pp. 262–264.
54. RM 10 is much longer than RM 7. Humility is there presented as the necessary and sufficient means of going to heaven. It envelopes obedience as well as taciturnity.
55. As a simple paraphrase of Cassian, *Inst*. 4.39, the chapter on humility has neither a preparation (except *quia mitis sum et humilis corde* of Th 14, which does not seem intentional), nor a sequel.
56. On this pessimism and this severity, see the article cited above (note 5), in *RHS* 50 (1974) 113–134.
57. Cyprian, *Ep*. 59.4,2; 66.4,2.
58. Basil, moreover, might have suggested to the Master an implicit ordering of his first exposition (Thp 24–53) to the doctrine of obedience to superiors.
59. Basil, *Reg*. 12, joins obedience to God and obedience to the neighbor, but the second comes into play only where Scripture stipulates nothing. The two obediences are juxtaposed, rather than superimposed.
60. That those whom one should obey according to *Reg*. 70 are indeed superiors, and not ordinary brothers or the assembly of brothers, is suggested by the last part of the preceding

question (*Reg.* 69), where it is prescribed that one should present one's 'excuses' to the superior (*huic qui praeest*), or rather, according to the Greek of *Short Rules* 119, confirmed by the Syriac (Q. 70), to the superiors (*tois proëstôsi*). These Questions 69 and 70 are united in the Little Asceticon, but are separated in the Greek text (*Short Rules* 119 and 38).

61. Must not nuances be added to the affirmations of J. Gribomont, 'Obéissance et Évangile selon saint Basile le Grand', in *VSS* 6 (1952) p. 213: 'The superior is not God's representative', and p. 214: 'the role of the "proëstôs" (in Basil) never goes so far as to incarnate the divine authority, to give a religious value to indifferent actions'? Moreover, have QQ. 69 and 70 been taken sufficiently into consideration in this remarkable article? The mention of *proëstôs* in the first citation (in the plural in Short Rules 119) does not appear in the list of the uses made of this word (pp. 203-204), and the citation of Lk 10:16 in the second does not appear anywhere, unless I am mistaken, in spite of its doctrinal significance.

62. *Hist. mon* 31; PL 21: 458bc (lacking in the Greek). The commentary which follows is reproduced in our note on Thp 50, although this passage of the Master depends on Cyprian directly. The two citations (Mt 16:24 and Jn 6:38) are found in RM 7.51-52 but in inverse order.

63. C. Butler, *The Lausiac History of Palladius*, I, (Cambridge, 1898) pp. 265-266. Nothing prevents the phrase of the *Historia—si quis velit ad perfectionem velociter pervenire*—from having influenced RM 10.5 = RB 7.5. The reading *veni* in Jn 6:38 is too common to prove a bond of dependence between the *Historia* and our rules (see *La Communauté et l'Abbé*, p. 229, notes 3-4; E.T. p. 196, nn. 31-32).

64. RM certainly depends on Cyprian, *De dom. or.* 14, and perhaps on the *Historia*, this latter also depending on Cyprian.

65. Cassian, *Conf.* 16.6.4-5.

66. *Conf.* 24.26.13 (Is 58:3 and 13).

67. *Conf.* 19.6.6. Cf. *Conf.* 19.8.3 (Is 58:13). Ph 2:8 is cited alone in *Inst.* 12.8.1 and 12.28.

68. Cassian never cites Lk 10:16. However, the authority of the ancients is glorified in *Conf.* 2.14-15, and that of the cenobitic tradition, especially in Egypt, in *Inst.* 2.5; *Conf.* 18.5.

69. See notably Jerome, *De obedientia*; CC 78; p. 552,12 (Lk 10:16b); *Reg. IV Patrum* 1.17 (Jn 6:38) *Reg. Patr. II* 9 (Lk 10:16).

70. Basil, *Reg.* 12, 64-71, 80-83.

71. Augustine, *Praec.* 7.1 and 4. Between these two phrases, the words *Ut ergo cuncta ista serventur . . .* (7.2) already sound like a conclusion.

72. *Praec.* 7,3: *semper cogitans deo se pro vobis redditurum esse rationem* (cf. RB 2,34; 64.7; 65.22).

73. Ex 20:12. Cf. *Ordo monasterii* 6: *Fideliter oboediant, patrem suum honorent post deum, praeposito suo deferant sicut decet sanctos.*

74. Augustine seems to be thinking of Ex 20:12 and Eph 6:1-2 rather than of Lk 10:16, which is indicated in the note by L. Verheijen. In conversation the latter has kindly given me his assent upon this point. Lk 10:16 moreover has been introduced into the Augustinian text by *Reg. Tarn.* 23. Jerome, *De obedientia* (N. 69) uses Lk:10:16 to lay the foundation for obedience to the 'fathers'.

75. Eph. 6:1-2. Cf. Col. 3:20.

76. RM 2.1-3 = RB 2.1-3.

77. Lk 10:16 is cited eight times by the Master. See *La Règle du Maître*, t. II, p. 489.

78. Cf. A. Zumkeller, 'Der Klösterliche Gehorsam beim heiligen Augustinus', in *Augustinus Magister*, t. I, (Paris, 1954) pp. 265-276, especially the conclusion.

79. Horsiesius, *Liber* 19 [E.T. *Pachomian Koinonia* III (CS 47)]. See our article 'Saint Pachôme et son oeuvre', in *RHE* 69 (1974) 425-453, specially pp. 448-450. Jn 6:38 and

Lk 10:16 play almost no role, it seems, in the Pachomian doctrine of obedience, unlike that of these texts. The citation of Jn 6:38 in *Les Vies coptes*, p. 125, 30 (Bo 64), is a secondary fact (cf. F. Ruppert, *Das pachomianische Mönchtum*, pp. 391–394), and that of Lk 10:16 in *Les Vies coptes*, p. 340, 6 (S 3b) does not deal with obedience.

80. Evagrius, *Sentences* 88–92, especially number 90.

81. See above, notes 69 and 74. Cf. Jerome, *Ep.* 125.15.

82. *Reg. IV Patrum* 1.13.

83. *Reg. IV Patrum* 1.5–6 citing Ps 132:1 and Ps 67:7.

84. *Reg. IV Patrum* 1.17 citing Jn 6:38 according to the example of Abraham and the apostles.

85. 'Ascetic' in the sense that it deals with the repression of self-will. But this repression is considered as a true necessity for salvation, not as a simple matter of spiritual perfection that is more or less optional.

86. It is true that Basil, *Reg.* 3 puts the community at the beginning, while strongly insisting later on the renunciation of all self-will, in a perspective of individual abnegation (*Reg.* 12 establishes a certain relation between the two themes). On the other hand, although Augustine does not speak of the renunciation of self-will in *Praec.* 7.1–4, he inculcated it already in *Praec.* 5.5–7.

87. Prol 2–3. In the Master the word *oboedientia* appears for the first time in Ths 40 = Prol 40.

88. RB 67.7 (cf. 49.10). *Quocumque ire* makes us think of Basil *Reg.* 80 (*Si oportet ire quocumque, non commonito eo qui praeest?*), whose conclusion takes on the same general tone as the end of Benedict's phrase.

89. RB 68. Cf. Basil, *Reg.* 69 and 82; Pseudo-Basil, *Admonitio* 6.

90. RB 71 and 72.6. Cf. Basil, *Reg.* 64 (reference omitted in our annotation, t. II, pp. 668–671, as well as in our Introduction, t. I, p. 34, n. 23).

91. RB 71.2.

92. RB 68.5 (*ex caritate*) and 71.4 (*omni caritate*). Cf. RB 7.34 (*pro Dei amore*).

93. RB 71.1 *Oboedientiae bonum.* See *La Communauté et l'Abbé*, pp. 286–287 (E.T. p. 240) and 470–472.

94. They are underlined, without particular reference to RM, by F. Ruppert, *Das pachomianische Mönchtum*, and pp. 356–466 and *passim*.

95. Notably those of Gal 5:16–17 and Lk 10:16.

96. On this subject see the fine pages of Ch. Péguy, *Deuxième élégie XXX*, pp. 398–400.

97. RM 5:19.

98. Prol 2.

99. The humility of Christ obedient unto death is explicitly given as an example to Christians by Saint Paul in Ph 2:5: *Hoc enim sentite in vobis quod et in Christo Jesu.*

Chapter VI

SILENCE

(RB 6)

COMPARED WITH THE TWO LONG CHAPTERS of the Master from which it comes, this little treatise of Benedict is one of the most compressed we have.[1] A quotation from a psalm, briefly commented upon, and two of Proverbs: to avoid bad words entirely and good words as much as possible. Two phrases to describe the attitude of the monk in the presence of his superior: complete silence or a respectful request. Finally, the prohibition of pleasantries and idle words. The whole thing is laconic enough to give the impression of a lesson in taciturnity, as if Benedict wished to join example to teaching.

Yet one cannot help finding this treatment of such a subject a little too rapid. Speech and silence are realities too rich and too important for us to be content with such summary directives in their regard. Is the matter exhausted by this double negative advice[2]: to utter no bad word for fear of divine punishment, and to forswear even good words out of a disciple's humility and respect for the master? Does this advice even go to the root of things? We would wish for a broader and more balanced program which would omit neither the value and necessity of speech, indeed of laughter, nor the conditions for its good use. We would like to be warned, too, of the dangers and perversions of silence.[3] We would also like silence to be explicitly related to its highest end. If the monk renounces speaking to men, is it not ultimately in order to speak to God?[4]

What follows in the Rule provides partial answers to these requests. First of all, we find an imposing organization of the praise addressed to

God, then some scattered indications on the good use of words to men,[5] and on a certain bad silence to avoid.[6] Nevertheless, we must admit that instruction on good speech is scarcely outlined, and the overriding, almost the exclusive, concern remains that of the present chapter: as much as possible to keep the monks from speaking.[7] 'At all times the monks should cultivate silence': this opening maxim of Chapter 42 on night silence expresses quite well the spirit of the whole legislation.

Such a doctrine may seem narrow and one-sided, especially at a time when dialogue is so esteemed. Still, in its poverty it expresses faithfully the constant and deep tendency of all monasticism, both cenobitic and eremitic, to speak as little as possible. *Tace* (be silent) is the central article of Arsenius' triple program,[8] and what Jerome admired more than anything in the Egyptian cenobites was their perfect community silence.[9] The first monastic rules established right from the start a strict discipline about speaking,[10] which was to be reproduced indefatigably, with some variations, by the later tradition.[11]

The presence of a chapter 'On Taciturnity' in the midst of the great spiritual treatises which open our rules is therefore full of meaning. It reminds us that monastic life consists essentially in imposing on oneself certain renunciations. The author of a monastic rule does not have the task, as does the moralist, of drawing up a complete, reasoned, balanced theory on the good and bad use of the tongue, but the task of calling for renunciation and imposing it. The way of monasticism is to renounce freedom in speaking as well as in acting, the free use of the tongue as well as of the will. There is nothing astonishing in this, since renunciation of marriage and worldly business is its starting point.

In his presentation of this renunciation the monastic legislator can be more or less penetrating in his analysis of motives, and pertinent in his use of the scriptural proof. These considerations are not without interest, but let us admit that they are not of primary importance. What matters above all is the establishment of an energetic tendency and an effective discipline by which the individual and the community are really silent.[12] Once practised, silence, like the other renunciations will show its spiritual fruitfulness and unveil its many meanings.

The Master and Benedict have been explicit about only two of these meanings: the flight from sin, and humility. From the genetic point of view this last meaning is of primary importance, for the chapter 'On Taciturnity', like that 'On Obedience' in our rules, has its origin in Cassian's description of humility.[13] In its literary element, the taciturnity proposed by our authors is the effort of self-effacement by restraint of the tongue, moderation of voice and reserve in laughter.[14] But both authors, especially the Master, have given a special character to this silence of humility by integrating it into the system of hierarchical relations between inferior and superior.[15] By so doing they have related it to the abbot's teaching, that is, to the divine word. One is silent in order to listen to God.

The disciple's humble silence is fortified in our rules by fear of sins of the tongue. These do not consist only of lies, frauds, injuries, abuse of oaths and other gross faults mentioned in the Instruments of good works and the Prologue. According to the Gospel, we must also cut off 'every idle word for which men will have to render an account on the day of judgment',[16] and again, according to the Apostle, every 'improper' remark which does not 'edify'.[17] Understood literally, these New Testament maxims amount to excluding every word which is not spiritual or of strictly practical necessity. As far as jokes are concerned, their exclusion is reinforced with the Gospel words, 'Woe to you who laugh'.[18]

Silence because of humility, the silence of the disciple, silence to avoid sin: these three aspects of taciturnity do not express all its riches but they do refer it to essential elements of the spiritual life. To recognize in silence a mark of humility is to attach it to the great effort of inner purification which leads to charity. To demand silence of the monk because he is a disciple is to make silence a religious attitude, the attitude of one who keeps himself alert to hear God. In this regard it is important to note that taciturnity combines with the general practice in monasticism, of scriptural 'meditation' during work; the combination is explicit in the Master and implicit in Benedict. In this way is prolonged all day long that hearing of the word of God for the sake of which one is silent at the office, at table, and at reading.[19]

And finally, silence as a flight from sin is also related to the divine word. If the monk abstains from speaking vainly or from laughing, he does so to obey the voice of Christ. If he avoids every remark which is not spiritually 'edifying', he does so to follow the Apostle's watchword. And the divine will which we thus obey only acts to open a passageway, through the buzzing of human conversations, to the ebb and flow of the eternal Word, the word of God to men and of men to God.[20]

NOTES TO CHAPTER 6

1. See t. IV, pp. 201 and 204. This proportion of 1/11 is very slender. The present section was written before we read A.G. Wathen, *Silence. The Meaning of Silence in the Rule of St Benedict*, Cistercian Studies Series 22 (1974).

2. See t. IV, pp. 237–238, and correct our note on RM 8.37 where we saw a 'third reason'.

3. Cf. Cassian, *Inst.* 11.3–4 (vanity); 12.27.5 and 6 (pride and anger); 12.29.2 (bitterness); *Conf.* 4.20.3 (pride); 16.18.1 and 4 (bitterness and spitefulness). See also the Apophthegma 'Poemen' 27 (judging others); Gregory, *Mor.* 7.60–61.

4. Cf. The Apophthegma 'Arsenius' 13; Sulpicius Severus, *Dial.* 1.17. What is said there about fleeing from men is valid also for silence.

5. See t. IV, pp. 278–280.

6. RB 7.44–48 = RM 10.61–65; RB 46.1–4 (cf. Augustine, *Praec.* 4.1).

7. RB 38.5; 42.1 and 9; 43.8; 48.5 and 18; 49.7; 53.23–24; 67.5. Several of these prohibitions aim at protecting the sleep or recollection of a neighbor.

8. Apophthegma 'Arsenius' 1. Cf. I. Hausherr, *Hésychasme et prière* (Rome, 1966) pp. 199–214.

9. Jerome, *Ep.* 22.35.2-4. Cf. Cassian, *Inst.* 2.10.1–2.

10. Pachomius, *Praec.* 8,31,33,34,59,60,68,88,94,116,121,122 (cf. *Inst.* 18. p. 59,6); *Ordo monasterii* 7 and 9; Basil, *Reg.* 8. 40–45, 53.136–137.

11. See for example Caesarius, *Reg. virg.* 9,10,18–20,22; Ferreolus, *Reg.* 7.22,25,29; *Reg. Pauli et Stephani* 18 and 37; Columban, *Reg. mon.* 2 and *Reg. coen.* 4,6,9,15.

12. *Taciturnitas* is not only the 'spirit of silence', but silence without further qualifications. See RB 42.1 and 9; Cassian, *Inst.* 12.27.5–6 and *Conf.* 16.18.3–4, where *silentium* and *taciturnitas* are interchangeable. The Master and Benedict have opposite preferences, the former for *tacere* and its derivatives (6/1), see latter for *silere* and *silentium* (1/5).

13. See *La Communauté et l'Abbé*, pp. 207–214 (E.T. pp. 179–185).

14. See Cassian, *Inst.* 4.39.2; his two last 'signs of humility' are found in RM 10.75–81 = RB 7. 56–61.

15. This modification, which is evident in the treatise on taciturnity, is already noticeable in the ninth degree of humility. See t. IV, pp. 319–321.

16. Mt 12:36, which is alluded to in RM 3.59 = RB 4.53; RM 9.51 = RB 6.8, and which RM combines with *Eph* 4:29. Cf. RB 67.4.

17. *Eph* 4:29 and 5:4, combined by RM 9.49; 11.49; 50.42 (cf. 5.8; 9.44 and 51), as well as Caesarius, *Reg. virg.* 19; *Reg. Pauli et Stephani* 37.2.

18. Lk 6:25 whose positive counterpart (Lk 6:21) is cited by RM 11.79. Cf. Basil, *Reg.* 8.

19. RB 38. 5–9; 48. 17–21.

20. This effort for verbal sobriety should moreover continue in prayer itself so that it may be 'pure' and true (Cassian, *Inst.* 2.10.3 and *Conf.* 9.36.1; RM 48.5 and 10–14; RB 20.4–5). Similarly, no declaration of humility (8th sign; 7th degree), but avowals (2nd sign; 5th degree) with the corresponding direction of the elder (3rd sign; this rudimentary dialogue is like the embryo of the conferences in which one submits one's problems to an elder).

Chapter VII

HUMILITY

(RB 7)

O UR EXCUSE FOR SPEAKING rather soberly on this chapter is that we have already commented on it in detail twice before.[1] In itself it certainly calls for the very amplest development. Its dimensions are enormous, especially in Benedict.[2] Its articulation in twelve degrees gives it the appearance of a Summa, and its place at the end of the doctrinal part of the Rule gives it the weight of a conclusion. Its role as a recapitulation results from a comparison with the two preceding treatises, for obedience and taciturnity are but manifestations of humility. Finally, the solemnity of its exordium, the generality of its first degree, its effort to embrace the whole spiritual life, from initial fear to the perfection of charity, make it look like a synthesis to which too much importance could not be attached.

In essence this synthesis reproduces a segment from Cassian, the journey from fear to charity traced by the Abba Pinufius.[3] Of the two great stages of this journey—exterior renunciation and humility—the Master and Benedict omit the first to give their entire attention to the second. Humility, already set in high relief by Cassian, becomes the very object of their treatise. The fear of God, instead of being its remote principle, constitutes its first degree. Cassian's ten 'signs of humility' are enriched with scriptural proofs and transformed into so many ascending steps, which makes them seem like an obligatory program and a method to be followed step by step. At the end of this ladder, a twelfth degree—the expectation of divine judgment—corresponds to the first. These two degrees at the beginning and end, taking up certain Basilian themes, frame the

117

description of humility towards neighbor, taken from Cassian, within that of humility before God.

Since this analysis of duties towards God is as detailed as the other, the whole ladder seems like a complete summary of the spiritual life. A biblical prologue claims for it this character of a Summa expressly: if 'anyone who humbles himself shall be exalted',[4] then to practise humility point by point is the necessary and sufficient condition for going to heaven. And in fact, at the other end of the chapter, a description of paradise lets us see, at least in the Master, what humility achieves in the next life. And charity, which Cassian made the goal of the ascent, is also attained here below by traversing the ladder, and it permits the monk to keep with sovereign ease everything which he labored to observe up till then. Thanks to charity, he can 'conserve humility' without difficulty now.[5]

Upon reflection, this schema of our rules presents more than one difficulty. One of the chief difficulties concerns transforming a list of 'signs' into a 'ladder'. Cassian was content to note several symptoms of humility; his list of ten signs was neither systematic nor exhaustive. The Master and Benedict substitute twelve 'degrees' for this enumeration, expressly said to be incomplete. This is to give Cassian's simple description a false air of being a gradated method; this is accentuated by certain more or less artificial progressions set up here and there between the degrees.[6]

Another point open to discussion is the elimination of the first stage in Cassian's itinerary: the renunciation of the affections and goods of this world. Certainly we understand that our authors refer this theme to another section of the Rule and here concentrate upon humility. But are they justified in presenting it as the only thing necessary? If their program is to be what it claims to be, a complete itinerary from earth to heaven, can it pass over in silence the first step on the way to perfection, which is this exterior renunciation which precedes and conditions the spiritual effort of humility?

These criticisms stemming from Cassian's point of view,[7] are supplemented by other causes of uneasiness, unique to the sensibility of our times. First of all, we are surprised that a synthetic representation of the ascent to God assigns charity so late and restricted a role. Besides the fact that love of neighbor is not even mentioned, the 'charity for the Lord' comes in at the end of the ascent, not at the beginning. The role of fundamental virtue, which seems to us to belong by right to charity according to the Gospel, is played by 'the fear of God' in our rules. This fear, analyzed in the first degree with a singular complacence, seems to envelop the whole ascent[8] and reaches its culmination in the twelfth degree. Is it not strange that one can 'climb the ladder of heaven' from one end to the other under the influence of this sentiment, which Saint Paul declared abolished,[9] without encountering the chief christian virtue, charity?[10] For this reason the present chapter seems like a preparation for christian spirituality rather than an exposition of it.

Finally, we are struck by another omission, that of grace. We must wait for the concluding phrase to hear of the Holy Spirit who purifies.[11] Like charity and in connection with it, the action of the Spirit is only mentioned at the last moment. It seems only to reward and complete human *ascesis*, not to arouse and sustain it. All during the ascent the monk has been set in the presence of the God who commands and judges, not of the God who loves, anticipates, and saves.

We could multiply observations of this kind; we could make a systematic tally of how this text fails to realize its own design or to satisfy our expectations. But when all was said, the task of perceiving the interest of the theme and the positive values which it contains would still remain. To this far more important task we wish now to devote ourselves briefly.

Humility is the word by which the Master and Benedict summarize all their doctrine, pushing to its limits a suggestion of Cassian. This abridgment is authorized by the Gospel: 'Whoever humbles himself, shall be exalted'. Taken literally and in its fullness, this word of Christ signifies that humility elevates man even to God and eternal life. According to the context of the three gospel passages which report this saying, humility is a matter of behaving humbly either in the most ordinary social life by taking the last place, or in religious society where the leader should look upon himself as a servant, or finally in the secrecy of prayer where it is right to recognize oneself as a sinner before God.[12] Humility then makes one pleasing to God and to men, here below and in eternity.[13]

But the gospel maxim assumes its full force only when we, with Saint Paul, recognize in it the expression of the mystery of Christ himself. Jesus has not only proclaimed it; he has lived it. The hymn of the Epistle to the

Philippians uses these same words to celebrate the two phases of his destiny: 'He humbled himself. . . that is why God has exalted him'.[14] The first stage, the crucifixion, is announced magnificently elsewhere in terms of *agapè*,[15] but the formula of Philippians has the privilege of embracing in its antithesis the whole paschal mystery, death and glorification.[16]

Thus the verb 'to humble oneself', like the verb 'to love', can express deeply the salvation accomplished in Christ. When it is said that 'Christ loved me and delivered himself for me', it is not useless to add that 'Christ emptied himself, taking the form of a slave. . . . He humbled himself, becoming obedient unto death, even to the death of the cross'. To descend from heaven, to ascend to heaven: does not the creed enclose the redemptive act of the Lord Jesus within this twofold movement of abasement and exaltation?

Our rules could have made explicit this Christological import of 'Whoever humbles himself, shall be exalted'. But they scarcely do so,[17] any more than the Master profited by his presentation of Christ as 'meek and humble of heart' at the threshold of the Thema.[18] Yet Christ remains indeed for him, as he said elsewhere, the 'Lord of humility'.[19]

In reading these words, we think of that 'humility of Christ' which recurs often in the fourth Book of the *Institutes*,[20] either with or without the 'poverty of Christ'. According to Cassian, the monk, by stripping and humiliating himself, enters into the mystery of Christ. He takes to himself the humility and poverty of Jesus. Just as the first phase of the existence of Christ Jesus consisted in depriving himself of his divine riches to become man and then sinking to the lowest place among men, so in the same way the monk first renounces all property, then all independence and all pride. These two renunciations are the two stages of one and the same movement of abasement, after the likeness and invitation of Christ. Cassian does not cite the words 'Whoever humbles himself, shall be exalted', but that is what he is treating. Whether he describes the cenobitic institutions of Egypt or reports the discourse of Pinufius, who sets forth their meaning, Cassian makes the very essence of cenobitism consist of humility.

That statement can be extended to the whole of monasticism, including eremitism. Several of the examples of obedience and humility given by Cassian in this book of the *Institutes* come from famous hermits.[21] More striking still is the fact that the book of the *Vitae Patrum* devoted to humility far overbalances almost all the others,[22] as if there were almost no other subject which inspired the Fathers of the Desert to so many apophthegms.

Monasticism is then a way of humility. In the cenobitic setting this way is called more precisely economic dependence, obedience, patience, effacement, as Cassian and Pinufius remind us every moment, and as a Faustus, a Caesarius, a Novatus were to repeat untiringly.[23] This program may appear discouraging, and it is, in fact, nothing less than the passion of Christ in which it makes the monk share. We can be grateful to contemporary psychologists[24] for warning us that this program is naturally dangerous and even unhealthy. It is indeed, unless a living faith in the mystery of Christ changes it into an 'exalting' hope.[25]

This faith can and should be penetrated by love. Cassian, the Master, and especially Benedict have suggested or said this.[26] But charity remains for them, at least in theory, the virtue marking the end, not the beginning or intermediate progress. There is here an undeniable divergence from our present-day perspectives, by which we appeal to love from the beginning and at every moment. Humility was for our fathers what love is for us—the key-word which sums up everything. Of charity they had a very high idea—too high perhaps—like the one modern people even yet usually have of the mystical life. These spiritual summits are spoken of only rarely and with reserve. As queen and synthesis of all virtues, implying, according to Saint Paul, the purification of all vices, charity is too sublime a thing for one to flatter oneself on having attained.

Nevertheless, this theory of charity as perfection does not so overshadow our authors as to make them miss other elements of scriptural teaching. Even if Cassian scarcely bothers with the twofold commandment of love, we have seen that our rules inscribe it in the place which belongs to it, at the top of their catalogue of good works.[27] For the Master and Benedict therefore, charity is not only at the end of spiritual effort, where it expels all fear and changes labor into a marvellous ease; it is also found at the beginning, as the great commandment to be observed before all and through all.

This correction, which nicely balances the teaching received from Cassian, should not, however, make us forget its importance. Not without reason does charity appear so late in the synthesis of the chapter 'On Humility', and in the discourse of Pinufius and in the corresponding schemes of the *Conferences*.[28] This presentation, inspired by the hymn to agapè in the First Letter to the Corinthians, has the merit of setting forth the demands of charity. By this means it guards against sentimentalism and the abuse of words. It costs nothing to speak about love, but acting according to love presupposes great virtue. The twelve preliminary degrees of our rules, like the 'signs' of Cassian from which they are drawn, aim precisely at establishing truth in this area. If we wish charity to be true, humility with all its train of connected virtues must also and first of all be 'possessed in truth'.[29]

This insistence on the conditions of true love goes so far as to assign a major role to the fear of God. Our astonishment at this might at first glance be warranted to some extent by the ancient sources themselves. The Master and Benedict make fear the first and most developed of the degrees of humility that the monk must traverse, but Cassian did not place it thus *at the heart* of the monastic life; in Pinufius' scheme, which serves as the source of our rules,[30] the fear of the Lord appears *before* entrance into the monastery, and draws the worldling there. This way of relegating fear to the preliminaries of the monastic life is already, very explicitly met, in the first Rules of Basil. Treating of charity at the beginning of his *Asceticon*, he declares frankly that fear is not a suitable motive for the relatively advanced Christians whom he is addressing.[31]

Yet it would be a mistake to oppose these statements of Basil and Cassian to the teaching of our rules. Basil writes a little further on that 'continual fear' is one of the effects of the constant remembrance of God which he extols. This fear is not opposed to charity, but associated with it.[32] Cassian, in the great schema of Pinufius which underlies our chapters 'On Humility', attributes to fear not only an initial conversion effect, but also a permanent role. Fear is both 'the beginning of salvation', and also its 'guardian', for it 'obtains purification from vices and the keeping of the virtues'.[33] It is therefore not only a preliminary to monastic life and a virtue pertaining to the threshold, but it makes its influence felt throughout the monk's *ascesis*, just as it does in the Master's teaching.

If Cassian, through the mouth of Pinufius, acknowledges this lasting effect of fear, this is doubtless because he remembers the distinction Abba Chaeremon made about the two kinds of fear, that of slaves and that of sons. The second accompanies charity and constitutes the 'treasure of the riches of salvation', according to a saying of Isaiah.[34] But this allusion to

Conference Eleven, which we emphasized in our previous commentary,[35] does not by itself explain the role of permanent 'safeguard' that falls to the fear of the Lord. To understand this better, we must re-read the earlier pages of Pinufius' sermon. There Cassian presents monastic renunciation as a 'crucifixion' and a 'death'. The cause of this spiritual crucifixion is precisely the fear of God, according to a saying of the psalmist.[36] By it all our wills and desires remain attached to the divine law and are put to death. The series of examples illustrating this crucifixion by fear already follows the scheme about to be clearly developed by Pinufius. We find in it, first of all, the renunciation of family affections, of material cares and property, then the renunciation of pride and its various manifestations, particularly resentment and impatience.[37] It appears thus that the whole effort of poverty and humility, in which the cenobitic life consists, is wrapped in the fear of the Lord.

Cassian had all this in mind when he put into Pinufius' mouth the saying that fear is the 'guardian of salvation', or the 'purification of vices and the guardian of the virtues'.[38] He was referring as much to the picture of the crucifixion of the cenobite which had just been sketched by the same Pinufius,[39] as he was of the theory of filial fear that was to be expounded in the *Conferences* of Abba Chaeremon. Whether you envisage it from the standpoint of the text of Isaiah or from that of the Psalm, the fear of God appears as a permanent, given element in the monastic life. It is not only at its origin, but at its heart.

The Master and Benedict are not diverging from Basil and Cassian, therefore, by proposing the fear of God with their well-known fullness and insistence in the first and last degrees of their ladder. To understand this doctrine of the ancients we must keep in mind its various scriptural roots and the complexity of the biblical language to which it conforms. Sometimes, under the influence of certain apostolic texts,[40] love is opposed to fear, and fear is declared abolished. Sometimes, in the whole Old Testament and many passages of the New, the fear of God is presented as a fundamental, always necessary, disposition, not at all opposed to love, but inseparable from it. Certainly the conclusion of the schema of Pinufius and of the chapter 'On Humility' in our rules describes the expulsion of fear by charity. But it would not be necessary to conclude from this that the 'fear of God' always means for Cassian, the Master, and Benedict that elementary fear of punishment which is expelled by charity. On the contrary, it is manifest that our authors often follow the common usage of the Bible in giving the expression 'the fear of God' its noble and undifferentiated meaning, which is pregnant with love.[41]

In this respect the conclusion of the chapter 'On Humility', far from furnishing a rule of general interpretation, represents an isolated case, an exception, for the Master and Benedict. The fear which is declared to be cast out by charity, does not even cover, it seems, the whole of the 'fear of God' described in the first degree. It is only a part, and the least lofty part.[42] This fear *of punishment* may be eliminated without the fear *of God* being removed.[43] Only the first disappears in the presence of agapè, according to Saint John, but not the second which was already love.

These considerations suggest that the ladder of humility in our rules is not at all a pre-christian way, conformed more to the Old Law than to the New, for all that it is penetrated with divine fear. They explain also that 'the fear of God' is the fundamental quality required by Benedict for more than one charge in the monastery.[44] The expression may sound curious to our ears, but the same is true of 'humility'. When by the light of Scripture we have recognized its true sense and richness, we ask if it is not irreplaceable as an expression of a great spiritual reality which is timeless: the astonishment and exultation of the believer in the presence of the Most High.

NOTES TO CHAPTER 7

1. See t. IV, pp. 281–370, and *La Communauté et l'Abbé*, pp. 251–266 (E.T. pp. 212–224) Cf. pp. 207–251 (E.T. pp. 179–224).

2. RM 10 is not longer than RM 11 and does not much exceed RM 7 and 8–9. On the contrary, RB 7 is out of proportion with what precedes and follows it, and with the remaining chapters of the Rule.

3. Cassian, *Inst.* 4. 39.

4. Lk 14:11.

5. RM 10. T. See our article 'Sur un titre de chapitre de la Règle du Maître portant des traces de Cassien non encore repérées', in *RHS* 51 (1975) 305–309.

6. See t. IV, pp. 283–291 and 312–326.

7. We could also point out the separation of Cassian's signs 2 and 3 (see *La Communauté et l'Abbé*, pp. 252–255; [E.T. 213–216]).

8. See RM 10.87 (cf. t. IV, p. 362). Paroxysm of fear at the twelfth degree: see t. IV, pp. 289–291.

9. Rm 8:15, 2 Tm 1:7.

10. Save for the addition *pro amore Dei* at Benedict's third degree (RB 7.34), a sort of inadvertence (see *La Communauté et l'Abbé*, p. 265 [E.T. 223] and 449–450).

11. RM 10.91 = RB 7.70. This phrase, unique to our rules, refers implicitly to Rm 5:5 (infusion of charity by the Spirit); Ez 36:25–27 and Ps 50:12 (Spirit and purity). See also 2 Co 6:5 (*in Spiritu sancto, in caritate non ficta*) and Cassian's commentary, *Conf.* 14.16.8–9. Moreover, although Cassian does not speak of grace in *Inst.* 4.39, he elsewhere notes its necessity for the ascent to charity (*Conf.* 11.9.1–2).

12. Lk 14:11, Mt 23:12, Lk 18:14.

13. Cf. Si 3:20, cited by RM 95.16.

14. Ph 2:8–9.

15. Ga 2:20, Eph 5:2 and 25. Cf. Jn 15:12–13, 1 Jn 3:16.

16. Compare the antithesis of Rm 4:25. The sacrifice of Christ also appears as a humble 'service' in Mt 20:28. Cf. Jn 13:1–5.

17. Except indirectly by citing Jn 6:38 and Ph 2:8 (RM 10.43 and 49 = RB 7.32 and 34). Still this last is deprived of the characteristic term (*humiliavit semetipsum*) which would expressly make Christ's obedience a model of humility.

18. RM Th 14, citing Mt 11:29. This very important citation (*discite a me* foretells the foundation of the *scola*) seems not to serve as an introduction to *De humilitate*. It is never repeated.

19. RM 13.72: *Christo humilitatis Domino.*

20. Cassian, *Inst.* 4.4,29,37. Cf. 4.5 and 37 (*paupertas Christi*). The *Qui se humiliat exaltabitur* is not cited either in *Inst.* 4, or apparently in the rest of Cassian's work. But *humilitas* is indeed the key word of this Book 4, where it occurs some thirty times and *obedientia* twenty times.

21. This is true not only of John of Lyco (*Inst.* 4.32–26), but also to some extent of the cenobites Patermutius and Pinufius (*Inst.* 4.27 and 30), whose exploits are probably transpositions of stories about anchorites. See 'Les sources des quatre premier Livres des Institutions de Jean Cassien', in *Aufstieg und Niedergang der römischen Welt*, (Berlin).

22. *Vitae Patrum* 5.15; PL 73: 953–969. Only Book 10 (*De discretione*) has a greater number of apophthegms.

23. Eusebius Gall., *Hom.* 36–45; Caesarius, *Serm.* 233–238; Novatus, *Sententia de humilitate*, PL 18: 67–70.

24. Cf. A. Klemp, 'Die Regula S. Benedicti und ihre psychologischen Korrelate', in *RBS* I, pp. 257–270.

25. RM 10.1 and 56 = RB 7.1 and 39.

26. Cf. Cassian, *Inst.* 4.27–28: Patermutius and the young nobleman act *pro amore Christi . . . pro nomine ac desiderio Christi*; RM 7.2 = RB 5.2; RM 10.55 = RB 7.38 (*pro Domino . . . propter te*). On the addition *pro De amore* (RB 7.34), see above, note 10. Cf. RB 68.5 and 71.4.

27. See our commentary on Ch. IV, above, notes 33–43.

28. Cassian, *Inst.* 4.39 and 43; *Conf.* 1 and 11.

29. *Inst.* 4.39.3: *humilitas vera . . . in veritate possessa.* This demand for truth—Cassian is thinking of verbal protestations of humility—comes back like a refrain (*Inst.* 4.8,9,23; cf. 4.24.1 and 4: *profunda cordis simplicitate . . . sinceram humilitatis oboedientiam*).

30. *Inst.* 4.39.1; 4.43.

31. Basil, *Reg.* 2 = *Long Rules* 4 (see t. IV, p. 307). Cf. *Prooem.* 3; PG 31: 895b.

32. Basil, *Long Rules* 5.3 (924b), alluding to Pr 8:13. The passage is missing in the first edition translated by Rufinus, but this edition does not ignore fear: see *Reg.* 138 = *Short Rules* 209 (Ps 118:120b; *a iudiciis enim tuis timui*).

33. Cassian, *Inst.* 4.39.1.

34. Cassian, *Conf.* 11.13.2.
35. See t. IV, pp. 349–351.
36. Cassian, *Inst.* 4.34 (Ps 118:120a: *confige timore tuo carnes meas*). This effect of fear on voluntary acts and desires recalls the first degree in our rules.
37. *Inst.* 4.35, lines 7–13, foretelling *Inst.* 4.39.1–2. See also *Inst.* 4.36.1–2.
38. *Inst.* 4.39.1.
39. The latter speaks again of the fear of God in *Inst.* 4.38 (Si 2:1).
40. Rm 8:15, 2 Tm 1:7, 1 Jn 4:18.
41. For the Master see t. IV, p. 361 (cf. pp. 335–336). For Benedict see below, n. 44. Cassian sometimes opposes fear and love (*Conf.* 11.6–12; cf. *Inst.* 4.39,43 and 6.19; *Conf.* 6,4 and 8.25.6), but he knows a fear pertaining to love (*Conf.* 11.13; cf. RB 72.9) and often mentions *timor Dei* alone as a general and fundamental disposition, associated with the remembering of God (*Inst.* 2.3.4; 4.34–35; 6.13.2; *Conf.* 7.3–4 and 7.24).
42. Thought of punishment in the first degree: see RM 10.11 = RB 7.11 (cf. RM 7.2 = RB 5.2, RM 9.41). The fear of God includes also the thought of eternal life.
43. In fact, *timor gehennae* (RM 10.90) is distinguished from *timor Dei* (RM 10.87), a sentiment which accompanies the disciple throughout the 'ladder of this life'.
44. RB 31.2; 36.7; 65.15 (cf. RB 3.11; 64.1; 66.4). Although Benedict replaces fear with love in the conclusion of RB 4.77 (see t. IV, pp. 219–220), his use of *timor Dei* and *timere Deum* is relatively more frequent than the Master's.

Chapter VIII

THE DIVINE OFFICE

(RB 8–20)

Section I. Continual Prayer and Prayer of the Hours (RB 16)[1]

THE ABRUPT MANNER in which Benedict begins his treatment of the divine office has always astonished readers and commentators. One enters immediately upon dry determinations about the horarium without any preamble to indicate the meaning of this body of rubrics. It is only towards the end of all this (RB 16) that Benedict thinks it well to expound the general plan of the hours and to furnish a scriptural justification for it. This first sketch of speculation on the office offered us by the Rule will be the point of departure for our reflections.

Benedict justifies the cycle of the hours by two Psalm texts: 'Seven times a day have I praised you'; 'At midnight I arose to praise you'.[2] The daily septenary thus founded on the divine word is something 'sacred'[3] in his eyes. To give it a correct interpretation which excludes night vigils from it, is enough to establish the 'cursus' of the office on the most indisputable base, a purely scriptural one.

Going by this simplified presentation, we might think that the *opus Dei* proceeded immediately from the inspired word. Consequently it is not without interest to refer to the corresponding passage of the Master.[4] We find there the word of the Psalmist certainly, but only by way of conclusion. Instead of opening the chapter like a peremptory oracle on which all rests, it ends the paragraph like a simple justification *a posteriori*. For the Master the ordering of the office has from the outset a different foundation: 'the custom of antiquity and the regulations sanctioned by the

Fathers'. The first justification of the office is to be sought, not in Scripture, but in tradition.

The Master, in speaking thus, sets forth a fact which is evident to every historian. A paleo-christian custom, fixed and specified by the Fathers of monasticism explains the arrangement of the office. Neither the number of the hours nor their determination results simply from Scripture. Scripture has doubtless furnished a group of suggestions decisive in establishing the cycle of the hours. The authors of treatises on prayer constantly connected each hour celebrated to persons of one or the other Testaments: Daniel and the psalmist, the apostles, and especially Christ. But if each hour can thus claim some text or episode of Scripture, sometimes even several, these are only scattered indications, often without explicit connection with the duty of prayer. It took the researches of several christian generations interested in constituting a system of hours of prayer to collect these texts and assemble them and to relate them to the Christian's prayer.

Does this mean that the series of hours is a mere human invention, to which Scripture furnished only a sort of pretext or illustration? That would be to fail to recognize the profound scriptural source from which all these searches sprang. If the writers of the third century in Rome, Carthage, and Alexandria took the trouble to propose times for prayer, their only concern was to respond, as best they could, to Christ's invitation: 'Pray without ceasing'.[5] This appeal for continual prayer, especially transmitted by Paul and by Luke, is the great spring which moved all ante-Nicene Christianity and monasticism. The Fathers never lost sight of the fact that this constituted the Lord's only precept in the matter. Their systems of hours are only proposals of human origin, most often stripped in their own eyes of any real character of obligation.[5bis] Only the precept 'Pray without ceasing' is obligatory. It was in trying to fulfil this that christian tradition discovered the utility of definite moments in which a person applies himself each day to prayer. Of course, these hours are only milestones in a day whose every instant should be filled with prayer. But experience shows that it is useful, even indispensable, given the weakness of man, to set for oneself moments of prayer so as not to let time roll by in dissipation of mind and concern for earthly things.

Prayer at certain hours is therefore something like continual prayer. It would not be legitimate to consider it as sufficient, but one can use it as a means of arriving at unceasing prayer. The function of the hours of prayer is not to dispense from the duty of continual prayer, but to recall it to memory and to outline its fulfillment. Starting from this outline, a person will tend more surely towards the perfect fulfillment of 'Pray without ceasing'.

Thus understood, the system of the hours conforms to the Lord's will, at the same time liberal and exacting. From Christ we have received no precise rule, not even that of 'three times a day', which he no doubt observed.[6] The Gospel rule goes far beyond every fixed observance. The Christian should pray 'without ceasing',[7] just as he should love with all his being. God is all, and the only homage that befits him is that of the totality of our time. But just because this demand is total, it cannot be expressed by any precise and universally obligatory precept. Instead, it resounds like an appeal addressed personally to each Christian. No one ever finishes responding to such an invitation. Each liberty is being perpetually solicited by a request both pressing and flexible, infinitely demanding without imposing anything materially. No human regulation could enslave this liberty or confine this dynamism. Beyond every individual habit and every collective custom, each person remains in the end solely responsible at every instant for the attention he accords and the response he gives to 'Pray without ceasing'.

The Fathers understood it this way. The first monks in their turn understood it this way.[7bis] In this perspective, to celebrate prayer at certain hours must have seemed hardly worthy of a Christian in love with perfection. Very early Clement professed only scorn for the hours of prayer: the gnostic prays everywhere and always.[8] This ambitious ideal was soon to be the object of concrete activities in monasticism. When the threat of a bloody death ceased to hang over every christian head, the monk tried to give his whole life here below the value of a martyrdom. The break with the world no longer consisted in defying the law and confronting torture, but in leaving society and living for God alone far from men. The value attached to the supreme sacrifice was transferred to an earthly existence totally consecrated to God. The present time was thus charged with a new value,[9] and Christ's appeal for continual prayer resounded with more force than ever. Thereafter, to pray without ceasing was no longer to be one of the Lord's directives among others; it was to be the *raison d'être* of lives freed from every temporal preoccupation. In his retreat the monk could apply the Gospel instructions literally. All the day and half the night would be devoted to uninterrupted prayer accompanying manual work. This continuity made the celebration of the traditional hours useless. Those at the beginning and the end of the night were kept, but the whole day was spent without offices. This at least was the original practice of the monks of Egypt;[10] this was also the ambition of the most fervent and strongest monks[11] in other regions, and not only in the circles touched with Messalianism.

However, this 'Egyptian perfection' soon seemed 'an inimitable rigor' for most.[12] Monasticism outside of Egypt was as a whole content to resume the cycle of hours of ante-Nicene asceticism, completed here and there more or less, by some new hours. But this apparent continuity of the monastic *cursus* with those of the preceding age should not mask the profound change brought about, especially among cenobites. The horaria of prayer proposed to isolated Christians became social rules constraining all the members of a community.[13] The prayer of the hours was no longer made in private, according to each person's desire. The monks gathered to celebrate it. That meant there was a passage not only from the privacy of one's room to a public gathering, and from liberty to obligation, but also from the indeterminate contents of an individual prayer to the precise *ordo* required by every communal celebration. We barely know what the third-century Christians included in their prayer of the hours. Surely the Lord's prayer, commented upon by all the treatises on prayer and already prescribed by the *Didachè*. Sometimes also, if we believe Tertullian, some selected psalms, accompanied by alleluia.[14] On the whole, formulas were both rare and brief, and they were prolonged by free and spontaneous prayer. Quite different is the canonical hour of the monks. It always included the recitation of psalms, a fixed and often large number of them, each followed by a prayer which lasts for a set time. Except for the morning, and sometimes the evening hour, these psalms were taken consecutively from the psalter. At the main hours, more or less obligatory scriptural readings completed the psalmody.[15]

The monastic office differs much then from the ancient christian prayer which it succeeded. Must we see in this transformation the return to a kind of legalism? Spiritual liberty seems to have given way to constraint, the boundless appeal of Christ was changed into a liturgical regulation, the mobility and diversity of graces had to bend to custom, invariable for each and uniform for all. To deny that there is a problem here would be the surest way to make it insurmountable. The communitarian office finds its legitimacy only in a clear recognition of its relationship to 'Pray without ceasing'. Those who bind themselves to it should never forget that it constitutes not an end but a means, not an ideal or a law come down from heaven[16] but a humble wise invention of men to respond better to Christ's appeal and to take common measures against their weakness. The only law for the monk as for the Christian of the first centuries was to pray without ceasing. The office was only a method for attaining this. The canonical hours should be seen as the pillars of a bridge thrown across the stream of time. The only purpose of these supports is to carry the road which will bestride the river and connect the two banks. Thus the meaning of the hours of the office is to provide the underpinnings for continual prayer. They can effectively sustain the effort of someone who wants to surrender to the Lord's invitation, but they would go right contrary to their purpose if they caused Christ's voice to be forgotten or lulled to sleep the restlessness of the christian soul.

Cassian understood this perfectly and proclaimed it in a capital page at the heart of his treatise on the office.[17] There he opposes the Egyptians' prayer, which is private, spontaneous, and unceasing, to that of the Easterners who gather by conventual obligation to celebrate only certain hours. The contrast appears to him wholly to the Egyptians' advantage. Their uninterrupted prayer is superior to the discontinuous offices; their spontaneous zeal has more merit than an observance imposed by the common life.

This means that the prayer of the hours remains directed to unceasing prayer, the regulated office to personal prayer, and common celebration to solitary heart-to-heart conversation with God. At first glance, this is wholly surprising to our modern minds, permeated with the superiority of liturgical worship over private prayer. But the astonishment ends when we reflect upon the profound difference in origin and nature separating the prayer of the hours from the Eucharistic liturgy. By its whole history and its very institution by the Lord, it is clear that the Eucharist is essentially an act of the Church. But the prayer of the hours flows from another evangelical source and has followed another course. To gather the christian assembly is not of its essence. The law of continual prayer, which stands at its beginning and end, is addressed directly to each conscience and is accomplished moment by moment in private life. It does not require that one leave home and assemble with others. 'When you wish to pray, close your door and pray to your Father in secret'.[18] More-over, the Christian is never alone. The 'we' of the Our Father is enough to place his most solitary prayer in the heart of the Church. If he joins with his brothers to pray, this may be in order to confer on his prayer a new value by giving it a visible communitarian dimension.[19] But it can also be—and this is what we monks especially seem to have in mind—to help each other, by dint of a common rule, to bear a personal obligation which each one feels too weak to discharge by himself. In this monastic perspective the office of the cenobite does not seem like a *nec plus ultra* but like a simple preparation for the prayer of the hermit or as a more or less permanent substitute for it. Its meaning is no different from that which covers every cenobitic observance, namely, that of a school or a substitute for the properly monastic life: intimate converse with God. It is a matter of approaching unceasing personal prayer by submitting to the pedagogy of a prayer celebrated in common at certain hours.

Thus, while 'Do this in memory of me' is necessarily performed in Church, 'Pray without ceasing' is expressed in common activity only acci-dentally. This contrast is verified in the history we have just sketched. It explains moreover the fact that Eucharistic worship has been constantly moulded and controlled by the hierarchy of the Church which has had the care of it, while the prayer of the hours developed by the free initia-tive of fervent souls and of monks. No doubt monasticism adopted the Eucharist from its beginnings, but without giving special emphasis to its celebration for a long time.[20] No doubt also the clergy were also progres-sively brought to celebrate the prayer of the hours, like monks, with a chosen few faithful until the time they began to say it alone in empty churches. But this change leaves intact the original and essential difference separating the two modes of prayer. One is official and public, necessarily presided over and regulated by the bishop; the other is private or domes-tic, a matter of personal devotion and charism. Such distinct roots will never permit the two to be confused, even when the Mass is reduced in appearance to a private ceremony, or the prayer of the hours takes a com-munitarian and quasi-public form. Moreover, in the last case, we must distinguish carefully the office of the canons and that of the monks. If the first has an official character from the fact of the hierarchical function ex-ercised by those who sing it, the second remains closer to its individual and charismatic point of departure. The canons' office and the monks' prayer by no means fall under the sanction of ecclesiastical authority by the same title or in the same degree. In the first case it is normal that the hierarchy control a form of worship which it has taken on. In the second, a great freedom belongs to societies whose true end is not to celebrate public worship before men in the name of the Church, but to lead their members to the secret and personal realization of 'Pray without ceasing' by means of a communitarian pedagogy.[21]

Admittedly these distinctions were soon more or less effaced to the extent that a type of monastery centered on serving the sanctuary and the task of worship grew up, especially in frankish, anglo-saxon, and germanic countries.[22] Even at Rome the basilica monasteries of the fifth and sixth centuries already doubtless represent a compromise of this sort between the monastic ideal and liturgical ministry. Certain traits of the office in the Master and Benedict show the clerical influences undergone in this hybrid milieu. But the rural communities envisaged by our two rules remain the purely monastic type. There the office keeps its primitive aspect as domestic prayer, without reference to any ecclesiastical responsibility. Far from being the function proper to a community attached to a sanctuary, this prayer is incumbent on each monk as a personal obligation which he must discharge wherever he is. The monks perform it not only all together in the oratory, but also, if need be, in little groups and even individually, in the kitchen, cellar, garden, the fields, or on a journey.[23] Manual work is imposed on the monks as an economic necessity and as an exercise of *ascesis* and a religious duty. The organization of the *opus Dei* must take account of the demands of the *opus manuum*. Both legislators were confronted with this delicate problem of adjustment. Although they resolve it differently, the Master mostly by granting occasional dispensations from the office, Benedict by admitting fewer exceptions and making the common observance more flexible,[24] it is clear that neither of them was writing for men whose only obligation was to execute the office punctually in choir. 'Nothing is to be preferred to the work of God'[25] is a maxim valid only in set circumstances. The arrangements Benedict made in the horarium of the office show that no subordination of the whole of claustral life to the conventual celebration of the hours is implied.

What then is the place of the divine office in the life of the monastery and of the monk according to our rules? It is impossible to answer this question without referring to 'Pray without ceasing'. Unfortunately

neither the Master nor Benedict bring forward this historical and ontolog-
ical root of the *opus Dei*. For lack of it, commentators have provided only
disappointing answers. For Delatte, 'the liturgy is the proper and distinctive work of the Benedictine, his lot, his mission. He makes profession in
order to be within the Church, a society of divine praise, one who glori-
fies God according to the forms established by the Church, the Church
which knows how to honor the Lord and which possesses the words of
eternal life'.[26] But this making of official praise in the name of the Church
the essence of the monastic vocation is to confuse the monk and the can-
on. For Butler, 'the public celebration of the divine office is the principal
service of the community'.[27] But although this time the reference to the
Church is less clear (perhaps subsisting in the word 'public'), the office is
still conceived as a collective task, and we do not see its relationship with
the personal life of the monk. The image of court service, borrowed by
Butler from Gasquet,[28] makes it appear as a work that is chiefly formal
and external. In addition, saying that the *opus Dei* is 'our principal duty'[29]
is to present it as one obligation among others, without our knowing its
relationship to those others and why it is superior to them.

For Herwegen, the office was also the work of the Church.[30] Although
he has some fine pages on the sanctifying value of the psalmody,[31] his
communitarian mystique constantly brings him back to the exaltation of
the office considered as the meeting of the community with God.[32]
Father Steidle's commentary is much more attentive to the history of the
hours and the teaching of the great monks on prayer. But he again affirms
the primacy of the office over private prayer, inasmuch as it is the 'prayer
of the monastic Church addressed to Christ'.[33]

It seems that we might come to a deeper understanding of the office by
considering it in the light of 'Pray without ceasing'. If the prayer of the
hours is ordered to continual prayer we immediately see its place in the
monastic day and its connection with the monks' other occupations.
There can be no question of opposing it to them as the sacred to the profane. The whole life of the monk is in essence a search for God, and effort
at prayer. But in this continual search and effort the hours of the office
mark the beats at which the monk can recollect himself. If need be, they
relaunch the impetus of incessant prayer. Seen this way, the office is not
one act of the monk among many, not even the principal or the essential
one; it is simply a particular way of doing the unique spiritual activity

which fills his whole day—a discontinuous, collective, regulated way which should sustain a life of prayer that is continual, private, and spontaneous.

This organic relationship of the office to the rest of the monk's day appears more clearly still if we examine the contents of each. We shall see in the following section that the ancient office was made up of psalms and *prayers*. Similarly, the monastic day consisted of manual work accompanied by 'meditation' and interspersed with prayers. It was customary for the cenobite and hermit always to accompany the activity of their hands with that of their mouths, that is, with the oral repetition of scriptural texts, which they called *meditatio*.[34] The psalter was one of the favorite texts used for this exercise. Thus the monk was doing the same thing at work as at the office; in both the time flowed by in the continual recitation of Scripture, and especially of the psalms.[35] Prayer was the response, both at work and at office, to this incessant hearing of the word of God. At the office the prayer was said after each psalm during a period of time determined by the superior who concluded it; at work prayer came and went more freely as it pleased the one praying, and according to the possibilities his work allowed. In this regard 'to prostrate frequently to pray' is the only rule formulated by Benedict and the Master.[36] But these different ways of praying do not prevent the prayer of the hours and prayer at work from looking alike; in each case there are short prayers punctuating the recitation of Scripture. Thus the prayer of the hours is not only ordered to prayer all day long; it is made up of the same elements and goes on in the same way. In virtue of this likeness it seems to everyone to be what it is in essence, namely, the momentary actualization, in a communal form, of intimate continual conversation with God during the course of work.

For analogous reasons the office is also in basic continuity with *lectio divina* and meals. During the two or three hours of daily *lectio* what is the monk doing but reading and listening to Scripture, learning it by heart or preparing to decipher it? The purpose of these studies is to furnish the memory with inspired texts to recite continually, either at the office or at work. Meals we know included reading then as now. But perhaps we do not grasp immediately the analogy established between the refectory, the oratory, and the workshop. The monk ate to the sound of reading, just as he worked while reciting texts,[37] and what he did while eating and working, he continued at the work of God. From morning to night, during diverse activities, hearing the word of God went on, arousing responsive prayer at more or less close intervals. The office was no exception to this rule. Rather than the irruption of the sacred into a profane time, it was the privileged moment when all business ceased and the word was listened to more attentively, and prayer responded more frequently and fervently.

But in underlining this way the basic homogeneity of the office with the spiritual activity which fills the whole life of the monk, we must reckon with certain facts that suggest the Master's and Benedict's tendency to establish a clearer and clearer separation between the *opus Dei* and the rest of the day. First of all, it is striking that neither of the two rules speaks clearly of the prayers which should intersperse the work. 'To prostrate frequently for prayer' is prescibed only in the *ars sancta*. Moreover, this precept follows an article on 'holy reading', which perhaps means that these prayers should be made especially during the time for *lectio divina*.[38] In any case, the legislative part of the Rule says nothing further about prayer during work. In RB the fact might be explained by Benedict's conciseness, for he does not mention *meditatio* again. But the Master is explicit on this point, and it is astonishing not to meet any allusion to prayer in so detailed a document. Apparently the only prayers in connection with the work are those said before and after it, to ask God's help and to give him thanks.[39] Might these prayers which framed the work have replaced prayers during the course of the work,[39bis] while work itself was accompanied only by 'meditation'? This suspicion is confirmed by the lenten observance. For it the Master established 'pure prayers'—that is, not preceded by psalms—to be made in common between the hours of the office.[40] It would seem that it was necessary to gather the community for saying such prayers, as if the individuals had no such habit. With Benedict, these collective prayers are replaced by *orationes peculiares* but nothing is mentioned about their being said during work.[41]

Thus there is reason to think that prayer which interrupts work was scarcely esteemed by these sixth-century cenobites.[42] If that is so, the office must appear under a new title as *the* prayer of the monk: it alone included prayers properly speaking, in addition to scriptural recitation. This phenomenon is to be connected with the evolution of the meaning of *opus Dei*.[43] Originally the expression meant the whole monastic *ascesis*. With the Master and Benedict, as well as with their contemporary, Caesarius, it refers only to the office. The prayer of the hours thus appears as a sacred act, in opposition to the profane occupations which fill the rest of the day. The immediate connection of these latter with the service of God is weakened, partly no doubt because work ceased to appear as a continual prayer.

This aspect of the office as separate is accentuated by the prohibition of work during the psalmody and the lessons. The tradition of Egypt, and also of Gaul in its wake, would have it that the monk kept his hands busy during the night office while listening to the biblical recitations.[44] Certainly this was primarily a matter of keeping awake during the long vigils. But nothing could show better the continuity of the office with the work day. But the Master makes no mention of manual activity at the work of God. And Benedict, repeating a passage of Augustine, formally excludes that sort of thing.[45] It seems then that an african and roman tradition, to which our rules belong, intended to give the office a less familiar and more hieratic style than it had in Egypt and Gaul. No doubt this character is due in large measure to clerical influence. A pachomian monk who meditated in his cell during his work, must have found it natural to work in the oratory while listening to Scripture. But a bishop like Augustine could see in this a profanation of the holy place analogous to those drinking bouts in honor of the martyrs which he exerted great efforts to prohibit in his church.[46] What disorders would occur if this monastic custom should spread among the faithful? The same repugnance might have existed in the monastic circles of Rome, so closely associated with the clergy and also little accustomed to manual work.

We see what is signified by this contrast between the egyptian tradition and a monasticism influenced by clergy. For seculars and their pastors the distinction between the profane and the sacred is indispensable. For monks for whom the service of God is the only and immediate aim of their whole existence, this separation has no such clear necessity. All times, all places, and all activities are capable of consecration and are compatible with prayer. 'All the places of the monastery should have the appearance of a church, and thus no matter where any gathering occurs, it will be in a place suitable and pleasant where prayer gives delight'.[47]

The Master says this, and yet we have just seen that already for him the office had taken on a sacred value which tended to cast other activities into the sphere of the profane. With Benedict this tendency only increased. The liturgical section is no longer presented in the course of the description of the day, but at the head of the legislative part of the Rule, in splendid isolation. The conflict between office and work, already introduced in RM, is settled by the solemn affirmation of a principle borrowed from the monasticism of Lérins: 'Let nothing be preferred to the work of God'. It could not be stated more clearly that prayer and work have quit their alliance. Henceforth the two 'works' exist side by side. The monk must leave one to run to the other.

Moreover, nothing is so revealing as the meaning the Master and Benedict give to the famous passage of the *Institutes* which they use in this connection. In Cassian's eyes, to answer the signal immediately was a fine act of *obedience*, and the monk could obey in an equally meritorious way if the signal drew him from his cell to call him to a common work.[48] Our two rules have repeated this description of immediate obedience when the signal sounds, but with them it is a matter of punctuality only *at the office*.[49] The meaning of the act has changed. No longer is it a matter of renouncing every private occupation to go to any common activity, but of renouncing one's work in order not to arrive late at the oratory. The conflict is no longer between self-will and obedience, but between profane work and 'the work of God'. This slip in meaning comes from a new preoccupation, that of defending the office against a certain activism. Cassian did not point out this temptation among the cenobites of Egypt.[49bis] It is characteristic of a monasticism where work and prayer are no longer as well integrated.

We must not, therefore, hide the fact that the work of God, at the time of our two rules, was in the process of becoming detached from the rest of life. With the Master, however, it was still the prayer of the hours, performed exactly at the hour decided upon and explicitly intended to give thanks for the time just past.[50] With Benedict, there is no more rigorous exactitude or reference to the occupation of the day. The office tends to become a *pensum* (task) independent of the hours to be accomplished when one can. This detachment of the *opus Dei* from other activities has as a sign, if not as a consequence, a material separation. Instead of the lightning-like gatherings of RM two signals are sounded between work and the office.[51]

The process of separation between the office and life is then more advanced in RB. But even if we take into account all the indications of this trend, whether common to the two rules or peculiar to the second, it remains true that the office in the time of the Master and Benedict still appears close to its origins and its first meaning. It is born of private prayer and meant to sustain it; it is also composed of these private prayers, that is the prayers after the psalms. This means that no rigorous distinction—still less, an opposition—can be established between public office and private prayer. The work of God does not appear primarily as a community act and social worship, but as the accomplishment of a personal obligation. Moreover, its community aspect does not confer on it a superiority over solitary prayer. In a monastic perspective common prayer seems rather an education with a view to solitary conversation with God. The accent is not placed on the exterior and aesthetic element, but on the application of the mind to the psalms and the purity of silent prayer. And if the office is scarcely conceived of as an official interview of the cenobium with its king, it is still less homage rendered in the name of the Church, pursuant to a mandate of, and in forms established by, the hierarchy. The monk is not a member of the Church specially assigned to public praise. He is simply a disciple of Christ who seeks to put into action, alone or with others, the command 'Pray without ceasing'.

The prayer of the hours offers him a first approximation of this ideal and at the same time a help in his effort to realize it more completely. It is not therefore a particular occupation, unique of its kind and without common measure with the others, but rather the momentary actualization of a constant effort. The office and the life make up one thing.

Section II. Psalmody and Prayer (RB 19–20)

If there is one point at which the Master is useful in throwing light on Saint Benedict, it is the structure of the office. In reading RB today we do not suspect that the ancient monastic office was composed of psalms *and prayers*. Yet these prayers, of which nothing remains in our modern office, were an essential part, or to say it better, the very essence of the ancient prayer. Each psalm of the office ended with a time of silence in which those present rose and prostrated themselves to pray. If RB in its extreme conciseness scarcely allows us to surmise this important fact, RM leaves no doubt about its existence.[52] But this calls into question the whole concept of the office to which we are accustomed.

Modern commentaries on RB agree in identifying the office with vocal recitation. As they represent it, the *opus Dei* of Saint Benedict consisted, as does ours, in an uninterrupted succession of psalms. Before and after the psalmody secondary elements such as versicles, hymns, lessons, long or short responsories, canticles, and litanies, whose careful enumeration fills the chapters of the *ordo officii*, only reinforce the impression of a continuous sequence of texts said aloud. The only element of silent prayer seems to be the final 'Our Father', at least at nocturns and the little hours. Even then there is no question of free prayer but of recitation in a low voice. Thus from end to end the office seems made up of recited formulas.

There is nothing suprising then if modern commentators think of finding Benedict's thought on the meaning of the work of God only in the chapter 'On the Discipline of the Psalmody' (RB 19). Since the divine office consists only in reciting texts, of which the psalms form the greatest part, one would think that this chapter on psalmody by itself constitutes the spiritual treatise on common prayer. The relationship of the chapter 'On Reverence at Prayer' (RB 20) to the office is not seen. This chapter on prayer seems to treat private prayer. No doubt the last phrase does speak of prayer *in conventu*, but since this community prayer seems to take place at the end of office, to judge by a famous text of Saint Gregory,[53] it seems like a simple conclusion or an appendix, leaving intact the notion of the *opus Dei* as an uninterrupted recitation. It would deal then with prayer made in common, but of a private character, and as such, outside the office in some way.

The usual interpretation sees in these two chapters then two distinct treatises, one on common prayer and the other on private prayer. We find thus in RB a distinction familiar to modern spirituality: on one hand, the liturgical office made up of a series of texts fixed by custom and pronounced aloud, and on the other, the prayer which each one makes interiorly and in silence, either alone or in a group. But if in reality the *opus Dei* of the ancients was made up not only of psalms and other recited texts, but also of prayers, it is clear that this current interpretation goes badly astray. In fact, the chapter 'On Reverence at Prayer' concerns the divine office just as much as does the chapter 'On the Discipline of the Psalmody'. These two chapters study in turn the two essential elements of the work of God: psalm and prayer, in the very order in which they come all during the celebrations. That Benedict has slipped into the second one a remark concerning prayer made in private, outside the office, in no way changes the primitive and primordial object of this chapter. Far from being an appendix treating an extra-liturgical form of prayer, it primarily concerns the liturgy. The prayer of which it speaks is not a side-dish to the office, but its very heart.

As we see, it is not only the meaning of RB 20 which is at stake here but the whole modern concept of the *Opus Dei*. For the ancients the office was by no means a mere declamation of texts. Silent prayer occupied a considerable place in it. To judge by the length of the prayer which the Master puts into the mouth of the excommunicated during the silence following each psalm,[54] each prayer could have lasted about one and a half minutes. That means that they often gave to prayer a time equal to that of the psalm. Also, when the Master was seeking a way to shorten the office in case of need, the first idea that came to him was to suppress two of the three prayers.[55] Such a method of abbreviation evidently supposes that the prayers are not short pauses between psalms, but prolonged interruptions. These facts should not be lost sight of when we read in Cassian, the Master, and Benedict that the prayer should be 'brief'.[56] This wholly relative brevity does not keep the prayers from constituting an important element of the celebrations, in terms of duration.

But such a quantitative fullness expresses only imperfectly the spiritual meaning recognized in the prayer. This meaning appears still better in the intensity required of the one praying. While the psalmody requires only a respectful bearing and an attentive mind, the prayer demands an intense effort of supplication. All the energies of body and soul are mobilized for this act. Tears flow,[57] sighs escape from a heart filled with fervor,[58] hands are extended as if to seize the feet of Christ.[59] Prayer appears not as a relaxation after the psalms, but as a redoubling of effort. Its silence carries a maximum of spiritual energy.[60] The very contrast of attitudes invites us to see in it the supreme act of the office. If the monk was seated to listen to the psalm, he rises to make the prayer;[61] if he said the psalm standing, he prostrates to make the prayer.[62]

Prayer is the crowning of the psalm therefore, both interiorly and exteriorly. Whether it takes the place of the *gloria* as was commonly the case in Egypt,[63] or it begins with a *gloria* as was probably the case with the

Master,[64] it has a close connection with the great Trinitarian doxology, both by its place at the end of the psalm and by its particular significance of homage and adoration.

But it is still too little to recognize in the prayer the strong beat and the spiritual summit of the office. We must go further and understand that it, and it alone, is *the prayer* of the office in the proper sense of the term. Saying psalms is not, of itself, praying. Admittedly many of the psalms are prayers, but a great number stem from different genres: eulogies of the man who fears the Lord, meditations on the destiny of the just and of the wicked, epic rehearsals of the exodus and the conquest, instructions and wedding-songs addressed to the king, Messianic oracles. None of all that is prayer in the proper sense. Even the psalms of praise are ordinarily presented as appeals thrown out to men, not as discourses addressed to God. But it is remarkable that the monastic office pays no heed to these differences of genres. With about two exceptions—lauds and compline—the hours are composed of psalms taken as they come. It is a complete jumble. No care has been taken to reserve the prayer psalms for the office. What is more, if we examine the antiphons of the roman monastic office, the greater part of which may go back to the time of our rules, we find no exclusive preference for words addressed to God. With these are often mixed words addressed to men, or simple impersonal statements.[65]

These facts show that the psalmody was not conceived of chiefly as a prayer. No doubt it was generally considered a song which rose towards God. Cassian in his time says we 'sing the psalm to the Lord',[66] and the Master says 'we should sing praises to the Lord with composure'.[67] But no one thought of giving the psalm the name *oratio* or any other name signifying prayer. Formally, prayer did not consist in the psalmody, but in the oration following it.

What then is the proper role of psalmody at the office? It prepares for prayer, it invites one to pray. Here an observation made above reveals its full importance. The psalms, we remarked are usually said as they occur, without any selection. This system of *psalterium currens*, even tempered by a weekly distribution, makes us think immediately of the *lectio continua* of the Bible, which occupies the best of the hours reserved each day for reading and constitutes the heart of the lessons at night vigils. Like the other books of Scripture, the psalter is chiefly the word of God, inspired writing. It is on this ground that the psalm precedes the prayer at the of-

fice. Before man addresses the word of prayer to God, he listens to the
word which God says to him.

No one has expressed this relation of prayer to psalmody more clearly
than Caesarius in one of his sermons:[68] 'Saying psalms is like sowing in a
field; praying (*orare*) is like burying seed and covering it over by ploughing
(*arando*) a second time'. '*Orare . . . arare*': the play on words cannot be
translated. The comparison he underlines shows the necessity of prayer
after psalmody. The latter sows the divine word in souls, as does every
scriptural reading. Then it is indispensable to make this seed penetrate to
the depths of hearts so that the vain thoughts of this world cannot remove
it from minds, like birds pecking at the surface of a field. That is the role of
prayer; it is like ploughing. By working on his own heart a man inserts
deeply into it the Word he has heard.

Prayer then is, first of all, meditation on the scriptural text. The divine
word, thus meditated on and assimilated, gives birth to a prayer: 'What
good is it to say psalms with faith if we neglect to petition God after we
have finished our psalms? Therefore when finished with the psalm, let
each person pray and petition the Lord in all humility, so that with the
help of God he may succeed in accomplishing by his works what he has
pronounced with his mouth'. This is the second act of prayer,[69] which
earns it its name. It originates, by way of meditation, from the psalmody,
considered as the proclamation of the divine word. The hearing of Scripture should precede prayer and engender it, because prayer is man's response to the Word of God.

This law of dialogue, in which God always has the initiative, is the same
which governs the most ancient prayer of the Church: the readings of the
liturgical assembly precede the prayer of the faithful and the priestly Eucharist. Thus the pair, psalms and prayer, reproduces at the monks' office
the structure adopted from the second century onward by christian worship, the heir of jewish prayer. Still closer to our *opus Dei* are the Easter
vigil and similar vigils in which each scriptural reading, sometimes prolonged by a meditative chant, ends in a prayer. These are so many different forms of the same spiritual instinct. The word of God is first; God
has first loved us. Man's prayer can only be a response to this appeal.
Hearing the word of God is the necessary preamble for every prayer.

But if the psalter in its totality as an inspired writing is the word of God
to men, it also abounds in men's prayers to God. Obviously it is this spe-

cial character which has earned its being chosen from among all the books of the Bible to nourish christian prayer. The psalmody, preceding the prayer, not only resounds as the word of God inviting to prayer; it also guides the prayer which it has aroused. God himself, by speaking, teaches man to answer him. Already in the psalm the human voice, praising and begging, is replying to the call of the divine voice. Thus the psalmody is both the scriptural preamble of prayer and the beginning of this prayer, rather like the invitatory at vigils, which is both the introduction to the psalmody and the beginning of it.

This double richness of the psalms is probably one of the deepest causes for the disappearance of the prayer. After what we have said about its importance, it may seem strange that it has completely disappeared from the office. No doubt the phenomenon is explained in good part by the 'horror of the void' that historians of liturgy find everywhere. Silence is generally a frail thing which puts up less resistance than do formulas to the negligence of men and the attrition of time. But in the present case this process of degradation must have been helped by the prayerful character of the psalter as a whole. To have said the psalm is already to have prayed. The more this aspect of psalmody was valued, the less indispensable did the prayer appear. Thus the psalm, originally meant to arouse prayer, could in itself be considered as a valid substitute and a sufficient prayer. What should have nourished prayer had also formidable capacity for devouring it. Otherwise it would be inexplicable that monastic prayer lost precisely the essential act which should have conferred on it its character as prayer.

The generalization of the *gloria* at the end of the psalm also no doubt facilitated this evolution. In the East at the beginning of monastic psalmody, the *gloria* was said only after psalms said antiphonally.[70] But in Egypt especially, these were far from constituting the bulk of the psalmody, as would be the case later in our two rules and in the roman office. Primitively, the psalm was ordinarily followed, not by the *gloria*, but by the prayer.[71] The situation is completely changed in the Master's and Benedict's milieu. Not only is the *gloria* customary after each psalm said antiphonally,[72] but it is also said at the end of the responsories[73] and even of the psalms said straight through without antiphons.[74] The Trinitarian doxology therefore concludes every sort of psalm. But this formula of praise too can be taken as an equivalent to the prayer. Like it, it is accompanied by a gesture of homage.[75] By its content it is a supreme act of adoration. Moreover, it answers the need to end each psalm in an explicitly christian perspective.

Thus the *gloria* also appears, on several grounds, as a possible substitute for the prayer. It served no doubt as an introduction to the prayer in RM.[76] We can then establish a parallel between the *opus Dei* of the monks and ecclesial prayer. Just as the priestly collect alone remained at the end of the prayers of the Mass, so the *gloria* alone has remained at the beginning of the psalmic prayers of the office. In both cases a formula remains the sole witness to ancient silent prayer.

Again, the generalization of responsorial and antiphonal psalmody has probably contributed to the elimination of the prayer. At the beginning when the greater part of the psalms were executed in the direct mode, that is, as solos without any intervention by those present, these latter, having remained seated in silence during the whole psalm, must have felt a need to give themselves to prayer. It was the only way for them to emerge from their situation as passive hearers and to exercise a certain activity, both corporal and spiritual. But with the extension of the responsorial and especially the antiphonal psalms, those present would find in the psalmody itself more and more satisfaction of this need of activity. Their voices rang out, and their bodies, at least during the antiphony, were compelled to stand in a somewhat constrained attitude.[77] Thus their increased participation in the psalmody no doubt removed from the prayer something of its attraction and its proper role.

If we have tried in many ways to explain the disappearance of the prayer, all these converging explanantions are none too many to account for such an astonishing phenomenon. This is not the place to retrace the history according to the documents.[78] We must, however, note that the prayer is the first thing the Master thought of when he envisaged shortening the office.[79] Already this silent prayer was less important in his eyes than the psalm which preceded it, or the *gloria* which introduced it. Already the word is more important than the silence, the recited text than the personal improvisation, the prescribed formula than the free effusion of the heart before God. In this area, as in the case of food, the exceptional authorizations foretell the general and definitive dispensation. Was the latter already in force in Benedict's time? In any event, the prayer no longer appears in the sixth century as the original and irreplaceable act which formally constitutes the prayer of the office. The psalm and the *gloria* can take its place in case of need. It is one way of praying, alongside the psalmody; it is no longer the pre-eminent prayer, and still less the unique prayer.

While the meaning of the prayer tends to fade, the psalm is increasingly conceived of as a prayer. Admittedly from the fourth century onward, the psalm is represented as 'sung to the Lord'. But if Cassian occasionally expressed himself this way,[80] all his attention still was directed to another aspect of the psalmody. What was important to him was that the psalm be understood and relished by the hearers as much as possible. From this derives the small number of psalms, the division of the long psalms into two or three sections, the slow and careful utterance of the one reciting them, and the changing of reciters in the course of the psalmody.[81] The only purpose of all these prescriptions is to enhance attention and intelligibility, while avoiding haste and fatigue. The spiritual profit of those present is the only thing considered. It is a matter of making the inspired text savory, so that souls are kindled for the prayer which is to follow.[82]

A change of perspective appears in the sixth century. No doubt the role of edification pertaining to the psalmody was not forgotten. The Master recommends to anyone who says the psalm that he 'note in his heart everything that he says', so that his soul draws profit from it.[83] But this recommendation comes only towards the end of the chapter. The chapter opens with considerations about the impeccable bearing which is required when singing in the presence of God.[84] Henceforth God is the principal hearer of the psalmody. He is the one chiefly addressed: to say psalms is a 'service accomplished before the divinity.'

Moreover, the precept of attention to the meaning of the words is itself transformed by this basic concern with honoring God. When the Master has finished speaking about the exterior bearing, he comes to the interior attention, but retains at first the same perspective of homage to the Lord. If every distraction must be avoided, this is because God would be insulted if he were left at the door (the mouth) while the devil was introduced into the house (the heart). On the contrary, heart and tongue must unite to pay the Lord their daily debt.[85] It is only after having given this motive for the duty of attention that the Master passes to the motive of edification that we pointed out above. Man's spiritual profit is only a secondary aspect of the psalmody. Moreover, the Master scarcely notes this aspect when he returns to the principal one: 'We must *cry out to God* not only with our voices, but with our heart as well'.[86]

Thus a sort of revolution was wrought in the psalmody from the time of Cassian to that of the Master. Instead of being primarily a message from God to man, it has become chiefly man's homage to God. These two conceptions are incarnated in some way in two kinds of psalmody and two corporal attitudes. In Cassian's time almost all the psalms were said in the direct mode; the one reciting was the only person to stand up, the monks remained seated to listen to the psalm as they would have listened to any other scriptural reading.[87] By the Master's time almost all the psalmody was sung antiphonally, which obliges the whole community to stand.[88] The hearers of the word of God have been changed into those who sing his majesty.

We can recognize the same meaning in another contrast between the Egypt of Cassian and the Italy of the Master. In Egypt the long psalms were divided into two or three sections; in Italy each psalm had to be said in full, and counted for only one 'imposition'. In the mind of the Egyptians the shortness of the psalm sections would make them more easily assimilated. For the Romans and the Master man's interest is less important than the glory of God. The psalm is a sacred whole which must be returned to the Lord as he gave it to us.[89]

This last fact should now be taken into consideration if we wish to perceive exactly Benedict's conception of the psalmody. Benedict seems indeed to be following the 'Egyptian' suggestions of Cassian by dividing the long psalms of vespers and vigils, and by having only one strophe of Psalm 118 said before each *gloria* at the little hours. Would it be that the principle of intelligibility has regained in him an importance which it had lost— or perhaps had never had—in monastic circles at Rome? This interpretation would find support in the prescriptions concerning the choice of singers and readers, for Benedict is careful to procure the edification of the hearers, both by the psalmody and by the readings.[90] Yet the attitude he recommends to the singers immediately afterwards consists precisely in the 'gravity' and 'fear' which the Master imposed as a duty on anyone singing psalms before God.[91] On the other hand, when we examine the chapter 'On the Discipline of Psalmody' (RB 19), we find in it no touch tending to enhance the aspect of reading and edification in the psalmody.

Quite the contrary, Benedict does not even have anything corresponding to the Master's indications on this subject,[92] while he emphasizes the aspect of the worship rendered to God by an introductory phrase, recommending faith in the divine presence in a special way at the office.[93] And if he ends with an invitation to 'make the mind agree with the voice',[94] this is a simple consequence of the principle that God and his angels are present. As in the Master's corresponding passage,[95] attention is demanded only in the name of the reverence due the Lord who is being addressed.

It seems then that the psalmody was for Benedict, even more than for the Master, chiefly a prayer. If he has taken account of Cassian's recommendations in dividing the psalms, nothing proves that he had rediscovered the primitive notion of psalmody as *lectio*, from which these recommendations proceeded. Perhaps his instructions about the choice of singers tend mostly to assure a certain exterior dignity of execution. That 'the listeners be edified' is moreover an indispensable condition for the psalmody's being a homage rendered to God by all.

The conception of the psalms as worship seems therefore to prevail more and more clearly as the sixth century proceeds. The psalmody still preserved from its origins the solo mode of execution, with the community intervening only to repeat the antiphon or the *responsio*.[96] But two centuries later almost nothing remained of this way of doing things, which connected the psalm with its primitive form as a lesson. When the custom was established of singing the psalms in two choirs, verse by verse, nothing any longer suggested that the psalm had originally been intended to be heard by those present and to arouse the prayer which followed it. The alternating psalmody that we still know lends itself as badly as possible to such an interpretation. Instead of listening in more or less complete silence, all those present are required to sing psalms from one end of the office to the other. Obviously the verse which one choir recites is not addressed to the choir opposite, but the two choirs are sharing the task of singing the psalm to God.

Thus the psalmody was to lose all significance as a word addressed to men and appear purely and simply as a prayer rising towards God. The disappearance of the prayer was to be the logical complement of this evolution. Thus the office lost one of its essential components. Instead of having a double rhythm—hearing and answering—it was to be only an uninterrupted recitation in which the voice of man and the voice of God mingle in one outcry. The divine word no longer rang out as a distinct message preliminary to prayer. The human voice would not be heard except under the cover of the inspired text. Only outside the office in the modern 'half-hour of prayer' would the prayer find again its autonomy, if not its spontaneity. This exercise is surely a necessary compensation for the loss of the prayers at the office. But it cannot be held to be a simple equivalent of these 'brief and frequent' prayers. Something has changed, either in the method of prayer, or in the concept of the psalms and the *opus Dei*.

With the Master and Benedict we have not yet reached that point. Even though the evolution has already begun, their rules retain enough connections with the past that today they can lead monasticism back, if it wishes, to that elementary pair, psalm and prayer, which still constituted in the sixth century the breathing rhythm of its prayer.[97]

Section III. Further Clarification on Continual Prayer and on Common Prayer

The pages above were written in 1965 and were intended even then for the present commentary, but they appeared first in the form of articles in 1966–1967.[98] Ten years after this first publication, we cannot neglect several studies which, appearing at the same time or afterwards, call into question our interpretation of the Rule. We shall begin by presenting these divergent views. Then we shall try to re-evaluate our own theses in this light.

In 1965 and 1966, I. Hausherr published a study on 'La prière perpétuelle du chrétien'.[99] The subject was not new to him, but his way of treating it differed quite a bit from his earlier publications. The great work of spirituality on *L'hésychasme*, which had appeared ten years earlier,[100] could be regarded as a model of intelligent and respectful sympathy for the doctrine of the ancient monks. In his new essay, Hausherr considered this monastic doctrine of continual prayer much more critically. Writing for the laity and searching for a form of constant prayer fully accessible to them, he turned this time to three doctors of christian antiquity, Origen, Aphraates, and Augustine, who understood the precept 'Pray without ceasing' in the same way:[101] to pray each day at certain determined times, and outside this explicit prayer constantly to perform good deeds, which constitute an existential and implicit prayer. This broad interpretation of 'Pray without ceasing' would be preferable to that of the monks. While

the latter try to realize the sacred word literally by an inhuman psychological tension and a dangerous doubling of attention, the great doctors remain closer to the true meaning of Scripture, of sane theology, and of
good sense, by demanding only an attachment of the heart to God, habitual and deep—but not necessarily conscious—in the faithful accomplishment of his will.[102]

In 'The synthesis of Saint Basil'[103] Hausherr thought he found a remarkable deepening of this doctrine of Origen, Aphraates, and Augustine. No doubt Basil required, in addition to good actions, an attendant
thought, the continual mindfulness of God, but this thought of God is not
superadded from outside to normal human activity. Far from opposing
this, it springs from it in a natural way and returns to penetrate it: each action is the occasion for thanking God and invoking his help.[104] Prayer and
work are not performed therefore in a parallel way, as two activities foreign to each other, but work itself is transformed into prayer by attention
to its present reality and its true finality.[105]

This study of Hausherr on the perpetual prayer of the Christian has received the enthusiastic support of O.du Roy in his book *Moines aujourd'*
hui.[106] He considers our interpretation of 'Pray without ceasing' as hesy-
chast, and does not find it consonant either with the sense of Scripture or
with the teaching of the Rule. In fact, Benedict does not extol a psychological effort at perpetual prayer. What he demands is simply faith in the
universal presence of God, the 'mindfulness' of the divine 'gaze' resting
continually on man. This faith accompanies the monk in all his tasks and
enables him to perform them with a complete liberty of spirit. To pray
and to work are not to be conceived as two rival operations on the same
level, but the first develops at a much deeper level than the second. Prayer
is the Holy Spirit present in our hearts beyond all explicit attention and all
striving of our mind. This mysterious operation, at the root of our liberty
does not interfere with the monk's activities, which can be true activities,
serious, well done, and by themselves constituting a true service of
God.[107]

Moreover, du Roy observes that Benedict in no way refers to 'Pray
without ceasing' in order to lay the foundation of the prayer of the hours.
In the Rule the office does not appear as a substitute for continual prayer
and a means of arriving at it. Taking it as such springs from an interpretation of history which sees in cenobitism a degradation of the eremitical

ideal of solitary conversation with God. On the contrary, du Roy thinks that Pachomius, Basil, and Benedict have opportunely rediscovered the ecclesial value of prayer, misunderstood in certain monastic circles. 'Where there are two or three gathered together in my name, there am I in the midst of them' (Mt 18:20). This is the word which lays the foundation for the community prayer of the cenobites.[108]

In this regard the opinions of du Roy agree perfectly with those of A. Veilleux, whom he does not cite. In his work on the liturgy in pachomian monasticism, published in 1968, Veilleux rejected our presentation of the office as a preparation for continual prayer. No doubt the pachomian monks did exert themselves to maintain this latter during their days, but their prayer gatherings in the morning and evening had a different purpose. Far from being ordained as means to private prayer, they aimed at obtaining the specific and irreplaceable good of common prayer, namely, communion in prayer. If Cassian does not refer to Matthew 18:20, certain pachomian texts cite this word of Jesus, fundamental to all cenobitism worthy of this name.[109]

Let us take up in order the objections raised by these three authors. They center around two principal questions: the interpretation of the words 'Pray without ceasing'; and the meaning of common prayer.

In regard to the first point we can inquire first about the explanation of the three great doctors cited by Hausherr. Do they agree? Are they satisfactory? Certainly Aphraates expounds a theory of implicit prayer, that of works, which corresponds with Origen's views,[110] but unlike Origen, he does not apply this theory to the interpretation of 'Pray without ceasing'.[111] Augustine in turn comments upon 'Pray without ceasing' but does not understand it merely as constancy in performing good deeds as does Origen.[112] According to Augustine, it is 'by continual desire, in faith, hope and charity' that a person prays without ceasing.[113]

Is this continual desire for true life conscious or not? Augustine is not precise on the point. We can only note that he assigns verbal prayer, made at definite hours, the role of controlling and rekindling the ardor of this continual aspiration. The latter will be more *effective*, if it is preceeded with more affective warmth at the prayer of the hours. It consists not only of desiring eternal life, but of *asking* God for it.[114] These expressions of Augustine's suggest that perpetual desire is for him not a simple uncon-

scious potentiality without determinate psychological acts. Rather it is a
matter of effectively producing prayers of petition, even though they do
not exclude all other activity and are not expressed in verbal formulas, as
at the prayer of the hours.

Such an interpretation of 'Pray without ceasing' goes far beyond the
simple well-doing extolled by Origen. By the relationship it establishes between continual prayer and the prayer of the hours, the latter giving new
impetus to the former,[115] it connects instead with the thought of Tertullian, whose work *De Oratione* Augustine doubtless remembered when
writing his Letter to Proba.[116] In line with his African predecessor, the
Bishop of Hippo seems to have envisaged continual prayer as a reality
homogeneous with the prayer of the hours, composed as it is of explicit
acts.

Understanding the words 'Pray without ceasing' in this way is to maintain what seems to be the true meaning of the Apostle's word. Nothing
indicates that Paul was thinking of an implicit prayer, as Origen would
have it. For the latter, as for many moderns, 'to act well is to pray'. Those
who wax enthusiastic about this interpretation do not seem to perceive
that the Alexandrine is *allegorizing* prayer, as was his constant procedure.
But 'to pray' in 1 Thessalonians 5:17 is to be taken in as literal a sense as
are the verbs which surround it: 'to rejoice' and 'to give thanks'. If Origen
believed he had to understand it otherwise, this was because, by pressing
the adverb in an exaggerated way—he took it to mean an absolute continuity, moment by moment—he set himself a false problem: 'How is it *possible* to satisfy such a demand? What must that 'prayer' be in order *to be
able* to continue without any interruption?'

To such questions commonsense could answer only one thing: all God
asks of us here is to do good. But nothing obliges us to engage in this artificial way of stating the problem. What the Apostle is inviting us to do is
constantly to maintain joy, prayer, and thanksgiving, each taken in its
proper sense. At every moment joy should prevail over sadness, prayer
over forgetfulness of God, and thanksgiving over ingratitude for his gifts.
No periodicity is indicated, of course, for the feeling of joy, or even for
the activities of prayer and thanksgiving. It is not a precise command bearing upon a fixed observance,[117] but a general indefinite invitation. Each person will reply to it as best he can, according to the fervor of his feeling and
the intensity of the acts and their frequency.

There is no limit to the effort thus demanded. The monks therefore are not deceived in proposing to pursue the effort as far as possible. Their interpretation of 'Pray without ceasing' in the sense of an unremitting conversation with God is more natural and truer than the allegorizing exegesis of Origen. It agrees in substance with Augustine's, whose 'continual desire' includes petitions made to God, as we have seen.

Whatever may be the value of this interpretation, the fact is that the monks set their hearts on conforming their life to it. This fact has been completely recognized by Hausherr. Even when presenting a different doctrine for the use of laymen in 'La prière perpétuelle du chrétien', he admits that monastic life has been conceived with a view to conscious prayer that is as continual as possible.[118] On the other hand, the author of *Moines aujourd'hui* attributes this ideal of perseverance in prayer properly so called, only to one particular monastic current, hesychasm. The rest of the monastic world, Basil and Benedict in particular, was alien to it. Thus Origen's broad interpretation could be preached to the Benedictines of our time. So it comes about that du Roy proposes to monks what Hausherr offered to laymen.

Let us see then what the case was among the ancient monks and with Benedict: did they know nothing about the ideal of continual prayer in the proper sense? Were they content with the saying 'To work is to pray'? It is not necessary to cite again the texts of monastic authors, Eastern and Western, already quoted, who describe or prescribe continual 'meditation' on Scripture during work. These documents, which surpass the limits of hesychasm on every side, show well enough that recitation of the Word of God was a commonplace observance. It served to support a prayer which continued amidst occupations.

Although this practice implies a certain doubling of attention, the young Basil extols it to his friend Gregory: 'What is happier than always to have prayer for a companion while working, and to have hymns, like salt as a seasoning for work? These consoling hymns maintain a state of soul that is joyous and without sadness'.[119] Later on, Basil was to reaffirm against the Messalian tendencies of certain monks that it is perfectly possible to pray and recite psalms during work. It is true that in this passage of the Rules some new details appear. The circumstances may demand that the psalmody be only 'in the heart' (Eph 5:19, Col 3:16), and in addition to the recitation of scriptural texts, Basil suggests a spontaneous thanksgiving which relates like prayer, to the work itself.[120] But these ways of doing it do not affect the fundamental principle, that one can and should ceaselessly praise God and invoke his help by explicit acts while working.[121]

Augustine too was not unaware that monks exerted themselves to think of God while working, and far from seeing in this a superfluous pretension, he admired and encouraged them. By the year 386 he noted that the manual work of the Egyptian cenobites was organized in view of two ends: to obtain nourishment for the body and not to turn the mind from God.[122]

Fifteen years later when Augustine was treating the work of monks, he spoke out, like Basil, against those who wished to do nothing but pray, sing psalms, and read the Scripture. 'A person can very well sing the divine songs while working manually. The voice of God will be a consolation for him who labors, like the rhythmic song of the coxswain (celeuma)'. Workers sing theater songs very well while working. 'What is to prevent the servant of God from "meditating on the Law of the Lord" (Ps 1:2) and from "singing to the name of the Lord, the Most High" (Ps 12:6), while doing manual labor?' And then, as if to dissipate every equivocation, Augustine speaks of the time that must be set aside to learn by heart the texts to be recited by memory.[123] Thus there is no doubt that the recitation of Scripture during work is formally recommended to monks by this author, who has been represented—wrongly, as we have seen—as the champion of a 'Pray without ceasing' that is purely implicit.

Moreover, we learn from the correspondence of Jerome that what Augustine proposed to the monks of Carthage was being done spontaneously in Palestine even by seculars.[124] Chrysostom, on his part, tries to persuade the lay people of Antioch that they could pray frequently, indeed continually, in the midst of their secular occupation. Nothing prevented them from praying interiorly, without voice or gesture, before the door of the tribunal, in the market place, at work.[125] In a less ambitious and more practical mode,[126] Chrysostom was preaching to his faithful the gnostic ideal of continual prayer held by Clement.[127]

And it was also the ideal of the monks. In this regard we must establish some connections. In the same Sermons on Anna, trying to reconcile 'Pray without ceasing' (Lk 18:1-8, 1 Th 5:17) with the prohibition against 'much speaking' (Mt 6:7), Chrysostom declared that 'Christ and

Paul have commanded short and frequent prayers to be made at short intervals'.[128] But this practice he was proposing to the laymen of Antioch is the very one which characterizes the prayer of the Egyptian monks, according to Augustine and Cassian.[129]

Thus the effort made towards continual prayer in a conscious way during the course of work was not only the practice of monasticism as a whole, it even touched certain lay circles, either in the form of verbal recitations or of interior prayers. Moreover, was it not to a secular audience that Basil in his Homily on the Feast of Saint Julitta proposed prayer appropriate to each occupation of the day and during part of the night?[130] If, with him as with Chrysostom, this was not a matter of reciting parts of Scripture, if even the prayer and thanksgiving were put in close relationship with the tasks to be done, it remains nonetheless that he, like Chrysostom, asked the simple faithful to make explicit and repeated acts of prayer all day long in order to observe the command to pray without ceasing.

It is hard to see therefore how the monks could have been content with a simple, implicit, metaphorical prayer such as Origen speaks of. It would have been all the more strange because the very type of work they took on themselves was determined, as Augustine just reminded us, by the aim of not turning their minds from God. In fact, keeping their souls attentive to God in the midst of all occupations seems to have been their constant concern. 'Meditation' on Scripture during work was practised by them generally, as a privileged means of maintaining this attention. If Benedict does not speak of it in specific terms,[131] we have no reason to suppose that he and his monks had abandoned or were unaware of it. It is rather one of those important points which even a rule as detailed as his could pass over in silence, because they were known and admitted by everyone.[132]

Although Benedict does not mention the exercise of meditation, he, following the Master, does treat at length the continual remembrance of God, faith in his presence and in his gaze.[133] This faith, which is constantly exercised during the day, is only intensified at the time of the office.[134] Someone has said that this is a matter of God gazing upon man, not man gazing upon God.[135] Nothing of the sort! The constancy of the divine gaze is evoked only to provoke a human gaze that will also be as constant as possible. 'Absolutely to flee forgetfulness', 'to remember always', 'to refrain oneself at every moment', 'to say always in one's heart', 'to take constant care', these expressions and others like them are to be taken at face value. They mean nothing but an attention ceaselessly renewed, conscious acts, and a discipline which, even though it is spiritual, demands nonetheless a psychic effort.

The fact that Benedict does not refer to 'Pray without ceasing' in order to establish the prayer of the hours, changes nothing in regard to the origin of this prayer. Even if relatively late authors such as the Master and Benedict make no mention of it,[136] the scriptural word remains historically at the origin of the system of the hours of the office. In this regard the fundamental text is Tertullian's *De oratione*, whose doctrine has marked a whole series of latin authors: Cyprian, Jerome, Augustine, Cassian.[137] Although a genuine literary and spiritual tradition, this line does not, it is true, include Clement, Origen, and Basil, but they have an analogous way of approaching the question of times of prayer, starting from 'Pray without ceasing'.[138] This scriptural word has therefore played a decisive role in searches which were bound to end in the constitution of our office, and we must return to it if we wish to find again its profound meaning.[139]

With this done we still have not yet established the office as *communal* prayer. This communitarian dimension is not suggested by the biblical text itself or by the Fathers' reflection on the subject, and the prayer of the hours only acquired it with the appearance of monastic communities.

Again, it has not been considered an enrichment by everyone. Cassian, we remember, saw in the common obligatory office only a substitute for solitary, free prayer. This judgment, which astonishes us, is better understood when we put it in the perspective traced by Tertullian. If, as he suggests, the prayer of the hours is only a beginning of the response to 'Pray without ceasing', then communitarian prayer, necessarily discontinuous, will easily appear as an approximation to incessant, solitary prayer. To this problematic of continuity and discontinuity inherited from Tertullian,[140] Cassian naturally enough joined the coupled elements of solitude and community. Thus the ordination of the prayer of the hours to continual prayer is embedded almost automatically in the ordination of cenobitism to eremitism.

Yet, this relation between the temporal and social aspects of the problem, as established by Cassian, may seem disputable. The resulting conception of the office is reproached for misunderstanding the proper merits of common prayer, and it is asserted that these latter appear clearly in certain scriptural passages, such as the word of Jesus: 'If two of you agree on anything, whatever they shall ask upon earth, it shall be done to them by my Father who is in heaven. For where there are two or three gathered in my name, there am I in the midst of them' (Mt 18:19–20).

Has this Gospel text played a role comparable to that of 1 Thessalonians 5:17 in the reflection of the Fathers on the prayer of the hours? One may doubt it. A certain number of ancient authors took it in a figurative sense: for them, the 'two or three' were not several disciples gathered together, but either the parts of the soul or of the human composite united in an interior harmony, or the pray-er united to Christ and to God.[141] Sometimes indeed, this spiritual interpretation expressly aims at maintaining the value of solitary prayer against an abusive literal interpretation.[142] Other writers, like Basil, used the second part of the text in its specific sense, but without reference to our problem: they invoked the presence of Jesus in the midst of his own, not to establish the value of common prayer, but to establish the necessity of some disposition of soul[143] or the indefectibility of the Church.[144]

Of the remaining texts in which common prayer is treated, many are found in the homilies of bishops, who seem to have been thinking chiefly of liturgical gatherings to celebrate the Eucharist.[145] Outside his treatment of the office,[146] Cassian mentions the first of these verses only in regard to 'the reasons why we are heard' and the occasional mention that Columban made of it scarcely goes beyond that.[147]

It did however, happen that Matthew 18:20 was applied to the hours said together. The Apostolic Constitutions make this application. If the bishop cannot assemble the faithful in church, the normal place of prayer, let them gather by houses; if not that, then let them pray alone or in twos or threes, in memory of Christ's word.[148] The Athanasian work *De virginitate* recommends that the virgin gather one or two companions, if she has them, for prayer, for the sake of the same word of the Lord.[149]

More interesting still are the citations made in regard to the cenobites' office. Yet they are less numerous and less clear than one would expect. Let us begin with two pachomian texts. At the beginning of what remains of his Regulations, Horsiesius cites our verse to warn against the 'scandal' which might occur 'in the place where two or three are gathered together in the name of Jesus' and where 'he is in the midst of them, as he said'.[150]

Does this refer specifically to the oratory and the gatherings for common prayer?[151] The lack of antecedent context scarcely permits us to affirm this reference with certainty, inasmuch as the considerations following it have no evident connection with the office, which Horsiesius will treat later. It might concern more generally the monastery and the common life.

The other text found in the Coptic Lives of Pachomius, certainly envisages the office, but makes only a doubtful reference to Matthew 18:20. The angel says to Theodore about the gathering: 'Do you not know that the Lord often comes into their midst . . . ?'[152]

Basil in his turn invokes Matthew 18:20 to establish a brother's obligation of celebrating Terce where he was working, if he could not rejoin the brothers in the oratory.[153] 'Two or three' suffice to draw the Lord's presence without the necessity that all assemble. This use of the text, close to that of the Apostolic Constitutions, does not oppose common prayer to individual prayer, but assimilates the prayer of some to that of all.

Moreover, it seems that Basil attached a real importance to prayer said in common at the hour of Terce. No doubt this was because of the example of 'unanimity' of the apostles gathered in the Upper Room to receive the Spirit.[154] It will be noted, however, that Long Rule 7, which refers expressly to the model of the primitive community, does not list communion in prayer among the benefits which recommend the common life. Although Rufinus' translation presents a phrase which seems to do so, comparison with the Greek text shows that he completely misunderstood Basil's thought.[155] What Basil had in mind in this passage was not the gathering of two or three to pray (Mt 18:19-20), but the concordant testimony of two or three witnesses (Mt 18:16). The absence of the theme of prayer in this systematic eulogy of the common life is something surprising.

To sum up, the meaning attached to common prayer in primitive cenobitism remains a poorly documented point. We must be resigned to this poverty, for which the Master and Benedict provide almost no remedy.[156] Surely nothing prevents our satisfying this lacuna with everything that can be suggested by our own experience and the communitarian sense of our epoch. But we should not lose sight of the discretion of the ancient sources. We are not obliged to make Cassian's construction our own, but we should keep this important fact in mind: the hours of prayer that we celebrate in common have their origin in the endeavours of generous Christians to obey individually the precept 'Pray without ceasing'.

Section IV. Eucharist and Communion

Monks of the twentieth century, accustomed to regard the Eucharist as the best part of their daily liturgy, are surprised to find no mention of it in the liturgical section of the Rule. Yet in antiquity this is not an isolated case. The *ordo officii* of many rules are equally blank on the Mass and communion,[157] and those that do treat the subject do so only in passing and as it were, accidentally.[158]

We find the same indirect and allusive character in the rare indications Benedict gives about this subject outside his chapters on the office. He speaks once of 'Mass' and 'communion' together, in connection with the reader's rite of entry into service on Sunday morning.[159] 'Communion' is mentioned by itself later in the same chapter, and it also figures, preceded by 'the peace', in the prescriptions concerning rank within the community.[160] We recognize the Mass in the 'service of the altar' entrusted to the monk-priest,[161] as well as in the 'oblation' to which is joined the commitment of young oblates.[162]

Even if we add two doubtful references,[163] this half-dozen furtive allusions scattered throughout the Rule seem to us very few, given the importance of the subject. The marginal place thus assigned to the Eucharist liturgy contrasts strangely with the privileged place it occupies in our esteem and in our usages. For us, as Dom Delatte wrote, 'the liturgy has its center in the Mass, in the Eucharist. The divine office and the hours are only the glorious retinue, the preparation or the radiation of the Eucharist'.[164]

The literary facts we have just pointed out speak for themselves. Yet we would love to know more precisely the sacramental practice they cover, to compare it with our own. This is not an easy thing to do. We can perceive without too much trouble what was done at the Master's monastery—daily communion outside of Mass in the oratory, and Sunday Mass at the parish church—, but the usage in Benedict's is less clear. The celebration of a Sunday Mass in the monastery oratory seems certain,[165] but the existence of a daily communion service remains unsure.[166] In any case, daily conventual Mass seems excluded both by the silence of the benedictine horarium about it and by all the information furnished by ancient monastic rules.[167]

This last point constitutes a major difference with present usage, whose origin is very ancient. Beginning with the carolingian era, communities of the great frankish monasteries met daily for a solemn Mass, preceded by a 'matutinal Mass' of quasi-official character and surrounded by private Masses celebrated by monk-priests at different altars. This 'system of Masses' of the high Middle Age, which has recently been studied thoroughly,[168] still governs our twentieth-century practice, account being taken of the disappearance of the matutinal Mass and the recent absorption of the private Masses into concelebration. Its primitive intention seems to have been the imitation of the celebrations of the Roman Church; the conventual Mass corresponds to the papal station, and the private Masses to Eucharists celebrated in parallel fashion in the other sanctuaries of the City.

Such an imitation implies the assimilation of each monastery to a city, indeed to Rome itself. It comes from the desire to venerate the sacred places, which are the altars and the relics enclosed there, and the saints who are the patrons there. The multiplication of these miniature sanctuaries, images of those in the City, and the necessity of honoring them by frequent celebrations probably explain the rapid growth in the number of clerics we see in the monasteries of the eighth century. Altars, Masses and monk-priests multiply in the same movement to correspond to the demands of the model of worship borrowed from Rome.

We need only evoke this liturgical movement of the high Middle Age to feel how alien are these conceptions, though noble and worthy of respect, both to the spirit of ancient monasticism reflected by the Rule, and to present-day monasticism, whose institutions and usages nevertheless remain marked by its results. Whether we like it or not, our daily Masses and our communities of monk-priests stem from that milieu. New justifications, taken from other spiritual currents, have come and still come to take the place of these original motivations, of course. Yet the recourse to the inspiration of the founders recommended by Vatican II,[169] while envisaging more directly the life-style and activities of religious, could not exclude their liturgical practices. Thus it is not beside the point to consider carefully the Eucharistic practice of ancient monks, in order to understand it better and, perhaps, to be inspired by it.

For that we must first of all give up a naive concept of progress. Too often the Eucharistic practice of the ancients is represented as a deficient state of affairs which was remedied little by little by a more fitting appreciation of the Mass and its importance. In reality, their weekly Mass, with a simple communion service on ordinary days, is *another* way, neither more nor less worthy than our own, of venerating and profiting by this great sacrament. In itself the daily repetition of an act enhances it no more than does its renewal once a week. Frequency is not without ambiguity. To introduce a rite into the daily routine is both to pay it homage and to make it commonplace—*quotidiana vilescunt*—to mark its importance and to weaken its impact. Inversely, spacing out the sacred celebration may seem either a sign of less interest—it is not worth spending time on every day— or a token of high esteem: the action is too sublime to be degraded, it should be reserved for solemn occasions.

In the case before us, the ancient monks' intention, like ours, was to give the Eucharist the best possible emphasis. They did so by reserving the Mass to Sundays and feasts,[170] while we do so by celebrating it every day. 'One, honoring it, dares not receive it daily, and the other, honoring it, dares not forgo it a single day'.[171] What Augustine said about communion, daily or otherwise, in his time, we can say about the two rhythms for the celebration of Mass, that of the ancient monasteries and our own. Both of them aim only to 'honor' Christ's institution. The divergence between them does not come from a greater or lesser esteem for the divine gift, but from a different choice of how to make it fruitful.

Objection might be made to this interpretation of ancient usage by pointing out the fact we observed at the beginning, the rarity and almost surreptitious character of references to the Mass in our rules. Does not this literary effacement of the theme show a mediocre esteem for the thing? But this is not, apparently, the true meaning of the facts pointed out. If Mass and communion are scarcely mentioned by the authors of rules, this is because, unlike the office, the Eucharist does not fall directly within their competence. As a gift belonging to the whole Church, it is presided over and regulated by the hierarchy. In such a case a monastic legislator has nothing specific to prescribe. While the monks can and should use creativity in the prayer of the hours, they have almost nothing to do at the Eucharist except conform to the norms of the local Church.

The reserve of the monastic rules does not, therefore, show a lesser appreciation of the Eucharist. But it draws our attention to the disparity between Mass and office. For us, who are used to joining these two forms of worship in our daily liturgy, indeed who establish an organic relation between them, it is salutary for us to be reminded that they did not enter in the same way into our liturgical *pensum*. First of all, the Mass, as we have said, is more a work of the Church concerning the whole body of the faithful than a task specific to monks. Moreover, it does not by its nature belong, as the office does, to the daily service of the monastic community. The prayer of the hours which are meant to sanctify the day must necessarily by repeated every day. No such necessity for the Mass exists. Its frequency is a matter of convenience, and therefore subject to variation according to circumstances and needs.

The weekly or twice-weekly rhythm, which seems to have been common in ancient monasteries as in the church at large then, was not immutable . 'Let the Mass take the place when the abbot—or abbess—judges it opportune', directed Bishop Aurelian of Arles during Benedict's time, envisaging celebrations more spaced out, it seems.[172] But on the other hand, daily Masses are attested here and there at that time. Augustine speaks of them more than once in regard to his episcopal city,[173] and Gregory the Great praised the holy bishop of Narni, Cassius, for having celebrated almost every day.[174] Yet the monasteries do not seem to have adopted this practice. The Eucharist appears in the daily *ordo* only in the form of simple communion outside of Mass.[175] This usage, coming from the Church of the first centuries,[176] corresponds to the idea that the Body of Christ is 'our daily bread'.[177] The Mass in´a particular way honors Sunday, the Lord's day, by commemorating his death and his resurrection.

This routine, which was probably in force in Benedict's monasteries as in those of the Master, is connected with the structure of the benedictine office. We know how carefully the Rule determines the measure of the elements of the daily horarium: work, reading, common prayer. The introduction of the Mass into this system compromises the balance. The Mass, joined to the office, weighs down the liturgical element at the expense of the other two. People will always be tempted to trim the prayer of the hours in order to re-establish the balance, as has been done in our days.

Moreover, the Mass is not inserted naturally into the daily cycle of the office. Its incomparable grandeur seems crushing compared to the simple hours of prayer. Inevitably it seems like their summit or their center; yet it has no intrinsic relation to the time which the office intends to sanctify. The same lack of relation to time means that it does not adequately replace an hour of the office. Such substitutions are attested in the ancient Church and monasticism, but only by way of exception.[178] The same can be said of the various combinations found here and there when Mass and the office come together.[179]

It seems then that a brief communion service is the daily Eucharistic rite in harmony with the office as Benedict conceived it. Thus Christ is received each day and is offered once a week on the day of his resurrection. In this way both the Mass and the Sunday are set in singular relief.

NOTES TO CHAPTER 8

1. This study and the following appeared in the form of articles in *RAM* 42 (1966) 389–404; 43 (1967) 21–33. We reproduce the text exactly, only modifying the annotation (entirely new notes are indicated by a *bis*). See the third section of this chapter for objections raised against the views developed here.

2. Ps 118, 164, and 62 (cf. RM 34.3; 33.1). The first of these verses was already used by Cassian in this sense, *Inst.* 3.4.3, who may have depended on Eusebius. See our article '*Septies in die laudem dixi tibi*. Aux origines de l'interprétation bénédictine d'un texte psalmique', in *RBS* III–IV, pp. 1–5.

3. RB 16.2. Cf. RM 42.3–4, where the seven hours are connected with the seven gifts of the Spirit; 43.2, where they are called 'canonical'.

4. RM 34.1–3, the text depends on Cassian (above, note 2). See t. V, pp. 512–516.

5. 1 Th 5:17. Cf. Rm 12:12, Eph 6:18, Ph 4:6, Col 4:2, Lk 18:1 and 21:36. The scriptural principle is expressly formulated by Tertullian, *De orat.* 24–26, and by Origen, *De orat.* 12.1–2. We shall return later (note 112 and following) to the interpretation of this latter. What matters here is that he, like Tertullian, refers to the words 'Pray without ceasing' before indicating the moments when prayer should be made. No express citation of the precept occurs in Clement, *Strom.* 7,7, or in Cyprian, *De dom. or.* 34–36, but the first develops a theory of unceasing prayer and mentions the hours only in contrast with this (40.3–4), while the second ends with an insistent appeal to pray without ceasing. Even Hippolytus, *Trad. Apost.* 41, enters into this perspective at the end, though very soberly.

5bis. This is especially true of Terce, Sext and None in the eyes of Tertullian, *De orat.* 25.5, who holds on the contrary that the morning and evening prayers are obligatory (*legitimis*), as they were in Judaism according to Philo, *De vita cont.* 27; Josephus, *Antiq. Jud.* 14,4,3 (priests); Letter of Aristeas 160. These two hours, which were *obligatory* for each of the faithful according to Tertullian, were to be the only two hours celebrated *in common* by the Egyptian cenobites, according to Cassian, who seems to be confirmed by the pachomian sources. Although not prescribed, Terce, Sext, and None are presented by Tertullian as a minimum. The same presentation of 'three times a day', also based on Dn 6:13, occurs in Origen, *De orat.* 12,2, but this minimum appears clearly as a 'duty' (a matter of morning, noon, and evening). Cyprian, *De dom. or.* 34, presents the celebration of Terce, Sext, and

None as an Old Testament practice (cf. Dn 6:13) prefiguring the mysteries of the New Testament, but he does not affirm clearly that these hours are obligatory, as he does later for those of the morning and evening (35). For Clement, *Strom.* 7.7.40.3-4, Terce, Sext, and None are celebrated only by 'some'. Hippolytus, *Trad. Apost.* 41, seems to enjoin the observation of all the hours without distinction, but those of morning and evening, unlike the others, are exempt from biblical motivations, which suggests that they are less discussed.

6. Dn 6:10,13. Cf. *Didachè* 8.3; IQS 10.1-3 and 8-10 (these lines of our primitive text render futile the criticism of O. du Roy, *Moines aujourd'hui* (Paris, 1972) p. 174, n. 2, who seems not have read them). See the preceding note for Dn 6:13 in Tertullian, Origen, and Cyprian. Under the influence of this text, or by tradition, the first two echo the primitive rule of 'three times a day'.

7. This 'without ceasing' of Paul, like the 'always' of Luke, is obviously capable of two interpretations, one strict (without any interruption), the other broad (without any long or disorderly interruption; cf. Augustine, *De haer.* 57). In this second sense, which is doubtless that envisaged by the sacred authors, the word lends itself again to a series of diverse interpretations, which do not however exclude the first sense as a limit and ideal towards which totend. We shall return to this.

7bis. In accordance with the normal sense of 'thus', these two phrases refer to what precedes, not to what follows (to correct A. Veilleux, *La Liturgie*, p. 319). The ante-Nicene Fathers have been cited in notes 5 and following. For the monks, see Jerome, *Ep.* 22.37 and Cassian, *Inst.* 3.3.8, both dependent on Tertullian, whom Augustine, *Ep.* 130.18 perhaps remembered also. In his turn Basil, *Long Rules* 37.3, goes from continual prayer accompanying work (1 Th 5:17, 2 Th 3:8) to the prayer of the hours, but without pointing out the connection of one to the other as clearly as the Pseudo-Basil, *Serm. asc.* 4; PG 31:877a.

8. Clement, *Strom.* 7.7, especially 40.3-4 regarding the hours. For the days, see 35.1-6 (cf. Origen, *Contra Cels.* 8.21-23).

9. For the meaning assumed by time in the Constantinian era, see G. Dix, *The Shape of the Liturgy*, 2nd edition (Westminister, 1945) 303-32, specially 305-8.

10. Cassian, *Inst.* 3.2. Cf. A. van der Mensbrugghe, 'Prayer in Egyptian Monasticism', in *Studia Patristica*, 2 (Berlin, 1957) 435-54.

11. Cf. the Apophthegma Epiphanius 3 (= *Vitae Patrum* 5.12.6), and the rule of Julian Sabas in Theodoret, *Hist. Rel.* 2; PG 82:1309.

12. Cassian, *Inst.* 3.1.

13. Even hermits generally lived in colonies or lauras, and obeyed common traditions in the matter of prayer.

14. Tertullian, *De orat.* 27. It deals with psalms 'answered' by those present, therefore said in a prayer gathering.

15. Cassian, *Inst.* 2.4-6.

16. As the 'Rule of the Angel' would have it (Cassian, *Inst.* 2.5; Palladius, *His. Laus.* 32.7). Still these sources are careful to present the office as a simple substitute for incessant prayer, for the use of the 'little ones' (Palladius, cf. Cassian, *Inst.* 3.1-2), or as a reduced measure adapted to the weakness of the majority (Cassian, *Inst.* 2.5).

17. Cassian, *Inst.* 3.1-2 (cf. *Inst.* 2.1 and 9; *Conf.* 1, *Praef.* 5). The use Cassian makes here of Ps 53:8 (*voluntarie sacrificabo tibi*) curiously recalls the notice of John Damascene, *De haer.* 80, on the Lampetians, a Messalian sect.

18. Mt 6:6. However, the ecclesial prayer of morning and evening, to which certain texts of the third century already allude, were to become daily in the following century.

19. Cf. Mt 18:19-20 (see below, our third section).

20. G. Dix, *The Shape of the Liturgy*, 326-7. Little by little the Eucharist was to take a central

place in the monastic life (*ibid.*, 332), but only later would people think of making it the center of the prayer of the hours. See the fourth section of this chapter.

21. Even the basilica-monasteries of Rome enjoyed a great autonomy in the organization of their office, as is shown by the diversity of traditions still flourishing in the twelfth century. We have the impression of a sort of anarchy in the time of the Master and of Benedict. Everything was in a state of flux at that period, with diverse practices jostling and influencing each other. These remarks, however, do not suggest that the return to this kind of anarchy would be beneficial at the present time.

22. See for example A. Häussling, 'Konventamt und Privatmesse', in EA 41 (1965) 294–304, particularly 297–301.

23. RM 55 and 56 (cf. 16.47–52, 20.1–11, 73.12–16, and 19–20); RB 50. See already Basil, *Long Rules* 37.4.

24. See t. V, pp. 589–616.

25. RB 43.3: *Nihil operi Dei praeponatur.*

26. P. Delatte, *Commentaire sur la Règle de saint Benoît* (Paris, 1913) 153 (E.T. [London, 1921] p. 134). In fact, the (hierarchial) Church did not give the divine office to monasticism; monasticism gave it to the Church.

27. C. Butler, *Benedictine Monachism* (London, 1924) 30.

28. *Ibid.*, 31.

29. A formula borrowed from the Declarations of the English Congregation.

30. I. Herwegen, *Sinn und Geist der Benedictinerregel* (Einsiedeln, 1944) 146.

31. *Ibid.*, 182–4.

32. *Ibid.*, 145 and 184.

33. B. Steidle, *Die Regel St. Benedikts* (Beuron, 1952) p. 179, n. 1.

34. Cassian, *Inst.* 2.12–15 and 3.2 (cf. Pachomius, *Praec.* 3, etc.); RM 9.45, 50.26 and 43 (cf. see below, note 131). What Cassian presents as obligatory for the Egyptians is only a 'permitted' practice for the Master. But account must be taken of the context, which is regulation of the use of words. 'Meditating' is done in a low voice and, as such, needs a 'permission', which the Rule grants once for all (see however RM 68). The obligation to meditate is recalled by Caesarius, *Reg. virg.* 20 and 22, Aurelian, *Reg. mon.* 24, *Reg. Tarn.* 8.14–16 (cf. Jerome, *Ep.* 46.12), Isidore, *Reg.* 5.5 (cf. Augustine, *De op. mon.* 17), Donatus, *Reg.* 20, Waldebert, *Reg.* 12.

35. Private psalmody is connected with the public office by Ferreolus, *Reg.* 12. On this text, unfortunately obscure, see G. Holzherr, *Regula Ferioli* (Einsideln, 1961) 55–6.

36. RM 3.62 = RB 4.56. See our article '*Orationi frequenter incumbere*. Une invitation à la prière continuelle', in RAM 41 (1965) 467–72.

37. Sometimes, in fact, the work is combined with a reading. Cf. RM 50.28–33, 53.38–41.

38. Cf. Jerome, *Ep.* 58.6 and 130.15, who may have inspired the Master; Origen, *In Gen.*, *Hom.* 11.3, Pelagius, *Ep. ad Demetr.* 23 and *Ep. ad Celant.* 24, Isidore 5.6.

39. RM 50.20 and 47–50. The thanksgiving after work is scarcely distinguished, as far as meaning goes, from the office which follows immediately. Moreover, it consists perhaps only of the sign of the cross and a *Deo gratias* (RM 54.5 and note). When travelling, the monk should pray every time a bad thought comes to his mind (RM 15.53–54), but this prayer, which is not given the name *oratio*, is of an occasional character. RB 52.3–4 speaks of particular prayers in the oratory, but it is not known when they took place.

39bis. Cf. *Vitae Patrum* 5.12.15 where the 103 prayers said by one of those present during a conversation is opposed to the prayer said only before and after the conversation.

40. RM 51–52.

41. RB 49.4–5. This program is particularly vague.

42. Had it ever been so in Italian monasticism? Cassian's descriptions in *Inst.* 2–3, concern only Egypt, not even the East. Cf. *Les Vies coptes*, p. 105,9–12 (Bo 34); p. 114, 21–23 (Bo 47).

43. Cf. I. Hausherr, 'Opus Dei' in OCP 13 (1947) 195–212. (E.T. *Monastic Studies*, 11, pp. 181–204). In RM 11.94–106, manual work (*opus laboris, carnalis opera*) is opposed to the provosts' work of surveillance, which is considered 'spiritual' work. Similarly, reading appears as *opus spirituale* (RM 50.16–17) in opposition to manual work. But *opus Dei* is reserved for the office.

44. Pachomius, *Praec.* 5,7,12; Cassian, *Inst.* 2,12–14 (private vigils only), Caesarius, *Reg. virg.* 15, Aurelian, *Reg. mon.* 29 and *Reg. virg.* 23, *Reg. Tarn.* 6. With the Master, work is not done in the oratory, but one can recite the office while working (cf. Basil, *Reg.* 107 = *Short Rules* 147) and even while walking: RM 16.50; 20.11; 55.17–18; 56.2–6; 73.16.

45. RB 52.1.

46. See F. van der Meer, *S. Augustin. Pasteur d'âmes* II (Paris, 1955) 351–65. (E.T. *Augustine the Bishop* (London and New York: Sheed and Ward, 1961) 514–25).

47. RM 53.64–65.

48. Cassian, *Inst.* 4.12. The occupation abandoned is not necessarily manual work, but can also be 'reading'.

49. RM 54.1–2, RB 43.1–3.

(49. bis) Note however the warnings of Pachomius, *Praec.* 141–142; cf. Basil, *Reg.* 107 = *Short Rules* 147.

50. RM 50. 17,23,35,52,55.

51. RB 48.12. On all this, see t. V, pp. 589–616.

52. RM 14.1 and 20. In regard to RB, see t. V, pp. 577–88.

53. Gregory, *Dial.* 2.4. Cf. RB 67.2.

54. RM 14.3–19. Cf. t. V, p. 583.

55. RM 33.46–47. Cf. RM 55.5–8.

56. Cassian, *Inst.* 2.10.2–3; *Conf.* 9.36. This recommendation of brevity is aimed quite specially at the part of the prayer which is accompanied by prostration (*Inst.* 2.7). For the two periods of standing which frame it, Cassian's expressions indicate a certain duration.

57. RB 20.3 (cf. 52.4); RM 3.63 = RB 4.57. Cf. Cassian, *Conf.* 9.27–30.

58. Cassian, *Inst.* 2.10.1, where the involuntary groan springing from fervor is opposed to the sighs and groans arising from negligence.

59. RM 48.12. According to Cassian, *Inst.* 2.7.2 hands are extended when one prays in the standing position.

60. Cassian, *Inst.* 2.10.1: *praecipue cum consummatur oratio*, which applies most particularly to the priestly ending of the prayer. The attention of the Egyptians is opposed to the negligence of certain Gauls, who see in the prostration a 'rest' (*Inst.* 2.7.3).

61. Cassian, *Inst.* 2.7.1–2.

62. RM 14.1; 47.6 and 48.10–12; 69.10 and note.

63. Cassian, *Inst.* 2.8.

64. See t. V, p. 582.

65. Modern breviaries have a series of antiphons which are found again almost uniformly in the most ancient antiphonaries. See R. Hesbert, CAO, I–II, n. 26–43.

66. Cassian, *Inst.* 2.4.4: *psalmos Domino cantaturus exurgit*; *Conf.* 23.5.9: *dum psalmum Deo canit.* Cf. Nicetas, *De psalm. bono* 7–10. The same author develops the other aspect equally (5–7 and 12). A synthetic formula occurs at the end (13): *et nos delectabit et audientes aedificabit et Deo suavis erit tota laudatio.*

67. RM 47.6.

68. Caesarius, *Serm.* 76.1. Later Caesarius sketched another schema: *aut orate aut psallite, ut et orando peccatorum veniam accipere et psallendo ad spiritalem possitis laetitiam pervenire* (*Serm.* 77.6). Here the prayer seems to precede the psalmody (cf. 1 Co 14:15). But such a presentation disregards the liturgical reality and is only justified for literary reasons: sadness (prayer) should end in joy (psalmody); cf. James 5:13–14. This second schema, though artificial, has at least the merit of indicating exactly the joyous climate of the psalmody (cf. below, n. 84) and one of the major objects of the prayer. In fact, this latter is constantly envisaged by the ancients as a petition for the pardon of sins. See Athanasius, *De virg.* 20; Nicetas, *De psalm. bono* 5; Caesarius, *Serm.* 72.3–4 and 77.2–3; RM 3.63 (= RB 4.57), and 48.2, etc.

69. In fact, however, Caesarius mentions the prayer *before* the meditation. These two acts, which our analysis distinguishes perhaps too rigorously, seem to develop at the same time: one meditates while praying.

70. Cassian, *Inst.* 2.8.

71. In the roman office of the last three days of Holy Week the psalms have no *gloria*. This is doubtless a trace of fifth-century roman custom. Towards the end of that century, the Pseudo-Jerome, *Ep.* 47.1; PL 30:293a, was still campaigning to add the *gloria* at the end of each psalm. It is true that his campaign aimed perhaps more precisely at the words *sicut erat*. Cf. Council of Vaison II (529), can. 5, Bruns II, p. 184.

72. RM 33.43–46; RB 17.2.

73. RM 46.9; RB 9.6–7 and 11.3. However, Benedict was content with a *gloria* at the end of the last responsory.

74. RM 55.5–7; RB 9.2. The *gloria* is said also after the initial verse of the little hours (RB 18.1).

75. RM 33.46–47 and note; 55.4–6; RB 9.7 and 11.3.

76. See above, n. 64.

77. RM 47.6. This concerns not only the solo singer, but all those present (cf. RM 69.10–11: this 'psalmody', in the course of which there is a danger of falling asleep, is not the solo of the singer, but the sharing of all in the antiphony; it is also this sharing which is aimed at in RM 33.46 and 52: *omnes psallentes* and RM 67.1–3: *fratres psallentes . . . psallentibus*).

78. See t. V, pp. 583–8.

79. RM 33.46–47; 55.5–8.

80. See above, n. 66. Cf. Cassian, *Conf.* 10.11.4–6, where the monk identifies himself with the inspired author, making his own the prayer of the psalm.

81. Cassian, *Inst.* 2.3–6 and 11–12.

82. Cassian, *Conf.* 9.26.1–2.

83. RM 47.15–17. At the same epoch, psalmody and reading were assimilated by Caesarius, *Serm.* 76.1, ed. Morin, 1, p. 303. Cf. *Serm.* 72.1; 75.2; 77.6. Compare the assimilation of the psalm responsory to the epistle and the gospel, all called *lectiones* in the texts of Augustine assembled by H. Leclercq, art. 'Psalmodie responsoriale', in DACL 14: 1945–6.

84. RM 47.1–8. This 'respectful gravity' should be recommended all the more urgently since the singing of psalms seemed to the ancients a joyous and pleasant exercise, indeed a little wanton if pushed to the extreme. Cf. *Consultationes Zacchaei* 3.6; Basil, *In Ps.* 1.1; PG 29:212bc; Nicetas, *De psalm. bono* 5 and 12; Augustine, *Conf.*. 10.33.49–50; *De ord.* 1.8.22; *Enarr. in Ps.* 132.1–2; *De op. mon.* 17.20. One hummed the psalms when leaving the office (RM 68.1–3). On the role of psalmody in pacifying the passions, see Evagrius, *Traité pratique*, 15, and the note of A. Guillaumont (SCh 171; pp. 537–8); Diadochus, *Chap. gnost.* 73, etc.

85. RM 47.9–14.

86. RM 47.18-20.

87. Cassian, *Inst.* 2.12.1. Cf. *Inst.* 3.8.4.

88. See above, note 77.

89. RM 33.45. The roman office also does not recognize the division of psalms.

90. RB 47.3 (cf. 38,12).

91. RB 47.4. Cf. RM 47.1,6,14.

92. That is, to RM 47.15-17.

93. RB 19.1-2 (with no parallel in RM).

94. RB 19.6-7.

95. RM 47.9-14 and 18-20.

96. In the difficult question of the nature of the ancient antiphony we follow provisionally J. Gélineau, 'Les formes de la psalmodie chrétienne', in *La Maison-Dieu* 33, (1953) 134-72. However, antiphony should not be assimilated too closely to responsorial psalmody. Some ancient witnesses, in particular Basil, *Ep.* 207.3, suggest the participation of all present, divided into two choirs, in the singing of the psalm itself.

97. An important vestige of the ancient conception of psalmody remains in the recitation of all the psalms of the psalter consecutively, without distinguishing those which are prayers and those which are not. To remove from the office certain psalms on the pretext that they do not belong to christian prayer would be to mistake the meaning of this continuous recitation of the psalter. Certainly a good number of psalms cannot be 'prayed', either because of their literary genre, or because of their pre-christian tenor and spirit, but all can and should be transformed into authentic christian prayer in the silent prayer which follows them.

98. See above, note 1.

99. In *Laïcat et sainteté*, II: *Sainteté et vie dans le siècle* (Rome, 1965) 111-66; reproduced in I. Hausherr, *Hésychasme et prière*, OCA 176 (Rome, 1966) 255-306.

100. See OCP 22 (1956) 5-40 and 247-285; reproduced in *Hésychasme et prière*, 163-237.

101. This agreement had already been noted by I. Hausherr, *Noms du Christ et voies d'oraison*, OCA 157 (Rome, 1960) p. 132 (reference to Augustine, *De haer.* 57, not yet to *Ep.* 130.18) and p. 155. (E.T. *The Name of Jesus*, CS 44 [1978] 130-1).

102. See especially *Hésychasme et prière* (we will refer henceforth to this volume) pp. 270-2. Cf. *Noms du Christ*, p. 155.

103. *Ibid.*, 272-306.

104. *Ibid.*, 273-7 (Basil, *Long Rules* 5) and 283 (*Long Rules* 37).

105. *Ibid.*, 284 (*Long Rules* 37).

106. O. du Roy, *Moines aujourd'hui*, 173-87. See pp. 180-84.

107. We summarize as best we can, pages 179-80 (cf. pp. 184 and 187).

108. *Ibid.*, pp. 177-8.

109. A. Veilleux, *La Liturgie*, 318-23 (cf. p. 284, n. 31).

110. Aphraates, *Dem.* 4; *Patr. Syr.* 1:137-182. See especially ¶¶14-16. This theory of the 'prayer of works' ends, moreover, with an invitation to zeal for prayer properly so-called. The same final recommendation in Origen, *In Ps.* 1,2; PG 12:1088c (this conclusion is not reproduced by I. Hausherr, *Hésychasme et prière*, p. 272).

111. Aphraates, *Dem.* 4.16 indeed cites Lk 18:1 (*Orate et nolite deficere*), but only to incite the reader not to neglect prayer properly so-called (see the preceding note).

112. Origen, *De orat.* 12. See also *In I Reg.*, Hom. I.9; *In Ps.* 1.2; *In Matth.* 16.22. In the light of this consistent teaching we can interpret in the same sense the less clear passage, *In Num.*, Hom. 23.3 (what interrupts the perpetual sacrifice of incessant prayer is sin; cf. *In I Reg.*, Hom. I.9). See also *Contra Cels* 8.21-23; *In Gen.*, Hom. 10.3; 11.3; 12.5.

113. Augustine, *Ep.* 130.18. Cf. *Enar. in Ps.* 37.14, close to Origen.

114. *Semper ergo hanc a Domino Deo desideremus.* We know that *desiderare ab aliquo* means 'to ask from someone' (cf. RB 33.5: *a patre sperare*). This feature of *Ep.* 130 is lacking in *Enar. in Ps.* 37.

115. A relation not indicated by Origen, *De orat.* 12; Augustine, *Enar. in Ps.* 37.14.

116. Compare Tertullian, *De orat.* 24–25 and Augustine, *Ep.* 130.18. Besides the general resemblance of the two arguments, note in Tertullian *admonitionem . . . admonitione* (25.5), and in Augustine *admoneamus . . . admonentes*, as well as *etiam* in one (25.1) and in the other. The letter to Proba dates from 410–411. Much later (428) in *De haer.* 57, Augustine considered prayer at certain hours sufficient to satisfy 'Pray without ceasing'.

117. It is not impossible, however, that Paul was thinking of a prayer as *berakhoth*, which pious Jews had to make in regard to every action of some importance. See M. Arranz, 'Les prières presbytérales des Petites Heures dan l'ancien Euchologe byzantin', in OCP 39 (1973) 50–52.

118. I. Hausherr, *Hésychasme et prière*, p. 280 and passim. Here Basil is put with the 'three great doctors' and contrasted with the monks. On the contrary, in *Noms du Christ*, p. 132 (E.T. 131) I. Hausherr put him with the monks and contrasts him with Origen, no doubt because he has attributed to him two inauthentic sermons. But he was right after all, because in fact Basil much surpasses Origen in the 'monastic' sense (see below, note 121).

119. Basil, *Ep.* 2.2, ed. Courtonne, pp. 7–8, l.44–51. The 'hymns' seem to be psalms and other liturgical texts (cf. l.47: 'hymns and chants' in relation to the office of matins). On the delight which is experienced in singing the psalms everywhere, see Basil, *In Ps.* 1:1; PG 29:212bc.

120. Basil, *Long Rules* 37.2. The pair, prayer-psalmody, structures this text from beginning to end. The development on 'thanksgiving', suggested by Eph 5:19, seems to refer to the psalmody. Another use of Eph 5:19 occurs in *Reg.* 107 = *Short Rules* 147: the brother who is prevented from sharing in the common psalmody should say the psalms mentally (*kata dianoin*, equivalent to *en tais kardiais*; not *consciencieusement* [conscientiously] as L. Lèbe translates it), even while working. Here again, Basil does not recoil from the mixing of two activities and the doubling of attention.

121. Cf. Basil, *In mart. Iul.* 3–4: the same doctrine, except that work, a monastic activity, is replaced by common actions such as eating and drinking (1 Co 10:31), putting on one's tunic and cloak, lighting the lamp, watching, sleeping. Compare this text with Origen, *In Ps.* 1.2; PG 12:1088, who could have inspired the connection of 1 Th 5:17 and 1 Co 10:31 and the connection to dreams, but who remains much vaguer and less demanding. For Origen, good actions are prayer. For Basil, it is a matter of making an explicit prayer in regard to each action. On thinking of God and thanking him while eating: on praying before and afterwards see Basil, *Ep.* 2.6; p. 12,25–35. Basil preaches the absence of distractions (*ameteôriston*), not only in prayer (*Short Rules* 201), but in all actions (*Long Rules* 5; *Short Rules* 202 and 306). Beside Ps 15:8, he invokes on this subject 1 Co. 10:31 (*Long Rules* 5) and Ps 1:2 (*Short Rules* 306): 'to give thanks' for everything, and 'to meditate day and night on the law' of God.

122. Augustine, *De mor. eccl.* I. 67. The trait is lacking in Jerome, *Ep.* 22.35. Augustine is copied by Isidore, *De eccl. off.* II.16.12.

123. Augustine, *De op. mon.* 17.20. The text is reproduced differently by Isidore, *De eccl. off.* II. 16.12; *Reg. mon.* 5.5.

124. Jerome, *Ep.* 46.12 (from Paula and Eustochium to Marcella); the text is copied by *Reg. Tarn.* 8. Compare Basil, *In Ps.* 1,1 (above, note 119).

125. Chrysostom, *Serm. de Anna* 4.5–6 (cf. *Serm.* 2.3).

126. Chrysostom mentions the hours of Terce, Sext, None and doubtless is only thinking of prayers spaced out as these are.

127. Clement, *Strom.* 7.7. Here it is a matter of unbroken continuity to such a point that the observance of Terce, Sext, and None seems superfluous (40.3–4). Account being taken of a certain vagueness, it seems that Clement is thinking, not of an implicit prayer (Hausherr, *Noms du Christ*, p. 143), but of explicit prayers (see particularly 35.6; 39:6; 49.4; 49.7). *Ouk antikrus* (49.6) seems to us to mean 'not openly', rather than 'not directly, not explicitly' (Hausherr): the prayer should be secret, but explicit. Cf. G. Békés, *De continua oratione Clementis Alexandrini doctrina* (Roma, 1942) p. 1, who translates it as *non aperte.*

128. Chrysostom, *Serm. de Anna* 2.2.

129. Augustine, *Ep.* 130.20 (compare moreover *Ep.* 130.18 with Chrysostom, *Serm. de Anna* 4.5: return to prayer reheats the lukewarm soul; *Ep.* 130.15 with *Serm. de Anna* 2.2: conciliation of 1 Th 5:17 and Mt 6:7); Cassian, *Inst.* 2.10.3 and *Conf.* 9.36.1. It will be noted that Augustine's discussion is not concerned with the frequency of these prayers, but with their brevity.

130. Basil, *In mart. Iul.* 3–4. See above, note 121.

131. The three uses of *meditare* (RB 48.23; 58.5) and *meditatio* (8.3) refer to the effort of memorizing the sacred texts. This meaning is, moreover, the most frequent one in the Master (RM 1.63 etc.); that of 'recitation' during one's occupations scarcely appears except in RM 50.26 and 43; 68.2. In this latter sense the Master uses just as easily *recensere* (RM 9.45; 50.26) and *recensio* (50.43), terms unknown to Benedict.

132. It is the same for the distinctive character of the monastic habit, as we shall say in the proper place.

133. See especially the first and twelfth degrees of humility.

134. RB 19.1–2.

135. O. du Roy, *Moines aujourd'hui*, 179–80.

136. Although *Orationi frequenter incumbere* (RM 3.62 = RB 4.56) is an invitation to continual prayer, as we have shown in RAM 41 (1965) 467–72.

137. See above, notes 5 and 7*bis*.

138. See note 5. Cf. Aphraates, *Dem.* 4.16, and Callinicos, *Vita Hyp.* 24.10 (Lk 18:1); *Les Vies coptes*, p. 85, 27 (Bo 10). and Evagrius, *Pract.* 49 (1 Th 5:17).

139. As I. Hausherr writes, *Hésychasme et prière*, p. 304, 'this ordinance [the seven hours of the office] . . . is . . . an attempt to make possible to a certain degree the precept of continual prayer'. It could not be put better. We have not 'claimed to show' anything else in these pages, in spite of the reserve shown in their regard by Hausherr, 'Pour comprendre l'Orient chrétien; la primauté du spirituel', in OCP 33 (1967) 351–69 (see p. 364).

140. Cassian, *Inst.* 3.3.8, depends literally on Tertullian and does not bring in the pair solitude-community. This question appears, on the contrary, in *Inst.* 2.1 (anchorites and cenobites of Egypt), in regard to the two major hours, and in *Inst.* 3.2 (Egyptian and Eastern cenobites), in regard to the three little hours. There Cassian is independent on Tertullian, but may, in the second case, be inspired by Palladius, *Hist. Laus* 32.7. See our article 'Les sources des quatre premiers Livres des Institutions de Jean Cassien', to appear in *Aufstieg und Niedergang der römischen Welt.*

141. Flesh and spirit: Cassian, *Conf.* 12.11.1; soul, spirit, body (?): Paulinus, *Ep.* 36.4; soul and body: Eusebius Gall., *Hom.* 52.1–4 (reproduced by Caesarius, *Serm.* 152.1) and 54.6. This interpretation goes back to Origen, *In Matth.* 14.3 (body and spirit, to which is joined the soul), followed by Ambrose, *In Luc.* 7.192–193 (cf. *De inst. virg.* 10–14) and Jerome, *In Matth.* 3; CC 77; 162–3. A variant is found in Isaias, *Log.* 7.2, ed. Draguët (*noûs* and *psuchè*); Philoxenos, *Letter to Patricius* 35 (*noûs, thumos, epithumètikon*). Man, Christ, and God: Aphraates, *Dem.* 4.11–12.

142. Thus Aphraates (preceding note). Cf. Basil, Short Rules 225: God is also present to a

single soul who keeps his commandments. Aphraates' thesis recalls the *agraphon* 'Where there is only one, I am there just as much', cited by Ephrem, *Comm. de l'Év. concord.* 14.24, ed. L. Leloir (Dublin, 1963) p. 135.

143. Basil, *Long Rules* 5.3 (fear of God); *Short Rules* (*ameteôriston*). Cf. *Short Rules* 225 (concord and obedience to the divine will). According to *Short Rules* 15 and 261, Mt 18:19 concerns the sinner's acceptance of his spiritual guide's remonstrances (cf. Mt 18:17–18 and 21.

144. Thus G¹ 94; Cyril of Alex., *Ep.* 55; PG 77:293a.

145. Thus Chrysostom, *Serm. de Anna* 5.1; Leo, *Serm.* 88.3 (Emberdays fast); Caesarius, *Serm.* 152.1. With Cyprian, *De unit.* 12, the accent is placed on 'unanimity', that is, on communion with the one Church (cf. above, notes 143–144).

146. Cassian, *Conf.* 9.34.1..

147. Columban, *Ep.* 4.2 (concord).

148. *Const. Apost.* 8.34.10. The source (Hippolyte, *Trad. Apost.* 41) does not have these considerations.

149. Athanasius, *De virg.* 10. The elliptical text can be clarified by the parallel passages of ¶16 and ¶20.

150. Horsiesius, Regulations 30–33; CSCO 160, p. 81 (E.T. *Pachomian Koinonia*, 2, CS46:208–9).

151. As A. Veilleux affirms in *La Liturgie*, p. 321.

152. *Les Vies coptes*, p. 196, 29–30 (Bo 184) and 333,34–35 (S⁶). This 'often' is a little surprising, since the gospel text is absolute. Would the author be thinking instead of Ez. 34:11–16, where the Lord announces his visit (cf. the sequel)?

153. Basil, *Long Rules* 37.4.

154. Basil, *Long Rules* 37.3. Cf. Ac 1:14 and 2:1–15.

155. Basil, *Reg.* 3; PL 103: 49SC; *Long Rules* 73; PG 31: 932C.

156. RM 20.5, which recalls the prayer of the Church for Peter (Ac 12:5) is about the only thing that can be cited. See also RM 14.25–26, but it does not concern the office. The two chapters the office (RM 47–48; cf. RB 19–20) say nothing about prayer as common.

157. Thus the *Ordo monasterii* 2; Caesarius, *Reg. virg.* 66–70 and *Reg. mon.* 20–25; Columban, *Reg. mon.* 7; Donatus, *Reg.* 75; Isidore, *Reg.* 6 (save for the final sanction); Fructuosus, *Reg.* I.2–3.

158. Cassian, *Inst.* 3.2 and 11; RM 45.14–15 and 17; Aurelian, *Reg. mon* 396b and *Reg. virg.* 406b.

159. RB 38.2. Cf. Gregory, *Dial.* 4.58: *cum missarum solemnia peregisset et mysteria sacrae communionis accepisset.*

160. RB 38.10 and 63.4. See t. I p. 104–5.

161. RB 62.6.

162. RB 59.2 and 8.

163. RB 35.14 (*usque ad missas*) and 60.4 (*missas tenere*).

164. P. Delatte, *Commentaire*, pp. 151–2 (E.T., p. 133).

165. RB 38.2. Cf. Fructuosus, *Reg.* II.13.

166. Cf. RB 38.10. See t. I, p. 105, n. 8.

167. See our 'Scholies sur la Régle du Maître', in RAM 44 (1968) 122–7; 'Problèmes de la messe conventuelle dans les monastères', in *Parole et Pain*, 20 (1967) 161–72. Aurelian, *Reg. mon.* 396b and *Reg. virg.* 406b, mentions general communion on Sunday after Terce (cf. Cassian, *Inst.* 3.2), outside of Mass apparently. The *Reg. cuiusdam* 32 also calls for communion each Sunday, and *Reg. Pauli et Stephani* 13 speaks of a daily communion, probably without Mass. Fructuosus, *Reg.* II.13 witnesses to Sunday Mass. Masses without a determinate frequency are mentioned by Caesarius, *Reg. virg.* 36 and Aurelian, *loc. cit..* Daily

Mass appears only in the Rule *Largiente Domino* 2 (after Terce in summer) and 3 (after None in winter). This Rule is carolingian.

168. See A. Häussling, *Mönchskonvent und Eucharistiefeier*, LQF 58 (Münster/Westfalen, 1973).

169. *Perfectae caritatis*, no. 2.

170. In the East Saturday must be added. See for example *Les Vies coptes*, p. 96 (Bo 25).

171. Augustine, *Ep.* 54.4. *Ille bonorando non audet quotidie sumere et ille bonorando non audet ullo die praetermittere.*

172. Aurelian, *Reg. mon.* 396b and *Reg. virg.* 406b. He has just prescribed a general communion on Sunday after Terce. If there were some question later of the Sunday Mass, it would be hard to explain this communion outside of Mass the same day. Therefore, it is question of leaving to the abbot's judgment the determination of the days on which Mass should be celebrated. Neither Sunday nor the feasts (the preceding phrase) are automatically solemnized by the Mass.

173. See A.M. La Bonnardière, 'Pénitence et réconciliation des pénitents d'après S. Augustin', I, in REA 13 (1967) 31–53, specially pp. 49–51.

174. Gregory, *Dial.* 4.58 (daily); *Hom. Ev.* 37.9 (almost daily). The homily, the first in chronological order, is addressed to the people, not to monks, and Cassius himself is not a monk. The Mass is represented as a means of propitiation, together with alms and tears.

175. RM 21–22; *Reg. Pauli et Stephani* 13. Cf. Cassian *Inst.* 6.8; *Conf.* 7.30.2; 9.21; 14.8.5, as well as *Historia monachorum* 2 (406b) and 7 (418–419).

176. See H. Leclercq, art. 'Communion quotidienne', in DACL 3: 2457–2465. This article, like that of A.M. La Bonnardière cited above (n. 173), does not distinguish between the Mass and simple communion at home. On the latter, see in particular Tertullian, *Ad uxorem* 2.5; Cyprian, *De lapsis* 26; Basil, *Ep.* 93; Jerome, *Ep.* 48.15.

177. Cassian, *Conf.* 9.21.2. Cf. Cyprian, *De dom. or.* 18.

178. Cassian, *Inst.* 3.11; Etheria, *Pereg.* 25 and 27 (cf. *Liber Mozarabicus Sacramentorum*, ed. M. Férotin [Paris, 1912] 723–31: *Ad nonam pro missa*).

179. Mass of Ember Saturdays in the roman rite, evening Mass of the vigils and Mass after the *orthros* in the byzantine rite, Mass of the days of penitence at the hour of None in the mozarabic rite. See our article 'Problèmes de la messe conventuelle', pp. 170–71, nn. 36–37.

Chapter IX

THE ABBOT'S COLLABORATORS

(RB 21 & 65)

T HE CHAPTER ON THE DEANS and the chapter on the provost are closely linked by mutual references.[1] Benedict mentions the two functions together in another passage as well.[2] It therefore seems fitting not to separate these two sorts of collaborators of the abbot.

Our commentary on them can be short, moreover, because Benedict himself does not show much interest in them. He does not favor, in principle, the office of provost, and wishes to do without it by means of deaneries;[3] the deans themselves he treats only with extreme sobriety.[4] The criteria for choosing them and the ways of deposing them are about all that is indicated in the little chapter *De decanis monasterii*.[5] In the rest of the rule there is little to be found on these *decani* or *seniores*, whose role seems to have lost the importance the Master attributed to it.[6] Insistence on the authority and responsibility of the abbot, on the one hand, and on fraternal relations, on the other: this twofold accent seems to have entailed a lessening of the attention previously given to the subordinate officers, the deans.

Has this decline in the dean's function in our Rule prepared for its more or less proximate disappearance in the benedictine tradition down to our day? In any case, it corresponds to Benedict's complex heritage, in which the Egyptian current transmitted by Cassian and the Master combined with other influences. As far as we know, only the cenobia of Egypt were divided into numerically equal groups, whether these were the houses of forty monks in the pachomian congregation or the 'decuries' and 'deaneries' pointed out by Jerome and Cassian. The communities for which

Basil, Augustine, and the Four Fathers legislated apparently included no such division.[7]

Then too, organization by deaneries appears in the West only where the Egyptian current was felt with some force. It is absent from the *Regulae Patrum* and from the rules of Gaul, where Augustine's influence was preponderant,[8] and is encountered only in the Italian family made up of the Master, Eugippus, and Benedict,[9] and in the following century in the Spanish family of Isidore, Fructuosus, and the *Regula communis*.[10] Even with Benedict, the augustinian influence doubtless tended to limit the system's importance and to blur its outlines.

While the dean's function loses its importance in our Rule, the office of provost finds there a reticent, but on the whole positive, welcome, which contrasts with its express exclusion by the Master. Again, the line of evolution which passes from one rule to the other has been prolonged in the tradition issuing from Benedict. Admitted by him with many reservations, the 'second' has remained under the name of *praepositus* or 'prior' throughout the centuries of benedictine monasticism down to our days. Thus posterity has preferred the provost to the deans, contrary to Benedict's formal recommendation, but not without a certain connivance with the legislator's undeclared tendencies.

Deans and provost. Without excluding each other,[11] these two functions tend to be opposed, especially in smaller communities. As they both aim to relieve the abbot, one seems to be enough and to make the other superfluous. The 'second', being almost indispensable anyway,[12] was in a better position to survive than the deans, whose usefulness depended too much on the number of monks they controlled.[13]

Thus has prevailed the kind of subordinate officer who had fewer biblical and ecclesiastical models to which reference could be made. If the typology of the deanery is quite rich, that of the provost is almost wholly lacking. In describing the deans, Benedict is manifestly thinking of the leaders of a thousand, a hundred and of ten who assisted Moses, as well as of the deacons established by the apostles; and the first of these models establishes an analogy between the abbot's deans and the priests around the bishop, themselves also referred to the 'ancients' surrounding Moses.[14] Cassian had already cited Exodus in regard to the leaders of ten, while the Master set them in parallel with the presbyterate of the Church, applying to them as to the latter the word of Christ: 'He who hears you, hears me'.[15]

On the contrary, the role of 'second' has few biblical analogues. Only once, among the Pachomians, is Joshua cited in this regard, as assisting Moses.[16] The only model the Master thought of, was that of 'Caesar-Elect', a purely profane figure.[17]

For a reason that has nothing to do with these biblical references, the division of the community into deaneries enjoys a certain favor today. This point is one on which people would gladly return to the Rule. Complaints are made, especially in large communities, about the inadequacy of human relations, since each monk remains fairly isolated in a group too big to encourage a warm social life. An intermediate structure between the whole community and its individual members is therefore advocated. Groups comprising about ten monks or fewer seem to correspond to this need.

What is especially desired of these groups is that they serve as a framework for fraternal exchanges. It is a matter of instituting discussion among the monks, so as to complete the vertical system of obedience to superiors by horizontal relations of confidence and friendship. Having chosen among themselves someone in charge, or an animator, the members of the group meet once or twice a week, sometimes sharing prayer and a meal. Eventually, group activities are envisaged, such as permanently insuring some community service, or economic applications, such as pooling the fruits of labor and the mutual control of expenses.[18]

Groups like this have begun to be restored in some monasteries. The point which interests us here is their relationship with the benedictine deanery which serves as their model or reference. On this, the Rule says so little that we must have recourse to other ancient monastic texts to get some idea, however imprecise, of its nature and purpose.

Beginning with the closest document, we come upon the *decada* of the Master, a group of ten monks ruled by two provosts. Its aim is to assure the continual surveillance of the men by their leaders. There are two of them, so that one of them is always present when the other is occupied or so that the ten may be divided. The provosts, always at the side of their subordinates, rebuke every failure to observe the Rule, especially in breaches of silence and behaviour. At table, in the dormitory, at work, while reading, out of doors, they recall the abbot's directives at every moment and impose the observance of them.[19] If their warnings are fruitless, they denounce the guilty person to the abbot.[20] It is also their duty to question the brothers about their thoughts, to receive their confessions and to make known to the abbot their temptations so he may remedy them.[21] Finally, the provosts are in charge of the chest which holds all changes of clothing for the decade. Thus they are the guardians of renunciation of property.[22]

A century before the Master, Cassian gave similar indications. In the cenobia of Egypt the head of the deanery had charge of the wardrobe and furnished all the clean habits.[23] At table he asked for what was missing.[24] But what the *Institutes* especially set forth is the spiritual role of the dean. The formation of the young monk seems to have been wholly his business. By painful orders the senior mortified the will of his disciple. In response to his manifestation of thoughts, he taught him to combat the vices, and guarded him from all illusion.[25]

Jerome, to whom we are indebted for the first description of the system,[26] shows the dean making the round of the cells, day and night, to comfort the tempted brothers and to incite the negligent to prayer. The 'decury' gathers around him both at the meal, which is taken in silence, and at the conference which is held afterwards until nightfall. Without giving then an instruction *ex professo*, as the 'Father' of the monastery has done before the meal, the dean points out to the group the examples of gracious behaviour, of silence and of restraint given by one or another brother. Again he comforts the weak and encourages the fervent to progress. Jerome points out finally that he collects his men's work and gives it to the steward.

We find analogous traits in the pachomian 'houses', although they were groups four times bigger.[27] The head of the house, assisted by a 'second', directed the work, watched over good order and renunciation of goods, gave two instructions a week, in addition to those of the head of the monastery. Part of the common prayer took place in the evening in each house. By houses also the brothers exercised different trades and assured the 'weeks' of service.

Thus there appears both numerous differences of detail between the four pre-Benedict testimonies we have just collected and their basic agreement on the purpose of the groups into which the monastic community was divided, whether they were called decade, deanery, decury, or house. This purpose, from which nothing shows Benedict and later authors

wished to depart, is very different from that of the groups recently established in monasteries. They concerned not fraternal exchanges but surveillance and direction. The dean, instead of being an animator chosen by the
group, was a true superior, delegated by the abbot. Like him, he was
sometimes called 'father'.[28] Far from cutting across the relationship of
obedience which ties the monks to the abbot, the deanery system constituted the first link of this chain. It belonged not to the horizontal dimension but to the hierarchical structure.

Another contrast is obvious. The ancient deaneries were not groups for
dialogue but for silence. The principal task of the Master's provost was to
keep the discipline of *taciturnitas* respected in all its points. Without going
into the same details, the preceding authors suggest rules of silence no less
strict.[29] The daily conference mentioned by Jerome has a precise purpose
of edification. It did not consist of exchanging ordinary remarks, but of
encouraging the members of the decury in the practices of asceticism, notably in silence. The dean repeated in a collective conversation the individual exhortations he had given at other times in his visits to the cells of the
brothers.

The groups in ancient cenobitism did not therefore aim at tempering silence any more than obedience. On the contrary, they tended to make
both of them more effective. Today monks gather in groups from time to
time in order to interrupt the tension of solitary conversation with God
by spontaneous conversations. Then they lived in a group under the direction of a master to sustain themselves in this perpetual effort of atten-
ding to God, of renunciation and of self-mastery. Today monks seek in
gatherings to disclose themselves to one another, in order to know and
love each other better. This care to know the others and to make oneself
known plainly does not appear in the texts we have just analyzed. The
only opening envisaged there is that of the disciple who manifests his
thoughts to an elder.[30]

We should not therefore conceal the deep differences that separate the
spirit of the ancient deanery from that of the groups recently restored. Yet
a certain harmony exists between the two proposals, and one may hope
that ours will let itself be guided by the sense of monastic values.

Moreover, we are happy to note that the two chapters examined here
include among these values several features whose importance is felt now-

adays with a particular sharpness. Benedict, by inviting the abbot to 'share his burden', opens the way to the sense of coresponsibility, which is more than ever necessary today.[31] By suggesting that he agree to the 'humble and reasonable request of the community' which asks for a prior, he opens to the desires of the brothers a possibility of expression of which the Master seems not to have thought. Not only does the principle of counsel find here a new application, but a certain initiative even seems admitted on the part of the subjects. And when Benedict adds that the prior will be chosen 'with the counsel of God-fearing brothers', he underlines again, in a no less personal way,[32] that the authority of the abbot, however full it may be, cannot do without the cooperation of the community, or at least of those who form the healthiest part of it[33] according to the standards of the Gospel and tradition.

NOTES TO CHAPTER 9

1. RB 21.7 and 65.12.
2. RB 62.7
3. RB 65.12–13. See *La Communauté et l'Abbé*, pp. 404–10.
4. RB 21, with its seven verses, is not even one-fifteenth of RM 11.1–107, a record of brevity.
5. See *Le Communauté et l'Abbé*, p. 289–306.
6. See t. I, pp. 53–54.
7. Yet it may be hidden in the *Ordo monasterii* 6–7, where the function of the *praepositus* at meals recalls Cassian, *Inst.* 4.17.
8. Perhaps the *senior* of these rules was sometimes a head of a group of ten, but there are no positive indications of it. The same is true for Columban, the *Regula cuiusdam*, Waldbert, and Donatus.
9. The *Regula Pauli et Stephani* falls in the came category as those mentioned in the preceding note.
10. Isidore, *Reg.* 9 and 13; Fructuosus, *Reg.* I. 3,6,8,20,21 and II. 12.
11. As the pachomian and spanish documents show.
12. Someone must replace the abbot when he is absent. Cf. Basil, *Long Rules* 45; RM 16.35 and 72.2 (cf. 93.66).
13. Gregory in his Letters and Dialogues had already named more than one *praepositus*, but never spoke of *decani*. The twelve monasteries of *Dial.* 2.3, although they numbered only twelve monks in the beginning, had true abbots in charge of them (cf. 2.4).
14. See *La Communauté et l'Abbé*, pp. 300–305.
15. Cassian, *Inst.* 4.7; RM 11.11 (Lk 10:16).
16. See *Les Vies coptes*, p. 139, 19 (Bo 78). The same Joshua is cited on p. 274,3 (S⁵ 126) and 338,4 (S³ᵇ), but as Moses' successor rather than as his assistant.
17. RM 93.63.

18. Apart from this last point, the indications given by O. du Roy, *Moines aujourd'hui*, pp. 135–140 (cf. pp. 67 and 288–290), correspond to what is done in one or another French monastery.

19. Besides RM 11 (cf. RB 21–22), see in particular RM 50 and 84 (cf. RB 48.17–18 and 56.3). There is no reason to oppose the 'disciplinary role' of the Master's provosts to the 'spiritual responsibility' of Benedict's deans (du Roy, p. 135).

20. RM 12; cf. RB 23.

21. RM 15; cf. RB 4.50 and 46.5–6.

22. RM 17.11 and 81.9–14.

23. Cassian, *Inst.* 4.10. Cf. Pachomius, *Praec.* 42,65,70,105.

24. Cassian, *Inst.* 4.17 (cf. above, n. 7).

25. Cassian, *Inst.* 4.8–9. See also 4.10 (obedience).

26. Jerome, *Ep.* 22.35. On the interpretation of ¶¶4–5, which always deals with the dean, see *La Communauté et l'Abbé*, p. 52, n. 1 (E.T. p. 40, n. 9 on p. 60).

27. According to Jerome, *Praefatio in Regulam Pachomii* 2 (cf. 6). We borrow the following details from the Rule and the Lives (in particular Bo 26).

28. See Jerome, *Ep.* 22.35.4: *unaquaeque decuria cum suo parente*. The criteria of choice are the same for the deans and for the abbot, according to RB 21.4 and 64.2.

29. See in particular Jerome, *Ep.* 22.35.2; Cassian, *Inst.* 2.15.1.

30. Cassian, *Inst.* 4.9; RB 4.50 and 46.5–6. Cf. RM 10.61–65 = RB 7.44–48, where the *senior* of Cassian is replaced by *abbas*. On the other possibilities of spiritual conversations in the Master, see t. IV, pp. 272–4.

31. Cf. A. van der Wielen, 'Coresponsibility According to the Rule of St. Benedict', in *Cistercian Studies* 9 (1974) 348–53.

32. At least in relation to the Master. For Basil, *Long Rules* 45.1, see *La Communauté et l'Abbé*, p. 190, n. 1 (E.T. p. 163, n. 7 on p. 174).

33. Compare RB 65.15 and 64.1.

Chapter X

THE DORMITORY, SLEEP, AND NIGHT SILENCE
(RB 22 & 42)

T HESE TWO CHAPTERS deal with the night, the first describing the
monks' dormitory and their rising, the second dealing with night
silence and what precedes going to bed. Although the chapters are
far removed from each other, they are connected, not only by their common object, but also by the fact that Benedict seems to have joined them
mentally: many features of the first chapter come from the section of the
Master which corresponds to the second.[1]

The common dormitory was not a primitive institution of cenobitism.
Only towards the beginning of the sixth century was it substituted, simul-
taneously in Gaul, Italy, and Byzantium, for the former dwelling in cells.[2]
This change, which doubtless constitutes the most important event in the
history of cenobitism in antiquity, was conceived by its promotors as a
palliative for the drawbacks of the cell in matters of renunciation of
goods, conduct, and good morals. To these moral and disciplinary
preoccupations were sacrificed the lofty values of solitude, recollection,
attention to God and to oneself which were associated in the mind of the
first cenobites with dwelling in cells. Cenobitism thus departed from its
eremitic origins, to which it owed the individual cell, and chose to
develop to the full the possibilities of surveillance, either hierarchical or
mutual, offered by the common life.

The return to the cells, which has been accomplished progressively over
several centuries and into which a number of Cistercian monasteries has
just rushed, brings us back, at least materially, to the state of things prior
to the Rule. What have been the historical reasons for this return and

what is its meaning? We would like to think that it marks a rediscovery of the primitive ideal of dwelling with oneself under the gaze of God.[3]

The monks' sleep begins early and ends early. Seculars also have their night watches, but they are generally put at the beginning of the night, not at its end. Watching does not mean the same thing in both cases. For one it means either prolonging the day's work, or compensating for it by relaxation, friendship, and pleasure. The others take their sleep when the sun goes down[4] and rise early to anticipate its rising with prayer. For this watch with God alone they profit from the calm hours which follow the night's rest rather than those when they are still throbbing with the excitements of the day.

The monks' sleep is brief.[5] The tendency to deprive oneself of sleep, as well as of food, is general in monasticism. The principles which inspire the *ascesis* of fasting are also valid for watching.[6]

Both fasting and watching were regulated for the ancients by the framework of the natural day and night. Their life did not roll along, as ours does, in an abstract time, cut into uniform hours, but in a time of changing duration, determined by the vicissitudes of the daily light. The revolution of the earth upon itself is almost the only parameter of our existence. That of the earth around the sun also fashioned the life of our Fathers and enriched it with an additional reference to the cosmos. Artificiality and monotony are the price we pay for the conveniences of our routine. No doubt monks would have something to gain by taking greater account of the great cosmic rhythms on which the Rule, like all ancient monasticism, built the horarium of rising and going to bed, of work and of reading, of meals and of prayer itself.

Monks sleep with all their clothes on, lying on hard beds,[7] in a room which remains lighted. Their rising is quick and followed immediately by the office. They sleep in a state of availability, 'always ready' to answer the signal and take up again the service of the divine praise.[8] This striking picture inevitably makes us think of the parables of Christ's return.[9] Whether Benedict thought of it or not, his monks resemble the servants in the Gospel who await the return of the master in the middle of the night. Night is the chief time for silence;[10] it is also the time of hope. It makes us desire the light, security, and joy which it lacks. Christ, who is all that for us, will return. We await his Day, which will shatter the night of this world.[11]

But before this final event, his awakening from among the dead and our resurrection from sin are also figured by each day's dawn. As children of the light and children of the day, Christians have no part in the shameful and sterile works of darkness. Their watches can only be spent in putting on Christ, taking up the weapons of light and preparing for the holy actions of the day.[12]

These pauline images give the monks' nocturnal schedule its deepest meaning and foundation. On this point, as on so many others, monastic observance only expresses in a visible way the inspiration of the New Testament. Going to bed at nightfall signifies the denial of the evil or vain things men engage in when the day is ended. Rising during the night and watching before dawn expresses the will to purify oneself, the desire for Christ, and the awaiting of the day.

This strange way the monks have of anticipating the hour of going to bed and of rising, of living *in advance*, is found in another area which we conjecture is in the background of the chapters on which we are commenting: sexuality. There too, the monks' behavior looks towards the end of time. By a costly choice and effort, they already make their portion consist of what will be the state of consummated humanity, which will be like the angels.[13]

It is a paradoxical fact that this renunciation constitutive of monasticism is not mentioned clearly even once in our Rule. Celibacy, total and perpetual continence, figures in it nowhere in specific terms. There is no chapter, no paragraph on the question. Poverty and obedience are the subject of treatises in which behavior is prescribed, motives indicated, and scriptural texts cited. There is nothing of the sort for chastity.[14] There are almost no allusions either to the virtue itself[15] or to the dangers threatening it.[16]

Certain prescriptions of our two rules are more or less certainly to be put among these measures favoring chastity.[17] Among them, 'Let each one sleep in a separate bed' aims concretely at the perversion of the instinct, and furnishes in addition the image of the monastic renunciation of its normal satisfaction. The monk is a solitary in this sense above all.[18] Benedict's silence, like that of the Master,[19] on this important point only shows how much for granted it was taken. Continence for the monk is like the air he breathes: the invisible and always present presupposition, the essential milieu of his existence.

We often recall nowadays that monasticism has a prophetic character. It must not be forgotten that this reference to the Bible refers essentially in the tradition to the solitude and chastity of some of the great prophets.[20] They are the models for monks, and this is their prophecy, that God suffices now for his consecrated ones, just as he will be all in all one day.

NOTES TO CHAPTER 10

1. See t. V, pp. 655–7, as well as the notes on RB 22, T,3,4, (borrowed from RM 29).

2. See t. V, pp. 664–97.

3. Cf. Gregory, *Dial.* 2.3, ed. Moricca, p. 81.14–82.11.

4. Except when the long vigil is celebrated (Cassian, *Inst.* 3.8–9; RM 49, etc.) but these celebrations were unknown to Benedict.

5. Cassian, *Conf.* 12.15.2 recommends three or four hours. Without going that far, the cenobitic texts are generally restrictive. In winter, it is true, Benedict is astonishly generous (RB 8.1–2), but the reaction of ancient commentators shows that they felt an anomaly here (see t. V, pp. 419–31).

6. See our commentary on RB 39–41 further on.

7. Cf. RB 55.15: *matta*. These mats can be used in the oratory (RM 19.25; 69.10) as well as in the dormitory (RM 81.31). See Gregory, *Dial* 2.11, ed. Moricca, p. 98, 12.

8. RB 22.6.

9. Mt 24:43–25:13; Lk 12:35–40. It is not certain that Benedict refers to them. Cassian, *Conf.* 8.3.4–5 thinks it necessary to allegorize them.

10. RB 42.1. See t. V, pp. 705–6.

11. Rm 13:11–12; 1 Th 5:1–4.

12. Rm 13:12–13; Eph 5:8–14; 1 Th 5:4–8. Cf. Jn 9:4.

13. Mt 22:30 and parallels.

14. This triad of 'evangelical counsels', usually absent from the ancient texts, is found however in Horsiesius, *Liber* 19 (obedience), 20 (chastity), 21–23 (poverty).

15. RB 4.64 = RM 3.70 (*castitatem amare*); RB 64.9 (*castum*). In RB 72.8 *caste* probably does not denote chastity any more than does 64.6. See E. Dekkers, 'Caritatem caste impendant. Qu'a voulu dire saint Benoît?', in *La Ciudad de Dios*, 181 (1968) 656–60.

16. Cf. RB 36.8.

17. RB 22.1, 3–4, 5 (cf. RM 11.118–119), 7 (see however t. V, p. 660, n. 36); 42.4 and 8–11 (but see t. V, p. 721).

18. On this primalry sense of *monachos* and its Syriac equivalent (alone, without a woman), see A. Guillaumont, 'Monachisme et éthique judéo-chrétienne', in RSR 60 (1972) 199–218, especially pp. 200–202.

19. Except for allusions to 'marriage' (RM 91.41) and to 'fornication' (5.6; 15.32). Cf. 11.118–119; 27.46 and all of chapter 80.

20. See Cassian, *Inst.* 1.1.2 (cf. 1.11.3) and 6.4.1; *Conf.* 21.4.2 (chastity); Jerome, *Ep.* 58.5 (cf. 22.36) and Cassian, *Conf.* 18.6.2 (solitude), etc.

Chapter XI

THE REPRESSION AND REPARATION OF FAULTS

(RB 23–30 & 43–46)

T HE PART OF THE RULE which we now approach is no doubt the one with the least present-day application. Excommunication and blows fell into desuetude a long time ago. The practice of accusations, penances, and satisfactions in their turn seems to be disappearing in many communities. This retreat from repressive measures and penitential gestures is accompanied by a feeling of embarrassment about the texts which prescribe them. Not only do corporal punishments seem barbarous and infantile, but the very principle of repression becomes a problem. Contemporary humanism opposes it as well as all overt constraint. Personal liberty, dignity, and responsibility seem to demand that each person do his duty and submit to the common law willingly, according to his conscience, not under the threat of sanction. We count more on brotherly help and communitarian warmth than on a penal code to repair mistakes and to sustain wavering good-wills. Moreover, is not the very existence of an arsenal of penalities enough to throw a cloud over the climate of mutual confidence and benevolence, optimism and joy, which constitutes the supreme blessing of a community?

Finally, the way in which many communities are evolving makes every system of sanctions frail. When the observances are constantly changing, a stable law no longer exists, in relation to which a fault can be defined and punished. What is penalized today may turn out to be a happy initiative and become the general custom tomorrow.

What has just been said of the system of repression applies also to self-accusation and spontaneous satisfaction, to the extent that these practices

185

are enjoined by the Rule and relate to violations of it. In addition, even when detached from the Rule's framework, such behavior risks seeming inappropriate in the atmosphere we have evoked. Voluntary humiliation is easily suspected of being masochism. It makes those who witness it uncomfortable and helps spread a sense of culpability. Is it not better discreetly to correct one's deviations and to rejoin the group without a fuss?

However summary these remarks may be, they suggest how far we are from Benedict in this area. The examination of these chapters will therefore be all the more interesting.

Our first concern should be with understanding the place allotted to the penal code in the literary and doctrinal framework of the Rule. We have expounded elsewhere[1] how Benedict divided the Master's treatise (RM 12–14), keeping in its original place the part about penalties (RB 23–30) while postponing to a later section the part about satisfaction (RB 43–46). Neither of these two groups of chapters thus constituted is easy to connect with what surrounds it.

On the other hand, the Master's treatise was connected with the preceding expositions by strong and interesting ties. Coming immediately after the long chapter on the provosts (RM 11), it presented the penal sanctions as the continuation of the educative efforts previously employed by the officers of the monastery, the provosts and the abbot. Up to Chapter Ten, the Master had traced a program in which the abbot teaches and the brothers learn. In Chapter Eleven he indicated how this doctrine was to be inculcated at every moment by the provosts and put into practice by their men. It is to 'all that' that our author explicitly refers when he passes in Chapter Twelve to the question of excommunication.[2] It is for not having paid attention to the warnings and reprimands of his provosts that they report a disedifying brother to the abbot.[3] The sanctions which follow, do not have a simply disciplinary significance, therefore. Their motive and their aim are of the properly spiritual order. The 'cause of God' and 'the cause of the spirit' are at stake.[4] This is a matter of making the divine precepts assembled by the Rule, taught by the abbot, and recalled in vain by the provosts, pass over into the conduct of a negligent or recalcitrant brother.

Thus the Master's penal code prolongs the great doctrinal exposition which fills the Thema and the first ten chapters of the Rule. The Rule began with a solemn reminder of baptism; the *scola monasterii* has as its only purpose the realization of the demands of baptism and the ripening of its fruit.[5] The treatise on excommunication in its turn obviously refers to the sacramental discipline of the Church. As the monastery succeeds to the baptistery, so monastic penitence imitates and refines ecclesiastical penitence. In the first case, the relationship of the two institutions is one of both chronological succession and analogy.[6] Here analogy alone remains. But in both cases the monastery only perfects the work or operation of the *mater ecclesia*.

Baptism and penitence. These two sacraments, as we know, are so intimately connected that they lend their names to each other: baptism is the first penitence, and penitence is the baptism of tears. In the same way, to the rite of profession by which the monk commits himself to serve God in the monastery corresponds the rite of reconciliation, which terminates the penitence of the excommunicated brother. The Master took care to mark this correspondence by prescribing the same gestures for the end of each ceremony. Like the newly professed, the penitent is again placed by the abbot in the hands of his provosts;[7] like him also, he should wash the hands of the brothers before communion and implore their prayers.[8]

This latter feature is not absent from the Benedictine Rule, since a request for prayer figures in the ritual of reconciliation as well as in that of profession.[9] The resemblance is scarcely noticeable, however, and the others are entirely absent. In addition to this effacement of the likeness between the two rites, Benedict did not continue the visible connection which linked the Master's treatise on penitence to the body of the previous teaching. With Benedict, the penal code is not only separated from the chapter on the deans,[10] but also from the spiritual part, by the long section on the office.[11] Thus in the Benedictine Rule the penal question is entirely isolated from the spiritual whole to which it was so clearly joined in the other Rule.

This state of things, which was not willed for itself,[12] should not keep us from restoring all their force to the connections distorted by Benedict. In particular we should recover the continuity between the spiritual section and the chapters on repression established by the common theme of the struggle against evil. Not for nothing does the *Explicit* of the Master's spiritual part define it as a method for 'fleeing sin'.[13] This theme of the 'purification from vices and sins' is recalled at every moment, especially in the conclusion of the chapters on the abbot and on humility,[14] and it leads straight into the section on penitence. If the primordial purpose of the Rule is to ensure that all offence against God be avoided, then it should with the greatest care provide for the reparation of faults committed, so that they are not committed again.

The Master, by establishing so close a relationship between the treatise on excommunication and the abbot's doctrine enforced by the provosts, draws our attention to a remarkable trait: the lightness of the faults committed, and consequently the severity of the sanction punishing them. According to the nine typical admonitions which he puts in the mouth of the provosts,[15] our author apparently foresees as matter for excommunication such small offences as speaking without being questioned or too loudly, laughing easily or saying something funny, adopting a careless attitude. Even if the list contains some more serious faults, such as lying, oaths, anger, insults, it still surprises us by the importance which it gives to such peccadillos. No doubt the fact of falling again after many warnings can be rated as 'contumacy' or 'contempt', but it remains that the smallness of the initial matter seems disproportionate to so serious a penalty as excommunication.

To dissipate the astonishment that we feel, it is not enough to invoke the ecclesiastical parallel of 'excommunications' inflicted on clerics for minor infractions of canonical discipline.[16] These excommunications are simple sanctions which last for a set time, without requiring for their cessation that the guilty party submit to major penitence and be reconciled.[17] On the contrary, the Master and Benedict put the brother excommunicated 'from the oratory' in a dramatic isolation from which he cannot escape except by undergoing the humiliating procedures of public penitence and by submitting to a solemn rite of reconciliation. The copying of major ecclesiastical penitence is here evident.[18]

The monk can therefore be put under the ban of his community, 'delivered up to Satan', constrained to a true penance, for having spoken too loudly two or three times. The monastic rule, while imitating the Church's penitential discipline, has manifestly departed from it by its heightened severity. The failures for which it demands public penitence are among those which the Church has never considered other than light sins,[19] from which the Christian purifies himself every day by the recitation of the Lord's Prayer[20] and by good works.

This refinement of the common conscience, which came to regard apparently light faults as grave, was accompanied by an extreme rigor in fixing the time limits for repentance. Although a sinner in the Church can defer as long as he pleases, even waiting for the hour of death to ask for penance, the Master only gives the excommunciated monk three days before he is flogged and shown the door.[21] Although Benedict sets no time for action, he scarcely seems less in a hurry to obtain the submission of the guilty person. In the monastery the presence of a sick member cannot be tolerated for long, even when he has been designated as such and been segregated. He must make reparation as soon as possible or else decamp.

From the lightness of the grounds and the briefness of the delays, the rigor of this repressive discipline is obvious. However, we should add that the penitence is also very short and, on the whole, light. Normally, the Master seems to have envisaged only a duration of a few days, even a few hours.[22] If we reckon with this last fact, our general impression is that of a sort of miniaturization of canonical penitence. The nature of the faults penalized, the time allowed for satisfaction, the required expiation— everything is reduced to a very small scale. Thanks be to God, truly grave faults scarcely occur in the monastic milieu. Moral effort and zeal for holiness bear therefore on lighter offences, and repression becomes in its turn simpler and quicker. Only the rites of reconcilation remain at least as ample as those of the Church, especially with the Master.

Ecclesiastical penitence is not the only model to have inspired our authors. Before and above it, the norm of Scripture directed them. Of all the penal passages of the New Testament, the most important is no doubt Matthew 18:15–17, where the Lord prescribes first rebuking the guilty person privately, then before witnesses, and finally in the presence of the Church, before expelling him 'as a heathen and a publican'. Most monastic legislators refer explicitly or implicitly to this fundamental charter, although they are far from always following it point by point. One retains only the preliminary warnings,[23] another the final separation.[24] As early as the *Iudicia* of Pachomius, however, we find the complete procedure sketched out,[25] and Basil reproduced it more than once.[26] The Master and Benedict, in their turn, visibly sought to conform to it, both in regard to the first excommunication and the definitive exclusion of the relapsed brother.[27]

The Gospel of Matthew furnishes monastic discipline with another directive: that of 'cutting off' like an incurable member, the brother who causes scandal (Mt 5:29–30). This is one of the texts which establish most clearly, according to Basil, the duty of expelling impenitents from the brotherhood.[28] Directly or indirectly Benedict based himself on it as well when he invited the abbot to 'use the knife of amputation'.[29]

Finally the pauline epistles are rich in directions on penal matters: the appeal to 'take away the evil one' from the midst of the Church by 'delivering up the guilty one to Satan',[30] the invitation to 'console charitably' this latter once the community has 'rebuked him enough',[31] the order 'to 'withdraw' from the disobedient 'so that he may be ashamed',[32] the advice to 'rebuke sinners in front of all'.[33] Basil profited by almost all these suggestions,[34] and Benedict introduced many of them into his penal system. They constitute one of its novelties in relation to that of the Master.[35]

From this collection of New Testament texts one lesson appears quite clearly: the christian community should remove sinful members who refuse to listen to its voice and who gravely erode its holiness. In ecclesiastical language this putting aside is called excommunication. The term and the process are found among the monks, but with them things are less simple. The monastic community, being more compact than the ecclesiastical society, has not only one arm, but two: excommunication and expulsion. Excommunication puts the guilty person under the ban of the community, but it does not expel him from the monastery. When it has had no effect, the graver sanction remains, expulsion from the community.[36]

Thus the New Testament texts prescribing the rejection of serious obstinate sinners are susceptible of two distinct interpretations and two graduated applications in the monastic world. It is not always easy to discern, by the text cited which concrete application was envisaged by the legislator.[37] Benedict makes a clear distinction: from the same passage of the First Epistle to the Corinthians, he cuts out one phrase which he applies to excommunication,[38] and another which he takes to mean expulsion.[39] It is impossible to show more clearly the dichotomy which the monks introduced into the single penalty foreseen by Saint Paul.

Exclusion, in its turn, can either be revocable—'up to three times'[40]—or definitive. The triple possibility of return is allowed, by the Master and by Benedict by reason of the three preliminary warnings which Jesus prescribed according to the Gospel of Matthew.[41] This is clear with the

Master. Thus the merciful dispositions of the Gospel, which they had applied first at the beginning of the penal procedures,[42] are brought into play again by our authors at the stage of the ultimate sanctions. Monasticism has multiplied the chances of salvation for the sinner by profitably using its intense common life.

Complete exclusion, especially if definitive, can, however, seem incompatible with other evangelical texts prescribing indefinite pardon[43] or implying that no one is holy enough to 'throw a stone' at his fellow.[44] Voices were also raised, first among colonies of hermits, then among cenobites themselves, against superiors and communities which threw back into the world their monks who were sinners.[45] Yet no monastic rule refused itself this right of exclusion, set down in the New Testament and ratified by the tradition of the Church. This decision is all the more justified in that rejection by a monastic community does not mean deprivation of all means of salvation.[46]

By comparison with canonical penitence and with its New Testament sources, the monastic discipline of major penitence stands out therefore by its zeal in pursuing the least sins and by the multiplicity of its efforts to correct sinners. These two traits, the second of which is particularly stressed by Benedict,[47] are found again in the related field of secondary penalties: excommunication 'from the table', flogging, various humiliations, privations of food and drink.[48] There also, Benedict's tendency was to outdo the Master. His penalties are more numerous and especially, since his text is much shorter, more frequent. Their abstract formulation, the absence of motivation, the place they often occupy at the end of the chapter all give them a harsher aspect. At the same time Benedict loves to add preliminary warnings and subsequent sanctions so that he establishes strings of penalties.[49]

Although the Benedictine Rule is relatively severe, compared to its immediate source, it is not for all that the product of a late development. The strict repression of the smallest failings goes back to the origins of cenobitism. The Pachomian Rule already abounded in penal clauses no less numerous or less dry than Benedict's.[50]

These remarks bring us back again to the problem we posed at the beginning, our allergy to a repressive organization which has always charac-

terized cenobitism, and which Benedict in particular tends rather to re-in-
force. The causes of the malaise are many. The most evident is the evolution of a society in which civil equality and respect for the person make
unthinkable such punishments as public humiliations and flogging.

Another cause arises within the Church itself. Ecclesiastical penitence
of the first centuries, already in full decline by Benedict's time,[51] has
already long ago been replaced, as far as we are concerned, by the wholly
different system of private confession. But monastic penitence was based
on that outmoded discipline, as we have said. There is nothing astonishing therefore if Benedict's chapters on excommunication and public reconciliation leave us perplexed. The only things that speak to us are the
few allusions he makes to the secret avowal of bad thoughts and hidden
faults,[52] but we would be mistaken if we saw here sacramental confession,[53]
for, to use modern terms, they were only the spiritual therapy of *ascesis*
and direction.

Yet this difficulty relative to major penitence does not affect the whole
penal system of our rules. If the whole system is repugnant to us, it is for a
deeper spiritual reason. Perhaps the primary point of departure is found
in the interpretation of the evangelical law itself. Several times already, in
commenting upon the Prologue, the Instruments of good works, and the
chapter on silence, we have met this disconcerting fact: the importance attached by our Fathers to precepts which to us seem secondary, the care
with which they strove to eliminate from their lives ways of behaving
which seem to us hardly blameworthy. Here again we find these ways of
behaving, the idle word or laughing, punished with an astonishing severity. The least material negligence, the least moral slackness were regarded
as faults demanding reparation.

This rigorism of the ancient monks supposes an acute sense of sin. It
witnesses also to an extraordinary seriousness in the way of understanding
the Gospel: not one iota of this law will fail to be accomplished. Abstaining from much talking and from laughter is not only one of the particular
points on which to obey the word of Christ; it is also the whole expression of this basic seriousness, of this inflexible attention to the God who
commands and the God who judges.

Such intensity towards the elimination of sin and the accomplishment
of the divine will can seem to us almost inhuman. We may regret that it
leaves little place, apparently, to values dear to us, like liberty, spontane-

ity, joy. Yet, it has its grandeur, which calls into question the facile humanism in which we may be tempted to be complacent. The penitential section of our rules reminds us that monasticism is a way of penitence in the full sense of the word.

The monastic life was so basically penitential that the ancient Church considered it a substitute for canonical penitence.[54] As Benedict says, it should be a continual Lent,[55] perpetuating that annual forty-day period which prepares the penitents for the Easter reconciliation. This notion, combined with the authority of the New Testament,[56] can help us understand how the penitential discipline of our rules was bearable for the monks of that time. Was not the undergoing of its rigors a placing of oneself in the very axis of the whole monastic life, thus realizing in a paradoxical but profound way the vocation of the monk to humility and to conversion?

NOTES TO CHAPTER 11

1. See t. V, pp. 723–6 and 791.

2. RM 12.1: *In his omnibus supradictis.*

3. RM 12.2: *monitus* (cf. RM 11.41,47,50,54,63,66,69,75,81,85) *et correptus* (RM 11.95).

4. RM 11.95 and 98.

5. RM Th 1–25; Ths 45.

6. See our commentary on the Prologue.

7. RM 14.71; 89.28. This 'reconsigning' corresponds also to the point of departure in the penal procedure (RM 12,1–3), in which the provosts have the initiative.

8. RM 14.74–76; 89, 29–30.

9. RB 44.4; 58.23 (*ut orent pro eo*).

10. By making into a distinct chapter (RB 22) the Master's passage on the dormitory (RM 11.108–121). Also RB 21 and 23 are no longer set in relation to each other by the 'admonitions' of the provosts-deans (see above, n. 3).

11. RB 8–20.

12. See t. V, p. 384 for the reasons which Benedict had in placing the liturgical section immediately after the spiritual part. The analogy of RB 19.1–2 with the first degree of humility is striking. Did not Benedict choose to locate the office, the privileged place for attention to God, as close as possible to the doctrinal considerations which underlie such an attitude?

13. RM 10.123.

14. RM 2.40 = RB 2.40; RM 10.91 = RB 7.70. Cf. RM 11.32–34, 40, etc..

15. RM 11.40–90.

16. See for example Council of Vannes (465), can. 14: seven days without communion for having missed a morning office: *Statuta Ecclesiae antiqua* 74–75 (excommunication for having sworn by creatures or sung at a meal).

17. See B. Poschmann, 'Penance and the Anointing of the Sick', (E.T. New York: Herder and Herder, 1964) p. 117. These sanctions correspond in the Master and Benedict, to the scattered penalties sometimes called 'excommunications' (see t. V, p. 763–88) in a weakened sense. A first example is the excommunication 'from the table, not from the oratory' (RM 13.60, etc.; RB 24.3, etc.).

18. See in particular our 'Scholies', pp. 156 and 273–5.

19. See for example Gregory, *Dial.* 4.41: 'Of small and very little sins . . . such as continuous idle talk, immoderate laughter . . .'.

20. Augustine, *Serm.* 17.5. (cf. RB 13.12–13). Cf. A.-M. La Bonnardière, 'Pénitence et réconciliation des pénitents d'après S. Augustin', in REA 13 (1967) 31–53 and 249–283 (specially pp. 49–53); 14 (1968) 181–204.

21. RM 13.68–73.

22. RM 14.20–26. Compare the *diuturna excommunicatio* of RM 82.26–27.

23. Augustine, *Ordo mon.* 10; *Praec.* 4.7–10. In these two texts the final sanction remains indeterminate.

24. Cassian, *Inst.* 2.16 (this does not refer to Mt 18:17, but to 1 Co 5:5). According to Basil, *Ep.* 199.22 this 'exclusion from prayers' with 'tears at the door of the church', is the first and more severe of the four degrees of the penitence imposed on fornicators.

25. Pachomius, *Iud.* 1 and 4 [E.T. CS46:175–9]. *Iud.* 3,6,7,8,10, are less clear but may refer to the same system. Elsewhere the *Iudicia* put degradation (*Iud.* 2: cf. 9 and 11) or being sent to the infirmary (*Iud.* 5; cf. 12) after the warnings. The three other collections do not speak of warnings or of 'separation'. Their penal system is different and does not seem to refer back to the Gospel.

26. Basil, *Reg.* 16 = *Short Rules* 3; *Reg.* 122 = *Short Rules* 47; *Short Rules* 232 and 293 (cf. *Long Rules* 36: a brother leaves a sinful community). In addition, we find the following texts cited by themselves: Mt 18:15 (*Short Rules* 178; lacking in *Reg.* 178), Mt 18:16 (*Long Rules* 7.3; deformed in *Reg.* 3) and Mt 18:17 (see below note 37).

27. RM 12.1–5 and RB 23.1–4; RM 64.1–4 and RB 29.1–3.

28. Basil, *Reg.* 26 = *Short Rules* 7; *Reg.* 76 = *Short Rules* 44; *Reg.* 175 = *Short Rules* 57; *Long Rules* 28.1.

29. RB 28.6.

30. 1 Co 5:2–13 (compare 1 Co 5:5 and 1 Tm 1:20). See below, notes 38–39.

31. 2 Co 2:6–8. The first verse is cited by Basil, *Reg.* 3 = *Long Rules* 7.3; *Reg.* 16 = *Short Rules* 3; *Reg.* 175 = *Short Rules* 57; the last verses are cited by RB 27.3–4.

32. 2 Th 3:6 (Basil, *Reg.* 28 = *Short Rules* 9; *Long Rules* 14; *Short Rules* 20); 2 Th 3:14–15 (Basil, *Reg.* 16 = *Short Rules* 3; *Reg.* 42 = *Short Rules* 25; *Reg.* 147 = *Short Rules* 53; *Long Rules* 14, without parallel in *Reg.* 7; in *Reg.* 16, Rufinus understood it as a matter of a separation *ad mensam*, no doubt by confusing *entrapè* with *en trapeza*).

33. 1 Tm 5:20 (Basil, *Long Rules* 28.1; RB 48.20 and 70.3; cf. Augustine, *Praec.* 4.9 and RB 23.3).

34. Except apparently 2 Co 2:7–8 (see above, note 31).

35. See t. V, pp. 747–50.

36. Basil, *Reg.* 76 = *Short Rules* 44, clearly distinguishes 'excommunication' (*aphorismos*) from subsequent 'cutting off' (*apokoptesthô*). The first is decreed without scriptural justification and is accompanied by fasting (*asitia*); the second is based on Mt 5:29–30 (above, note 28). See also *Long Rules* 51 (*aphorismos* alone, with a possible allusion to 2 Th 3:14, as in *Reg.* 122 = *Short Rules* 47, where the verb *anamignusthai* re-appears; but specially *Reg.* 71 = *Short Rules* 39 and Long Rules* 29, this last moreover uses the verb *katamignusthai*).

37. Thus for the citations of Mt 18:17 in Basil. To the four texts cited at the beginning of note 26, add *Reg.* 28 = *Short Rules* 9; *Reg.* 73 = *Short Rules* 41; *Long Rules* 36 (complete separation); *Short Rules* 261 (moral condemnation).

38. 1 Co 5:5, cited by RB 25.4. Cf. Basil, *Reg.* 77 = *Short Rules* 164.

39. 1 Co 5:13, cited by RB 28.6. Cf. Basil, *Reg.* 30 = *Short Rules* 86; *Long Rules* 47 (expulsion); *Short Rules* 155 and 281 (expulsion). The analogous phrase of 1 Co 5:2 is cited by Basil, *Reg.* 122 = *Short Rules* 47; *Long Rules* 28,1 (expulsion); *Short Rules* 84 (expulsion) and 293.

40. RM 64.1; RB 29.3.

41. See RM 64.4. Cf. our article '*Per ducatum evangelii.* La Règle de saint Benoît et l'Évangile', in *Coll. Cist.*, 35 (1973) 186–98, specially pp. 193–4.

42. RM 12.1–5 and RB 23.1–4 (above, note 27).

43. Mt 18:21–22 (seems instead to concern private pardon).

44. Jn 8:7 (exclusion, a spiritual death, is like being stoned).

45. See our article 'L'anecdote pachômienne du *Vaticanus graecus* 2091. Son origine et ses sources', in RHS 49 (1973) 401–19.

46. Even if one sees the world as the devil's city (RM 88.14).

47. See t. V, pp. 724–726, 737–745, 756–761. The progressive reconciliation described in RB 44 makes us think of the degrees of penitence enumerated by Basil, *Ep.* 199.22; Council of Nicea (325), *can.* 11; Council of Arles (443–452), *can.* 10–11; Felix III, *Ep.* 7 (488); PL 58: 925d–926a.

48. See above, note 17. See t. V, pp. 826–828 for flogging, a punishment inflicted on clerics as well as on monks.

49. Cf. t. V, pp. 787–8.

50. The *Regula Pachomii* is half as long as RB, and has about fifty penal clauses in it, about twice as many as RB.

51. See for example C. Vogel, *La discipline pénitentielle en Gaule des origines à la fin du VIIe siècle* (Paris, 1952) pp. 116–118.

52. RB 4.50; RM 10.61–65 = RB 7.44–48; RB 46.5–6. See also RM 15 and 80.

53. The abbot or *senior* to whom one confessed was not necessarily a priest; moreover the Church then knew only one type of sacramental penitence: public penitence, with its substitute *in articulo mortis.* See B. Poschmann, (above, n. 17). E.T. pp. 120–121 on confession-direction.

54. See C. Vogel, (above, n. 51), pp. 132–8; B. Poschmann, E.T. p. 113–16.

55. RB 49.1.

56. See the evangelical and pauline texts analyzed above. If the penitential discipline of the ancient Church has been profoundly transformed, these scriptural texts, which constitute the other major branch of monastic penitence, remain a question for us today.

Chapter XII

OFFICIAL SERVICE AND MUTUAL SERVICE
(RB 31–41)

F OOD IS THE CHIEF OBJECT of this section, which begins with the directory for the cellarer and ends with the treatise on fasting. The cellarer is occupied mostly, if not exclusively, with the food storeroom and the wine cellar, with the kitchen and eating utensils. His colleagues, the guardians of the tools and the other objects, are only mentioned later, by association of ideas.[1] With the weekly kitchen servers the theme of meals soon returns again, and runs from the chapter on reading at table through the three chapters on food, drink, and fasting. If the series has some interruptions, these are clearly connected with the chapters about meals if we examine even slightly the Master's texts which are their source. Renunciation of goods, which Benedict completes by the distribution of what is necessary, was prescribed by the Master in connection with the cellarer's office;[2] the sick, the old, and children were treated by the Master in connection with the hour for meals.

Such a down-to-earth subject should not offer much scope to a commentary like ours. But even at first reading we notice a good number of spiritual directives whose recurrence and convergence give this section a sort of higher unity independent of the theme of food. To take into consideration the various needs and infirmities,[3] to be careful not only of things but also of persons, especially the weakest,[4] to spare another and to forbid oneself every sadness, trouble, or murmuring,[5] to remain humble,[6] to serve in charity and to work for the 'reward':[7] these repeated touches, and others like them, constantly changed the practical discourse into a moral exhortation.

Compared with the Master, Benedict gives few specific regulations. He seems to worry less about the details of the actions to be performed than to state the spirit and the way in which they should be done.[8] The ordering of works and rites to which his predecessor was specially attached gives way with him to a dominant preoccupation with the good of souls. Partly under the influence of Augustine, Benedict is interested in their individual differences,[9] their inmost feelings,[10] and their mutual relationships.[11] We have here a presentiment of what will become manifest at the end of the Rule in the chapter 'On the Order of the Congregation' and in the Appendix, in the chapters on obedience in impossible things, and on good zeal.[12]

This section demands our attention first of all then, because it is full of humanity. The long chapter on the cellarer which introduces it, is a good example of this. Benedict draws the moral portrait of this personage with a certain partiality. Perhaps he already sees him as more than the one responsible for the food, an officer of more scope.[13] It might also be that the location of this chapter, the first dedicated to a function of this kind, moved him to make the cellarer a sort of prototype for all the officers charged with material goods.[14] In any case, Benedict took a remarkable interest in this *cellararius*. The directory he writes for him surpasses in length that for the abbot at the end of the Rule, which it so much resembles. And these directives do not only insist, as did the Master, on the care of objects and subordination to the abbot, but also, in a new way, on the humility and goodness of which the cellarer should give proof in his relations with the brothers, on his solicitude and responsibility for the sick, children, guests, and the poor, and finally on the help and precautions by which he himself should benefit in order to keep his soul in peace. In regard to this first department chief, the model for the others, Benedict recommends all that he was to inculcate in the following chapters until the end of the Rule: attention to fraternal relationships, mercy towards the weak and the wretched, respect for those who serve, so that drudgery does not render their self-sacrifice fruitless.

It is not enough to grasp the psychological and moral content of this section, however. On a deeper level it offers great interest in understanding the cenobitic life and its structures. Reserving to specific studies the question of renunciation of goods and of *ascesis* in food,[15] we will reflect here on the meaning of *service* and its relations with some connected data: the refusal of individual property, the distribution of what is necessary within the community, largess outside, and obedience.

'To serve' is indeed the first watchword to emerge from these pages. The two latin forms in which it appears—*ministrare* and *servire*, with their derivatives—each translates a different greek verb in the two great pauline texts to which Benedict himself refers explicitly or implicitly. *Ministrare* (*diakonein*) is the official service of the deacon which our Rule evokes in relationship to the cellarer.[16] *Servire* (*douleuein*) is voluntary and spontaneous servitude, the mutual service of Christians in charity, to which Benedict alludes in characterizing the task of the weekly servers.[17] Their service, moreover, is not only 'mutual' and 'by rotation', but also as regulated and official as that of the cellarer-deacon. Therefore we are not surprised that Benedict occasionally calls it a 'ministry'.[18]

'They who have ministered well gain for themselves a good standing' (1 Tm 3:13); 'Serve one another mutually in charity' (Ga 5:13). These are the two scriptural roots of this notion of service which defines, for Benedict, the functions of the cellarer, the weekly servers, the infirmarian, and, we could add, the guest-house cooks[19] and all the other department chiefs in the monastery.

Yet these two words of Saint Paul evoke two New Testament scenes which were probably present in Benedict's mind. To speak of the deacon's ministry is to recall the institution of deacons reported in chapter six of Acts. Although Benedict seems to think of this episode more specifically in the chapter on the deans than here,[20] it is significant that the original task of the first deacons in Jerusalem was the very one over which the cellarer presides: 'the service of tables'.[21]

On the other hand, the recommendation to 'serve one another in charity' makes us think of the foot washing at the Last Supper. Before and after Jesus' act, explicit words relate the act to the charity with which he loved his disciples, and they are invited to act in the same way towards one another, in the same spirit.[22] We note that the washing of feet is exactly the rite by which the hebdomadaries finish their week, according to both Benedict and Cassian.[23] Thus their service appears as the imitation of Christ and obedience to his commandment.

The institution of the first deacons and the Last Supper are then the two backdrops which appear behind the persons of the cellarer and the

weekly servers. But Acts and the Gospel do not illustrate only the two
chapters devoted to these officers. The Book of Acts is also represented—
this time in the form of explicit citations—in the two little chapters dealing with renunciation of goods and the distribution of what is necessary.
The Gospel furnishes the chapter on the sick with its double initial motivation, to which can be added several allusions in the treatise on the cellarer. Let us look at all this more closely.

Benedict, following Augustine, establishes the community of goods and
the distribution of what is necessary 'to each according to his needs' on
the example of the primitive Church.[24] This time it is chapter four, not
chapter six, we are dealing with. The motive behind the institution of
deacons (Ac 6:1–6) was the distress of certain widows not sufficiently provided for. But this situation, in which some members of the community,
not the whole community, were in need was preceded by a period when
all the faithful, according to Luke's account, had 'laid down their goods at
the feet of the apostles', and received from them what was necessary,
'each one according to his needs' (Ac 4:34–35). This original state of affairs lives again in the monasteries: like the apostles, the abbot receives
and keeps the goods pooled by the brothers. He also presides over the distribution of what is necessary, watching that all receive not an equal quan-
tity, abstractly determined by an arithmetical division, but what pertains
to each person and his real needs.

This picture of the first christian community, so evidently proposed by
these two little chapters of Benedict's, gives way in the chapter on the
sick to the scene of the last judgment according to St Matthew. There
Christ declares: 'I was sick, and you visited me . . . . What you have
done to one of these littlest ones, you have done to me'.[25] But the sick
are not the only 'little ones' to whom Christ has bound himself. Guests
are in the same category, as are the needy of any kind. Benedict was to
recall this expressly at the beginning of the chapter 'On receiving
guests',[26] but he seems to have remembered it already in recommending
that the cellarer 'take care of the sick, the children, the guests and the
poor with all his solicitude, knowing for sure that he will have to render
an account for all these persons on the day of judgment'.[27] Moreover, he
cites to the same cellarer Jesus' word about 'those who scandalize one of
these little ones'.[28]

With these words of the Gospel we have apparently just about completed the review of the New Testament passages to which the Rule refers in this section about service.[29] It remains for us to scrutinize these texts and draw them together, setting forth their implications and relationships. Nothing will help us penetrate further into the meaning of the multiform service regulated by Benedict, and of the cenobitic life itself.

Considered apart from their scriptural origins, the ministry of the cellarer-deacon and the 'mutual service of brothers in charity' are quite different things. The deacon has an official, permanent function, which he holds from the Church and fulfils in the name of the Church. On the contrary, when Christians serve each other mutually, they are indeed obeying a precept of the Lord, but in an informal and intermittent way, in the spontaneity of their heart and each according to his own grace.[30] Moreover, the deacon's ministry has a set object: to administer the goods of the Church and to use them to help certain particular needs, either those of the widows, at the origins of the institution or, more broadly, various categories of needy persons. In mutual service this specificness is lacking. Each one serves his brother according to circumstances and with his own resources, according to the infinite variety of concrete situations and the appeals of charity.

When we pass from this scriptural and ecclesial model to its monastic application, several differences appear. First of all, as we remarked when speaking of the vocabulary, the 'mutual service in charity' tends to become organized and institutionalized. When Benedict alludes to St Paul's word, he is speaking of the weekly servers in the kitchen. Although he, unlike the Master, does not state the modalities of this weekly rotation precisely, he too is obviously thinking of an obligatory and organized turn from which 'no one should be excused'.

Are these weeks of regulated service a pure creation of monastic milieu, suggested perhaps by some secular institutions?[31] We cannot help relating them to the weekly duty of the classes of Levites in the service of the Temple as glimpsed in a passage of Chronicles.[32] The first monastic text which specifically mentions 'table service by turns each week' comes from the pen of the biblist Jerome and it resembles this page from Chronicles.[33] Christian cenobites might have been inspired here as elsewhere by a biblical precedent, and this trait might be among those which assimilate the monastery to the Temple, as well as to other figures of the Church.[34]

But this scriptural counterpart of the institution does not hinder it from specifying in an unexpected way the Apostle's general invitation 'to serve each other in charity'. To us, this is what matters at the moment. From an indeterminate piece of advice whose application is left to the grace and good will of each person, cenobitism has drawn a precise regulation which uniformly constrains all members of the community. Without excluding other more spontaneous forms of service,[35] 'cenobites serve each other' essentially in this obligatory and regulated tour of duty.

The evolution we are analyzing is entirely like that which leads from St Paul's words, 'Pray without ceasing', to the punctual, communitarian celebration of the seven offices by day and one at night.[36] In each case we pass from a piece of indefinite New Testament instruction to a specific observance which makes it concrete. We can only admire the will to obey the word of God which inspires such observances. Yet this obedience attains its end only if the application is made with constant and conscious reference to the principle, if the monks who celebrate the office and serve at table always remember the words 'Pray without ceasing' and 'Serve mutually in charity'. Never should these counsels lose their universality for them, their inspiring and creative power, their flexibility and their indefinitely urgent force. While these counsels are incarnated in observances, they should also remain operative in the whole of life.

If the pauline principle of mutual service is made singularly specific in our Rule, the diaconal ministry of the cellarer, on the contrary, finds there a sort of enlargement and generalization. Instead of succoring the needs of only some, it extends to all the members of the community. Of course, Benedict recommends particularly to the cellarer 'the sick, the children, the guests and the poor',[37] but beyond these special needs, the cellarer must be 'like a father to the whole community'. Indeed he must feed all the brothers. None of them can provide for his own subsistence. All of them are voluntarily deprived, without personal resources, entirely dependent on the community which they make live and which makes them live.

The monastic society which the cellarer serves is, therefore, less the image of the Church at the moment of the deacons' institution (Ac 6:1–6) than of the wholly primitive Church described in the preceding chapters of Acts. The needy to be provided for are not only widows and other underprivileged persons, but all members of the community without exception. Monasticism, surmounting the distinction between the haves and have-nots supposed by the affair of the widows, returns to the original state of things, where no one called anything his own, where all was held in common and distributed to each according to his needs. Not by chance does Benedict, following the Master, legislate on renunciation of goods and the distribution of what is necessary in the prolongation of his chapter on the cellarer. Indeed, the cellarer's ministry implies this perfect community of goods and this complete dependence of everyone on the monastery.

Such a situation also explains the extreme attention given by Benedict to the relation of the cellarer with the brothers. In a society where money is of no use each person is literally at the others' mercy. The lot of the individual depends on the good will of his neighbor, and specially of those who hold some office. When the impersonal medium of money is absent, everything becomes an affair of direct relations between persons. From this arises the vital role of charity in the daily life of such a society as well as in its principle. The primitive Church had already experienced it: 'murmuring' is quick to arise when one must rely on the zeal and impartiality of another for the satisfaction of one's needs.[38] Every day the members of the community and those in charge must give proof that all are effectively but one heart and one soul as at the beginning.[39]

This is why Benedict insists so much that the cellarer show himself humble, affable, and good. This officer is, in regard to all the brothers, in the same position of superiority as is the infirmarian in regard to the sick or the porter to the poor. Healthy or sick, strong or weak, able or disabled, all are radically in a situation of subjection and impotence. All are 'little ones' whom he must keep from 'irritating' by making them feel their dependence.[40] Reciprocally however, the cellarer cannot use what he holds to obtain for himself the least thing, even the most indispensable aid.[41] In his turn he must ask, and another must give to him. In the monastery everyone is in the happy necessity of obtaining graciously from another everything he lacks.

Renunciation of goods, therefore does not only suppose charity; it demands it. As an effect and a sign of union of hearts, it deprives those who

embrace it of the protecting screen of possessions, and hands them over
defenceless to each other. No more intermediate objects or services. The
relationship is an immediate one of heart to heart. The objectivity of exchanges, the anonymity of buying and selling gives way to personal relations which should be those of pure charity.

Still, Benedict does admit that the monk may manifest his needs.[42] For
him dispossession does not go so far as to forbid asking for oneself, though
this was the heroic norm of Basil, the Egyptian cenobites described by Jerome, and still, at the beginning of the sixth century, of Fulgentius.[43] According to this primitive rule the monk so renounced himself that he left
to those in charge of the community the care of discovering his needs and
satisfying them. Then the abandonment is total; each one commits himself to the discretion of God and his representatives, trusting in the Providence of the one and the clear-sighted charity of the others.

But the cenobite gives up not only the right to use freely the goods of
this world or even to ask things for himself. One of the most precious
things he renounces is the power to give. Since he no longer has
anything of his own, he may not give alms according to his heart's in-
clination. The charity which made him put his goods and energy at the
disposal of his brothers no longer allows him to do works of charity personally to those outside the monastery.[44] This great christian work of
mercy he can exercise only indirectly and impersonally, corporately and
by delegation, specifically, through the hands of the cellarer and other officers.[45]

In this task of almsgiving the cellarer finds again the primitive function
of his ecclesial prototype, the deacon. But he exercises it in a particular
form, as the agent of a society of renunciants who furnish by their goods
and labor what he gives to the poor, without themselves being the witnesses
or agents of this gift. Deprived of this commerce with the misery of the
world, the brothers run a certain risk of losing sight of it or of perceiving it
in an unrealistic way. Hardness, dryness, and depersonalization in regard
with the wretched are risks inherent in the situation of men who have
nothing further to give because they have abandoned all. The Master,
shrewd educator that he was, seems to have thought of this when he offered each brother the possibility of personal sacrifices destined for the
poor.[46] We do not see why in our time visible connections of this sort

could not be established between the personal renunciations of the monks and the collective generosity of the monastery.

Analogous remarks can be made about the relationships of the monk with the sick of his community and with the guests which it receives. In regard to these two categories Benedict cites the words of Christ in the scene of the last judgment: 'I was sick and you visited me . . . . I was a stranger and you took me in.' With the Master, help to both these groups was still open to everyone: 'the brothers should vie with one another in visiting, comforting and serving the sick brothers', and the guests had as guardians two brothers who changed each week.[47] With Benedict, as already with Augustine, the care of the sick was reserved to an infirmarian, and permanent officers also took care of guests. Christ's words are directly addressed therefore only to some brothers who specialize in these tasks. Such a specialization is indeed a guarantee of seriousness and efficiency in the service of these persons, but here again cenobitic organization places official machinery between the monk and the needs of his neighbor. As a result, the majority of the brothers may stand at some distance from the suffering Christ.

Moreover, we find here again what we noted in regard to the kitchen service: the Word of God is enclosed, as it were, in the institution it raised up. The admirable impetus of obedience to the divine precept forged a rite, an observance, an organization which should ensure the perfect and perpetual execution of the precept within the monastic community. But the institutional form which was created also enclosed the word of life as much as it incarnated it. Like the choral office and 'Pray without ceasing', like the weekly service and 'Serve each other mutually in charity', the statutes of the Rule on the care of the sick and of guests cannot rob the Lord's words of their universal resonance or of their enduring leavening power. Beyond and beside the apparatus which assures their regular execution, they should still be heard by every person and they should make every heart restless.

'Whatever you have done for one of these little ones, you have done it for me'. The scene of judgment which we have just heard evoked in regard to the sick and the guests, should, to be concluded, be related to the foot-washing. This latter, we remember, is given as the model for hebdomadaries.[48] In one citation Christ reveals his mysterious presence in all human distress; in the other he shows himself the servant of men, who provides for their needs. In the one he suffers and receives; in the other he acts and gives. In the judgment scene, Christ is *he who is served* in the person of the needy; in the foot-washing, he makes himself *the one who serves*, the model of the servant.

These two scenes therefore define two aspects of christian service and its relationship to Christ. Jesus is both he whom we serve and the model for our service. In the sick, the guests, the poor, and needy persons of every kind—and each monk, as we have said, is radically a needy person by his profession—it is Christ we serve. In doing this, however, we also imitate Christ in his earthly life, Christ, who did not come to be served, but to serve and to give his life as a ransom for many.[49]

It is the same with service therefore as with obedience. 'He who hears you, hears me': to obey a superior is to *obey Christ*. But by doing this we also obey *as Christ did*. 'I have not come to do my own will but the will of him who sent me'.[50] In regard to both service and obedience, Christ is the model of our actions and the person to whom they are addressed. From these two complementary points of view spring forth endless stimulations to obey and to serve.

In the line of obedience, the figure of Christ to whom our actions are directed is that of the Lord who commands through superiors. In the line of service, he is the universal brother and the man of sorrows who suffers in his littlest ones. Jesus is our example of obedience by his attitude towards his Father; he is the model for our service by his attitude towards men.[51] And the will of his Father, which he obeys, is specifically that he serve men by loving them and giving his life for them. Thus obedience and service combine to give the monk the full experience of Christ.

NOTES TO CHAPTER 12

1. At least in the Master, for Benedict bestows on them besides a similarity to the weekly servers (cf. RB 32.3 and 35.10–11).
2. In addition, renunciation of goods and holding things in common lead in some way to the gift of self in mutual service, while the distribution of what is necessary is prolonged in the chapters on food and drink.
3. RB 34.2; 37.2–3; 40.3. Cf. RB 35.3 and 39.1.
4. RB 31.3,9,15; 36.1,6,10 (*cura*).

5. Sadness: RB 31.6–7,19; 34.3; 35.3; 36.4. Perturbation: RB 31.19; 41.2. Murmuring: RB 34.5; 35.13 (cf. 38.10); 40.8–9; 41.5.

6. RB 31.7 and 13 (*humilitas*); 34.4 (*humilietur*) 38.2 (*elatio*).

7. Service: RB 31.8; 35.1,6; 36.1,4,7,10. *Merces*: 35.2; 36.5; 40.4.

8. See t. VI, pp. 1237–9; *La Communauté et l'Abbé*, pp. 310–12; 457–9; 516–18.

9. RB 34.1–5 (Ac 4:35); 40.1 (1 Co 7:7).

10. See above, notes 5–7.

11. RB 31.6–7,13–14,16–19; 34.3–5; 36.1–5.

12. *La Communauté et l'Abbé*, pp. 322 and 438–503.

13. *La Communauté et l'Abbé* 310–11 and 314. Cf. RB 31.3–5 and 15: the abbot determines how far the cellarer's domain extends; his province seems therefore to go beyond the cellar, as that of the *oeconomus* in Jerome, *Ep.* 22.35.6, and Cassian *Inst.* 4.6 (clothing) and 10.20 (work) goes beyond meals (*Inst.* 4.18 and 20; 5.40.1). Similarly, the *cellarius* or *custos cellarii* of the *Reg. Orientalis* 25 keeps the clothing, tools, etc. See also Horsiesius, *Lib.* 26 (Boon, p. 127,5–6).

14. Cf. Basil, *Reg.* 112 = *Short Rules* 148; *Short Rules* 156.

15. See our later chapters on RB 33 and 39–41.

16. RB 31.8, citing 1 Tm 3:13 (cf. RB 64.21). See already *Reg. IV Patr.* 3.26–27.

17. RB 35.6 (*sub caritate invicem serviant*): cf. Ga 5:13 (*per caritatem servite invicem*).

18. RB 35.10 and 38.6 (cf. t. VI, pp. 1044–1045). Moreover it is not sure that *ministerium* and *ministrare* always connote an official function. With the Master, *ministerium* and *servitium* seem interchangeable (cf. RM 23.53 and 27.40; 31.2–3).

19. RB 53.18.

20. Cf. RB 21.1 (Ac 6:3).

21. Ac 6:2. This service, like that of the kitchen, is carried out by the hebdomadaries, but under the control of the cellarer, who is permanently in charge of the job. Moreover, the text of Acts should doubtless be understood in a broad sense, closer to the cellarer's function than to that of the weekly servers.

22. Jn 13:1,14–15,34–35.

23. RB 35.9; Cassian, *Inst.* 4.19.2 (express reference). Cf. t. VI, pp. 990–3 and 1014.

24. RB 33.6 (Ac 4:32); 34.1 (Ac 4:35).

25. RB 36.1–3 (Mt 25:36 and 40).

26. RB 53.1 (Mt 25:35). Cf. RB 53.7 and 15.

27. RB 31.9. Formally the last words echo Mt 12:36 but the whole phrase supposes Mt 25:31–46.

28. RB 31.16 (Mt 18:6).

29. RB 37.1 appeals only to 'nature'. Also, it does not deal directly with service.

30. Although the foot washing, at least as a rite of hospitality, seems like a strict obligation which should be carried out literally (see t. VI, p. 1265, n. 82).

31. Herwegen, who is fond of these connections, points out none here.

32. 2 Ch 23:8: *Levitae . . . veniebant per ordinem sabbati cum his qui impleverant sabbatum et egressuri erant, siquidem Ioiada pontifex non dimiserat abire turmas, quae sibi per singulas ebdomadas succedere consueverant.* This last proposition seems to be Jerome's gloss. It is lacking in the Hebrew and Greek, which stop at 'classes' (*turmas* = *ephèmerias*). On these latter, see 1 Ch 23.6 (levites) and 1 Ch 24.19; Lk 1:5,8 (priests). *Ephèmereutai* is the name given to kitchen servers and refectory servers by Palladius, *Hist. Laus.* 32.11 (cf. 61.6).

33. Jerome, *Ep.* 22.35.4: *mensas quibus per singulas ebdomadas vicissim ministrant.* Cf. *Praef. Reg. Pach.* 2: *ut . . . in ebdomadarum ministerio sibi succedant per ordinem.*

34. See our article 'Le monastère, Église du Christ', in *Studia Anselmiana*, 42 (Rome, 1957)

25–46. Note that the weekly change is made in accordance with 2 Ch 23:8, on the sabbath day. Cf. RB 35.7–11.

35. Cassian, *Inst.* 4.19.1; 4.20; 4.30.4 (cf. *Conf.* 20.1.3).

36. 1 Th 5:17: RB 16.1–5 (see our previous commentary).

37. RB 31.9. This phrase refers to Mt 25:31–46 (above, n. 27), a text of general significance, not to those which concern the deacons in a special way.

38. Ac 6:1. Still it deals with the later situation in which only the widows are involved.

39. Ac 4:32. Cf. Augustine, *Praec.* 1.2.

40. RB 31.16 (Mt 18:6).

41. RB 31.17.

42. RB 31.7 (cf. 31.13); 33.5 and note. Cf. Caesarius, *Reg. virg.* 42.

43. Basil, *Reg.* 91,92,94 = *Short Rules* 131,132,135; Jerome, *Ep.* 22.35.6; Ferrandus, *Vita Fulg.* 52 (t. II, p. 677).

44. Basil, *Reg.* 98,99,186 = *Short Rules* 100,87,91 (cf. *Short Rules* 302).

45. RM 16.34–37 and 27.49–51; RB 31.9 (cf. 53.15; 55.9; 66.3).

46. RM 27.47–51.

47. RM 70 and 79. There is no trace of an infirmarian in the Master, though C. Gindele, 'Zur Frühgeschichte klösterlichen Krankendienstes', in *SMGBO* 84 (1973) 451–8, thinks he has found one.

48. Mt 25:31–46 (RB 31.9, etc.); Jn 13:1–17 (RB 35.9).

49. Mt 20:28.

50. Lk 10:16; Jn 6:38. See our commentary on RB 5, above.

51. Not in an exclusive sense, of course, for he also obeys man and serves his Father.

Chapter XIII

THE RENUNCIATION OF PROPERTY

(RB 33)

HERE AS ELSEWHERE,[1] Benedict condemns property dryly and vigorously. His purpose seems more practical than doctrinal: he is concerned with extirpating this 'vice', not discoursing upon it. The only motivation he gives is itself more juridical than spiritual: the prohibition of ownership is based on dispossession of self, that is, on the subjection of the monk to the abbot.[2] Benedict has recourse to Scripture only late and soberly, citing two short phrases of Acts.[3]

This theoretical motivation and scriptural illustration are of great interest, however dry they may seem, as we shall discover. Yet it is difficult to grasp their full significance, if we do not bear in mind the developments of the doctrinal tradition which is here condensed. Benedict depends especially on the Master, Cassian, and Augustine in this matter of renunciation of goods.[4] It is important therefore to throw light on what little he tells us, by examining what these authors taught.

The Master's considerations on renunciation of goods are far from presenting the same orderly aspect as do his expositions on obedience,[5] but nonetheless his method of exposition is quite similar in both cases. It consists of presenting the virtue under discussion in a progressive way, setting out markers which little by little guide the reader towards the fullness of his teaching.

In the matter of obedience, it will be remembered, the Master first of all established, in his commentary on the third petition of the Our Father, the need to do the will of God, and to that end, not to do one's own will.[6]

Then he showed that the will of God is signified to the faithful and to the monks by their respective 'teachers', the bishops and abbots; from this it follows that we must submit ourselves to these teachers.[7] Finally, a general exposition, twice repeated, describes the qualities of obedience and celebrates its greatness.[8]

In regard to renunciation of goods we see appear successively three themes which develop by successive touches throughout the Rule and converge in two formal treatises at its end. However, these themes are far from impressing themselves equally upon our attention.

The first and most evident theme is that of the daily bread which God gives his servants. This begins with the commentary on the fourth petition of the Lord's Prayer, that is, just after the first foundation of the doctrine of obedience and in explicit relationship with it: if we do the will of God, we are justified in asking him for 'our daily bread', just as workers expect a salary (*merces*) from their employer and slaves receive from their master the ration of food which enables them to live (*annona*).[9] The theme, thus rooted in the Lord's Prayer, soon develops into a series of exhortations, the first very short,[10] the others rather more extensive,[11] to expect everything from Divine Providence. Since God thinks of us, our primary concern, indeed our only concern, should be to 'seek the kingdom and its justice', as the Gospel says.[12] All our thoughts should be turned towards the care of our soul and its eternal destiny, not towards things necessary for the present life, which God will surely obtain for us.

This doctrine on Providence appears to have no relationship with renunciation of goods, but in reality it is its primary foundation. We see it clearly when the Master in Chapter 82 undertakes to write his first treatise on the question. A solemn exordium at the beginning repeats the theme of indifference to the goods of this world and of exclusive preoccupation with the kingdom: 'All these things shall be added to you'.[13] On this base the Master then places the demand for renunciation of goods: 'Therefore since the Lord provides us with all these necessities and it is the concern of the abbot alone, with God, to supply everything, why should the disciple dare to do or to have or to demand anything for himself?'[14] Other arguments and scriptural texts can be invoked in support,[15] but the former is indeed the principal one, as is shown by its repetition at the end of the paragraph: because each brother is sure to receive everything necessary, he has no need to possess anything of his own.[16] Renunciation of goods is chiefly a corollary of faith in Providence.

Yet this passage of Chapter 82 also appeals to the solicitude *of the abbot*, as the reader will have noted. The abbot functions as mediator between the God who is Providence, and his servants. In the name of the Lord, he provides for the upkeep of the brothers. This mediation of the human superior does not give rise to solemn affirmations founded on Scripture, as in the theory of obedience.[17] It is introduced a little surrepticiously into the theory of renunciation of goods. Yet the Master is not mentioning it here for the first time. Three times already in Chapters 1 and 7 he has called specific attention to it. Bad monks 'do not want to have an abbot to look after all their needs',[18] and 'fancy that it is pleasing to God and preferable that they themselves should think about their own bodily needs';[19] on the contrary, good cenobites 'are not obliged to think of their temporal needs, thanks to their abbot's solicitude . . . sure as they are, by obeying simply, to provide for all their other interests, both of body and of soul'.[20] Although these remarks on the abbot's role are brief and made in passing, they prepare for mention of him in Chapter 82. They constitute a second series of texts, much more discreet than the first, but along with it they converge in the treatise on renunciation of goods.

Finally a third series of notes tends to the same end. Two juridical definitions are inserted in the treatises on the abbot and the cellarer.[21] Citing and commenting upon the same *sententia regulae*, they lay the principle that 'the temporal possessions of the monastery belong to everyone and to no one'. Therefore no brother can possess anything as his own. Only the abbot disposes sovereignly of persons and goods.[22]

These are the three currents which flow together in the Master's Chapter 82. All the elements we have just distinguished[23] are found united there: the appeal for detachment founded upon faith in Providence; the insertion of the abbot in the activity of Providence; the prohibition of possessing anything, now motivated by the universal solicitude of God and of the abbot. This simple vigorous argument drawn from the Sermon on the Mount (Mt 6:25 and 34) is strengthened by a pauline citation: 'No one in the service of God entangles himself with secular affairs if he wishes to please him to whom he has engaged himself'.[24] The Gospel and the Apostle therefore agree: when 'seeking the kingdom' or 'serving God', religious engagement requires disengagement from the things of this world. 'No man can serve two masters'.[25] One must choose on this earth between concern for oneself and concern with pleasing God.

This citation of 2 Timothy 2:4 should be noted carefully, for, appearing here for the first time, it will replace Matthew 6:24–34 in the reminders of this doctrine which mark the last chapters of the Rule.[26] The most important of these repetitions is the long discourse of Chapter 91, which constitutes a second treatise on renunciation of goods. Addressing himself to the parents of 'the son of a noble', the Master develops again, with an abundance of scriptural and patristic illustrations, the necessity of stripping the monk of all property.[27] Here, however, he is no longer treating objects possessed within the monastery, but outside, not of remaining in a state of non-possession, but of entering that state. Reversing the chronological order, the Master speaks of this initial dispossession only from Chapter 87 onward, after having promulgated in Chapter 82 the permanent prohibition of the *peculiare* (personal property). This renunciation demanded at the beginning is based, moreover, on clear *testimonia* of the Gospel, the most important of which are the call of the rich young man,[28] the demand to renounce everything one possesses to become Jesus' disciple,[29] and the saying in the Sermon on the Mount: 'Where your treasure is, there will your heart be also'.[30]

Chapters 82 and 91 are therefore the Master's two formal treatises on renunciation of goods. Several passages in between them deserve at least some mention, for various reasons. In Chapter 86, to begin with, the Master again preaches detachment from earthly things and confidence in Providence in connection with the monastery's agricultural lands.[31] In the following chapter he tackles the problem of the renunciation of goods for the postulants, and some spiritual considerations precede the different juridical solutions expounded at length.[32] Then he sums up these considerations in the ritual of profession.[33] Finally the long chapter on the formation of the lay postulant ends by forbidding restitution of the new brother's goods brought to the monastery, in the event he apostatizes.[34] This juridical note contains a *sententia regulae*[35] which reminds us of those in Chapters 2 and 16.

In its rich variety this is the spread of the Master's texts about property. If we try to locate this complex theory in the doctrinal assembly of the Rule, two principal connections appear immediately: renunciation of goods touches both obedience and work.

The first of these relationships is so close that renunciation of goods and obedience form a kind of pair which appears many times. Beginning with the commentary on the Our Father, as we have seen, the notion of God as master and the Providence of Christians (fourth petition), the basis of the renunciation of goods, flows from the accomplishment of the divine will (third petition) which makes us the 'workmen' belonging to this master. At the other end of the Rule, where the doctrine of renunciation of goods has reached maturity, it is presented in the same way *immediately after* the discourse on obedience. Thus the abbot proposes to the postulant first obedience to the Rule, and then renunciation of his goods, the second a condition of perseverance in the first.[36] The same sequence holds true in the profession ceremony: the new brother first pledges himself to obey, and then—if need be—he offers his goods to the monastery along with his person.[37] Then the long chapter on the lay postulant (RM 90), which is a veritable treatise on obedience, ends on a note about this brother's goods, again considered as a pledge of perseverance.[38] But especially in the following chapter (RM 91) the pair appears in full light: after one long exposition on obedience, we find another, of equal length, on renunciation of goods. Everything happens as if the case of the lay postulant and that of the 'son of the nobleman' provided the Master with pretexts for proposing for one last time, one right after the other and in the same breadth, these two interdependent and inseparable themes.

In all these passages the order is the same: renunciation of goods *follows* obedience. This observation, which could be extended to the whole Rule,[39] invites us to compare the Master's sequence with that usually presented by his favorite author, Cassian. In the *Institutes* obedience and renunciation of goods form a pair just as much, but they are set in inverse order: detachment *precedes* humility and obedience.[40] This presentation was familiar to many ancient authors, who connected it sometimes to 'the call of the rich young man' in the Gospels: 'Go, sell what you possess . . . , then come, follow me',[41] this last word being applied to interior renunciation and especially to obedience.[42]

Yet this is not the order adopted by the Master. In his chapter 'On humility' where he follows Cassian, he does not breathe a word about detachment, the introduction to humility and obedience according to his source.[43] No doubt because of its practical implications, the theory of renunciation of goods is deferred by the Master to the second part of the

Rule, which deals with material organization and observances.[44] But this literary reason does not explain everything. It is valid for the general ordering of the Rule, but it does not account for the particular passages in which we have observed the same order. To understand these we must now examine more closely the relationship which the Master establishes between obedience and disappropriation.

To do this we need only run over the two consecutive chapters of the Rule in which renunciation of goods appears: first, as the object of a long note about clothing (RM 81. 9–20) and then in the first formal treatise mentioned above (RM 82). According to the note about clothing, it is not enough that the brothers' clothing be kept in common chests in which no one can hide some personal object. It is also necessary that every article to which a brother seems attached be taken away from him by his provosts and given to another, 'so that self-will will not assert itself in this brother' (*ut non extollatur propria in fratre voluntas*).[45] This maxim, which is repeated twice in the following treatise and once again in regard to postulants, [46] expresses clearly the bond between the two types of behavior: appropriation is a manifestation of self-will. Consequently, we can add, disappropriation is a corollary of obedience. The monk must renounce all property chiefly because material objects are rich ground for that affirmation of the carnal self which is *propria voluntas* (self-will).

In addition, the Master taken pains immediately afterwards to explain the deep meaning of the desire to possess, in terms of pauline anthropology: 'For whatever his soul seeks to obtain for him must instead be denied to him. For the spirit opposes the desires of the flesh (Ga 5:16–17); wherefore the man of God is spiritual, not carnal'.[47] Spirit, soul, flesh: this triad, in which the middle term oscillates between the two extremes, is already known to us from the theory of obedience.[48] What the Master is saying here about the desire to appropriate is only a specific case of his teaching on self-will. Both of them are 'desires of the flesh' stirred up by the devil and contrary to God. The sinful soul, captive of the flesh, pleads for it. Only the spirit resists and embraces the divine will. The mission of monastic superiors is to come to its aid and make it triumph, so that each of their subjects becomes truly a man of God, a spiritual man. And this they do both by mortifying self-will and by taking away private property.

But the case just envisaged, concerning an article of clothing, an object of complacency and affectation, is a specific and superficial case, not yet reaching the depths where the spirit of poverty unveils its most radical demand. The doctrine is affirmed in its full rigor in the following chapter, which treats renunciation of goods *ex professo*. There the Master considers the 'three things necessary to life': clothing, footwear, and food. While all persons, to whatever social category they belong, bestir themselves and labor to obtain these three things, the servants of God have been ordered by their master not to worry about them. Their only desire should be to arrive at eternal life, their only concern to 'seek the kingdom of God and his justice'. In return for this, the Lord will furnish them with everything necessary for the present life.

We see to what lengths the Master here pushes the demand for renunciation of goods. It amounts to nothing less than renouncing that concern for self which is the very instinct for life. In this regard the true cenobite entrusts himself entirely to divine Providence, which provides for his needs by means of the abbot. Without resources or security of his own, he receives everything from another. Renunciation of goods is an exit from self, an abandonment to another, an act of hope.

This 'other' to whom the monk entrusts himself is no doubt God, but God acting through a visible institution and person: the monastery and the abbot.[49] By this fact renunciation of goods again proves itself analogous to obedience and connected with it. Obedience consists in renouncing our own will and doing the will of God as signified to us by his representative, the abbot 'teacher'. In the same way renunciation of goods consists in relinquishing concern for our subsistence, expecting everything needed from this superior. And the two attitudes are not only similar. The first is a condition of the second: he who does only the will of God and of his abbot can count on God and the abbot for his upkeep. This sort of contract between the Lord and his 'workmen' was already sketched, we remember, in the commentary on the fourth petition of the Lord's Prayer,[50] but the mediation of the abbot was still lacking there. With that included, the contract is stated clearly in a passage from the chapter 'On Obedience': the monk is perfectly secure both in temporal and spiritual matters; let him only obey God through his superior, and God will by the same channel provide for all his needs.[51] The will of God is communicated by the abbot, and the Providence of God likewise works through the abbot. The latter is the sensible sign by which the cenobite clings to the divine will and, in return, entrusts himself to the God who is Providence.

Renunciation of goods, as the negative phase of this second movement, is therefore again related to obedience. Earlier it appeared to us as an extension of obedience: to renounce one's own will is especially to deny oneself all private property. By means of this implication we now perceive that a relationship of conditioning has been added: obedience *permits* the monk to count on God and on the abbot, and therefore no longer to possess anything private. We must go even further: it *obliges* the monk to reject possessions and concern with self. This is indeed the order established by the Lord. In his service, the *peculiare*, the little private hoard conceded by civil law to slaves, is not allowed.[52] Such a reserve would insult the divine master. His servants owe him all their strength, all their activity, and all their thoughts, and he in exchange becomes responsible for *all* their needs.[53]

Obedience and renunciation of goods are therefore two organically related components of one and the same state: the service of God. One cannot be embraced without the other. If our author ordinarily goes from obedience to renunciation of goods his thought sometimes moves, at least implicitly, in the reverse direction. Indeed, detachment from earthly things, signified and realized by disappropriation, is in its turn the condition for a total engagement in the spiritual work of obedience. Does not the first word of the Prologue exhort the reader to 'leave aside his other thoughts'?[54] To make himself entirely attentive and obedient to the rule, he must first of all cut off his 'other thoughts' and cares of this world, and this is what renunciation of goods aims to do radically. The same sequence appears in filigree in the *ars sancta*: just before calling for a consideration of the last things and an effort at conversion, including obedience,[55] the Master proposes 'hoping for one's sustenance not from the work of one's hands alone, but rather from God',[56] by an act of hope which is at the root of both renunciation of goods and of detachment regarding work. Finally, although the postulants' *promise* to obey the Rule and the abbot precedes their renunciation of goods,[57] obedience *in act* comes only afterwards. In reality, if not in treatment, renunciation of material goods comes first.

Whatever the order in which they are arranged, obedience and renunciation of goods form a pair. Both consist in throwing oneself on God: the obedient person takes the divine will for his law; he who renounces riches wishes to have no other riches than Christ.[58] Both of them are a choice for the spirit,[59] a conversion to things on high,[60] a bet on eternity.[61]

This orientation towards the next world is also one of the traits which connect renunciation of goods with another complementary attitude: detachment in regard to the fruits of work. To be spiritual, to desire solely the things on high, to care only for eternal life—these attitudes demand not only that one renounce all possession; certain profits coming from work must also be renounced. To work is indeed a duty, as the Master recalls more than once, basing himself on the teaching of Saint Paul,[62] but spiritual persons discharge it as a duty, that is, out of obedience to God, and not for fear of lacking what is necessary or for self-interest, as seculars do. They prove this purity of intention by some significant renunciations. Part of the provosts' manual work is remitted so that they may be freer for their spiritual task of surveillance;[63] what the artisans produce is sold at cheaper prices as a sign of disinterestedness;[64] field work is renounced as an occasion for dissipation and a pretext for infringing the law of fasting.[65]

These manifestations of detachment are closely united to renunciation of goods, not only as signs of conversion towards the next life, but also because they imply the same abandonment to Providence. This theme of confidence in God, the master and father who takes care of us, is the foundation of both the appeals to reduce the work[66] and the treatise on renunciation of good.[67] The same scriptural *testimonia* are invoked: in both, the Sermon on the Mount invites the monk not to be concerned about the next day and to seek the kingdom;[68] in both, the servant of God does not entangle himself in worldly affairs.[69]

The interest of this connection lies in showing that the Master, in the matter of temporal goods, is not content with demanding the dispossession of individuals. He also requires a certain detachment from the community itself. Not that he forbids collective property, as happened here and there in ancient monasticism.[70] On the contrary, he acknowledges the monastery's right and duty to hold possessions.[71] But he at least wants the spiritual character of the servants of God to be impressed upon the use of these goods, on the style of work, and on the profit drawn from it. Thus renunciation is to be not only an individual, but also a collective thing.

In legislating thus about the brothers' work, the Master is manifestly addressing chiefly the abbot, the guardian of the Rule, the head of the community and the all-powerful administrator of its goods. He, first of all, must give proof of disinterestedness, must abandon himself to Providence and must act as a spiritual man. In his usual way, however, our author does not call on the abbot by name. It is Benedict, as we shall see, who was to summon the abbot and lay on him this collective detachment as a personal obligation.

Benedict has summed up his predecessor's many developments on this question in a simple note in his chapter 'On the abbot'.[72] He will not speak of it again later: in regard neither to the deans nor the cellarer, neither at the beginning of his two texts on renunciation of goods nor in regard to postulants or profession or the 'son of the nobleman'. This way of transferring to the abbot a series of directives of the Rule is quite Benedict's style. Here as elsewhere he renounces detailed legislation and assigns everything to the superior's decision,[73] simply reminding him of the principles. And as elsewhere also, he forewarns the abbot against failure, a thing the Master did not allow himself to envisage.

The abbot then should guard against neglecting the salvation of souls and being too solicitous about temporal interests. The temptation is particularly dangerous in a case of penury. To ward it off the abbot should recall the words 'Seek first the kingdom of God' of the Sermon on the Mount, and, 'Nothing is lacking to those who fear him' of the Psalmist.[74] The first of these citations lay at the heart of the Master's appeals for confidence in Providence.[75] He did not use the second, but cited the following verse of the same Psalm to illustrate the same thought.[76]

These facts underline the close relationship of the benedictine note with different passages of the Master to which they correspond. To all appearances Benedict remembered these passages while drawing up his note for the abbot. Carrying the whole responsibility of the monastery, in temporal as well as in spiritual matters, the superior is more exposed than anyone to the temptation of preferring one to the other. A certain abbot of Soracte once did this by sending his monks to work outside the cloister, to the detriment of their souls, to bring back to the monastery the oil they were lacking.[77] Benedict, on the contrary, according to Gregory, gave a poor man the little flask of oil that remained to him, and later had the flask thrown out the window rather than keep it through lack of faith.[78] In both cases God multiplied the oil miraculously in response to the disinterestedness and faith of his servants. These two incidents in the *Dialogues* together form a complete commentary on the present note in the chapter 'On the

abbot': the conduct reproved by our Rule is represented by the abbot of
Soracte, the recommended conduct by the abbot of Cassino. Divine Providence confounds the first and justifies the second by a dazzling intervention.

Benedict thus sets the head of the monastery face to face with his duty,
and after that avoids this theme of collective disinterestedness and abandonment to Providence. 'To hope for one's sustenance not from the
work of one's hands alone, but rather from God':[79] this instrument of the
ars sancta is missing in his 'instruments of good works'. Correlatively, the
chapter forbidding field work (RM 86) is omitted, while several passages
of the Benedictine Rule indicate the adoption of this work, at least in
cases of necessity, with all the resultant consequences for the horarium,
attendance at the office and meals.[80] Benedict maintains the prescription
to sell things more cheaply than seculars do,[81] surely, but he relegates it to
the end of the chapter on artisans,[81] tempers it with a restrictive adverb
(*aliquantulum*) and abstains from defining the motive too precisely.[82] It is
true that this same chapter begins with a feature that shows in Benedict a
very keen sense of the preeminence of the good of souls over all material
interest: any artisan who is too proud of the advantages he secures for the
monastery is forbidden to practise his trade. However, this remarkable
application of the principle set forth in the chapter 'On the abbot' gives
rise to no commentary which would reveal the significance. The struggle
against independence and haughtiness, the leit-motiv of the whole Rule,
receives more attention than the theme of the primacy of the spiritual.
This remains implicit, not formulated.

On the whole, the doctrine of collective disinterestedness and abandonment to Providence undergoes a certain regression in Benedict. Circumstances have changed, and it is necessary to incite the monks to earn their
living rather than to moderate their appetite for gain. Concern for souls
remains dominant, but its concrete manifestations are to be revised.[83] The
legislator prudently leaves that to the abbot's conscience.

But what we must especially note here is that the theme of collective
detachment is no longer connected with that of renunciation of goods.
The Master clearly joined them by making them spring from a common
root: the doctrine of abandonment to Providence. In Benedict, the only
passage of the chapter 'On the abbot' which sums up this doctrine does
not explicitly concern either of these themes: the abbot is warned against

the invasion of temporal cares, but no precise conduct is traced out for him. In fact, the passage doubtless deals with the monastery revenues and the brothers' work, therefore with collective detachment rather than with individual renunciation. When Benedict treats this last, he makes no mention of Providence.[84] Thus personal disappropriation and community disinterestedness cease to seem like two complementary modalities of one same attitude of confidence towards our Father in heaven.

The relationship of renunciation of goods to obedience is marked by Benedict soberly but vigorously. Two short phrases in Chapters 33 and 58 state it in almost the same terms: the monk can possess nothing, since his own person is no longer in his power.[85] This maxim in the juridical style, equivalents to which are found in more than one monastic legislator,[86] makes us think of the slave-laws of antiquity. Yet the slave could possess a *peculium* (private savings) which is specifically forbidden the monk. For him dispossession is as complete and perpetual as obedience.

The Master saw the relationship of the two patterns of behavior from a spiritual point of view: property appeared as one of the characteristic manifestations of 'self-will', that is, of the desire of the flesh, and as a blow at the service of God, in which devotion to his will and abandonment to his Providence should be without reserve. As a consequence of his extreme conciseness, Benedict sums up these spiritual considerations, duly illustrated by Scripture, in a dry juridical formula. The conflict of the flesh and spirit, disencumbering oneself in order to serve God, the search for the kingdom and its justice to the exclusion of every other care, all that has disappeared to give place to a simple legal rule.

These observations lead us to consider the use Benedict made of the sum of the Master's texts. The Master's doctrine on renunciation of goods unfolded, as we have seen, in three series of texts which in turn presented God as Providence to his servants, the abbot as provider for his monks, and the dispossession imposed on them under the solicitude of God and of the abbot. In Benedict's summary, Providence no longer appears: this central piece of the theory of disappropriation has vanished. The abbot is no longer presented by Benedict as the agent of Providence supplying the needs of the brothers,[87] but he does insist on his prerogatives and his supervision: the abbot's permission is required for every act by which material objects are disposed of,[88] and everything necessary must be asked of him.[89] Notes of this kind stem from the Master's third series of texts. Finally, of this third series Benedict has kept scarcely more than one of its juridical notes about dispossession (RM 16, 58–61). He has even made it more evident,[90] developed it[91] and added specifications.[92] His only concern is with defining the statute on renunciation of goods with exactitude and to apply it with rigor.

This statute consists essentially in the total dependence of each monk on the abbot. It is true that Benedict, under Augustine's influence, introduces into the statute the famous maxim of Acts: 'All their goods were held in common',[93] but this citation does not affect it much. In referring to the Church of Jerusalem, Benedict, unlike Augustine, omits 'the one heart and the one soul', which was the spiritual foundation of the community of goods.[94] Moreover, his citation of Acts is scarcely more than a re-expression in scriptural terms of the Master's maxim: 'The goods of the monastery belong to everyone and to no one'.[95] With him the stress was not on 'belongs to everyone' but on 'belongs to no one'. It is the same with Benedict who follows his phrase 'let all things be common to all' with the negative counterpart: 'let no one call anything his own'.[96] For both rules the fraternal sharing of goods is much less important than the entire stripping of individuals under the abbot's authority. To the degree that Benedict was later to be interested in the unequal distribution of necessities, as Augustine had conceived it according to Acts,[97] so here he passes rapidly over the holding of goods in common, the sign of union of hearts.[98] He is keenly interested in 'giving to each according to his needs' and in establishing brotherly relations in peace, but he does not go so far as to rethink in a perspective of communion the basically individualist and vertical notion of renunciation of goods that he draws from the Master.[99]

We find then in regard to disappropriation the same contrast we have already observed on the subject of obedience, between our rules and the rule of Augustine. There is nothing astonishing in this: the two patterns of behavior are so closely connected that the perspective adopted by the legislator necessarily affects both of them. Augustine starts from the community, the union of hearts: this is, first of all, signified by the holding of goods in common; in addition, it requires the obedience of all to one superior. The Master and Benedict start from the salvation of the individual and its demands. The first of these is the renunciation of self-will and obedience to the 'teacher', which implies in turn renunciation of goods. Community is a secondary reality, especially in the Master.

Yet we would be wrong to oppose the two perspectives absolutely. In the area of disappropriation they partially meet because both envisage this virtue in a social and hierarchical framework inspired by the primitive Church. The thing is evident for Augustine: the Church of Jerusalem is proposed as the immediate model. The reference to Acts is equally clear in Benedict, who follows Augustine in this. But this reference is not less present and important in the Rule of the Master, even though it is much less apparent.

The Master does not limit himself to citing Christ's words in the Gospel: 'Go sell what you possess . . . . He who does not renounce everything cannot be my disciple'.[100] These words in themselves only invite a man to strip himself once and for all of the goods he owned. They do not imply a subordinate relationship to the community and its leaders. Such a relationship only appears in the evocation of the Church of Jerusalem, from the beginning of Acts[101]: the faithful bring their goods and lay them at the feet of the apostles,[102] who in return distribute them to each according to his needs. But the Master alludes to these scenes of the primitive Church, not only in the two passages where he brandishes the specter of Ananias and Sapphira,[103] but also, apparently, when he has the abbot say to the postulant: 'Sell what you possess and bring the whole price here before me, so that I may distribute it to the poor in your presence'.[104] Besides the evident allusion to Matthew 19:21 ('Go sell what you possess and give to the poor'), this phrase seems to allude to Acts: the product of the sale is not distributed to the poor directly by the one who gives it up, but is 'brought before' the abbot, who makes the distribution. The abbot here holds the place of the apostles.[105] Although the beneficiaries of the distribution are not the members of the community, as in the Acts, but the poor in general, as in the Gospel, the operation takes place in Church, hierarchically, under the control of the community's head.

It is true that this phrase envisages only one of the modes of initial disappropriation, alms given to the poor. But the example of Acts continues to haunt our author's mind when he thinks of the other mode (donation to the monastery),[106] and the state of non-ownership in which the brothers live.[107] And in fact, the whole statute on cenobitic poverty is based on that of the primitive community: it is not only a matter of liquidating one's personal property one day, but also of putting everything in common, every day, with one's brothers,[108] in dependence on the abbot, the successor of the apostles. No doubt this theme of the common life is very discreet in the Master. No doubt, also, the express reference to the example of the apostles 'distributing to each according to his needs' is lacking. Yet the social and economic *reality* instituted by the Rule of the Master is cast just as much in the image of the primitive Church as is the monastery of Augustine or of Benedict. Its scriptural prototype is not in the Gospel, but in Acts.[109]

When we have recognized the common relationship of the different forms of cenobitism to the model of the apostolic church, we can discern more exactly what makes them different. This difference is not so much in the institutional, as in the spiritual and literary, order. It consists chiefly in the more or less clear and developed reference made by the authors to the text of Acts. The most complete and explicit use of it is Augustine's. With him the Church of Jerusalem is the unique and perfect model of his foundation. He follows the entire program point by point: union of souls and hearts, individual renunciation of goods, the community of goods, the distribution of necessities by the superior according to each one's needs.

On the contrary, the Master makes only fragmentary, scattered and sometimes veiled allusions to Acts: the goods are put 'at the feet' of the superior; all fraud will be uncovered and punished, as in the case of Ananias and Sapphira. Their unfaithfulness, of which Augustine did not think at all, receives full attention. Acts is invoked explicitly only to condemn the vice of property, while the positive motives for renunciation of goods are taken up elsewhere.

With Benedict, the reference to Acts reclaims part of the importance and clarity it had for Augustine. Benedict does not neglect the sad lesson of Ananias and Sapphira, but he pays attention chiefly to the positive example of the first believers. Of these he does not note their spiritual communion, but only—and in order of increasing importance—their holding goods in common, the absence of private property and their unequal distribution of necessities.

NOTES TO CHAPTER 13

1. See RB 54–55 and 58–59. To these chapters we join here RB 34 and 57, as we have done in t. VI, pp. 859–977 (VIIth Part).

2. RB 33.4; 58.24–25.

3. Ac 4:32, cited by RB 33.6.

4. See t. VI, pp. 875–81.

5. See the commentary on RB 5, above.

6. RM Thp 24–53.

7. RM 1, 76–92. Cf. 11.1–14.

8. RM 7.1–74; 10.30–60; 90.1–59. Only RM 7 treats of 'the qualities'.

9. RM Thp 54–56. More precisely, *annonam* is here connected with *operariis* and *mercedem* with *mercennario*. Elsewhere, *annona* is coupled with *servorum* (16.30) as well as with *operariis* (16.27).

10. RM 3.49, where *a Deo sperare* is perhaps equivalent to *[Deus] rogatur* of Thp 56, according to one meaning of *sperare* (followed by *a*) which is found in RB 33.5.

11. RM 11.94–106; 16.1–26; 86.1–17. Cf. RM 23.2

12. Mt 6:33, cited by RM 11.103 and 16.14. With other witnesses, the Master omits *primum* which makes the command more categorical: the kingdom must not only be sought before, but to the exclusion of, the rest. It is the same in RM 82.15.

13. RM 82.1–15, citing Mt 6:25 and 33.

14. RM 82.16–17.

15. RM 82.18 (2 Tm 2:4) and 19 (cf. 81.9–20); 82.20–22 (Ac 5:1–11).

16. RM 82.23–25.

17. RM 1.82–92; 11.1–14. These affirmations are doubtless supposed here.

18. RM 1.68–69.

19. RM 7.34–35.

20. RM 7.53–54.

21. RM 2.48–50; 16.58–61. These notes have a precise echo in RM 82.17.

22. See in RBS II, pp. 13*–18*, our review of P. Blecker's study, 'Roman Law and *Consilium* in the *Regula Magistri* and the Rule of St Benedict', in *Speculum*, 47 (1972) 1–28.

23. These elements already mingled in certain earlier passages: the human mediation of the cellarer appears in RM 16.11 and 27–31 (theme of Providence), and that of the abbot in RM 2.48–50 and 16.58–61 (juridical notes); the opposition between care of the body and care of the soul intervenes in RM 7.34 (note on the abbot).

24. RM 82.18, citing 2 Tm 2:4.

25. Mt 6:24 (cf. RM 91.13–14). In this phrase and in the following (*Non potestis Deo servire et Mammonae*; cf. RM 13.10; 16.5,16,22), *servire* translates the greek *douleuein*. The same latin verb is used to translate the greek *strateuomenos* in 2 Tm 2:4, where the Vulgate has *militans*, but the Master's version has *serviens*. The notion of 'service of God', so familiar to the Master, can then refer either to Mt 6:24 or to 2 Tm 2:4, without counting many other biblical texts which use it. In the Master's eyes it closely connects the two words of the Gospel and the Apostle.

26. See RM 86.18; 91.11.

27. RM 91.8–70.

28. Mt 19:21, cited by RM 87.13–14 and 39; 91.18,44,55,71.

29. Lk 14:33, cited by RM 91.15 (cf. 86.17).

30. Mt 6:21, used in RM 87.7 and 89.19, with a characteristic inversion. Cf. RM 91.14 (an allusion to Mt 6:20).

31. RM 86.1–17, citing notably 2 Tm 2:4 and Lk 14:33.

32. RM 87.5–24, using Mt 6:21 and 19:21; Ac 4:34–35 and 5:1–11.

33. RM 89.17–23 (Mt 6:21).

34. RM 90.88–95.

35. RM 90.95.

36. RM 87.2–4 and 5–24.

37. RM 89.8–16 and 17–23. In this last passage obedience is closely associated with stripping.

38. RM 90.3–67 and 88–95.

39. The Rule is composed of two parts: *Actus militiae cordis* (Pr–10) and *Ordo monasterii* (11–95). Although both of them treat the two virtues, the theory of obedience has its center of gravity in the *Actus*, and renunciation of goods its center in the *Ordo*.

40. Cassian, *Inst.* 4:39 and 43; these two progressions reflect the steps of initiation described in *Inst.* 4.3–6 and 8–12 (see t. IV, pp. 344–6 and 363). It is true that in *Inst.* 4.3.1 humiliation precedes stripping, but this time obedience is not included in humility. On the other hand, the insight on obedience (*Inst.* 4.8–12) preceeds that on non-ownership (*Inst.* 4.13–15), but we are not dealing with a chronological sequence.

41. Mt 19:21.

42. See Paulinus of Nola, *Ep.* 24.5–9; Macarius, *Hom.* 21.1–4; PG 34: 656–657 (does not cite Mt 19:21). The verb *sequi* is one of those expressing obedience in the Master. See RM 7.4; 7.8 (cf. Mt 4:22); 7.52 (Mt 16:24). It is therefore possible that the Master is thinking of obedience when he cites *sequere me* from Mt 19:21 (see above, note 28). See also Isaias, *Log.* 14.54; CSCO 294, p. 270; Gregory, *Mor.* 32.42–43 and *Hom. Evang.* 32.1–2.

43. See above, note 40.

44. Cf. note 39.

45. RM 81.17.

46. RM 82.19 and 31; 87.18. Cf. 90.8.

47. RM 81.18–20. The division of the phrases and the translation are doubtful.

48. RM Thp 28 and 1.80. See the commentary on RB 5, notes 9 and 28, above.

49. RM 82.23–25 (cf. 82.16).

50. RM Thp 54–56. See above, note 9.

51. RM 7.53–54. Cf. note 20.

52. The Master makes no allusion to this right, which he denies implicitly by his condemnation of the *peculiare*.

53. Cf. *omnia* and *omnibus* in RM 82.16 and 25 (cf. 16.22). The same thought occurs in Cassian, *Inst.* 6.7.2, paraphrasing 2 Tm 2:4.

54. RM Pr 1; *dimitte alia modo quae cogitas*. The verb *cogitare*, in RM and in the version of Mt 6 which he uses, expresses temporal 'care'. In RM 2.50 as well the thought goes from non-possession to obedience.

55. RM 3.50–67.

56. RM 3.49. See t. IV, pp. 156–7 and 202–3.

57. See above, note 37.

58. RM 89.21–23; 91.8,70.

59. RM Thp 28 and 1.80 (obedience); 81.18–20 (renunciation of goods).

60. RM Thp 45–47 (obedience *sicut in caelo*); 82.11 and 86.13–16 (renunciation of goods: *superna cogitare, desiderare*), cf. 91.14 (Mt 6:20: *thesaurum in caelis*) and 91.44 (Mt 19:21: *thesaurum in caelo*).

61. Obedience: RM Thp 30–33 and 53; 1.90–92; 7.53–56, and all of chapter 90. Renunciation of goods: RM 82.4–10 and 12–15; 86.8–13 and all of chapter 91.

62. RM 50.1–7; 69.12–15; 78.18–24; 83.10–22; 85.6–7.

63. RM 11.94–106.

64. RM 85.1–7.

65. RM 86.1–27.

66. RM 11.99–106.

67. RM 82.12–15.

68. Mt 6:31–34, cited by RM 11.100–106 and 82.12–15.

69. 2 Tm 2:4, cited by RM 82.18; 86.8; 91.11.

70. *Vita Alexandri* 7–8, 18–19, 27, etc.; PO 6:662–663, 671–672, 678; Gregory, *Dial.* 3.14; ed. Moricca, p. 165,21 – 166,1 (Isaac of Spoleto).

71. RM 86.18–22.

72. RB 2.33–36.

73. See t. I, pp. 55–7.

74. RB 2.35 (Mt 6:33) and 36 (Ps 33:10).

75. See RM 11.103; 16.14 and 25; 82.15.

76. RM 16.8 (Ps 33:11). Compare RB 19.3 (Ps 2:11a) and RM 47.4 (Ps 2:11b). In each case Benedict cites the verse or half-verse which precedes that cited by the Master.

77. Gregory, *Dial.* 1.7; Moricca, pp. 46,6–47,9. It is the provost Nonnosus who redresses the situation by his faith.

78. Gregory, *Dial.* 2.28–29. Cf. Cassian, *Inst.* 4.25. The episode recalls Cyril of Scythopolis, *Vita Euth.* 17.

79. RM 3.49.

80. See t. I, pp. 46–8. Cf. t. V, pp. 589–616; t. VI, 1190–1203.

81. RB 57.7–9.

82. See t. VI, pp. 937–49.

83. This revision does not seem to me to go as far as O. du Roy claims, *Moines aujourd'hui*, pp. 269–79. Benedict remains on the level of applications; no principle is at stake.

84. *Sperare* doubtless does not have the meaning of 'to hope' in RB 33.5. See above, note 10.

85. RB 33.4 and 58.25. Cf. RM 16.58–61; 87–89.

86. See the note on RB 58.25.

87. It is true that Benedict expatiates on the distribution of what is necessary by the abbot (RB 33.5 and 34.1–5; 55.18–22), but he makes it less the motive of renunciation of goods than the counterpart of it. In addition, the abbot is not put in relation with Providence.

88. RB 33.2 and 5; 54.1–3; 55.17.

89. RB 33.5.

90. By constituting it as a separate chapter (RB 33). On the other hand, RM 82 is annexed to the chapter on clothing (RM 81): see RB 55.

91. We go from six lines (RM 16.58–61) to thirteen lines (RB 33) to which are added the ten lines of RB 54, entirely new by comparison to the Master.

92. Cf. RB 33.2 (*dare aut accipere*); 33.3 (list of objects); 33.4 (motivation); 33.6 (scriptural citation); 33.7–8 (sanction). However, the four verbs enumerated by RM 16.59 are a series of specifications which Benedict did not keep. The same is true of *sententia regulae* which follow.

93. Ac 4:32c, cited (in the imperative) by RB 33.6.

94. Ac 4:32a, cited by Augustine, *Praec.* 1.2.

95. RM 16.61 (cf. 2:48).

96. Ac 432b, cited by RB 33.6. Note the inversion. The final position which results for this word of Acts gives it an importance which is confirmed by the verbal resonances of RB 33.2 (*ne quis praesumat aliquid . . .*); 33.3 (*aliquid*); 33.5 (*nec quicquam*).

97. Ac 4:35, cited and commented on by RB 34.1–5 and 55.20–22.

98. He will not return to it either in RB 55, or in RB 58, two chapters which, however, repeat RB 33–34.

99. The communitarian aspect of the renunciation of goods is not absent from the Master's thought (cf. RM 2.48–49 and 16.61: *omnium est*; 91.52–54), but it has only a secondary importance. Compare *Regula IV Patrum*, which begins like Augustine from unanimity (1.5–6), but continues immediately with obedience (1.8–18), while the norms for disappropriation do not appeal to the example of Acts. (2.17,29–31,34–35).

100. Mt.19:21 and Lk 14:33. Paul's word to Timothy (2 Tm 2:4), another key text of the Master, scarcely goes any further.

101. Except for the allusions in the Gospels to a certain common life led by Jesus and his disciples (Lk 8:3; Jn 12:6).

102. Ac 4:34–35 and 5:1–2.

103. RM 82.20–23 (note *omnia . . . ante pedes apostolorum*) et 87.24.

104. RM 87.14–15 (note *omne . . . ante me defer*). Cf. 87.21: *omnia . . . defer*.

105. Cf. Rm 1.82–89; 11.5–12; 14.13–15.

106. RM 87.19–24 (cf. above, notes 103–104).

107. RM 82.20–23.

108. Aside from the initial contribution, there are revenues from work and acquisitions (RM 16.59).

109. Acts influences the Master as a model, not only by the direct reminiscences of the text, but also through the institutional tradition of cenobitism.

Chapter XIV

ABSTINENCE AND FASTING
(RB 39–41)

RESTRAINT IN EATING is not the object of any theory in our rules. For the Master and Benedict it is obvious, without need of justification, that the monk should practice fasting and abstinence. They limit themselves to saying that fasting, like chastity, should be 'loved',[1] because each is an essential component of the monastic life. 'To chastise the body' according to the word of St Paul, and 'not to be fond of soft living', 'not a heavy drinker', 'not a big eater'[2]—these few maxims complete the meager body of teaching on this point in our two rules. In the institutional part our authors are content to fix a triple norm: the ration of food, the ration of wine, the hour of the meals.[3] The three chapters treating these points are essentially practical. Only a few furtive annotations let us glimpse the meaning that the Master and Benedict attach to these observances

This laconic style and this lack are more noticed today because the meaning of food restrictions and even their practice are less and less familiar to us. For a quarter of a century the Church has suppressed almost all vestiges of the fasts and abstinences traditionally imposed on the faithful. The observances proper to the monks, already very enfeebled, are tending at the present time to diminish or disappear. Instead of one or two meals a day according to the seasons, we take today three meals a day all year round, exactly like seculars, and like them, too, many communities avail themselves of snacks and coffee-breaks. There is no question of pushing back dinner to the afternoon or the evening.[4] To mark the 'fast' we are generally content to reduce the rations a little for breakfast and dinner. Where abstinence exists, it applies to scarcely anything but meat. Often it is limited in almost a symbolic way to one or two days a week.

The rationing of food and drink would lend itself to more subtle observations.[5] On the whole, however, contemporary monasticism may be said to be very attentive to the tender consideration Benedict prescribes for the weak, while his demanding norms find little echo. Everything happens as if—and this is often said—the human race had fallen into such a state of feebleness that any corporal *ascesis* the least bit serious must be renounced.

This explanation, we must confess, leaves us dissatisfied. When man feels a need intensely, he finds the strength to obey it and the means to organize his life as a result of it. If *ascesis* no longer has its place in our lives, it is because we no longer feel its importance. We have as much strength as our Fathers had, but we employ it differently. Monks have abandoned fasting not because of a lack of health, but because they no longer had a reason to fast.

Our weakness in this regard is therefore chiefly a spiritual matter, requiring spiritual explanations. One of the deepest of them is no doubt the extroversion of the human dynamism, which, having cast aside effort on self, has invested itself wholly in working with things.[6] *Ascesis*, the specific activity of the monk, is today devoured by work. Work mobilizes all energies and, by its implacable rhythm and demand for productivity, imposes the eating schedule and physical conveniences which are conditions for such work. Already in the Benedictine Rule the correlation is evident between the adoption of agricultural labor and certain relaxations of the observance.[7] Modern monasticism is engaged, for better or for worse, in the whirlwind of activism around it, and has pushed this process to its ultimate consequences.

The resulting situation, like many others, seems justified by considerations drawn from Scripture. Contemporary Christianity, and the monastic world with it, is especially sensitive to what seems in the New Testament like a disavowal of jewish, pagan, or Gnostic asceticism. Christ eating and drinking with sinners seems opposed to the austere John the Baptist.[8] We remember Christ's indifference to rules of legal purity.[9] Peter, set in the midst of animals forbidden by the Law, heard God command him: 'Kill and eat';[10] Paul often rejects the distinctions between days and foods.[11]

The fasting and abstinence of monks seem too much like scrupulous observances for which the Apostle had a cautious charity, but declared to be without foundation. In the name of christian liberty do we not have the right to abandon such practices?

The objections just sketched are not new. They found a champion in Jovinian in a debate on asceticism which marked the end of the fourth century. The refutation of Jovinian by Jerome, like that of other opponents by Philoxenus of Mabbug, shows that they were taken into consideration by the defenders of asceticism.[12] At the same time so brilliant a company of authors as Basil, Augustine, Evagrius, Pelagius, and Cassian elaborated an ascetic doctrine in which *encrateia* or 'continence' plays an important role. The Master's and Benedict's rules about food can only be understood when connected with this body of traditional doctrine, to which they refer both by their vocabulary and by their terse remarks.

One of the first things our teachers are careful to do is remove every appearance of Judaism or Manichaeism.[13] Food in itself is neither pure nor impure. Only what comes from the heart of man, his desires, deserve such designations.[14] Restrictions about food therefore do not aim at protecting a man from an objective stain coming from without, but at purifying his heart, mortifying his desire, and freeing his spirit.

Considered from this point of view, continence seems like a personal affair whose measure necessarily varies from one individual to another. To fix universal norms is impossible, except the maxim found in Acts: 'To each according to his needs'.[15] But if the concrete measure of food and drink cannot be determined, once and for all, the principle of *ascesis* is valid for everyone. Anyone who aspires to perfection should restrain his eating and drinking to what is truly necessary for him. To discern this essential minimum, desire is not a valid criterion; still less is pleasure. An effort is required to separate the true need of nature from abusive appetites and illusory attractions.[16]

Since *encrateia* is a subjective purification, it cannot be limited to abstention from certain foods. The appetite for nourishment is only one of the desires emanating from the human heart. Inseparable from the others, it ought to be treated within the framework of general therapy of vices. But it is true that in the midst of all these, *gula* (gluttony) holds a very special place which we can rate first in many ways. The appetite for eating is a primary, irrepressible need whose satisfaction is indispensable for life, and thus it can never be entirely eliminated or sublimated.[17] Its incessant, compelling urgency sets it aside from other desires. Some, like sexuality, are not less natural, but none of them is as immediately essential. From this results its key position[18] and its value as a test for the whole moral effort. By it a man begins to discipline himself, and by it the tone of his *ascesis* is constantly verified. It is a general law which rules most especially the area of sexuality. Not by chance do Evagrius and Cassian make gluttony the first vice and lust the second.[19]

The monk fasts therefore to preserve chastity. He also fasts to sustain the struggle against any defect from which he particularly suffers.[20] Fasting and abstinence are general, all-inclusive expressions for the resolution to attain purity. The same was true for the ascetic struggle then as for the political struggle now. For the monk of the fourth century as for the non-violent protester of the twentieth, fasting witnesses to the intensity of the pain, the gravity of the concern, and the will to overcome evil.

Fasting plays, therefore, a universal role, like that of prayer, with which it forms a fighting partnership according to the biblical tradition sanctioned by the Lord himself: 'This demon cannot be expelled except by prayer and fasting'.[21] To this influence dietary continence has over the whole spiritual life corresponds the extension of *encrateia* over the whole field of *ascesis*. The Fathers, with a kind of unanimity, warn against a narrowly material notion of temperance.[22] Temperance is a general virtue which moderates not only the appetite for eating but all the desires. 'Everyone in a contest abstains from *all things*'.[23]

Continence in regard to food should therefore suggest a more interior discipline. While abstaining from nourishment, the monk should remind himself of the parade of vicious thoughts from which he has still a greater obligation to abstain.[24] Bodily food is not bad in itself as the vices are.[25] This mental transfer of the morally indifferent material object to the whole array of disorderly inclinations, which are the only true evils, takes place in connection with food as well as property.[26]

So 'in the interests of the soul', one 'chastises the body'.[27] In using this latter expression the Master, Benedict and many other Fathers were obviously thinking of St Paul.[28] They applied the pauline formula chiefly to fasting, which in antiquity was the most characteristic and most used corporal discipline, if not the only one. Seen as a corporal punishment, the fast has an obvious relationship with penitence, either voluntary or imposed. The role which it played in the penalties of excommunication is well known. When we remember the close relationship which the ancients established between the monastic life and penitence, we are not surprised at the importance attributed to fasting in this way of life.

To the words of the Apostle 'I chastise my body' are joined his other words, 'I bring it into subjection'.[29] Fasting is a means of 'subjecting the body',[30] or again, 'of taming the flesh', as Basil and Augustine say.[31] This of itself is linked with the equally pauline image of the struggle between the flesh and the spirit.[32] Even if these two principles are too easily assigned to the body and the soul, we are surely not mistaken in seeing in fasting a sign and a privileged instrument of the triumph of divine grace over sinful nature, and of rationality over instinct.

The influence of philosophical notions, as we have just encountered in regard to spirit and flesh, appears again more extensively in the definition of the ideal of frugality our christian sages propose. It is significant that Augustine's Rule ends its exposition on continence with a fine maxim inspired by Seneca: 'It is better to need less than to have more'.[33] Happiness does not consist in possessing and consuming much, but in having few needs and satisfying them at small expense. It is the ideal of *frugalitas* or *parcitas*,[34] which Benedict echoes by using this latter word[35] and by recommending twice that God be specially thanked when one's needs are less well met.[36] Basil had already celebrated in a similar way the royal dignity of the Christian, who like a wise man knows how to be content with little.[37]

Although this determination to live modestly was influenced in its formulation by pagan wisdom,[38] it has its root in the biblical love of poverty. Simple and inexpensive nourishment befits a Christian, a monk,[39] inasmuch as his retreat from the world is supposed to turn him from the preoccupations and embarrassments caused by a life of good cheer.[40] The exclusion of meat and wine is motivated in large part by this concern to eat and drink poorly.

Instead of spending money to satisfy artificial needs, the monk will give alms to the truly needy. This is how the Egyptian monks acted, who were celebrated by Augustine, Rufinus, Palladius, and Cassian.[41] This is what Leo recommends to his faithful, and Diadochus to the ascetics who read his works.[42] When the Master and Benedict invite the monk in two suc-

cessive maxims to 'love fasting' and to 'relieve the poor', there is no doubt
that a connection of cause and effect unites these two 'instruments'.[43]
This relationship between continence and charity is shown in a touching
way in a passage of the Master where we see the spiritual brother give up
part of his daily allowance of food for the sake of the poor.[44]

It is obviously Christ in the person of the poor who receives the monk's
voluntary sacrifice. More directly, the monastic fast on Wednesdays and
Fridays, like that of Lent, is motivated by the desire to share the sufferings
of Christ.[45] Inversely, the presence of the risen Bridegroom forbids fasting
on Sundays and in Paschaltide.[46] *Ascesis* in regard to food is, therefore,
not a simple conquest of self. It has a properly christian significance, an explicit relationship with Christ.

This religious sense of the fast is enriched by the great scriptural examples to which our authors refer, from Moses and Elijah to St Paul and the
infant Church,[47] including John the Baptist and Jesus himself. In the beginning Adam was forbidden to eat one certain fruit, and the use of meat
and wine did not begin until after the flood, according to Genesis, so that
to abstain from them seems like a return to paradise.[48]

Fasting prepared Moses and Elijah to see God. For Daniel it preceded
revelations and visions. Why would it not be for us as well the condition
of certain charisms?[49] In fact, contemplation is had at this price, and the
taste for God is obtained only by renouncing the taste for earthly nourish-
ments.[50] Reciprocally, the energy to fast is drawn from spiritual taste and
divine contemplation.[51]

Again, fasting is an imitation of the angels,[52] a weakening of man so
that the power of God may dwell in him,[53] a refining and lightening of his
spirit.[54] These few aspects, taken from among many others expressed by
our texts, let us glimpse the many meanings attached to restrictions on
eating. Just as a written document produces indefinitely various meanings
for those who read it, so does an exercise of *ascesis* for those who practise
it. In this regard, fasting is like silence.[55] These two great renunciations,
touching fundamental realities of human life, can be interpreted in a thousand ways and can stir up spiritual experiences which are always new.

This richness of meaning explains the considerable interest taken by the
ancients in the discipline of eating. There is no account of a holy monk
which does not say how he ate and drank, sometimes noting with preci-

sion his successive regimens.[56] We observe a contrast and a progression between the two chief monastic ways of life: relatively generous regimen of the cenobites gives way to the anchorites' increased austerity.[57]

Should we see in this interest in food some kind of materialism? This reproach would be hard to reconcile with the commonplace accusation of despising the body which is brought against this patristic spirituality impregnated with Platonism. We can ask, on the contrary, if true realism is not on the side of an *ascesis* which in no way separates the body from the soul in the spiritual effort, and which imposes very concrete renunciations to signify and support the thrust towards God. Is not the 'angelism' of which the Fathers are accused to be attributed instead to us, who are inclined to disdain observances and to make spiritual progress consist in a purely interior journey? And if there is materialism somewhere, it might be less in the austere generosity of these old monks than in the comfort and activism in which we delight.

In any case, the fact is that fasting and abstinence seem to have pertained to the very essence of monasticism since the beginning. St Paul says of chastity, and Benedict repeats about abstinence: 'Every one has his unique gift from God'.[58] These are personal gifts, no doubt, but together they define a specific human and christian type, the type of the monk. There exists a monastic gift, grace, and charism, and this charism consists specifically in renunciation. Renunciation of sexual intercourse and delicate eating, of independence and of speaking, of property and prestige—we could go on and on listing the different abstentions which make up the way of being a monk. Each of these is a gift of God which makes us renounce some relative good in view of his absolute good. That is how *ascesis* in eating and drinking operates. By delaying somewhat the satisfaction of desire, it liberates something for God. We can hardly conceive how it could be absent in such a concert. How could the most powerful human appetite escape the monastic charism of renunciation?

We must not let ourselves be deceived by the reservations with which the ancients frequently surrounded their presentations of fasting.[59] Reading them, we get the impression that they were already tending towards the quasi-absence of *ascesis* that we know today. In fact, they were ordinarily dealing with ascetics who were more convinced of the necessity of fasting than conscious of its spiritual implications. It was necessary therefore to insist on the limits of observances, on the deep meaning of as-

ceticism, on the virtues of the interior man. But this spiritual effort of in-
teriorization presupposes an exterior practice which serves as its
matter.We are too tempted to forget that. Today when this practice
scarcely exists, we no doubt have less need for appeals for moderation and
for interiority than we do for stimulations to concretize our search for
God by actual renunciations.

The life of the monk should be a continual Lent, says Benedict, and
Jesus says that when the Bridegroom is no longer present, his friends will
fast.[60] These words and others like them should command the attention
of the monks of today. At this price the joy of spiritual desire is obtained,
the joy of constantly finding again the Bridegroom who is always absent.
At present we are better supplied with speculations than with observances. If someone would again experience fasting and would communicate that experience, he would contribute more to promote monasticism
in our time than all the authors who are writing on the theology of the
monastic life.

The necessity and the difficulty of such a renewal are greater in that we
live in a consumer society. 'To diminish one's needs rather than to increase
one's possession's.[61] Is this augustinian maxim, the expression of monastic
thought of that time, not the exact opposite of an economy founded on
exciting and satisfying needs that are always growing in number? Yet such
is the wisdom proposed by Benedict, following Augustine.[62] At the very
heart of the famous benedictine discretion, which is too often taken as a
synonym for easiness, is found this demand for corporal restrictions 'so
that souls may be saved'.[63]

NOTES TO CHAPTER 14

1. RM 3.13 = RB 4.13. Cf. RM 3.70 = RB 4.64.
2. RM 3.11-12 = RB 4.11-12; RM 3.40-41 = RB 4.35-36.
3. RM 26-28 = RB 39-41.
4. Our horarium of rising and retiring, which is almost uniform at all seasons, would
eliminate most of the significance of the variations in meal times prescribed by Benedict. See
t. VI, p. 1172.
5. Our main meal has more dishes than the Rule foresees, but there is no wine in many
countries.

6. Cf. our article 'Le procès des moines d'autrefois', in *Christus*, 12 (1965) pp. 113–28, specially p. 121.

7. See t. VI, pp. 1190–1203.

8. Mt 9:9–17; 11:16–19.

9. Mt 15:1–20 (eating without washing hands). Cf. Mk 7:1–23.

10. Ac 10:9–16. Cf. Ac 15:1–35.

11. Rm 14:1–23 (cf. 1 Co 8–10); Col 2:16–23; 1 Tm 4:3–5; Tt 1:15.

12. Jerome, *Adv. Iovin.* II. 5–17; Philoxenus, *Hom.* 10 (392–394).

13. Basil, *Long Rules* 18; Augustine, *De mor. eccl.* I. 65–73; Jerome, *Adv. Jovin.* II. 6 and 16; Palladius, *Hist. Laus. Prol.* 9–14; Diadochus, *Cap.* 43–44; Philoxenus, *Hom.* 11 (449–454). Cf. Cassian, *Inst.* 5.22; Gregory, *Mor.* 30.60.

14. Mt 15:1–20; Mk 7:1–23.

15. Ac 4:35 cited by Basil, *Long Rules* 19.1 and *Short Rules* 252; *Short Rules* 131, 135, 148 = *Reg.* 91,94,111, in regard to food, and by Augustine, *Praec.* 1.3, the source of RB 34.1 and 55.20 in a larger context, which is also that of Acts. Same principle in Basil, *Reg.* 9; Cassian, *Inst.* 5.5.1; RB 40.1 without the citation.

16. The opposition between need and pleasure, necessity and sensuality is met everywhere. See for example Basil, *Hom. de ieiunio* 1.4; Cassian, *Inst.* 5.8; Gregory, *Mor.* 30.61–62; Ambrose, *De virg.* II. 8 (cf. Titus Livius, *Hist.* 21.4.6). On nature and desire: see Philoxenus, *Hom.* 11 (427–431 and 441–47).

17. Cassian, *Conf.* 5.16–23: we leave 'Egypt'; we do not destroy it. Since sexual desire appeared only after the fall, it is often considered less 'natural' than the desire of eating.

18. Cassian, *Conf.* 5.25: the spirit of gluttony introduces all the others (cf. Mt 12:43–45). Cf. Gregory, *Mor.* 30.58–59.

19. Evagrius, *Antirrh.* I–II; Cassian, *Inst.* 5–6 (cf. *Conf.* 5.4–6). On the connection between gluttony and lust, see Basil, *Hom. de ieiunio* 1.9; Jerome, *Adv. Iovin.* II.7; Diadochus, *Cap.* 43 and 49–50; Philoxenus, *Hom.* 10 (402); RM 27.48, etc.

20. Cassian, *Conf.* 5.14. Cf. Pelagius, *Ep. ad Celant.* 22; Pl 22:1214–1215.

21. Mk 9:29 (cf. Mt 6:5–15 and 16–18.

22. See notably Basil, *Hom. de ieiunio* 1.10 and 2.5–7; *Reg.* 8 = *Long Rules* 16–17; *Reg.* 88 = *Short Rules* 128; Cassian, *Inst.* 5.10–11; Diadochus, *Cap.* 42.

23. 1 Co 9:25, which deals chiefly with food. Cited by Basil, *Reg.* 8 = *Long Rules* 16.1; *Long Rules* 18; *Hom. de ieiunio* 2.3 in this restrained sense. Generalization in Diadochus, *Cap.* 42 (cf. Palladius, *Hist. Laus., Prol.* 14).

24. Pelagius, *Ep. ad Celant.* 22.

25. Cassian, *Inst.* 5.22. The movement from outside inwards (indicated above, notes 13–14) is here repeated, and generalized.

26. Cf. Cassian, *Conf.* 3.6–10.

27. RM 3.11. See our 'Scholies', p. 266. Cf. Pelagius, *Ep. ad Celant.* 22: *ut castigatione corporis erudiatur animus.*

28. 1 Co 9:27a, cited by RB 4.11 (cf. 2.28 and 30.3).

29. 1 Co 9:27b.

30. Cf. Basil, *Reg.* 8 = *Long Rules* 16.1; Cassian, *Inst.* 5.17–19; Philoxenus, *Hom.* 11 (478), etc.

31. Basil, *Hom. de ieiunio*, 1.9; Augustine, *Praec.* 3.1. Cf. Augustine, *De mor. eccl.* I, 67: *pro sufficientia domandarum libidinum*; Novatus, *Sententia*; PL 18:70c: *proper domandum sanguinem et carnem.*

32. Gal 5:16–25. Cf. Basil, *Hom. de ieiunio* 1.9 and 2.1–3; Philoxenus, *Hom.* 11 (455–458). One of the 'fruits of the spirit' moreover is *encrateia* (Gal 5:23), as Basil notes, *Reg.* 8 = *Long Rules* 16.1.

33. *Melius est minus egere quam plus babere.* Augustine, *Praec.* 3.5. Cf. Seneca, *Ep. ad Luc.* II. 6. See also Chrysostom, *In Iob.* 80; PG 59:437–438.

34. Augustine, *Praec.* 3.4 (*frugalitatem*) et 5 (*parcitate*).

35. RB 39.10. Cf. 40.6 (*parcius*).

36. RB 34.3 (cf. Augustine, *Praec.* 3.3–5)' 40.8.

37. Basil, *Hom. de ieiunio* 1.3 (*oligarkia*). Cf. Jerome, *Adv. Iovin.* II. 11.

38. Again it would be necessary to take account of the convergent influence of certain New Testament texts, as Ph 4:12; 2 Co 6:10.

39. Basil, *Long Rules* 19.2 (= *Reg.* 9; cf. RB 55.7) and 20.1–3.

40. Jerome, *Adv. Iovin.* II. 8 and 10–11.

41. Augustine, *De Mor. eccl.* I. 67; *Hist. mon.*18.1–2; Palladius, *Hist. Laus.* 32.9; Cassian, *Inst.* 10.22.

42. See A. Guillaume, *Jeûne et charité dans l'Église latine, des origines au XIIe siècle, en particulier chez S. Léon le Grand,* (Paris, 1954); Diadochus, *Cap.* 43.

43. RM 3.13–14 = RB 4.13–14. Cf. *Passio Iuliani* 46 (t. IV, p. 143).

44. RM 27.47–51. Cf. Gregory,*Dial.* 2.1: Romanus gives Benedict the bread of which he deprives himself.

45. *Hist. mon.* 7; PL 21: 419ab; *Reg. Macarii* 39. On Lent and the Paschal fast see RM 53.19–25 and 55–58.

46. Paschaltide: see Cassian, *Conf.* 21.18–20; RM 28.39. Sunday: Cassian, *Conf.* 21.20.3; Caesarius, *Reg. mon.* 22.

47. See 2 Co 11:27 (involuntary fasts?); Ac 13:2–3 and 14:23.

48. Basil, *Hom. de ieiunio* 1.3–5; Jerome, *Adv. Iovin.* II. 15.

49. Basil, *Hom. de ieiunio* 1.9 and 11 (cf. 6): Palladius, *Hist. Laus.*, *Prol.* 14.

50. Philoxenus, *Hom.* 10 (406–410, etc.); *Hom.* (471–478, etc.).

51. Cassian, *Inst.* 5.14.4; Diadochus, *Cap.* 44; Philoxenus, *Hom.* 11 (426).

52. Basil, *Hom. de ieiunio* 1.3,9. and 2.6; Philoxenus, *Hom.* 11 (424).

53. Cf. 2 Co 12:9–10. See Basil, *Hom. de ieiunio* 1.9; Jerome, *Adv. Iovin.* II. 6.

54. Philoxenus, *Hom.* 10 (354–358, 406–410, 418, etc.).

55. See our commentary on RB 6, above, notes 12–13.

56. See for example *Hist. mon.* 1 (395a), 2 (405c–406a), 6,7 (411d); Palladius, *Hist. Laus.* 11.4, 18.2, 38.10 and 12–13, 45.2.

57. Compare Jerome, *Ep.* 22.35.4 (*vivitur pane, leguminibus et olere, quae sale et oleo condiuntur*) and 36.1 (*pane et sale*). On bread, the hermits' only food, see Cassian, *Conf.* 2.19 and 12.15.2 (cf. *Inst.* 4.14 to complete *Inst.* 4.11 and 22: regime of the cenobites), confirmed by the *Apophthegmata* Agathon 20 and Serenus 1.

58. RB 40.1, citing 1 Co 7:7. The sliding of the reference is significant (cf. above, note 1). Although Benedict is dealing with wine, he extends the axiom to the whole *victus* (RB 40.2).

59. Notably Cassian, *Inst.* 5.10,21–22, etc.

60. RB 49.1; Mt 9:15. Cf. Philoxenus, *Hom.* 11 (484–485).

61. Augustine, *Praec.* 3.5 (above, note 33).

62. RB 34.3; 40.8.

63. RB 41.5 (cf. RB 64.17–19).

Chapter XV

WORK, READING, MEDITATION

(RB 48)

I N THIS LONG CHAPTER on the occupations of monks, Benedict furnishes
very few spiritual reflections. While the corresponding chapter of the
Master (RM 50) shows a constant concern with having the brothers
avoid every sort of sin, Benedict is content to establish a timetable, without commenting on the moral and religious meaning of this horarium.[1] A
nice opening maxim and one remark about the summer harvest are the
only doctrinal annotations he gives us. They deserve being considered
with all the more attention.

'Idleness is the enemy of the soul', proclaims the opening sentence. This
condemnation of idleness echoes the preamble of the Master who bases
himself on a saying of Proverbs: 'The idle man is a prey to his desires'.[2] It
also resembles a saying of Ecclesiasticus: 'Idleness teaches any number of
vices'.[3] The underlying current here seems to be that of the Sapiential
books, which contain more than one warning against idleness, laziness,
sleepiness and other vices of the same kind, whether in regard to the free
man to whom the discourse is addressed, or to the slaves under his command. Basil, in treating of monks' work, appeals to two of these texts,[4]
and Cassian cites several of them, notably those we have just seen.[5] Our
monastic authors rise from the worldly good sense of the Israelite sages,
anxious about poverty and the other temporal drawbacks of inertia, to a
more spiritual concern: this fault does harm to the soul, it contravenes the
will of God and incurs his punishment.

This is therefore the first doctrinal root of this legislation on work. It is
recognizable in the initial maxim and it continues to the last recommenda-

tions. From one end of the chapter to the other, Benedict's major concern is that no one 'spend his time in *otium*' or 'remain idle'.[6] The monk should always 'be occupied'[7] either in work or in reading.

However, a second scriptural current springs up discreetly in the middle of the chapter when Benedict gives 'our Fathers and the apostles'[8] as a model for monks. This time he is dealing not with occupations in general —either reading or manual work—but only with the latter. It is clear that Benedict was thinking especially[9] of the example and teaching of the apostle Paul, which Anthony and the other Fathers of monasticism took as their rule.[10] Basil, Augustine, and Cassian in particular made long commentaries on these pauline texts and proposed them to monks.[11]

According to this teaching the Christian should take care of himself and not be a burden on others. He has in justice the duty of earning his bread.[12] In addition, he should by his work earn the means of helping the needy, especially those prevented from working by the apostolic ministry.[13] Although Paul himself was devoted to the ministry and consequently enjoyed the right of not working, nevertheless he practised work voluntarily in order to provide an example.[14]

This is the teaching that Benedict, like the Master,[15] considers normative for 'true monks'. In itself it does not impose any particular work, not even that of harvesting, which was the occasion of Benedict's reference. Although the monk is constrained to work, he remains free to choose his livelihood, and he should do so taking into account the demands of his vocation. According to this criterion, Basil recommends some trades and counsels against others.[16] According to Cassian, the Egyptian monks were no less careful to avoid tasks incompatible with their *ascesis*. The more prudent of them abstained from agriculture as harmful to self-attention and to concentration of thought.[17] The Master also rejects field work for similar reasons—the preservation of tranquility and maintenance of fasting.[18] Basil, on the other hand, sees in such work the model of what is suitable for monks. This difference means that the practical judgment on the suitability of a given work can vary, without calling the fundamental values of the monastic life—separation from the world, simplicity, *ascesis*—into question.

Benedict does not even seem to make a judgment of this kind. In the case he envisages, gathering the harvest is a simple economic 'necessity', imposed by 'poverty'. Such work certainly has its inconveniences. The

Master had already noted them, and his fears are proven justified *a posteriori* by the mitigations to which Benedict had to consent by reason of the fatigue occasioned by this heavy labor.[19] But if in the circumstances the monks cannot otherwise 'live by the labor of their hands', they should devote themselves to such labor with courage and joy. These works are debatable in theory, but in the circumstances they are vested with the authority of apostolic precept. The thesis may reject them, but the hypothesis obliges us to admit them.

We may regret that Benedict mentioned 'our Fathers and the apostles' only in passing and in reference to an extreme case, so that his appeal to the great pauline teaching lacks clarity. But taking account of his extreme sobriety in giving doctrinal justifications, we should rather be pleased that the harvest forced him to refer to the traditional teaching, in at least summary form. We know thus the underlying meaning of benedictine work. Benedict did not mean to perform a social and civilizing work, as some moderns would have it,[20] or simply to prevent his monks from being idle, as others imagine.[21] The first group represents Benedict as a hardy innovator, breaking with the eschatological bent of his predecessors and engaging monasticism in tasks useful to humanity here below. The second group believes that the ancient monks—Benedict with them—saw in work only an ascetic pastime. In reality Benedict stands exactly in the line traced by the Fathers, without claims of originality or civilizing designs, but also without losing any of the various motivations of the tradition. For him work is not solely an ascetical exercise, an occupation to expel idleness. It is also an obligation towards the neighbor; the monks should earn their living and give alms.

'Manual work' is not, however, the only activity filling the monastic day. A part of it is also assigned to 'divine reading'. In reading the first sentence of our treatise we even have the impression that the two occupations share the time about equally. In fact, work much prevails over reading, especially in summer. Without entering into the rather subtle reckoning of the hours that Benedict devotes to each occupation,[22] we can say in summary, basing ourselves on the Rule of the Master and the general run of rules, that three quarters of the day are assigned to work and one quarter to reading. But this last part is not considered the last in importance, but rather the first: the best hours of the day are reserved to *lectio*.[23]

Moreover, although reading properly so-called occupies only a limited time, it is prolonged during the other occupations by the exercise of 'meditation'. The texts read and learned during the hours of *lectio* are then 'meditated', that is, repeated by mouth and heart during the work hours.[24] Thus the entire day rings with the divine Word. The part assigned to it seems secondary, but is in fact limitless.

The role of *meditatio* should be underlined, for later monasticism has lost even the notion of this vital exercise. Rightly has someone protested recently against the famous formula *Ora et labora* (Pray and work), wrongly presented as a complete summary of the monk's life. In fact, as was said, a third term should be added: *Ora, labora, lege* (Pray, work, read).[25] We in our turn would readily plead for one further enlargement of the formula: *Ora, labora, lege, meditare*. Without meditation the monk's day is incomplete. Continual prayer lacks its support, reading lacks its prolongation, and work lacks its accompaniment. This work of meditation truly deserves a place among the fundamental elements of the monastic life, for it binds the chief occupations together and cements their unity.

Meditation is the necessary complement of reading, for it makes the Word present in the midst of work. Reading produces its fruits of continual prayer by means of meditation. Because he repeats what he has just read, the monk at work hears God constantly and can reply to him frequently. But the relationship between the two activities is reciprocal. If reading calls for meditation to continue it, meditation in its turn presupposes the reading from which it springs. One must have read for several hours in order to meditate all day long. Meditating during work requires having 'applied oneself to reading', listening to Holy Scripture and fixing it in one's memory.

This mutual relationship of *lectio* and *meditatio* reminds us of the mutual relationship of the divine office and the precept 'Pray without ceasing'.[26] Just as the prayer of the hours at regular intervals relaunches the effort of continual prayer, so the hours of reading sustain unceasing meditation. It is very significant that the first christian author to prescribe reading for three hours at the beginning of the day based this observance on the same considerations by which Tertullian and Jerome had justified the prayer of the hours. In terms based on those of his predecessors, Pelagius writes to Demetrias: 'Although you should consecrate the whole of your life to the work of God, and absolutely no hour should pass without spiritual prog-

ress—must you not "meditate on the law of the Lord day and night"?[27]—
still there should be a determined, regulated number of hours when you
apply yourself more fully to God and which impose on you, as though by
law,[28] an unremitting mental attention. The best thing, therefore, is to
keep the morning, that is, the best part of the day, for this work. Thus until the third hour of the day the soul will exercise itself in the spiritual
combat in which it must engage every day.'[29]

What follows in the text shows the contents of these three hours reserved
for God. *Lectio* and *oratio* alternate. It is a 'reading frequently interrupted
by prayer'.[30] The text read is Holy Scripture, the nourishment of the
soul. The time of reading should fill the soul, like a meal, with 'enough for
the whole day'.

Thus, for Pelagius, the meaning of these three continuous hours of
prayerful reading is analogous to that of the five or six or seven discontinuous 'hours' of psalmody and prayer which mark out the monk's day. In
this precise form neither observance can claim any fixed scriptural foundation, but both of them respond, explicitly or implicitly,[31] to the same
general appeal of the Lord: 'Pray without ceasing'. Christ's disciple, in
order to obey this divine order more surely, obliges himself 'as though by
law' to reserve certain times in which to seek God. By doing this he does
not think that he has satisfied a precept and fulfilled his obligations. On
the contrary, he thinks of the observance as only a minimum. Far from
being all-sufficient, it only tends to sustain a limitless effort towards the
consecration to God of the whole of one's being, activity, and time.

This ordering of the hours of *lectio* to the rest of the day is especially envisaged from a practical point of view in the rest of Pelagius' text:
Demetrias should show in her dealings with men all day long the spiritual
fruits of her commerce with God. Reading teaches a person how to behave in life; it regulates and corrects conduct. But this predominant moral
concern does not exclude another consideration, the one which interests
us here. It will have been noticed that Pelagius wanted Demetrias 'to meditate on the law of the Lord day and night', outside the times of reading.
The morning study is therefore prolonged by meditation all day long. It is
the downbeat in a listening to God which aims at being continual. Its resonance in life does not consist only of good actions, but also of attention.

But Demetrias, living in the midst of her family, could not avoid the distractions which interrupted this effort. The 'meditation day and night'

recommended to her remained a somewhat theoretical ideal. It is different for a monk separated from the world. It is in a writing about monastic life, Augustine's *De opere monachorum*, that we meet the best description of this relationship between *lectio* and *meditatio* that we are seeking to clarify. Augustine first recommends 'meditating' and 'saying psalms' to monks while they are working,[32] and then adds: 'Nothing hinders them . . . provided they have leisure time devoted to learning what they will repeat from memory'.

These *seposita tempora* are none other than the hours of reading. They appear then as the time when the monk fills his memory with the texts he will recite during work. If he is going to remain in contact with God all day long by means of his Word, he must apply himself to it entirely for several hours. A restriction of work time and a lack of income are entailed, which should be compensated for by subsidies from the faithful, according to our author.[33] Leaving aside the last point, the important thing is that Augustine, more clearly still than Pelagius, sets *lectio* in relationship with the *meditatio* prolonged during the day. After him, Caesarius and his successors illustrate the same idea in a slightly different form: when the common reading in the refectory or at work ends, meditation in the heart should not cease.[34]

Augustine and Pelagius, these two contemporaries who were so violently opposed to each other in another area, not only agreed on this point, but it is also in their work that we find attested for the first time the custom of devoting three hours a day to reading. As we have seen, Pelagius wanted these hours to be the first three of the morning, considered the best. According to the *Ordo monasterii* attributed to Augustine, the brothers should apply themselves to reading from the sixth to ninth hour, before the meal.[35]

Thus was established a discipline not observed in Pachomius or Basil, nor among the Egyptian monks described by Jerome and Cassian,[36] namely a fixed space of time, at a specific moment, when the monk devoted himself exclusively to reading, all other business being suspended. The Gallo-Frankish tradition, stemming from Caesarius, observed the pelagian norm of the first hours of the day, but reduced it somewhat, especially for women.[37] The Italian and Spanish monasteries readily allocated three hours to reading, if not from the sixth to ninth hours as preferred by the *Ordo monasterii*, at least at other times in the middle or at the

end of the day. Everywhere in the West, monks and nuns obliged themselves to these two or three hours of reading a day.

Thus takes form the monastic horarium, composed of an alternation of
reading and work. These two occupations proceed from one and the same
root: the will of God. We know from Scripture, particularly from St
Paul, that man, the Christian and the monk, should work. The duty of
reading the sacred books is less clearly defined,[38] but it flows, as we have
said, from the invitation to pray without ceasing. By means of prayerful
'meditation', itself pronounced blessed by the Bible,[39] the two great scriptural directives join in one simple and harmonious practice. The monastic
day is one. Under the apparent variety of occupations, it unrolls the same
continuous chain of obedience and attention to God.

Work, reading, meditation. These three acts are of such importance
that it will be useful to recall briefly their nature. Work, often designated
as 'corporal' or 'manual' work,[40] is always conceived as a productive or
remunerative activity.[41] This is a matter of earning one's living, as we
have said. In itself, no honest trade is excluded, but the conditions placed
by the monastic life are demanding. They are very well suggested by
Basil,[42] and imply in particular the qualities of silence, recollection, and
the possibility of 'meditating' and praying.

Like the French word *lecture* (and the English word 'reading'), the Latin
lectio is an ambiguous term, being able to designate both the act of reading
and the text which is read. *Lectio divina* should be understood in the latter
sense. It designates the divinely inspired text, Holy Scripture. *Vacare lectioni divinae* therefore means to apply oneself to the Bible. Pelagius and
the Four Fathers mean the same by the expression *vacare Deo*[43]: to open
the Bible is to meet God. Jerome, Pelagius, and Augustine[44] all note that
prayer has its place in this reading, and the first two say that it should interrupt the reading 'frequently'.

The Master and Benedict in the Instruments of Good Works express
themselves in the same way: 'To listen willingly to holy reading, to devote
oneself frequently to prayer'.[45] Here the 'good will' or 'pleasure' with
which the reading should be listened to, corresponds to the 'frequency' of
the prayer. This word 'willingly' (*libenter*), which is also found in Caesarius,[46] aims at the repugnance at reading which seems to have increased as
the cultural level declined. Whether made in common or in private,

whether perceived by the ears or by the eyes, reading weighed heavily on some. Fulgentius showed his disfavor towards those of his monks who neglected it, and Benedict had to rebuke this negligence severely.[47]

We would be wrong to regard this aversion to reading as unique to an age in which instruction was less widespread and reading harder. The difficulties pertain to every age, for they stem from man's spiritual laziness and from the austere nature of this book, the Bible. Even today most monks would doubtless have trouble in remaining two or three hours every day in close contact with the sacred text. And as for reading it in public, we scarcely do it anywhere except at the office and in small doses.

Too often it even happens that our readings in the refectory are devoid of any religious character. We can recall in this regard that one of Benedict's concerns was the quality of the readings made to the monks. What he chiefly feared, apparently, was the reading of 'apocryphal' or scarcely orthodox books.[48] To this danger is added in our days that of superficial, distracting, and worldly readings. Whether they deal with history or current events, whether they aim at instructing monks about the past or keeping them abreast of the present, one can ask whether they do not also set monastic communities in a climate alien to the search for God.

After these brief statements about work and reading, it remains to define *meditatio*. The nature of this exercise is beginning to be better known in the light shed on it by some good works[49] of the last thirty years. We know now that the simple translation of the word is misleading. It is not the wholly interior act which our 'meditation' is, but a process both oral and mental, a recitation which occupies the mouth as well as the mind. This means that it consists not only of forming ideas and sentiments, but also and in the first place, of saying a text.[50] This text is naturally taken from the Book *par excellence*, the Bible.

Meditation, like reading, gives way to prayers which interrupt it.[51] The monk replies then to the divine Word which he has recited. The frequency of these prayers, always short in principle, depends on the nature of the work one is doing while meditating. For meditation normally accompanies manual work. The possibility of meditating is, as we have said, one of the criteria of work that is truly monastic.

Yet, the texts which speak of meditation do not always associate it with work. Sometimes the monk 'meditates' during reading times, whether the recitation of the scriptural text takes the place of reading, or the monk must learn texts by heart with a view to saying them at the office or at work. In this latter case, *meditari* takes a slightly different meaning from what we have admitted up to now. It is not merely recitation, but repetition with a view to learning by heart. This exercise of memorization, which demands the control of a teacher or recourse to the written text,[52] can only be made when one is not occupied, that is, during the hours of *lectio* and free time.

It is only in this latter sense and in connection with times when the monk is not working that Benedict uses the words *meditari* and *meditatio*,[53] and he does so three times. For him this is a kind of study. This meaning already predominated in the Master, and is the only one represented in our Rule. Does this mean that Benedict was ignorant of the other meaning, or that he relinquished the traditional exercise of 'meditation' during work? We have already given our opinion on this subject[54]: Benedict's silence can only be an accident. Several rules speak of meditation-study without neglecting to mention meditation-recitation.[55] Benedict's Rule, like some others,[56] indicates only the first of these ways of 'meditating', probably without excluding the second. No doubt this is the effect of the tendency, already perceptible in his neighbor Eugippius,[57] to reserve *meditari* and *meditatio* to memorization done outside of work. However this may be, the omission seems to us regrettable. The absence of all allusion to meditation upon Scripture during work is one of the points where we feel most keenly the need to clarify and complete our Rule with the data collected from monastic tradition.

It is not easy to draw applications for our times from this historical data. Work has assumed an enormous importance in our modern psychologies. There is less need to arouse monks to it than to keep them from being completely absorbed in it. In this regard, the 'meditation' of the ancients cannot be a great help as long as our memories, atrophied by wholly different methods of education, have trouble retaining the smallest text. On the other hand, reading, to say nothing of the other means of communication, presents infinite possibilities and facilities. However little intellectual or even technical the work may be, it is so draining that the mind can only with difficulty apply itself to holy reading and find in it a peaceful diversion.

Do these transformations we have just sketched render absolutely null and void the program traced by the Rule in this chapter? We do not think so. Experience proves that the monastic soul of today, guided by these principles, can discover the equivalents of scriptural *meditatio*—such as the repetition at regular intervals of a single verse drawn from daily reading—and by them, renewed forms of prayerful work, just as it can, as formerly, nourish itself from the Bible and draw from it its prayer, with the new means at its disposal. For this it needs only to be given, together with the light of tradition, a framework of observances like that traced in the Rule.

In this regard the flexibility and realism that Benedict shows are an example to us. When we see him specifically regulating the time needed for each occupation and, as a result, displacing slightly the regular hours of the office, these arrangements, which were quite original in their day, encourage us to search for the balances we need, and for the personal and communitarian time schedules which allow them. This search for the better use of the times separating the hours of prayer fixed by the Rule should respect these hours. If the Rule's horarium of office shows traces of a time division which is now outmoded, the design behind it remains at the heart of the monastic vocation, namely, to sanctify time by letting ourselves be recalled, indeed disturbed, at short and regular intervals by the service of the divine praise.

NOTES TO CHAPTER 15

1. See t. V, pp. 589–604.
2. RB 48.1; RM 50.1–2 (cf. Pr 13:4 LXX: *In desideriis est omnis otiosus*).
3. Si 33:29: *Multam enim malitiam docuit otiositas.*
4. Basil, *Long Rules* 37.2, citing Pr 31:27 (*Panem otiosa non comedit*) and 6:6 (*Vade ad formicam o piger*).
5. Cassian *Inst.* 10.21.1 citing Pr 28:19 and 23:21; *Inst.* 10.21.4, citing Pr 15:19 and 13:4, as well as Si 33:29; *Conf.* 24.2.2, citing Pr 13:4 and 21:25.
6. RB 48.18,23,24.
7. RB 48.1. The texts of the Sapiential books and their use by Basil and Cassian have work alone in mind, but Benedict joins *lectio* to them as a means of occupying the monk and keeping him from being idle.
8. RB 48.8.
9. Besides Paul and Barnabas (1 Co 9:6), he might have Peter and his companions in mind (cf Isidore, *Reg.* 5), whom we see fishing even after the Resurrection of Christ (Jn 21:2–3).
10. Athanasius, *Vita Antonii* 3, Citing 2 Th 3:10. Cf. *Vita Ant.* 44, 50 (agriculture), 53.
11. Basil, *Long Rules* 37.1–3 and 42.1; *Short Rules* 207 = *Reg.* 127. Augustine, *De op. mon.* 3.4–22.26. Cassian, *Inst.* 10.7–19; *Conf.* 24.11.4–5.

12. See specially 2 Th 3:7–12. Cf. 2 Co 12:13; 1 Th 2:9 and 4:11–12; Tt 3:14.

13. Ac 20:34–35; Eph 4:28.

14. In addition to the above texts, see Ac 18:3; I Co 4:12 and 9:6,12,15,18.

15. RM 50.6; 53.40; 78.18–24; 83.13–16.

16. Basil, *Long Rules* 38.

17. Cassian, *Conf.* 24.4 and 24.12.4.

18. RM 86.

19. See t. VI, pp. 1190–1203.

20. See E. Delaruelle, 'S. Benoît et la civilisation de son temps', in *Le Christianisme et l'Occident barbare* (Paris, 1945) 399–432; J.R. Palanque and E. Delaruelle, 'Le rôle temporel de l'Église du IVe au VIIe siècle', in *Inspiration religieuse et structures temporelles* (Paris, 1948) 77–106, specially pp. 97–8.

21. See L. Cognet, 'Spiritualité monastique et laïcs d'aujourdhui', in the bulletin *Ecoute* (La Pierre-qui-vire), 164 (15 May 1968), Supplement, pp. 19–20, and our criticism in *Ecoute*, 165 (1 July 1968) 27–31. See our study 'Travail monastique', in *Ecoute*, 95 (Nov. 1961) 1–12, and 96 (December 1961) 2–7, which had already appeared in shortened form as *Moines*, in *Témoignages, Cahiers de la Pierre-qui-Vire* (April 1953), (Paris, 1953) 122–38.

22. See t. V, pp. 591–604. Benedict gives reading more than the traditional three hours (see p. 598 and note 27).

23. Pelagius, *Ep. ad Demetr.* 23; PL 30:37b, followed by Caesarius, *EP. II ad virg.*; PL 67: 1132d.

24. See above our study on the office, Ch. VIII, n. 34–35.

25. See J. Winandy, 'La spiritualité bénédictine', in J. Gautier, *La spiritualité catholique* (Paris, 1953) 13–36, specially 33–4.

26. See our study on the office.

27. Ps 1:2.

28. *Velut quadam lege.* These words are found exactly thus, except for an inversion, in Cassian, *Inst.* 3.3.8. Pelagius repeats Tertullian's formula, *De orat.* 25.5 (*quasi lege*), as Cassian was to do after him. His whole phrase (*Quanquam . . . debet tamen . . .*) recalls Tertullian's argument, *De orat.* 24–25, and more precisely the form given to it by Jerome, *Ep.* 22.37 (*quanquam . . . tamen . . . debemus*).

29. Pelagius, *Ep. ad Demetr.* 23. Cf. *Ep. ad Celant.* 24; PL 22:1216.

30. *Lectionem frequenter interrumpat oratio.* Cf. Jerome, *Ep.* 58.6 and 130.15.

31. The reference is explicit in Tertullian and Jerome, implicit and indirect in Pelagius, who depends on them.

32. Augustine, *De op. mon.* 17.20: allusions to Ps 1:2 (cf. Pelagius, *Ep. Ad Demetr.* 23) and to Ps 12:6.

33. According to Ferrandus, *Vita Fulg.* 28, Fulgentius and his monks often received these subsidies.

34. Caesarius, *Reg. virg.* 18 (refectory) and 20 and 22 (work); Aurelian, *Reg. mon.* 24 and *Reg. virg.* 20 (work); *Reg. Tarn.* 8. 11–12 (table); Donatus, *Reg.* 20 (work) and 33 (table).

35. *Ordo monasterii* 3. Cf. Augustine, *De op. mon.* 29,37 (no precise detail about the horarium).

36. Jerome, *Ep.* 22.35.7: the monk applies himself to reading 'when the work is done'; Cassian, *Inst.* 4.12: *operi manuum seu lectioni*, without further precision. The mentions of the third hour (Cassian, *Conf.* 10.10.8; cf. Jerome, *Ep.* 23.1) and the second hour (Jerome, *Ep.*43.1) are too difficult to interpret for one to draw therefrom an attestation of an observance. According to the *Vita Patrum Jur.* 126, Eugendus gave himself to reading after the work.

37. See t. V, p. 594, n. 17.

38. 1 Tm 4:13 (*Attende lectioni*), invoked by Ferreolus, *Reg.* 19, is about the only text that can be cited.

39. Ps 1:2.

40. Augustine, *De op. mon.* 17,20 (*corporaliter*); RM 50.7 (*corporalis hoc est manuum*), etc. This mention of hands is scriptural (Ac 20:34, 1 Co 4:12, 1 Th 4:11, Eph 4:28). It may have been suggested also by the need to distinguish work from all other *labor* or *opera*, notably the *opus Dei* (*ascesis* or the office). The expression *opus laboris* (RM 9.19, etc.) seems to answer the same necessity.

41. The case of Paul of the Porphyrian desert (Cassian, *Inst.* 10.24), too often considered as representative, constitutes in reality an exception. According to Jerome, *Ep.* 125.11, the egyptian monasteries constrained their recruits to work less by economic necessity than to prevent them from being idle. In fact, each monk's work produces more than he consumed (Cassian, *Inst.* 4.14). The surplus was given away in good works (*Inst.* 10.22; cf. Augustine, *De mor. eccl.* I. 67; *Hist. mon.* 18.1-2; Palladius, *Hist. Laus.* 32.9). Augustine, *De op. mon.* 21.25, admits that those who were not used to manual work in the world were dispensed from it.

42. Basil, *Long Rules* 38, recommends various handicraft trades and agriculture; Jerome, *Ep.* 125.11. the weaving of willow branches and rushes, gardening and the raising of bees, making fishnets, and copying books. The last satisfies the soul as well as earning one's living manually. Cf. Palladius, *Hist. Laus.* 38.10; *Vita Caesarii* I.44.

43. Pelagius. *Ep. ad Demetr.* 23; *Reg. IV Patr.* 3.10.

44. Jerome, *Ep.* 22.35.7; 58.6 and 130.15 (*frequenter*). Pelagius, *Ep. ad Demetr.* 23 (*frequenter*); *Ep. ad Celant.* 24 (*crebrae orationum vices*). Augustine, *De op. mon.* 29.37, followed by Isidore, *Reg* 5.6. Cf. Cassian, *Conf.* 24.10 and 24.11.2 where *lectio* and *oratio* are associated, but without a set time.

45. RM 3.61-62 = RB 4.55-56. *Lectiones sanctas libenter audire, orationi frequenter incumbere.*

46. Caesarius, *Serm.* 75.3 and 196.2.

47. Ferrandus, *Vita Fulg.* 52; RB 48.17-20. See also Ferreolus, *Reg.* 19.

48. RB 9.8; 42.3-5; 73.3-6. Cf. t. I, pp. 143-5 and 171-2; t. V, pp. 711-12.

49. See H. Bacht, *Das Vermächtnis des Ursprungs* (Würzburg, 1972) 244-64.

50. This recitation can be purely interior, by force of circumstances. See Basil, *Reg.* 37.2.

51. L. Th. Lefort, *Les Vies coptes*, p. 105,9-12 (Bo 34); Cassian, *Inst.* 3.2; Caesarius, *Reg. virg.* 20: *meditatio verbi Dei et oratio de corde non cesset* (the words *et oratio* are omitted by Donatus, *Reg.* 20; similarly, Aurelian, *Reg. mon.* 24, avoids speaking of prayer during work, and substitutes the formula of Caesarius, *Reg. virg.*. 18: *meditatio sancta de corde non cesset*, which dealt with meals; on this tendency to eliminate prayer from work, see our section on the office, notes 38-42).

52. RM 50.12-14 and 64-69; 57.7-13. *Reg. Pauli et Steph.* 14-16.

53. RB 8.3; 48.23; 58.5 (this last is less clear).

54. See our section on the office, n. 132.

55. Thus RM, the *Regula Tarnantensis* and Isidore. For the detailed references, see our article 'Les deux fonctions de la *meditatio* dans les règles monastiques anciennes', in RHS, 51 (1975) 27-40.

56. Thus the *Regula Patrum II*, the *Regula Pauli et Stephani* and Fructuosus. The opposite is much more frequent (Pachomius, Caesarius, Aurelian, Ferreolus, the *Regula Orientalis*, Donatus, Waldebert. See the article cited above).

57. Eugippius, *Reg.* 36.1. See our article 'Quelques observations nouvelles sur la Règle d'Eugippe', in *Benedictina*, 22 (1975) 31-41.

Chapter XVI

THE ORATORY AND PRIVATE PRAYER
(RB 52)

THIS CHAPTER ON THE ORATORY of the monastery surely contains nothing more personal or more moving than the short phrase in which Benedict indicates ways of private prayer: 'If anyone wishes to pray in private, by himself, let him enter and pray quietly, not in a loud voice, but with tears and application of heart'. Neither the Rule of the Master nor that of Augustine, whose recommendations are combined here, furnished Benedict with this feature.[1] Although Augustine had mentioned private prayers made in the oratory outside the offices, he was thinking only of protecting them against the noise of profane works. Benedict is also concerned with the noise caused by those who pray, and do so in a loud voice. Not content to forbid it because of the embarrassment caused to others, he sketches as a counterpart the marks of true prayer: tears which spring from a heart that is intensely attentive.

This description makes us think immediately of the chapter 'On Reverence in Prayer'. There, too, Benedict contrasted two ways of praying; one that he advises against, and one that he recommends: 'We should recognize that it is not by multiplying words that we shall be heard, but by purity of heart and tears of compunction'.[2] In each case hypertrophy of the external element—abundance of words and loud noise—is reproved, and the accent is placed on the same spiritual elements: the heart and tears.

These elements are found together a third time in the program of lenten *ascesis*: 'prayer with tears, reading, compunction of heart'.[3] Benedict's insistence on this point and the consistency of his teaching are remarkable.

Following the Master, he made 'daily confession of past faults, in prayer, with tears and groaning', one of the instruments of good works.[4] But in the institutional chapters of the Rule he adds to this borrowed maxim a series of marks which go beyond it. To the tears, of which alone he spoke then, he now adds their interior source: the heart itself, which should be pure, intensely applied, and touched by compunction.

If we wish to penetrate this benedictine doctrine of prayer, we must do more than prove that his vocabulary bears the imprint of a spiritual tradition of which Cassian is for us, as he was for Benedict himself, the best known representative.[5] It is above all in Scripture that we must seek its inspiration. 'Not in much speaking . . . not in a loud voice': these two defects against which Benedict warns us are both attached to the same passage of the Sermon on the Mount in which Jesus, criticizing Jews and pagans, defines the characteristics of Christian prayer.

In regard to the first—the 'much speaking'—the matter is evident: 'When you are praying', says Christ, 'speak not much, as the heathens do. For they think that in their much speaking they will be heard'.[6] The relationship of the second defect to the gospel text is not clear at first sight, but we discover it by going back through a series of patristic passages which reprove the 'loud voice'. It seems that in the Fathers this criticism of loud prayer is based on Jesus' word: 'When you pray you shall not be as the hypocrites, who love to stand and pray in the synagogues and corners of the streets, that they may be seen by men . . . . But you, when you pray, enter into your chamber, and having shut the door, pray to your Father in secret'.[7] From Clement to Cassian, passing through Tertullian and Cyprian, the authors of treatises on prayer have constantly drawn from this text a condemnation of loud prayer and an invitation to pray softly.[8] The advertising of prayer which Christ condemns can result from the voice as well as from visibility. The secret place in which he wishes us to enclose ourselves is a matter of silence as well as of walls and a closed door. We must learn to pray with our mouth closed, in our heart.

This interpretation of the evangelical counsel particularly recommends itself where literal application was impossible for lack of a private 'chamber' in which to shut oneself for prayer. There are days and hours when Christians should pray together, and places of prayer where they can be found praying side by side. In these circumstances Christ's word does not lapse but is understood as the discretion each person should show in keeping his prayer to himself, in his conscience.[9] For cenobites deprived of private cells and always living in common rooms, this form of secret prayer is the only one possible, and always necessary. Just as the dormitory is substituted for the cell as the place of rest, so the oratory replaces it as the place of prayer.[10] Then the only secret chamber where the monk can address the Father is his heart.

But in passing from the order of seeing to the order of hearing, from place to conscience, the counsel about secrecy was open to a new meaning, which it did not fail to take on in the Fathers and in our Rule. In giving it, Jesus had in mind the absence of vanity, uprightness of intention, and the will to please God alone. To this demand for religious sincerity and purity is joined, and sometimes substituted, for it is our author's concern for interiority. Since the heart has become the place of secret prayer, this prayer is set against not only ostentation, but also irreverence and superficiality.[11] To pray loudly would be to insult God by supposing that he needs to hear our voices. To pray in silence is to recognize that his glance penetrates to the depths of the heart.[12] There the true spiritual encounter occurs: the heart in deep faith addresses the God it knows to be present.

Another shift in meaning affects the neighboring pericope, where Jesus forbids 'much speaking'. The motive given by the Gospel is that 'our Father knows what we have need of'[13] Sobriety of language in praying is therefore a matter of faith: although the heathen treat God as a man whose attention must be attracted by a flood of words, Christians believe in his providence, which has nothing to do with such persistence. But to those who use this text, such homage to the omniscient Father is associated with, or gives way to, a concern with attention and purity. If prayer should be brief, this is in order to avoid the distractions caused by human weakness or provoked by the devil.[14]

Thus two successive prohibitions of the Gospel—'Do not pray in public', and 'Do not use many words in prayer'—have engendered in christian tradition a reflection which goes beyond their immediate significance. From them has resulted a doctrine of prayer according to which one should pray quietly, in the secret of one's conscience, and without many words, with complete attentiveness. These two articles are precisely those which we find in inverse order in Benedict's chapters on prayer and on the oratory. They converge in what we can call *une mystique du cœur*. *Puritas cordis, conpunctio cordis, intentio cordis*: not for nothing is the word 'heart' repeated each time by Benedict's pen. The heart, as the place of secret prayer, is also the place of sobriety and attention.

The heart expresses itself by tears, and these are heard by God. Anna, the mother of Samuel, is the type of this prayer of the heart, with tears which surely obtain what she asks.[15] Hezekiah and the psalmist furnish other examples.[16] These tears, and the compunction of which they are the sign, can have different motives: sorrow for having sinned and desire for the next life, dread of hell and pain felt for one's neighbor's faults.[17] They spring forth at all the stages of spiritual progress, from the initial fear of punishment to the love of the perfect for things eternal.[18] Whatever the occasion, they disclose one important event: man's heart has been touched by the word of God.

The entire spiritual life, from its humblest beginnings to its highest states, is thus encompassed within Benedict's short formulas on prayer with tears. If confession of sins especially figures in one of them,[19] the 'purity of heart' of which another speaks constitutes, according to Cassian, the aim and perfection of all *ascesis*, the equivalent of charity and the place of contemplation.[20]

Nevertheless, it is not certain that we should understand this benedictine 'purity of heart' in the sublime, all-embracing sense of the *Conferences*. In the present passage of the Rule the reality is perhaps more modest and transitory: the purification of heart which occurs in the very act of fervent prayer. Purity, the ideal and permanent condition of prayer, is also its momentary companion in a more ordinary and verifiable way. When does the heart become pure if not when one is praying?

Whatever the precise meaning of the expression in the present context, this demand for 'purity of heart' illustrates the relationship of prayer to the whole ascetic effort. Prayer is inseparable from a life of virtue tending to complete purification of soul.[21] Certain connections must be brought out, in detail. The basic conviction of God's presence, inculcated at great length in the first degree of humility, is again Benedict's first and fundamental recommendation about one's attitude at the office.[22] Abundance of words and loud talking were first rebuked in the chapters on silence and humility, before being rebuked in the counsels relative to prayer.[23] The right way of speaking to men—in few words and quietly—also pleases God. In each case the underlying disposition is the same, humility.[24]

Finally, divine grace makes its effect felt in both areas. At the end of the treatise on humility, the Master and Benedict, going beyond Cassian, point out that the complete purification of the monk and his blossoming in charity are the work of the Holy Spirit.[25] When it comes to prayer, Benedict alone, going beyond the Master, observes that prayer can be prolonged 'under the effect of an affection inspired by divine grace'.[26] We know already from Augustine, to whom Benedict perhaps owes this touch,[27] that this apparent infraction of the rule about short prayer is not a relapse into 'much speaking'. But Augustine did not adduce grace in this regard. Benedict's mention of it here is original. It reminds us of the regulation to recite the verse 'O God, come to my assistance' at the beginning of each day hour.[28] Like other patristic authors,[29] but in his own way, Benedict points out that prayer is not only addressed to God, but also comes from him.

Prolonged prayer, prayer with tears. The two facts are attested in Gregory's biography of our saint.[30] Perhaps, as Gregory suggests, they were even habitual traits of his, which seemed to those around him characteristic of his religious make-up.[31] In any case, his invitations to 'tears of compunction', combined with his corresponding condemnations of laughter,[32] are among the things which make us feel how far we are from him and his spiritual universe. Not laughter but tears; not recreations but recollection; not amusements but compunction. Benedict's spiritual ideal is that of the ancient *penthos*,[33] and of the joy which the Spirit spreads about in the soul in the midst of penitence and expectation.[34]

NOTES TO CHAPTER 16

1. See t. V, pp. 617–35, specially p. 629–32.

2. RB 20.3.

3. RB 49.4. Compunction can be joined to prayer with tears (see t. VI, p. 1233), but also to *lectio*, as is seen in Gregory, *Dial.* 4.49; Moricca, p. 307,9–14 (Cf. Cassian, *Inst.* 5.14.1; *Conf.* 1.17.2).

4. RB 4.57 = RM 3.63.

5. See t. V, pp. 573–4 and 629–32. Besides Cassian, cf. *Historia monachorum* 1; 397b–398b.

6. Mt 6:7. The Vulgate translates in the same way the two different greek words (*battalogèsete* and *polulogia*) using *multum loqui* and *multiloquio*.

7. Mt 6:5–6.

8. Clement, *Strom.* 7.7.49.6: the 'chamber' is the soul, where one can pray by a simple

thought, according to the *agraphon* 'Think (conceive) and I shall give', several times cited by Clement (*Strom.* 6.9.78.1.; 6.12.101.4; 7.12.73.1; cf. 7.7.41.3); Tertullian, *De Orat.* 17.3–5; Cyprian, *De dom. or.* 4; Cassian, *Conf.* 9.35.

9. Tertullian, Cyprian, and Cassian deal with the inconvenience noisy prayer causes one's neighbor.

10. See t. V, p. 722.

11. Before allegorizing Mt 6:6, understood of the 'chamber' of the soul (see above, note 8), Clement took in its obvious sense the text of Mt 6:5 (*oude emphanôs tois pollois euxetai*). Cyprian also seems to associate the different senses, visual and auditory, external and spiritual. Tertullian deals only with the sound of the voice, but thinks also of respect for God and neighbor, without excluding the rejection of ostentation. Cassian thinks only of the secret of the heart and of silence, with the original preoccupation of hiding the prayer not only from the brothers, but also from demons.

12. This act of faith is but a prolongation of Christ's assertion: 'the Father sees in secret' [of the chamber], in Mt 6:6.

13. Mt 6:7–8. Just before using Mt 6:5–6 (note 11), Clement, *Strom.* 7.7.49.6, alluded to the prohibition of *polulogos*.

14. Augustine, *Ep.* 130.20; Cassian, *Inst.* 2.10.2–3 and *Conf.* 9.36.1; RM 48.5 and 10–11. Cf. Chrysostom, *Serm. de Anna* 2.2.

15. Cf. 1 Sm 1:10–13 and 26–27. See Clement, *Strom.* 6.12.101.4; Cyprian, *De dom. or.* 4; Chrysostom, *Serm. de Anna* 2.2–3. The case of Anna is mentioned again, but for other ends, by Origen, *De orat.* 2.13,16; Augustine, *Ep.* 130.20.

16. Is 38.2–5 = 2 Kgs 20.2–5; Ps 38:13.

17. Cassian, *Conf.* 9.29.

18. Gregory, *Dial.* 3.34 (cf. 4.49).

19. RB 4.57 = RM 3.63. Cf. Cassian, *Conf.* 9.11 and 9.15.1.

20. RB 20.3. See Cassian, *Conf.* 1.4–13 (cf. *Conf.* 9.14–15).

21. Cassian, *Conf.* 9.2–6; 10.14.1–2. 'Prayer' for Cassian, as for Evagrius, is moreover synonymous with 'contemplation' and this presupposes *puritas cordis* and charity (*Conf.* 1.4–13). This state of purity-charity is exactly what the Master and Benedict, following Cassian, *Inst.* 4.39.3 (cf. 4.43), propose as the destination of the spiritual ascent (RM 10.87–91 = RB 7.67–70). From Cassian's point of view, the place assigned by Benedict to the treatise on prayer, immediately after that of humility crowned by charity, is not without significance.

22. Compare RB 7.10–30 (= RM 10.10–41) and RB 19.1–2.

23. Compare RB 6.4 and 7.57 (= RM 8.35 and 10.76) with RB 20.3 (*non in multiloquio*); RB 7.60 (= RM 10.80) with RB 52.4 (*non in clamosa voce*).

24. Cf. RB 20.1–2: *cum humilitate . . . cum omni humilitate.*

25. RM 10.91 = RB 7.70.

26. RB 20.4.

27. Augustine, *Ep.* 130.19–20, citing particularly Lk 22:43 (Christ in agony prolongs his prayer). Cf. Chrysostom, *Serm. de Anna* 2.2: Anna 'multiplies her prayers'.

28. RB 18.1.

29. Origen, *De orat.* 2 (Rm 8:26); Evagrius, *De orat.* 59 (1 Sm, 2:9 LXX) and 63 (Rm 8:26); Cassian, *Conf.* 9.15.2 (cf. 9.25 and 10.11.6: Rm 8:26).

30. Gregory, *Dial.* 2.17 (prayer with tears *ut consueverat*); 2.27 (two days of prayer *more suo*).

31. In the *Dialogues*, the habit of prayer with tears is attributed only to a small number of people: See *Dial.* 3.33 (Eleutherius); 4.49 (Anthony and Merulus); 4.58 (Cassius). Occa-

sional tears: *Dial.* 1.7 and 12; 4.40,49,57. Recommendation of tears: *Dial.* 3.34; 4.60–62. Continual prayer: *Dial.* 1.10; 4.16,17,20.

32. RB 4.53–54 = RM 3.59–60; RB 6.8 = RM 9.51; RB 7.59–60 = RM 10.78 and 80.

33. We are thinking of I. Hausherr's important work, *Penthos. La doctrine de la componction dans l'Orient chrétien*, OCA 132 (Rome, 1944). E.T. *Penthos. The Doctrine of Compunction in the Christian East*, (Kalamazoo, 1982).

34. RB 49.6–7. See t. VI, p. 1234..

Chapter XVII

THE MONASTERY AND THE WORLD

(RB 53 & 66)

B ENEDICT'S CHAPTER ON HOSPITALITY shows a curious contrast between its beginning and its end. It stipulates first of all that guests
are to be welcomed as Christ, with an enthusiastic veneration. It
ends by forbidding the monks to speak with them.[1] Between these two
extremes the discourse shifts several times from one attitude to the other.
Against a background of extreme respect and goodwill for the guest a
series of negative remarks stands out. If we begin with prayer for the newly arrived, this is to counteract diabolic illusions. The fast is broken in
their honor, but only by the superior; the community continues to
observe its usual fasts. Among the motives which lead to honoring guests,
one tainted motive is pointed out, the fear of the rich. Finally, their kitch-
en should be separate 'so as not to disturb the brothers'.[2] However disparate these remarks are, they all show a certain reserve towards persons who
are welcomed with such warmth in principle. From different points of
view the inconveniences of the welcome appear, and measures are taken
against them.

The same contrast appears in the other major chapter about hospitality,
that on the porters. There, too, all is at first only eagerness to open and to
answer, religious respect and fervent charity. But soon afterwards the
door closes, and severe judgment is pronounced on monks going outside:
trips outside are not good for their souls.[3] Wide is the reception, but strict
the cloister. Those from outside belong to the world where the monks
avoid going, and they can feel they are both venerated and suspect, received
with open arms and kept apart.

259

Such contrasting impressions stand out within the whole collection of scattered texts which in one way or another touch on the relations of the monastery with the world. In one place Benedict recommends 'guests and the poor' to the cellarer; he honors 'the guests and pilgrims' by reserving the abbot's table for them, and shows solicitude and consideration for the stranger monk.[4] In another place, he warns those going on a journey against omitting the canonical hours, forbids them to eat outside the monastery, submits to the abbot's control every exchange of letters or goods with the outside; he foresees the troubles that will be caused by the stranger monk and the need to dismiss him; he is anxious over the pollution undergone in the world by the brothers returning from a journey, which they will transmit to their brethren who stayed at home.[5] This last feature, which occurs in chapter 67, comes immediately after the chapter on the porters. In a significant way Benedict has transferred there indications which the Master gave about journeys in another context.[6] So every journey appears as a regrettable exception to the rule of cloister which has just been formulated in concluding the chapter 'On the porters'.[7]

Benedict's glance then fixes in turn the positive and negative aspects of the world outside the cloister, not without dwelling more on the second. This alternating consideration scarcely differs from that of the Master, whose chapters concerning visitors go from a deferential and eager welcome to the imposition of obligatory work and a strict surveillance.[8] And besides our two rules, the whole of monastic tradition illustrates the same law of alternation. Sometimes there are found appeals to receive the guest like Christ,[9] and at other times—no doubt more frequently—there are restrictive measures of every kind which affect either the monks' trips into the world,[10] or their relationships with strangers coming to the monastery,[11] or exchanges of letters and gifts with them,[12] or finally the ways of receiving guests, which should not derogate from monastic simplicity or compromise the austerity of the rule.[13] More than once the porter appears in these texts as the agent by whom the rules of cloister are established and maintained. He is present in this capacity already in the Rule of Pachomius,[14] and is entrusted by the *Regula Orientalis* with the application of norms coming from the Second Rule of the Fathers,[15] and by Caesarius with that of the two articles from Augustine's *Praeceptum*.[16] In both cases he is made the guardian of principles established by earlier documents which had not as yet mentioned him.

Benedict's two chapters offer us excellent examples of this constant shifting between love of men outside the monastery, and fear of the world which envelopes them. Representative of a common thought in this matter, they propose to our reflexion with all the more weight the twofold theme of reception and separation. Separation is already known to us as an essential note of the 'school of the Lord's service',[17] while the cellarer's ministry has shown us the duty of hospitality.[18] It remains to consider these two themes together, in combination and relationship.

If the chapters 'On Receiving Guests' and 'On the Porters of the Monastery' speak first of reception and then of separation, a kind of logical priority still belongs to the latter. At the beginning of every monastic vocation and every monastic community we find an exodus. The monastery's welcome is the welcome of a society established outside the world, and the restrictions which accompany it are the permanent consequence of this step of fundamental retreat.

Scriptural motivations for hospitality are not lacking. Among all the texts of the New Testament which recommend it, and many of them are found in the monastic rules,[19] Jesus' word rings out with singular vigor: 'I was a stranger and you took me in'.[20] Benedict makes it the exergue of his chapter 'On Guests'. To exercise hospitality is to receive Christ.

Separation also answers an appeal of Christ and is defined in relation to him. In establishing his 'school of service' the Master thought he was obeying the Lord's invitation: 'Take my yoke upon you, and learn of me'.[21] Because he is 'a soldier for God', the monk 'does not entangle himself with secular business'.[22] According to Basil, leaving the world has a still broader motive; in the last analysis it results from the great precept of the love of God. To love him is to do his will and accomplish his commands. This work demands incessant attention, and an undivided heart and mind. In order never to lose sight of God and what he commands, the Christian must get away from those who live in forgetfulness and negligence. The discourse on the love of God and neighbor ends therefore in the decision to live apart. Thus a person obeys the appeal of the Gospel: 'If any man will come after me, let him deny himself, and take up his cross, and follow me'.[23] To be separated from the world is to follow Christ.

Separation and hospitality are therefore two manifestations of the same love: following Christ and receiving Christ. The following draws us out of the world, but there again he comes to us under the appearances of those who are in the world, and we receive him. Then the love which has provoked the separation is verified in the hospitality. The monk who has left the world for love of God and men should prepare himself for the welcome and should await the coming of him who said: 'I was a stranger and you took me in'.

But if promptness in receiving Christ is the touchstone of a true separation for the sake of Christ, this in its turn should put its mark on the reception. This is not a matter of making the house of God worldly, but of leading into it someone who comes from the world while delivering him from his worldly burden. It is Christ who should enter, not the devil. But every man carries within himself both the one and the other. Benedict's fear of diabolical illusions is not empty. Apart from the phantastic events of the egyptian desert of which he is thinking, a real spiritual risk is run with each arrival. Not only does the guest bring in the noise of the world and its sin, but the monk himself is also an equivocal creature. Between them the world threatens to take shape again each time. That is why it is important, according to the Rule, that they pray together before embracing.[24] Contact should not be established between sinful, worldly personalities but between regenerated spirits directed towards God by prayer. We ask that prayer dissipate the false appearances of the flesh and manifest what is at the bottom of each person, his relation to God, the real being.

But 'prayer before the peace' does not aim only at the 'illusions of the devil', as Benedict says. This motivation, which comes from the Master,[25] is combined in him with another no less profound consideration in which we recognize the most ancient *lex orandi* of the Church. The Master declares that thanksgiving to God should precede all human communication. The first act to be done together is to thank the author of the meeting, before exchanging the peace. Although the Master refers only to an anecdote of Jerome, of which he keeps a more or less accurate memory,[26] we inevitably think of the great liturgical tradition which makes the kiss of peace the 'seal' of common prayer.[27] By reason of this traditional order, mutual charity appears as the fulness and overflow of love for God. The communion of each person with his brother is the result of the communion of all with the Unique. The bond of love uniting Christians has a divine nature; it is established in prayer. It is this liturgical custom, well known to the Master,[28] which he recognized, rightly or wrongly, in the story of Jerome invoked here. The reception of guests in the monastery is only a particular case of this law of christian experience. There also, and there especially, the point of meeting should be, not the world, but God.

Just as prayer comes before the peace, reading of the divine law should precede the signs of 'humanity', that is, the meal.[29] Again, we do the man the honor of considering him more than a man. Sharing is begun by prayer and continues in hearing the word of God. The monks offer their guest the best of their life, the whole of their life. They treat him as one of their own; as reading 'edifies' them,[30] so it should 'edify' him as well. The meeting continues on a level that is resolutely religious.

The same underlying conviction marks the special regard shown to the poor and strangers, who are preferred to the rich. 'Fear' of them and the 'honors' which this earns them makes one think of the diabolical illusions denounced earlier. Will the guest be received for Christ and as Christ, or for the sake of Mammon, as a representative of the prince of this world? The refusal to reckon according to the social scale[31] extends to a complete overthrow of worldly values.[32] The most despised are those most honored. 'He who humbles himself shall be exalted'.[33] At the guest house as well as within the monastery it is sharing in the humiliations of Christ that deserves being considered and exalted in the visible reception of strangers and in the recesses of the heart seen by God alone.

All these honors accorded the guest—the salutation, prostration, water for the hands, the washing of feet—are added to the simple 'reception' mentioned by Christ in the last judgment scene: 'I was a stranger and you received me'. In this passage of Scripture hospitality appears as one of the works of mercy by which are relieved physical misfortunes: hunger and thirst, lack of shelter and clothing, the sufferings of imprisonment and sickness. Material giving, which the gospel chiefly envisages, is surrounded in our rules by a train of quasi-divine honors. A work of mercy has become in them an act of religion. The word of Christ, declaring himself concerned with whatever is done to the littlest ones, has wrought this transformation of a charitable service into a liturgy. The monks recognize him in their guests and bring to his reception the fervor he one day complained about not finding in the Pharisee's welcome, while a sinful woman showed him these marks of love and veneration.[34]

The edification that we strive to provide for the guest in reading Scripture to him also goes beyond the letter of the gospel text used as the exergue of the chapter. But this step aims less at Christ than at the Christian. The spiritual food which nourishes the monks we offer to this brother in the faith.[35] By this sharing and by the sharing of prayer the outsider is integrated into the community of those who seek God. Such an assimilation created no difficulty for Benedict's two inspirations—the author of the *Historia monachorum* and the Master—for both of them seem to have been thinking of the reception of 'brothers' in the full sense of the term, that is, of monks.[36] But with Benedict it is otherwise. With him the single category of *hospites* apparently includes every sort of arrival, laymen as well as consecrated persons. Generalizing the directions given by his sources, Benedict seems to apply to all comers the rites conceived for the reception of monks.[37] A daring extension which results in a presention even to the secular guest not only of the mystery of Christ hidden in him, but also of his own vocation to listen to God and to answer him, to hear Scripture and to pray.

The whole of Benedict's chapter 'On Guests' from beginning to end, in its rite of welcome and in its protective measures, proceeds therefore from the same concern for welcoming someone from the world without introducing the world. A true house of God receives him, and it should lose nothing of its religious character from that reception. Far from letting the world's spirit enter there, the house of God should communicate the spirit of Christ to those whom it welcomes.

We should recognize our present-day weakness in this regard. The way in which monasteries receive their guests today does not differ much from secular hospitality, whether it is that of private persons or of the hotel industry. Religious gestures are nearly absent, and the conversations are often only friendly chatter. There is no reason to be astonished at our inability to direct this relation to God. It reflects the deep weakness of a monasticism that dares less and less to be what it is. In a monastery the quality of the hospitality depends on the vigor of the separation.

Thus our thought returns to the separatist tendency of monastic life, the inextricable complement to the spirit of welcome. The separation in question is not solely or chiefly a matter of physical remoteness and visible quaintness, of lonely places and distinctive dress, of odd practices and silence. These things are only signs and instruments of the essential separation, the renunciation of sin and conversion towards God. Their insufficiency as well as their necessity were apparent to Basil from the first days of his withdrawal.[38] Later, when he made leaving the world a requirement of love for God, he thought chiefly of leaving self.[39] Rufinus, his translator, says it more clearly still: 'What we should leave is not only men who live badly, but also our own disorderly and ill-regulated habits.'[40]

This is the spiritual separation in view of which so many barriers have been established between the monastery and the world. We should neither cover over nor regret that they create a permanent tension between the two milieux. It is inevitable. Already in the time of the Master this organic law of all monasticism worthy of the name was being proven: monks and their way of life are not understood or appreciated by many laymen.[41] Far from being a bad sign, this lack of comprehension may indicate that the monastic life is fulfilling its function and attaining its end. This will be the case at least if the cloister and exterior differences are effectively aimed at the transformation of one's being in God. The separation from the world which is inherent in the monastic vocation is healthy and fruitful when it attacks the world's sin which the monk carries within him, and when it sustains his effort towards communication with God and holiness.

The separation of which we speak is not only on an equal footing with truly spiritual hospitality. It conditions the entire radiation of the monastic life on the outside, or to say it better, it is identified with it. The Rule says nothing about apostolate in the contemporary sense of the word,[42] but it demands the guest's edification by divine law,[43] and it wills that 'God be glorified' by the example of disinterestedness the monastery gives in its commercial relations.[44] It is by living according to his faith before men, without being afraid to be different from them that the monk has an effect on them, if God wills.

NOTES TO CHAPTER 17

1. RB 53.1–15 and 23–24. See t. VI, pp. 1262–87.
2. RB 53.5,11,15,16.
3. RB 66.1–5 and 6–7.
4. RB 31.9; 56.1–2; 61.1–5 and 8–11.

5. RB 50.4; 51.1-3; 54,1-5; 61.2 and 6-7; 67.3-5.

6. See RM 66-67.

7. RB 66.6-7. Cf. RM 95.17-21.

8. See RM 65 and 71-72; 78-79. Cf. t. VI, pp. 1255-61. There is an analogous curve in regard to welcoming clergy in RM 76-77 and 83.

9. *Les Vies coptes de S. Pachôme*, p. 109 (Bo 40) = G¹ 40 = Denys, *Vita Pach.* 33, citing Mt 25:40; *Hist. mon.* 7 (418d), citing Mt 25:35 (cf. *Hist. mon.* 1.[403a]: 'like an angel'); Cassian, *Inst.* 5.24: *suscipiens in vobis Christum; Reg. Macarii* 20 (allusion to Mt 25:35); Isidore, *Reg.* 23, citing Mt 10:40-42; Waldebert, *Reg.* 3, citing Mt 25:40.

10. Going out in pairs: Pachomius, *Praec.* 56, followed by *Reg Tarn.* 2.2 and *Reg. Orient.* 22; *Ordo monast.* 8; *Reg. Macarii* 22; and *Reg. Patrum III* 8-9. Cf. Gregory, *Reg.* 11.26 = *Ep.* 11.44; *Reg.* 12.6 = *Ep.* 12.24. Prohibition or limitation of going out: *Hist. mon.* 17; *Reg. Orient.* 26; Caesarius, *Reg. virg.* 2; Ferreolus, *Reg.* 20; Isidore, *Reg.* 1 and 24; *Reg. Tarn.* 2.6-3.1 and 4.4-5; 12.9 – 13.3. Different rules: Pachomius, *Praec.* 54-55 (cf. *Reg. Orient* 41) and 57 (cf. *Reg.* 2.3); Augustine, *Praec.* 4.26, followed by *Reg. Tarn.* 17.2-18.12; *Ordo monast.* 8, followed by *Reg. Tarn.* 17.2-18.12.

11. Pachomius, *Praec.* 53, followed by *Reg. Orient.* 41; *Vies coptes*, p. 109 (Bo 40 and parallels, see note 9); Basil, *Ep.* 22.1; *Long Rules* 32.2 and 45.1-2; *Short Rules* 188 = *Reg.* 32; Cassian, *Inst.* 4.16.2; *Reg. IV Patrum* 2.36-42; *Reg. Patrum II* 14-16, followed by *Reg. Orient* 26; *Vita Patrum Jurensium* 172; Caesarius, *Reg.* 38 and 40, followed by Donatus, *Reg.* 57; Isidore, *Reg.* 24; Fructuosus, *Reg.* I.8.

12. Augustine, *Praec.* 4.11 and 5.3, followed by Caesarius, *Reg. virg.* 25 and 43 (cf. *Reg. mon.* 1 and 15), and by *Reg. Tarn* 19.1-2 and 3-4; Aurelian, *Reg. mon.* 5-6 (follows Caesarius); Donatus, *Reg.* 53 and 60 (combines Caesarius and Benedict); Waldebert, *Reg.* 3; *Reg. Orient.* 26 and *Vita Patrum Jur.* 172; Isidore, *Reg.* 24; Fructuosus, *Reg.* I.8. See Cassian *Inst.* 4.16.2.

13. Basil, *Long Rules* 20; Augustine, *Serm.* 355.2; Caesarius, *Reg. virg.* 39-40, followed by Aurelian, *Reg. mon.* 48 and Donatus, *Reg.* 57-58.

14. Pachomius, *Praec.* 53-54.

15. *Reg. Orient.* 26. Cf. *Reg. Patrum II* 14-16.

16. Caesarius, *Reg. virg.* 25 and 43. Cf. Augustine, *Praec* . 4.11 and 5.3.

17. See the commentary on the Prologue above.

18. See the commentary on RB 31-41.

19. RM 12:13, cited by *Reg. Macarii* 20; 1 Tm 5:10; Heb 13:2 (cf. Gn 18-19; see *Hist. mon.* 1; 403a); 1 Peter 4:9.

20. Mt 25:35.

21. Mt 11:29. See RM Th 14 and Ths 45.

22. 2 Tm 2:4, cited by RM 82.18, etc. Cf. RM 3.22 = RB 4.20.

23. Mt 16:24. See Basil, *Reg.* 2, whose continuous exposition is broken into pieces in *Long Rules* 2-6. The gospel text is already cited by Basil, *Ep.* 2.1 as the motto of an ascetic program founded upon separation from the world.

24. RB 53.4-5.

25. RM 71.5-8.

26. RM 71.9, alluding to 71.3-4, where Jerome, *Vita Pauli* 9, is cited. Either the Master made a mistake (see the note), or else Jerome's words *dum . . . miscerentur* meant 'before embracing' for him.

27. Tertullian, *De orat.* 28.

28. See *La Règle du Maître*, t. I, p. 80.

29. RB 53.9. Previously, the 'prayer' to which the guest 'is led', is no doubt the office

celebrated in the oratory before the meal. The guest is integrated into the monastery's life of prayer.

30. RB 42.3; 47.3.

31. See already *Vita Abraham* 3; PL 73: 284c; *Vita Patrum Jur.* 172.

32. RB 53.15. See our article 'Honorer tous les hommes', in RAM 40 (1964) 129–38.

33. Lk 14:11, cited RM 10.1 = RB 7.1.

34. Lk 7:36–46. The foot washing is the only one of these marks of hospitality to be found in our rules. See RM 53.43, which refers to Luke's scene. The washing of feet was already associated with hospitality in 1 Tm 5:10. Cf. Pachomius, *Praec.* 51, which seems to refer to Jn 13:14.

35. *Domesticis fidei* (RB 53.2) seems to refer more precisely to consecrated persons. See 'Honorer tous les hommes', pp. 135–6 and p. 138, note 38.

36. About the Master, see t. VI, pp. 1374–5.

37. With the corrective, however, of *congruus honor* (RB 53.2): the *domestici fidei* (i.e. consecrated persons), being 'specially' honored, have perhaps claims to special rites. Already Pachomius, *Praec.* 51, seems to reserve to them the washing of feet and sharing in the office. This *maiori honore* of the Pachomian Rule corresponds to a note in the Greek Life: visitors are received *pros to axion hekastou* (G¹ 28). The extension wrought by Benedict is already sketched in RM 78. T (see t. VI, p. 1374, note 393), but only regarding the work imposed on guests.

38. Basil, *Ep.* 2.1–2.

39. Basil, *Reg.* 2 (493b–494a) = *Long Rules* 6: physical withdrawal seems a necessity in view of self-abnegation (Mt 16:24), that is, renunciation of one's own will. We think of the views developed by Cassian, *Conf.* 1.5–7; 3.6–8, etc.

40. Basil, *Reg.* 2 (493c): *et ita non solum ab hominibus non recte agentibus, verum etiam a nostris ipsis inordinatis et incompositis moribus secedamus.* These words are missing in *Long Rules* 6.1 (926c).

41. See RM 24.20; 58.5; 95.21.

42. Paradoxically, on the other hand, the Rule invites the 'neighboring Christians' (seculars) to intervene in the abbatial election to prevent the accession of a bad superior (RB 64.3–6). This feature clearly shows that the monks' liberty, and more generally their state of separation, was not a sort of juridical privilege which they enjoyed unconditionally, but a simple means to their sanctification. It could act against its own purpose and then should be suspended.

43. RB 53.9.

44. RB 57.7–9.

Chapter XVIII

THE MONASTIC HABIT

(RB 55)

I N READING THIS CHAPTER 'On the wardrobe and footwear of the brothers', we might wonder if there is enough matter for a separate commentary. It seems only to prolong two treatises we have already examined,
those on control of eating and on renunciaton of goods. It picks up this
latter not only by its last section, which renews the condemnation of
private property and the norms for the distribution of what is necessary,
but also by most of the regulations of the first part, obviously meant to
prevent the monks from appropriating any garment. 'To give', 'to
receive', 'to turn back'—these words recurring in every phrase clearly
show Benedict's dominant preoccupation.

We think immediately of asceticism in eating when three times we read
another key-term, 'to suffice'.[1] What is more, the list of authorized garments is introduced at the beginning of the chapter by the characteristic
formula *sufficere credimus* (we think it suffices), preceded by a little prologue based on that to the chapter on wine. Benedict's recognition of differences of climates here corresponds to the respect he professed for personal charisms about drink.[2] In each case the legislator is careful to do
right by different needs, while laying down an 'average' norm which
shows 'what suffices for monks'. Although our chapter, like the two of
the Master from which it is derived,[3] is located very far from the treatise
on food, Benedict connects them by the way he regards clothing. Basil
had already treated these two subjects one after the other, applying the
same principles to them.[4] Significantly, Benedict uses in regard to the col-
or and thickness of the habits a basilian phrase dealing with food.[5] In his

thought, as in that of the great eastern theoretician, clothing is considered
first of all from the point of view of *ascesis* and 'continence', and in this
they both differ from the Master.

By these two great themes, therefore, this chapter is connected with questions already studied. Yet, it has its own interest. Clothing, footgear, and
bedding are differently used than food and drink. While they satisfy urgent
bodily needs, they are not brutally appropriated as are the latter. Since they
are external to the body, they can be put on or taken off, kept for personal
use or put at another's disposal. Their separate existence and their durability
not only open them to a certain disappropriation, but provide them as well
with the possibility of special meaning. By putting them on or taking them
off, a man shows what he wishes to be or not to be, to do or not to do, to
undergo or to avoid. Attached to his body and associated with his action,
they represent the person and signal the role he means to play.

The way the monk dresses signifies, therefore, what he is. Much more,
it partially constitutes his very monastic being. From this fact springs the
moderate but serious attention which ancient monks constantly gave to
their dress. This fact by itself suggests that we should not let the present
chapter pass without examination. We are also invited to do so by the
confused and shifting situation in which monastic circles find themselves
today, precisely on this subject.

Until quite recently monks and nuns wore a conventional habit, each
piece of which was connected, through a long series of transformations,
to an article of the outfit prescribed by the Rule. People spoke of the
'tunic', 'cowl' and 'scapular'. In fact, the articles so named barely corresponded, either in form or purpose, to the things mentioned by Benedict.
The habit was very far from what it has been originally, and it was no less
far from the way men and women dress in our time, and this fact constituted another anomaly in regard to the benedictine habit which, although
quite distinct from that of seculars of the times,[6] did not differ from it fundamentally. Finally, this very great difference from ordinary dress caused
the habit, in some places, to be worn only inside the cloister. Outside,
monks wore the more discreet garb of the secular clergy.

This state of things is changing rapidly since the clergy in countries of
Catholic tradition began to abandon the cassock. The monks, following
their example, tend to go out in a simple clergyman's suit or even without

any insignia. Within the cloister modern work-clothes have appeared, varying by community, sometimes not uniform within the same community, often with nothing to distinguish the monk from a secular workman. In places where this garb has a distinct style and a certain uniformity, it tends to become usual and the former habit reappears only for general gatherings in refectory, chapter, and choir. In other places the monks dress uniformly for these common gatherings, but are more or less free to dress as they please at other times. Finally, while certain monasteries keep the traditional habit completely and constantly, others have only a choir garment which is put on for prayer, with no special uniform habit the rest of the time.

This in broad outline, is the situation at the moment we are composing this commentary. By the time it leaves the printing press, the situation will doubtless have changed. The uncertainty to which it witnesses moves us to examine carefully the principal texts in which the Fathers of monasticism articulated their thoughts on the subject.

The first and most important is Question 11 of Basil's *Asceticon*, soon divided into *Long Rules* 22 and 23. According to Basil, 'the right dress for the Christian' should have the same characteristics as his food. Both should be simple, cheap, easy to obtain, and reduced to a minimum. Having chosen the last place in society, the disciples of Christ should dress accordingly: no one should feel himself beneath them in rank. This humility in dress, Basil added in his second edition, was to make the Christian resemble John the Baptist dressed in camel's hair and the Old Testament prophets dressed in goatskins.[7]

But the fundamental text on which our author's thought dwelt is Paul's maxim: 'Let us be content with food and covering'.[8] A simple covering is what the Christian's garb should be. In the beginning God gave the man and woman tunics of skins to hide their nakedness. This first purpose of clothing has added to it another natural function, to warm the body and protect it. Nothing further should be sought. Neither pleasure of the eyes nor elegance should be taken into account.[9] Nor should the garments vary according to circumstances, so that one thing is worn outside and another inside the house, one thing by day and another by night.[10] Poverty (*aktèmosunè*) requires that we have one sole garment for these different uses. It is up to us so to design it as to satisfy all needs.

This unique, coarse, invariable garment will necessarily differ from ordinary dress, which men love to make pleasing to the senses and especially suited to different roles. This distinctive character was not willed by Basil for its own sake, but was to him a happy consequence and full of advantages. By their original dress our 'Christians' will be both more united among themselves and more separated from the sinful world.[11] *Koinônein* and *idiazein*, communion and separation: we recognize here the two great characteristics of the type of life defined in the first Rules.[12] The basilian ideal of a community of separated persons finds its expression in the habit. But while communion received a more developed treatment at the beginning of the *Asceticon*, Basil here puts the emphasis on distinction. Christians, set apart and made conspicuous by their habit, will feel more obliged to act as they should. The wearing of a characteristic habit will be a 'pedagogy' for their weakness. It will constantly remind them, as well as those who see them, of their resolution to lead a perfect life, of which it is a sign.

This special way of dressing will, Basil thought, present the note of *kosmiotès* desired by the Apostle when he enumerated the qualities of the bishop or described the apparel of a christian woman.[13] Both should be *kosmios*, that is, decent, well-dressed, but with a decency according to specifically christian norms,[14] as just indicated. These are equally valid for footwear: it should be simple, easy to obtain and practical, and nothing more.

When he came to the belt, Basil appealed to rather different considerations. First of all, he demonstrated the need for it by the example of biblical saints: John the Baptist and Elijah, Peter and Paul, Job and the Lord's disciples, all wore this thing. To this scriptural proof is added a practical reason which pertains to the theory of clothing: if clothing is not to prevent a man from working and is to keep him warm, it must be held close to his body by a belt. The example of Christ girding himself to wash his disciples' feet, in the second edition, corroborates this practical argument.

Finally Basil returns to the number of garments. He makes it a duty of poverty, we remember, to have only one garment for all purposes. Surely he now wished no one to possess several of these all-purpose garments. Again, this is a matter of *aktèmosunè*. What is more, the Gospel forbids it: 'Let him who has two tunics give one to him who has none'.[15]

This work of Basil deserved analysis in detail, for it shows better than any other the meaning of the monastic habit, as well as his references to

Scripture and the ascetic tradition of the Church. Once or perhaps twice before, Basil dealt with the habit for his ascetics,[16] but he did not explain the reason for the poor, strictly functional, and unique garment that he extolled then as now, and he did not observe either that these marks of the monastic habit set apart those who wore it and united them among themselves. Here, on the contrary, he furnishes an effort of reflection that will remain, unfortunately, without parallel. Evagrius, Cassian, Dorotheos and others were to be interested in the monks' habit, but their perceptions, all of which owe something to Basil, were not to equal his vigorous theory, both original and traditional.

The best thing about these views, is doubtless not the biblical literalism that Basil shows in regard to the belt and the two tunics. More detached from the letter, the evocation of the poor coarse garment of John the Baptist and the prophets, or that of Christ girding himself to serve, touches us more. But most important of all is the series of texts from the First Epistle to Timothy cited by Basil. According to the first, 'Having food and wherewith to be covered, with these let us be content' (1 Tm 6:8). This sentence of the Apostle, drawn from a pericope condemning avarice, well defines the spirit of poverty, simplicity, and liberation from the worries of the world which animates a disciple of Christ and is recognized even in his dress. We think for example, of the passage in the Sermon on the Mount where Christ exhorts his hearers not even to worry about food and clothing.[17] Jesus condemned worrying about the morrow. Paul dissuades us from seeking more than is necessary. The liberating appeal which resounds in these two texts is transmitted by Basil, when he cites and comments upon the second. The term 'covering' used by the Apostle evokes for him an extreme simplicity which reduces clothing, as in a philosophical definition, to the sole function of covering.

To be content with little, indeed with only what is strictly necessary is the scriptural maxim that governs the theory of clothing. Further on, Basil alludes again to two passages of the Epistle to Timothy in which Paul recommends being *kosmios*.[18] The first, concerning women, is the more significant. The Apostle reproves external finery, and invites women to replace it with the spiritual adornment of good works. This criticism of feminine elegance, together with analogous statements of St Peter,[19] are prominent in the *De habitu virginum* (On the Dress of Virgins) of Cyprian. This author even draws, in his *Testimonia*, a general maxim

valid not only for virgins but for every christian woman: 'A woman
should not be adorned in a worldly way'.[20] In support of this rejection of
all 'worldly adornment', the *De habitu virginum* develops a copious argument which is based sometimes on censure for the 'flesh' or the 'world'
and other scriptural appeals for renunciation, and sometimes on the philosophical notion of nature, all adornment being considered a deceitful and
antinatural artifice.

Such considerations, which one finds long before Cyprian,[21] differ
hardly at all from those which Basil asserted a century later to recommend
encrateia (continence) in general, and especially in regard to clothing.
From the New Testament to the *Long Rules*, we can trace a line passing
through the christian asceticism of the first centuries. What Peter and
Paul, Clement and Cyprian had said of women's clothing, Basil radical-
ized, applying it to men's clothing. His teaching about the habit was not
basically new; it had deep roots in tradition and scripture. But Basil was
innovative in the rigorous way he pushed it to its ultimate conclusions
and by the biblical literalism he associated with it.

The most original result of this systematization was to set off the notion
of a genuine uniform for 'Christians'. If this corresponds to a social fact—
the appearance of a new class of ascetics—Basil had the merit of expressing
clearly what it signified, connecting it with his general concept of an asceticism that was both separate and communitarian. The profound reason
for the monastic habit, valid for all times, is thus formulated once for all.
Though the forms of dress can change, the principle retains its value
throughout the ages for all cenobitism analogous to what Basil instituted,
indeed for all monasticism.[22]

This permanent significance in spite of changes is the very thing that is
often lacking in the explanations given by Basil's successors. All of them
have a penchant for interpreting symbolically the different articles of the
monastic habit. Although these exegeses were able to teach the monks of
that time, although they even remain interesting in indicating the monastic virtues represented by the habit, they have nevertheless the inconvenience of being connected with one or another article of clothing. When
these articles disappear or are changed, the lesson attached to them
vanishes or changes with them. Moreover, theories of this kind often prefer ingenious and edifying but artificial symbolisms to the true reasons for

the habit. They thus cover over the real purposes and permanent norms of the habit, obscuring thereby the very notion of the type of life to which they belong.

Evagrius, in the Prologue of his *Practikos*, seems the first to interpret the monk's habit this way.[23] To tell the truth, his explanation can gain authority not only from an exegetical tradition which took pleasure in allegorizing scriptural remarks about clothing,[24] but more specifically from a suggestion furnished by Basil himself in his chapter on the monks' belt. In connection with Job, whom God commanded: 'Gird up your loins like a man', Basil observed that to put on a belt is 'the symbol of manly courage and promptness in action'.[25] Evagrius interprets the belt differently; for him it was a sign of chastity, but he recognized in the *analabos* of the egyptian monks the same symbolism relative to action.[26] Thus each of the six pieces of the monastic outfit finds a particular meaning by more or less clearly opposing one of the eight principal vices, whose analysis and cure were one of the major purposes of the *Practikos*.[27]

The habit symbolizes, therefore, the soul of the monk, and an exegesis of it is a happy introduction to a work treating it. To Evagrius' eyes, it was essentially a 'symbolic vestment'. It would not have been had it not been 'so different from the dress of other men'.[28] But this difference remains unexplained. It is not, as with Basil, due to the very nature of the habit, that is, ultimately the monks' resolution to live according to the will of the Creator and the law of Christ. It is a simple difference of fact, a social given, from which the author only draws the profit of instructing the monks on the virtues of their state. The monastic habit, separated from its essential and evangelical reasons, tends to become pure convention.

The same can be said of a greek apophthegm whose latin translation Benedict must have read in the *Vitae Patrum*. Innocence, the cross, and fortitude he saw signified by the three pieces of clothing he mentions.[29] The same allegorical line is found in Cassian, who depended closely on Evagrius,[30] and if the author of the *Institutes* was inspired as well by Basil, it was to borrow from him chiefly what seems to us the least useful part of the Basilian Rule: the enumeration of biblical saints who wore the belt.[31] Basil's spirit is, however, recognizable also in Cassian by a certain insistence on work and poverty.[32] His general theory of clothing, based on the Apostle's word, is indeed that of the great Cappadocian doctor:

clothing should only 'cover', that is, hide nakedness and protect from cold, without conceding anything to vanity.[33]

Unlike Basil, however, Cassian was afraid not only of elegance. He also feared that reverse vanity which tries to distinguish itself by abjection. He was thinking less of the situation of the monk in society than of his relationship with his brothers in religion. In this new perspective the uniformity of the habit becomes an essential point. The monk owes it to *esprit de corps*, to respect for tradition, and to the virtue of humility to dress like the other monks, without singularity. These considerations are aimed especially at the wearing of the hairshirt, but they also have a general significance in relation to the favorite theses of Cassian about the apostolic origin and quasi-ecclesial character of monasticism. Under the influence of such preoccupations the basilian teaching is notably changed. That his 'Christians' should wear the same habit was for Basil only a corollary, noted in passing, of the principles ruling the christian way of dressing. Cassian was less concerned with these norms and much more interested in the uniform, which appears no longer as a simple consequence of the norms, but as an important aspect of *ascesis*.

Moreover, the chief value of this common habit, in Basil's eyes, was the visible separation it established between the world and the ascetics, and the 'pedagogy' which resulted from it for them. This role is developed at length in the *Long Rules*, but is scarcely mentioned in the *Institutes*.[34] Instead, Cassian wanted to attenuate the singularity of the monastic habit. In the most original chapter of his treatise, he warns westerners against a servile imitation of the egyptian model. Neither the climate nor the customs permit them to dress this way. Our habit should not shock seculars, but edify them. To understand these recommendations accurately it is important to see that they were aimed not at the basilian theory of clothing, but at the particular articles whose symbolic exegesis Cassian, following Evagrius, had just given.[35] The principle of a distinctive habit remains intact therefore. But instead of its pedagogical value to those who wear it, it is its aptitude to edify or shock others which claims the author's attention. The difference in clothing between monks and seculars is considered from the seculars' point of view, not the monks'. This is a new consideration and of great interest; it completes Basil's views and corrects Evagrius', putting the habit back in a realistic perspective.

To the basilian and evagrian themes which fill the first Book of the *Insti-*

tutes, Cassian later, in Book IV, adds elements from the Pachomian Rule. Cenobites have the right to a certain number of articles of clothing, of which he draws up a restrictive list.[36] Changes of clothing are kept in a common wardrobe, under the guard of superiors and provosts.[37] These arrangements are dictated by a spirit of poverty, that is, mortification and renunciation of goods combined. A rite of clothing marks the admission of postulants, and their secular clothing is kept to be returned to them should they leave.[38] By this ceremony, which precedes the year of probation, the new monk is made to understand that nothing any longer belongs to him, not even the clothes he wears. Incorporated into the community, entirely assimilated to his brothers, he has lost all independence and pride. Although the principal accent is placed on this subjection, the fact that one cannot carry off the monastery's things if one returns to the world, suggests something else: this habit is connected with the divine service and shares in its holiness.[39]

These regulations of pachomian origin are almost the only ones which the Master and Benedict, like many authors of rules, have retained from Cassian, whose theoretical considerations were not repudiated, but judged out of place in a rule. With them, moreover, the clothing takes place not at the beginning, before the year of probation, but only after it. This new order, which is general with the latin monks, stems no doubt from a more acute sense of the sanctity of the habit and of the conditions required to wear it worthily.[40] This at any rate is the reason given by the Master: as a sacred thing and sign of belonging to God, the monastery's habit should only be given deliberately.[41] No less clearly, the same author has in mind a habit different from that of seculars, from whom it elicits either respect or ridicule.[42] This distinctive character, which is constantly supposed by Gregory the Great at the end of the century,[43] was certainly not absent from the habit of Benedict's monks.

The sketch of doctrinal and institutional history that we have just traced permits us to answer now the questions posed by the present situation. In the light of this history the timeliness of an *aggiornamento* is perfectly obvious. The so-called 'traditional' habit does not correspond sufficiently to the authentic norms of tradition. Its anachronism makes us think of the exoticism rebuked by Cassian. Its practical inconveniences set it in contradiction with the law of work and poverty. Being more conventional than functional, it is not in the great realist and ascetic line of Basil. It has the merit of clearly setting apart those who wear it, but it does so in an arbitrary way, without relation to the monastic vocation itself. Atemporal, it does escape the pressures and fluctuations of fashion, but its picturesqueness appeals too much to the eye, and the desire for aesthetic effect is not absent.

The disaffection of today's monks for this dress would therefore be altogether legitimate if they were at the same time anxious to create a true monastic habit again. Unhappily, the rather widespread tendency to dress purely and simply like seculars indicates not only a lack of imagination but something more grave, the absence of convictions on the very nature of the monastic life. Fear of setting oneself apart and compromising oneself is not a healthy sign for monks. Whatever the stated motives, this refusal of visible separation reflects a profound lack, a lack of the conversion and *ascesis* which separate monks from the world spiritually and in reality.

We should not therefore lazily retain a conventional habit, nor should we dress exactly like seculars, but adopt a manner of dress that corresponds to the traditional and present-day purpose of monastic life. In this regard the principles laid down by Basil remain valid. Poverty, simplicity, and humility should be the fundamental marks of this new habit. It should be distinctive and uniform, too, but with a distinction which results naturally from the marks above and which flows from the monastic profession instead of designating it extrinsically and arbitrarily. Moreover, we should have the courage to wear it everywhere, outside as well as at home, for nothing is more degrading for a monk than to act out religious folklore behind the cloister and to camouflage himself as a secular when he goes out.

Finally, there is another duplication to avoid. When the monks gather to pray in the church, there is no reason why they should put on a special garment. The whole of ancient monasticism, including Benedict, knew nothing of such a choir garment.[44] For men entirely consecrated to God, putting on such a particular garment for prayer makes no sense. The hours which flow between the offices are not for them a profane time, but the time when they work at praying ceaselessly. This consecration of their whole life is signified by the unique habit which they wear in every circumstance.

NOTES TO CHAPTER 18

1. RB 55.4,10,15. Cf. RB 39.1,3,4 (= RM 26.1–2); 40.3 (cf. RM 27.5,6,10,27,28). See t. V, p. 654, n. 25.

2. RB 55.1–4. Cf. RB 39.1 (*sufficere credimus*); 40.1–3.

3. RM 81–82. See t. VI, pp. 909–35.

4. Basil, *Reg.* 9 and 11, where *continentia* translates *encrateia* (*Long Rules* 16–20 and 22–23).

5. RB 55.7; cf. Basil, *Reg.* 9 (complete the apparatus of sources, t. II, p. 618, according to the note on p. 619).

6. Despite the assimilation suggested by RB 55.9 (*propter pauperes*). This latter certainly leaves room for differences. See our article 'Moines aujourd'hui?', in *Benedictina*, 19 (1972) 227–38 (= *Autour de saint Benoît*. [Bellefontaine, 1975] 137–58).

7. Basil, *Long Rules* 22.1, citing Mt 3:4 and Heb 11:37.

8. 1 Tm 6:8, cited by Basil, *Long Rules* 22.2 (here and following, the second edition has its equivalent in the first, unless the contrary is noted).

9. Same condemnation of vanity in Basil, *Reg.* 142 = *Short Rules* 49.

10. See also Basil, *Reg.* 129 = *Short Rules* 90.

11. Basil, *Long Rules* 22.2 (end) and 3. The division into paragraphs breaks a continuous argument.

12. Basil, *Long Rules* 6 (separation) and 7 (community), in the opposite order from that of *Long Rules* 22.2–3.

13. 1 Tm 2:9 and 3:2, cited by Basil, *Long Rules* 22.3.

14. We understand this way, with Rufinus (PL 103:504b) the phrase *tou kosmiou dèlonoti kata ton idion tou christianismou skopon nooumenou* (PG 31:980d). Another interpretation is given in D. Amand. *L'Ascése monastique de S. Basile* (Maredsous, 1948) 219, and L. Lèbe, *S. Basile, Les Règles monastiques* (Maredsous, 1969) 99.

15. Basil, *Long Rules* 23 (end), citing Lk 3:11. In *Reg.* 129 = *Short Rules* 90, Basil thinks rather of Mt 10:9–10 (cf. *ktèseós*, recalling the *ktèsesthe* of the Gospel). Even here (*Long Rules* 23), Mt 10:9 has just been cited in connection with the belt.

16. Basil, *Ep.* 2.6 (date: 358–359); 22.2 (uncertain date: 364?).

17. Mt 6:25–34.

18. 1 Tm 2:9–10 and 3:2.

19. 1 Peter 3:3–5.

20. *Mulierem ornari saeculariter non debere.* Cyprian, *De habitu virg.* 8 (directed also to married women); *Test.* 3,36. In the two passages Cyprian omits *en katastolè kosmiô* (*in habitu ornato* or *ordinato*), that is, the words cited by Basil, no doubt because they seem to justify a certain decorum. Moreover, *kosmein* (*ornantes*) is translated by *componentes*.

21. See the citations of 1 Tm 2:9–10 in Clement, *Paedag.* II.127.2 and III.66.3; Tertullian, *De cor.* 14.2; *De orat.* 15.2 and 20.2. In Books II and III of his *Pedagogue*, Clement has long sections on the clothing of both men and women; Tertullian is the author of a work *De cultu feminarum* and *De pallio*. Cf. Gregory, *Hom. Ev.* 6.3.

22. Much less emphasized than the aspect of separation, the 'common' element is formulated by Basil in quite general terms (identity of *skopos*) in order to be able to be applied to all monks, even if Basil was thinking more specifically in terms of genuine communities.

23. Unless the tradition represented by the Apophthegm Nau 55 is prior. Evagrius, *Praktikos*, Prol 1, claims to report 'a teaching of the holy Fathers'. (E.T. *Evagrius Ponticus, Praktikos*, Cistercians Studies Series 4 [Spencer, Mass., 1970]).

24. See the references to Philo and Origen in A. Guillaumont, *Évagre, Traité pratique*, t. II, SCh 71 (Paris, 1971) 484–91. Saint Paul freely uses this image, either in a general way to evoke the 'putting on' of the new man (Rm 13:14; Eph 4:24, etc.), or in enumerating the different symbolic pieces (Eph 6:13–17).

25. Basil, *Long Rules* 23, citing Jb 38:3. *Andreia* is the virtue of the *anèr*. The belt in the apophthegm Nau 55 also symbolizes the same thing.

26. Evagrius, *Praktikos*, Prol. 4: *ergasian* recalls the *erga* of Basil, *Long Rules* 23 (981b), and *anempodiston* is read in him a little further on. For *peristellousès*, cf. *Long Rules* 22.2 (980a): *peristellein*, but the meaning is different. A. Guillaumont, SCh 71, p. 491 connects the *melotes* of Evagrius, the sign of poverty, with *Long Rules* 22.1 (Heb 11:37).

27. See our article 'Les sources des quatre premiers Livres des Institutions de Jean Cassien', in *Aufstieg und Niedergang der römischen Welt*, (forthcoming).

28. Evagrius, *Praktikos*, Prol. 1.

29. Apophthegm Nau = *VP* 5.10.115, recalling the same time Basil, Evagrius, and Cassian. Similarly Dorotheus, *Instruct.* 1.14–19. (E.T. *Dorotheos of Gaza. Discourses and Sayings*, Cistercian Studies Series 33 [Kalamazoo, Michigan, 1977]).

30. Cassian, *Inst.* 1.3–5, 7–8; 11.2. The method is extended to the exegesis of footwear (*Inst.* 1.9.1). See our article cited above (note 27).

31. Cassian, *Inst.* 1.1 (cf. 1.11.3). Same literalist tendency occurs in connection with *melotes* (1.7), the staff (1.8) and the footgear (1.9).

32. Work: *Inst.* 1.2.3: 1.5 (evagrian exegesis, but made realistic by the scriptural citations added by Cassian); 1.11.1 (cf. Basil, *Reg.* 11). Poverty: *Inst.* 1.6 and 10 (*vilitas*).

33. Cassian, *Inst.* 1.2.1, citing 1 Tm 6:8.

34. Cassian, *Inst.* 1.2.1; *sic ab huius mundi separentur ornatu*.

35. Cassian, *Inst.* 1.10. The egyptian articles, of which Cassian has 'omitted nothing'. are those enumerated in *Inst.* 1.3–9 (cf. the introduction of *Inst.* 1,3). The *illa . . . quae superius commemoravimus* are, it seems, the *zona* and the *vestis* (*Inst.* 1.1–2), that is the basilian pieces, to which are added perhaps the egyptian articles not criticized: *analaboi, palliolum* and staff (*Inst.* 1.5,6,8).

36. Cassian, *Inst.* 4.13. Cf. Pachomius, *Praec.* 81; Horsiesius, *Liber* 22.

37. Cassian, *Inst.* 4.10. Cf. Pachomius, *Praec.* 42, 65, 70, 105, and *Leg.* 15; Horsiesius, *Lib.* 26. The benedictine term *vestiarium*, missing from these texts, appeared already in Augustine, *Praec.* 5.1.

38. Cassian, *Inst.* 4.5–7. Cf. Pachomius, *Praec.* 49.

39. Moreover, everything in the monastery is sacred (Cassian, *Inst.* 4.19.3; 4.20). On the taking of the habit as a sign of change of life, see Denis the Areopagite, *Hier. eccl.* 6.3.4.

40. See t. VI, pp. 1348–9.

41. RM 90.74–78. Cf. RM 90.86: *Christi . . . habitus*.

42. RM 95.17–21.

43. See our article 'Sub regula vel abbate', in *Coll. Cist.* 33 (1971) 240 (E.T. in *Rule and Life*, Cistercian Studies Series, 12). On the thesis of D. De Bruyne and O. du Roy (the benedictine monk dressed like a secular), see the article cited above (note 6).

44. According to Pachomius, *Praec.* 102, the monk should only *take off* his sandals and cloak, and that for meals as well as for the synaxis. Cf. Palladius, *Hist. Laus.* 32.3 (the belt and *melotes* were taken off for Communion); Cassian, *Inst.* 1.9.2 (shoes were removed for the celebration of the Eucharist; cf. Ex 3:5 and Josh 5:16).

Chapter XIX

THE FORMATION OF POSTULANTS

(RB 58)

BENEDICT'S CHAPTER on the way of receiving brothers astonishes us today by its harsh and defensive tone. The severity of the reception given the postulant seems to us hardly believable. The four or five days at the door, the difficulties, the rough treatment shock our sensibilities as well as disquiet our concern for recruitment: do they want to make the house of God repulsive, to discourage good will?

The rest of the text tends to take this same hostile line. No doubt there is the question of 'winning souls' and of expecting a 'true search for God' manifested by 'application to the divine office, to obedience and to humble matters'. But these positive features are accompanied by sinister predictions, by repeated warnings—Rule in hand—,by irrevocable promises demanded after solemn admonitions. Surrounded with such precautions, commitment takes on a somber and dramatic character, which is climaxed with a threat of damnation. Nothing could be less attractive than this negative presentation, this threatening tone, this repressive machinery. Is this the way one enters the service of the God who is love?

In addition, we are surprised to see the novices so strictly set apart. This segregation, which seems to outdo the separation imposed on the guests,[1] scarcely allows the aspirants to know the community they must soon enter and remain in the rest of their life. What do people want to hide from them, to make them live this way, not in the midst of, but off to one side from, those who are going to be their brothers?

Several other questions come to our mind about profession. This act is manifestly the essential point of the treatise. The whole formation is directed at preparing the novices for it, and the rest of the chapter only describes it and marks the consequences. This insistence on the 'promise' made once for all seems to give the juridical aspect of the monk's commitment the chief emphasis. Everything seems reduced to the signature of a contract in good and proper form, which will bind the conscience for eternity. Is taking this 'yoke' deliberately, and observing this 'law', no matter at what cost until death the only problem of monastic formation and life?

Moreover the interval of time allowed before so grave a commitment seems too short. Although Benedict has considerably increased the interval foreseen by the Master,[2] this 'entire year' and 'prolonged deliberation' are still a small thing compared to the stakes, nothing less than the person's destiny for time and eternity. Contemporary man and the Church itself no longer agree to such a speedy probation. A preliminary postulancy of six months or a year, three years of temporary vows, other periods of reflection before the novitiate or after it, none of all this seems superfluous to us in taking such a decision seriously.

But all these difficulties are less grave than a last one, the nub of the matter: the difficulty we experience in regard to the perpetuity of the promises. In this chapter and the next Benedict obviously has nothing more at heart than assuring this perpetual consecration.[3] For him, as for the Master,[4] all means, including economic pressure, are good for obtaining the perseverance promised. We may ask the value of a fidelity sustained in such ways. Above all, however, the very insistence on perpetual promises does not appear to us self-evident. Is it really necessary to impose this on the monk?

Since monastic life is a charism freely imparted by the Spirit, perhaps it has not done well to imprison itself in this legal harness. 'The Spirit breathes where he wills', says Jesus—and why not also when he wills? Rather than demand perseverance in the name of juridical arrangements, we could, it seems, let it result from a continued choice, realized on the personal level by a free and constant adherence to the Spirit.[5] We would thus avoid several of the inconveniences noted above: the legalistic and negative presentation of the monastic life, the hesitation of postulants to settle down in it, and the need for longer and longer delays, the dramatization of commitment at the end of a novitiate polarized by the choice to be made, to say nothing of the harshness the monastery showed until recently to its 'apostates'.

A commitment that was not perpetual, but temporary or even without definite duration, would correspond not only to the concern for liberty and authenticity very widespread in our world, but it would also be warranted on the buddhist model, where leaving the pagoda is always permitted. At a time when christian monasticism is trying to get a foothold in the countries of Asia, this example would especially draw attention.

Before treating this crucial point of the perpetuity of the vows, we should make a few remarks about the different questions posed to us by Benedict's text. The repelling harshness of the reception is more understandable in an age of religious vitality, as the first centuries of cenobitism seem to have been. Communities grew quickly then,[6] and recruitment does not seem ordinarily to have caused much anxiety.[7] In such a situation, a head of a monastery would think less of finding recruits than of being sure about their quality.

Moreover, the 'difficulties' set in the way of candidates, do not exclude marks of affectionate concern for them. At the same time he was praising Benedict for his severe manner of discerning vocations,[8] Pope Gregory recommended that another abbot give the kindest and most encouraging welcome to some postulant.[9] Benedict himself at the end of his Prologue adds to the Master's text a paragraph of encouragement for beginners.[10]

The roughness of the probation is paralleled, moreover, by its relative rapidity. The rougher the trial, the shorter it can be.[11] Inversely, less energetic treatment must be prolonged. A relationship exists therefore between two of the surprising aspects of the probationary methods of ancient monasticism. Its vigor partially explains its brevity. If today we find the period of probation insufficient, this is doubtless because our gentler methods oblige us to take more time.

Another factor acts in the same direction: the relaxation of social pressure on the monks to persevere. Basil had already noted it and the Council *In Trullo* had repeated it: it was the Church's development in these centuries which stirred the hierarchy both to punish more severely the failure of consecrated virgins, and to lower the age at which the consecration of widows and of children was held to be irrevocable.[12] In both cases the intensification of the demands was motivated by the consolidation of Christianity within society, for general consensus made apostasies more difficult.

Inversely, we may add, the weakening of christian society diminishes the support received by those consecrated, and makes prudence more necessary. This has happened in our time. The initial trial, which was formerly quite short, tends naturally to be longer as social pressure relaxes and leaves the individual more and more only to his own resources.

The segregation of novices in a separate house is not so much intended to hide unpleasant things from them[13] as to make the step of profession more impressive. No one enters the community except someone who commits himself for good. Once the threshold is crossed, one cannot step over it again. This is another instance where the postulant is made to reflect on the gravity of the decision he is going to make.[14]

We return thus to the heart of our difficulties: the perpetuity of the vow of monastic life. Either explicitly, as in our rules, or implicitly, monastic profession was universally considered by tradition irrevocable. Although here and there men were admitted to the monastery for a time and shared in the common life without being obligated to it,[15] a radical difference was made between them and the monks. It was not a temporary monasticism, but an external sharing in the observance. For only commitment forever makes the monk.

This voluntary fixity in one state is not incompatible with the liberty of the gifts of the Spirit. The monastic charism is one of fidelity. What the Spirit from the beginning has asked of and given monks is precisely a self-consecration forever. The gifts of God are without repentance:[16] this axiom, stated by Paul in regard to Israel's vocation, is also valid for the alliance concluded by the Lord with those who give themselves entirely to him in the Church.

If therefore 'the Spirit breathes where he wills', we could not add in the present case 'when he wills'. The interpolation would be still more inappropriate since this word of Christ pertains to statements on the new birth wrought by water and the Holy Spirit, that is, baptism.[17] This gift, more than any other, is without repentance. This voice of the Spirit, which we hear without knowing whence it comes or whither it goes, is not a charism of transient prophecy, but the very grace of faith perpetually offered to those who have been reborn.

The Spirit breathes where he wills, but there he breathes without intermission. What is true of baptismal regeneration is also true of monastic

profession. Not by chance do the two commitments have the same definitive character, for the second repeats, confirms and specifies the first.
This relationship of monastic profession with baptism, clearly brought
out by the Master,[18] gives christian monasticism its own character distinct
from its pagan homologues. The philosopher can retire from the world
for a while; the *bonze* can leave the pagoda, as he entered it; but the christian monk, like the Jew before him,[19] makes a pact with the living God
for all eternity. Baptismal confession and monastic profession have the
same structure. The monk, like the neophyte, is bound by a 'faith'[20]
which unites him to Christ and which he cannot deny.

This gift of person to person distinguishes monastic commitment from
the simple quest for wisdom and makes it resemble christian combat, indeed martyrdom. As the one consists in remaining faithful to Christ until
death, so monasticism strives to maintain until death its resolve to renounce the world for Christ. These two actuations of baptism, the second
of which seeks to reproduce the first,[21] draw from their sacramental source
the same energy and the same constancy. They have before them the
same sign of Christ crucified. The death endured by Jesus calls the monk,
like the martyr, to hold on without defection until the end.[22]

This gift of the person to the personal God, the characteristic mark of
our monasticism, makes profession an inviolable consecration.[23] Anyone
who gives himself to God cannot take himself back, for God does not let
go. The apostasy of the monk is analogous to that of the believer. Whatever the mercy of the Church towards either, they cannot keep from
seeming like faults, and grave faults, without shaking christian monasticism and Christianity itself to the foundations.

Since the monk's commitment is so serious, we can understand that
Benedict, following the Master and tradition, saw the novitiate less as a
formation than a probation. It is not so much a matter of instructing the
novice as of measuring his resolution and his faith. But this disposition to
constrain oneself by vows is not a simple matter of the human will. By imposing perpetual bonds upon himself, the monk not only forearms himself against his own changeableness, like Ulysses fastened to the mast; this
denial of his own frail and changing being, already stamped with grandeur, is coupled with an invocation. The chant *Suscipe me* (Receive me)
makes this decision both a gift to God and a prayer.

Thus the ring of grace laid out at the beginning closes upon itself and makes a circle. First comes proof that the postulant's spirit 'comes from God', gained by the signs given that he'seeks God'; then comes the request that the Lord 'receive' him.[24] Perseverance thus becomes an act of hope. The human promise of fidelity, rooted in God, is entrusted to the grace of God for its fulfilment.[25]

NOTES TO CHAPTER 19

1. See t. VI, p. 1319. Cf. p. 1393.

2. See t. VI, pp. 1322 and 1352–1353. Cf. p. 1395.

3. See t. VI, pp. 1353, 1358, 1396.

4. Cf. RM 87–91, notably RM 90.92–93 and 91.35–41; RB 59.3–6.

5. We find this commentary on Jn 3:8 (cf. Greg., *Dial.* 2.21) and the following suggestion in a report presented to the Congress of Benedictine Abbots of 1970 (no. 106 - Schema D/2, pp. 1–2).

6. See *Vita Caesarii* 2.47 (the two hundred nuns of Arles; some years after Caesarius' death, Aurelian founded a new monastery); Gregory, *Dial.* 1.1 (the two hundred monks of Fondi) and 2.3 (the twelve dozen monks of Subiaco); *Vita Patrum Jur.* 25 (the one hundred five nuns of La Balme; Romanus and Lupicinus also founded several large monasteries of men). The enormous size of pachomian monasteries is well known.

7. Gregory, *Reg.* 8.30; 10.18; 11.54; 13.4 gives evidences of four cases of monasteries combined with others for lack of monks, but the two last documents indicate the wholly exterior reason for the deed, namely the Lombard invasion and ensuing insecurity. However, see *Reg.* 11.13.

8. Gregory, *In Libr. I Reg.* 4.70. See our article '*Discretione praecipuam.* A quoi Grégoire pensait-il?' in *Benedictina*, 22 (1975) 325–7.

9. Gregory, *Reg.* 6.47. Cf. *Hom. Ev.* 19.7 (a postulant *devote susceptus*) and 38.16 (the same *diu regulariter protractus quandoque susceptus est*).

10. RB Prol 46–49. Cf. RB 2.32: aims at increasing the flock.

11. Cf. Cassian, *Inst.* 4.3 and 32–33: a period of ten days represents a 'very long' time (subjectively, given the conditions), when one is subject to all sorts of rebuffs and humiliations.

12. See t. VI, pp. 1366–7.

13. Cf. Denys, *Vita Pachomii* 33: guests should not be scandalized by the unedifying young monks; so they do not let them enter.

14. RB 58.14–16. Cf. RM 88.1–10.

15. See RM 79, 29–34 and 87.60–65; RB 61.1–3. Moreover, with Benedict and probably also with the Master, it was a matter of monks coming from elsewhere, and not of seculars who try their hand at monastic life.

16. RM 11:29.

17. Jn 3:3–8.

18. RM Th 8–25; Thp 1–11. See above our commentary on the Prologue.

19. See the Rule of the Community of Qumran (IQS V.7–13; V.20–VI.1; VI.13–23).

20. See 1 Tm 5:12 (the defection of a widow). Cf. Basil, *Ep.* 199.18.

21. See RM 7.59 and the note.

22. RM Ths 45–46 (cf. Thp 11); RB Prol 45 and 50.

23. Cf. Basil, *Long Rules* 10.2 (*anatetheikosin*); 14 (*anatheis, hierosulos, anathèma*); 15,4 (*hagiasmon, anathèma, kathierousthai*). Cf. *Ep.* 199.18 (*skeuos hieron anatethen*) and 44 (*hierosulia, kathierômenon*).

24. RB 58.2 (1 Jn 4:1), 7–8, 21 (Ps 118:116). To the *Suscipe* the Master adds the verse *Confirma* (Ps 67:29), another prayer. See RM 89.24–25.

25. The primacy of God, as originator and receiver of the vow, is strongly marked in RM 89.6–11. By the verse *Confirma* (preceding note), the monk asks God to 'confirm what he has accomplished'.

Chapter XX

THE PRIESTS IN THE MONASTERY
(RB 60 & 62)

T HE TWO CHAPTERS on priests, which we combine here,[1] are separated in the Rule by the chapter on stranger-monks (RB 61). This discontinuity suggests immediately that the monastic priesthood was not for Benedict a separate theme to be treated by itself under its different aspects. Priests who become monks and monks who are ordained priests are instead, in his eyes, specific instances of two general questions: the conditions for admittance, and rank. The 'priests who wish to dwell in the monastery' make their appearance as one group of aspirants among others, and they are dealt with after the lay candidates and before the monk-postulants. In their regard the problem of rank is raised for the first time, and it continues to preoccupy the legislator when he treats the stranger-monks,[2] and then the monks who are ordained priests; finally in RB 63 he creates a synthesis in which he disengages some general principles.

The relationships of our two chapters with their neighbors show well enough that Benedict was scarcely thinking of elaborating a special statute and spirituality for the monk-priest. The same conclusion can be drawn from the fact that the appeal to obedience and humility, which resounds in both chapters, is very similar to the recommendations addressed to each of the officers and specialists in the monastery: deans, cellarer, artisans, and provost.[3] The same must be said of the condition laid down for the ordination of a monk to the priesthood, 'that he be worthy'.[4] In a particularly concise way Benedict is here expressing the consistent concern which causes him to enumerate carefully the qualities required for each office.

We can say therefore that neither the priesthood in itself, nor its union with the monastic state, is particularly scrutinized by our author. In this regard, it is worth noting that the fine maxim *magis ac magis in Deum proficiat* (let him progress more and more towards God), which is about the only citation or reminiscence in the second chapter, does not come from a text about the priesthood. Cyprian wrote this phrase in a letter addressed to certain 'confessors' who were not showing themselves equal to their position; after having gloriously confessed the faith, they were lacking in the most necessary virtues, notably *disciplina* and humility.[5] Cyprian wanted these prestigious persons to give good example to everyone.[6] The exhortation to 'progress more and more in the Lord' was addressed therefore to Christians whom one splendid deed had raised to honor, and who were running the risk of being satisfied with this success.

We see the analogy with the monk-priest of our Rule: like the confessors at Carthage, he might rest on the fact of having been judged 'worthy to exercise the priesthood', and no longer seek to progress. His ordination, like the act of 'confession', sets him on a pedestal where he runs the risk of becoming proud and forgetting that he remains subject to the 'discipline of the rule'. This maxim of Benedict's, seen in connection with its source, does not show any particular reflection on the specific requirements of the priesthood. The priesthood is simply considered as one of those religious dignities which can compromise moral effort, and harm humility and the other virtues.

Once we have situated these chapters in their context and recognized the weak specificness of their content, we must add at once that they bear witness to Benedict's keen interest in the priesthood. This new aspect is apparent as soon as we compare the Benedictine Rule with other monastic rules, notably with the Master's.

All in all, priests and clerics appear rarely in the rules. Augustine's Rule several times mentions a 'presbyter' who enjoys supreme authority in the monastery while remaining outside it.[7] This person, the priest delegated by the bishop to govern the monks, is known to us from other documents,[8] but the evolution of cenobitism would soon tend to reject this exterior control by clerics in order to leave the full authority with monastic superiors.[9] The same tendency is perceived in the documents of which we shall speak.

A little after Augustine, the Rule of the Four Fathers treats of clerics coming to the monastery. They are given full liturgical honors, but they may not stay and dwell there. Only the *lapsi* can enter the community, to do penance there. Stripped of all privilege, they disappear wholly into the mass of brothers.[10]

At the beginning of the following century the Master's legislation shows some development, but remains in the same line. Priests and clerics are received at table with all the honors due them,[11] and the arrival of a gift of blessed bread from a priest gives rise to the same demonstrations of respect.[12] The Master doubtless did admit priests to dwell in the monastery, unlike the Four Fathers, but he firmly laid down two conditions: first, the priests will have only honorific privileges, and no effective power over the community; then they will work with the brothers, like all the guests.[13] This regulation flows logically from the definition laid down at the beginning: priests are considered as strangers to whom hospitality is given. This initial phrase traces a sharp demarcation between the two societies to which belong the priests and those who receive them. On one side is the monastery, and on the other 'the churches'.[14] The first has only the abbot as its head; the priests' power is limited to the second.

If we add to these three texts a short paragraph by Aurelian of Arles, a contemporary of Benedict, we shall have almost completed the list of rules which speak of the priesthood in some way.[15] Aurelian's little chapter treats of the ordination of monks to the priesthood and diaconate, making this depend exclusively on the abbot's will.[16]

Each of Benedict's two chapters can therefore be placed in relation with a previous or contemporary rule. The first, 'on the priests who wish to dwell in the monastery', is connected immediately with what the Master had written on the subject. The second, relative to monks being ordained priests, has its parallel in Aurelian. Thus Benedict *combines* two cases, one envisaged by the Master, the other by Aurelian. In this matter he is more complete than either of his colleagues.

This fact already indicates the important place occupied by the question of the priesthood in our Rule. In addition, the length of the two benedictine chapters is considerable: their combined text is slightly shorter than Chapter 83 of the Master. Finally, without abandoning the defensive attitude of his predecessor, Benedict went far beyond what the Master foresaw. All this shows the interest he took in the matter.

The first original mark of our Rule in relationship to its predecessors is that priests are admitted into the community. The priest is no longer an exterior authority, as with Augustine, nor a stranger who may not remain, as with the Four Fathers, nor a guest kept on the periphery of the community, as with the Master. He can become a true member of the community. By opening the door to him, even though reticently, Benedict shows that the relationships between cenobitism and the clergy were changing. The monastery was thereafter strong enough, and its hierarchy sure enough of itself, to receive without excessive risk a person belonging to the hierarchy of the Church.

The tentative integration described by our chapter 60 is not entirely new. Beyond the exclusion of the Master and the Four Fathers, Benedict returns to a polity of assimilation inaugurated at the beginnings of egyptian cenobitism, by Pachomius himself.[17] In Palestine several of the monks mentioned by Cyril of Scythopolis, beginning with the great Euthymius, were already priests when they entered the laura. In the West, before and after Benedict, other cases can be cited of clerics becoming monks in a cenobium.[18]

Benedict's second original mark, in comparison to the Master, is to envisage the promotion of monks to sacred orders. On this point he does not follow Pachomius' example,[19] but ratifies a widespread custom. Not only are the *Lives* written by Cyril of Scythopolis full of examples of monks ordained deacons or priests for the service of their community, according to a custom later codified by Justinian,[20] but among the numerous priests and deacons met in the monasteries,[21] more than one was doubtless consecrated in the course of his monastic life. In any case, this is what happened, according to Pope Gregory, to one monk of Praeneste whom his abbot 'had ordained priest' by reason of his great merit.[22] The same Gregory intervened personally three times to recommend to the local bishop the request of an abbot or community in Sicily to have one of its members ordained.[23] Without moving ahead to this epoch later than Benedict, we can cite from the first quarter of the sixth century a monastery in Byzacene which enjoyed the right of having ministers ordained 'who celebrate the divine mysteries for us',[24] a right which was recognized a little later as belonging to all the monasteries of the region.[25]

The roman and african documents we have just mentioned unanimously indicate the purpose of these ordinations: to have monks who can celebrate the Eucharist at home and among themselves, without needing to go out or to call in an outside priest.[26] This was certainly the motive, and the only motive, Benedict had in mind when writing his Chapter 62. Not by chance does this text mention no other priestly function than the *officium altaris* (duty at the altar). The celebration of the Eucharist, much less frequent then than now, is the only activity offered the monk-priest. It is a singular situation to have a priest confined in principle to his liturgical functions, while the care of souls and the government of the community are assured by lay pastors![27]

The priesthood, even confined within these narrow limits, represents a considerable contribution to monastic communities. It obtains for them a sort of liturgical self-sufficiency which reinforces their independence and strengthens their enclosure. The Master's monks surely had to go out on Sundays and feastdays to hear Mass at the parish church.[28] Benedict's monks heard it in their own oratory, which thus becomes the equal of a secular church, equipped to have regular celebrations with its own ministers.

The monastic *scola* was therefore no longer merely a society parallel with the Church, like it by its teaching authority but deprived of sacramental powers.[29] Thereafter it became more like its model and less dependent on it. Either by the admission of priests among the monks or by the ordination of monks to the priesthood, the adoption of the priesthood made the monastery a largely autonomous ecclesiastical entity. By this fact communications with the secular Church, either by the presence of monks at the parish services or by calling diocesan priests to celebrate at the monastery,[30] were condemned to disappear. The monastery was both more integrated with and more separated from ecclesiastical society.

The monk-priest, as a member of the hierarchy, is in the paradoxical situation of a leader without troops, a pastor without pastoral responsibilities. His subordination to the abbot and the other lay officers causes problems. To join sacramental power and authority in one and the same person, and to place an abbot-priest at the head of the community, would therefore seem opportune.

In fact, this solution was much favored both in the West and in the East,[31] but in the centuries we are studying it was far from becoming the rule or even a custom. Although here and there we can point out texts where *presbyter* seems synonymous with *abbas*,[32] most of the documents reflect a keen awareness of the distinction between the two charges: when the abbot-priest is met, he is called *abbas ET presbyter*. Sometimes, moreover, this person had already been a priest before being elected abbot,[33] so we could not say that the union of the two dignities was willed for itself, as is surely the case when a monk receives both of them at the same time.[34] Even then, however, a contingent motive may be at work.[35] Reasons of this sort certainly explain the priesthood of a Fulgentius and a Sabas, imposed on them in the course of their abbatial career.[36] If we add the fact that a monk-priest was in some way predisposed to the abbatial office, either by his eminence in the community,[37] or by the singular virtues and general esteem supposed by his ordination,[38] we begin to wonder whether the cumulative function of abbot-priest was imposed for its intrinsic advantages or whether it resulted most often from accidental and varied causes.

However this may be, this pluralism was never erected into a system. Severinus, the great abbot of Norica, remained a layman,[39] as did Lupicinus and Eugendus at Condat.[40] The African Felix, the colleague of Fulgentius, seems also, to have done so and Fulgentius himself was and would have remained a layman except for the chance circumstance of which we have spoken.[41] In Palestine it was the same for Sabas.[42] It is remarkable that this last and his contemporary Eugendus expressed the same repugnance for the priesthood, and that they reproduced the objections formulated by Pachomius a century and a half earlier.[43]. At the end of the fifth century these holy abbots kept a keen awareness of the drawbacks of the priesthood for monks, even superiors. The priesthood is in fact a secular 'dignity',[44] which may cause trouble in monasteries by arousing the pride of some, and the ambition and jealousy of others.

Closer to our Rule, the Master did not conceive of the abbot as other than a layman.[45] Benedict gives no sign of having abbot-priests in mind. Was he one himself? Gregory, his biographer, nowhere says so,[46] though he notes that the Abbot Servandus, his friend, was a deacon.[47] But to evaluate these two facts correctly, we must examine the whole of the *Dialogues*. We see then that the mention of *diaconus atque abbas* Servandus is something unique in the four Books of this work. Of the some twenty-five abbots mentioned there,[48] no one else is called priest or deacon. Once, indeed, Gregory observes that one of them 'was not in holy orders',[49] and this fact is noted without comment as something natural and self-evident. It seems then that, at the end of the century, the pontiff considered the lay abbot the normal thing in Italy. Yet, the fact that Maximian, the roman abbot whom Gregory does not identify as a priest in the *Dialogues*, is presented as one in a passage of the *Homilies*,[50] should make us very cautious. Other abbots may have been priests although the *Dialogues* do not say so.

Gregory's correspondence gives rise to similar observations and uncertainties. If the abbot-priests or deacons are more numerous there—some ten out of about seventy[51]—it should be noted that four of them, perhaps five, resided outside Italy[52] and that one of the remaining cases is uncertain.[53] On the whole, the very great majority of the abbots on Italian territory and in the adjacent islands seem to have been laymen. This fact seems confirmed by a series of letters in which Gregory protests against the abuse of powers by clerics over monasteries.[54] If the abbots of these places had been vested with sacred orders, they would not have had to suffer the pretentions of their secular colleagues. Also, the communities which had a priest in their midst or who asked for one, are equally suspect of not having a priest as their abbot.[55]

Yet it may be that in the *Letters*, as in the *Dialogues*, Gregory sometimes neglected to mention the clerical title of the monastic superior.[56] This suspicion is aggravated by a curious fact: of the small number of priest-abbots or deacon-abbots mentioned in the correspondence, the greater number are at fault or under accusation, and the Pope inflicts sanctions or grants a grace to them.[57] The necessity of distinguishing in this matter between the abbatial office and the priesthood—these two functions are treated differently—may have led Gregory to mention expressly here the sacred order which would have remained implicit elsewhere.

It is difficult, therefore, to affirm that the Italian abbots in the sixth century were usually not priests, deacons, or clerics, as the gregorian literature suggests at first sight. If, however, we can accord a certain confidence to the indications of this literature, it seems that Benedict, a lay abbot, represented the general rule, and his friend, the abbot-deacon Servandus, the exception. The Benedictine Rule, like that of the Master, would thus stand in the contemporary perspective of a non-clerical abbot. In it the monk-priest is really—and paradoxically—subordinated to a lay superior. As a simple liturgical officer, he must give way in the pastoral sphere to the officers of a monastic hierarchy which is not clerical.

The strangeness of this situation only reflects the essential anomaly of monastic communities, groups of perfect Christians which are not churches.[58] To assure the sacramental life of these communities two solutions were available: recourse to the ministry of the secular clergy; and the constitution of their own clergy. The first, which seems to have been that of Pachomius and Horsiesius,[59] was still, at the beginning of the sixth century, the only one envisaged by the Master. In accepting the second, Benedict did not bring about a revolution in monasticism—it was already a practice before his time—but he at least parted company from his predecessor in refusing to maintain the monasteries in a purely lay state.

The two chapters we have studied mark, therefore, an important stage in the history of latin cenobitism. The priesthood and with it the Eucharistic celebration were officially installed in monasteries. The way was thus opened to that proliferation of priests and Masses which was one day to develop. Yet nothing presaged such an evolution. The priesthood remained rare and functional, ordered to community celebrations which did not even take place daily. After ten centuries of clerical monasticism, this state of things exercises an undeniable attraction upon our generation.[60]

NOTES TO CHAPTER 20

1. Besides the study in *La Communauté et l'Abbé*, pp. 327–47, a comparative analysis with RM 83 will be found in the article 'Les chapitres de Benoît and du Maître sur le sacerdoce', in *Benedictina* 20 (1973) 6–8.

2. RB 61.11–12, with express reference to RB 60.4–8. However, the motive of promotion, for the clerics as well as for the stranger-monks, is no longer clerical dignity, but the *vita*. In its turn RB 62.6 speaks of *vitae meritum*, a formula repeated in the general rule of RB 63.1 (cf. 21.4; 64.2). Between the two chapters on priests, Benedict's thought has been modified by considering the case of the stranger-monk. See t. VI, pp. 1378–9.

3. RB 21.2–5; 31.4–7 and 12–16; 57.1–3; 65.1–6 and 13–21.

4. RB 62.1. Compare RB 2.1; 21.6; 63.14; 64.5; 65.20, where this *dignus* is repeated. The expression, familiar to Benedict, does not seem to refer especially to the ritual clause in the matter of priestly ordinations, which we find for example in Gregory, *Ep.* 1.15 and 42; 6.28 and 42; 8.15 (compare the negative formula of *Ep.* 12.12 and 48). This clause moreover is absent in Aurelian, *Reg. mon.* 46.

5. Cyprian, *Ep.* 13.6. The priest Rogatian, who directed the group, received no special exhortation. Humility: see *Ep.* 13.3.1 (cites Is 66:2); 13.4.2–3. *Disciplina* (good morals): *Ep.* 13.3.2; 13.6.

6. *Ep.* 13.3.1 (cf. 13.5.1). We think of RB 60.5.

7. Augustine, *Praec.* 4.9 and 11; 7.1–2. Cf. *Ordo monast.* 6, where *pater*, similarly juxtaposed to *praepositus*, could designate the bishop Alypius, the presumed author (see L. Verheijen, *La Règle de saint Augustin*, t. II, pp. 153–4 and 164).

8. See *Les Vies coptes*, p. 99 (Bo 28 and parallels; however the motive invoked by the bishop disappears in Denys, *Vita Pach.* 27); Cyril of Scythopolis, *Vita Euthymii* 5. Pachomius is a monk, but Euthymius? The office of 'archimandrite and exarch of monks', whether cenobites or hermits, of which Cyril speaks, *Vita Sabae* 30 and 45, seems a little different. Were these diocesan superiors, elected by the monks, necessarily priests? In any case, Sabas was, and also Gerontios and Passarion. Authority of the bishop over the monks: Council of Chalcedon (451), *can.* 4; Orleans (511), *can.* 19, etc.; *Reg. Patr.* III, 2; Gregory, *Ep.* 7.35,etc.

9. For the interventions of the bishops, see the Councils of Arles (about 455) and Carthage (535–536), cited in *La Communauté et l'Abbé*, p. 343, n. 3 and p. 347. Regarding priests, it is significant that Caesarius, *Reg. virg.* 25 and 35, suppresses the *presbyter* mentioned by Augustine, *Praec.* 4.11 and 7.1. The same in *Reg. Tarn.* 18.16; 19.1; 23.1–3. The intervention of clerics in monasteries is forbidden by Gregory, *Ep.* 4.11 (Syracuse); 5.1; 6.29; 7.43; 8.15 (Ravenna); 6.46 (Pesaro). The terms of the first two letters recall in a particular way RM 83.1–2.

10. *Reg. IV Patrum* 4.14–19. The refusal of honors to the *lapsi* concerns those who are visiting, but doubtless extends to those who become monks.

11. RM 77.

12. RM 76.

13. RM 83.

14. RM 83.1–2. See also RM 83.18. Compare Gregory, *Ep.* 4.11 and 5.1 (above note 9).

15. Beyond these, about the only citations to be made are Pachomius, *Praec.* 51 (= *Reg. Orient.* 40); Caesarius, *Reg. virg.* 36,38–39,46,53,64; *Reg. Patr.* II.7 (Cf. RM 93–94); *Reg. Patr. III* 2,4,13; Fructuosus, *Reg.* II, 2.

16. Aurelian, *Reg. mon.* 46.

17. *Les Vies coptes*, p. 96, 22–27 (Bo 25 and parallels). The redaction of Denys, *Vita Pach.* 24, where it is a matter of 'living under the rule', and of 'submitting oneself to the father' (abbot) and of 'great humility', is particularly close to RB 60.

18. Cyril of Scythopolis, *Vita Euth.* 5 (Euthymius) and 16 (John and Kyriôn); *Vita Job.* 4–5 (John hides his quality as bishop); *Vita Cyr.* 4 (Anatolius); Cf. Theodore of Petra, *Vita Theod.* 8 (Basil). *Vita Patrum Jurensium* 13 (two clerics); *Vita Sequani* 4 and 6, in Mabillon ASOSB 1:250 (Sequanus, priest, enters at Réomé); Gregory, *Ep.* 12.35 (the cleric Pancratius).

19. *Les Vies coptes*, p. 96, 10–22 (Bo 25 and parallels). Benedict could have known this example given by Denys, *Vita Pach.* 24. However, he found in Denys, *Vita Pach.* 35 (= G² 37) a case of a monk ordained by the counsel of Pachomius (See *La Communauté et l'Abbé*, p. 330, n. 1).

20. Cyril of Scythopolis, *Vita Euth.* 16 (Domitian and Domnus, deacons); *Vita Job.* 8 (John, a bishop but unknown as such, is proposed for the priesthood after six years); *Vita Cyr.* 7 (Kyriakos, successively deacon and priest); *Vita Abraam.* 4 (Olympios, deacon, then priest and second superior). Cyril himself became a priest, according to the *Incipit* of the Lives of Theodosius and Theognios. When Sabas refused to let any of his monks be ordained (*Vita Sab.* 19), complaints were made to him as though this were an anomaly. The very many monks ordained for the service of secular churches constitute a different category. Justinian, *Nov.* 133.2 (four or five priests, deacons and clerics for a monastic church). Cf. Council of Chalcedon, *can.* 6.

21. Cyril of Scythopolis, *Vita Euth.* 26 and 48 (Thallelaios and Nil, priests); Eugippius, *Vita Sev.* 19.5 and 41.1 (Lucillus, priest); 19.3 (Amantius, deacon). On the priest and two

deacons of the monastery of Byzacene, see *La Communauté et l'Abbé*, p. 342, n. 5. The *Vitae Patrum Jur.* names the deacon Sabinian (52-58), the priest Antiodiolus (163), the deacon Valentine (165), and speaks of *the* priests under the abbacy of Eugendus (148 and 151; cf. 133-134). See also Gregory, *Ep.* 6.56 (*the* priests and deacons at Lérins); 6,62 (Athanasius, priest; cf. *Dial.* 4.40); 9.28 and 11.48 (Domitius, priest); 11.14 (Constantius, priest); 12.35 (Pancratius, deacon). This last was ordained in the course of his monastic life. Very probably it was the same for the priest of Byzacene mentioned above.

22. Gregory, *Dial.* 3.23.

23. Gregory, *Ep.* 6.42 (S. Hermas, Palermo); 9.92 (Praecoritanum, Palermo); 12.48 (Leontium). See t. I, pp. 109-10.

24. Letter of the abbot Peter to Boniface of Carthage, in Labbe, *Concilia*, t. IV, 1644b. The primate is the one to ordain.

25. Council of Carthage (536), in Labbe, *Concilia*, t. IV, 1785b. The local bishop should ordain.

26. See especially Gregory, *Ep.* 6.42.

27. See our article 'Le prêtre et la communauté monastique' in *La Maison-Dieu*, 115 (1973) 67-9. Of course, should occasion arise, the monk-priest can exercise some pastoral function, including that of abbot, as we shall see, but it is by accident and not as priest. Under this latter title, the monk-priest is not even the judge of whether to admit guilty brothers to the Eucharist which he distributes, this judgement being reserved to the abbot. See *Vitae Patrum Jur.* 151 (cf. RM 80; Dorotheus, *Instr.* 9.99). In Gregory, *Ep.* 9.37 (= *Reg.* 9.107), the priest Valentine who excommunicates the monks, could well be the abbot, as his complaints later on other subjects suggest.

28. See t. I, p. 104, n. 6 (cf. our 'Scholies sur la RM', pp. 122-7). To the examples already given of this practice ('Scholies', p. 126, n. 34). add Justinian, *Nov.* 133.2; Gregory, *Ep.* 6.42. It existed therefore in Benedict's time and even after him.

29. In the Master, the lay abbot distributes Holy Communion only *extra missam*.

30. Cf. RM 45.17; 93.8-11. See also Gregory, *Ep.* 6.42. This system which was in vigor with the Pachomians (Bo 25; G¹ 27), was effaced in the later texts (G² 23; Denys, *V. Pach.* 24), which substituted for the secular priest the monk ordained before entering the monastery.

31. See *La Communauté et l'Abbé*, pp. 341-42, and in addition Cyril of Scythopolis, *Vita Euth.* 5,16 (Euthymius); *Vita Sab.* 19 (Sabas) and 88 (Cassian); *Vita Joh.* 3 (John); *Vita Abraam.* 2 (Abraamios). According to Gerontios, *V. Melaniae* 49,67, the author is a priest. The same for Hypatios (Callinicos, *V. Hyp.* 13), Marinus of Lérins (*Vita Patr. Jur.* 179), the two abbots of whom Ferrandus speaks, *V. Fulg.* 29, Fortunatus in Byzacene (Labbe, *Concilia*, t. IV, 1785a). Of the four priests of the monastery of Hadrumetum (Labbe, ibid. 1646d), the first, Valentine, seems to have been the *praepositus* or *abbas* with whom Augustine dealt (L. Verheijen, *La Règle de S. Augustin*, t. II: 99-100), and his three successors could also have been abbots. See also *Reg. Patr. III* 4, and Georges, V. Theod. Syk. T. 21,41,130.

32. Gregory of Tours, *Lib. de glor. conf.* 9; PL 71:836ab. Eugippius, *V. Sev.* 37.1 says of Marcianus: *postea presbyter . . . monasterio praefuit.* The same is called *presbyter noster* (11.2; 46.1), a title given to his predecessor Lucillus (44.5; cf. 45.2), when the one and the other is superior of the monastery. It is useless to suppose with R. Noll (Note on 11,2, p. 128) that *presbyter = senior.* Everywhere in Eugippius, the word designates the priesthood of the second degree. Note that Eugippius, according to Paschasius' Letter-Preface, was himself a priest, and also abbot, according to *V. Sev.* 37.1

33. Thus Euthymius in Palestine, Fortunatus in Byzacene, Lucillus in Norica, Sequanus in Burgundy. Cf. Georges, *V. Theod. Syk.* 130 (John).

34. Thus Aelian, successor of Seridos at Gaza, according to Barsanuphius-John, *Ep.* 575, cited by L. Regnault, *Maîtres spirituels au désert de Gaza* (Solesmes, 1967) pp. 151–2. Cf. Georges, *V. Theod. Syk.* 41 (Philoumenos).

35. Aelian, a simple lay postulant, no doubt had need of priestly authority to impose himself on a monastery where he had not yet even been received among the monks.

36. Sabas also had need of authority to face an opposition. As for Fulgentius, the bishop hoped thus to stabilize him (Ferrandus, *V. Fulg.* 31).

37. Cf. RB 60.4. This place 'after the abbot' is that of the 'second', that is, the designated successor of the abbot, according to RM 92–93.

38. RB 62.1 and 6. The *electio congregationis* is found in Gregory, *Ep.* 9.92 (cf. *Ep.* 6.42), and in Caesarius, *Testament*, ed. G. Morin, in *Rev. Bén.*, 16 (1899) p. 103. With a community of men choosing one of its members for the priesthood, such a choice is like a scrutiny before the abbatial election.

39. As appears in Eugippius, *V. Sev.* 9.3; 16.4; 23.2. This lay abbot had three priests as his successors (above, n. 32).

40. *V. Patr. Jur.* 134. Romanus, their predecessor, was on the contrary ordained priest (ibid. 18).

41. See above, n. 36.

42. Here, however, the objection of the opponents (*V. Sab.* 19: 'He has not orders') suggests that in refusing the priesthood Sabas was departing from a widespread custom in Palestine, at least for the large communities.

43. *V. Patr. Jur.* 133–134; Cyril of Scythopolis, *V. Sab.* 16 (Mt 11:29) and 18 (*tès philarchias archè . . . hè tou klèrothènai epithumia*). Cf. G¹ 27 = G³ 36: *archè logismou philarchias ho klèros* (G² 23 and G⁴ 32 are not as close). This sentence of Pachomius concerns directly the ordination of monks, not superiors. On the refusal of this latter, see G¹ 28 and parallels (Pachomius): *Les Vies coptes*, p. 393 (Horsiesius).

44. Cf. *V. Patr. Jur.* 133.8: *inligari dignitate quam abrenuntiantes ac remotos minime convenit adfectare.* On the special relation which links the monk-cleric to the bishop and to the secular Church, see for example Conc. of Arles (455), in Labbe, *Concilia*, t. IV, 1024e; Eugippius, *V. Sev.* 41.1; Gregory, *Ep.* 1.42 and 12.35; Ferrandus, *V. Fulg.* 31. Benedict himself indicates it (RB 62.9).

45. RM 83.9.

46. We cannot deduce it from *Dial.* 2.8 (preaching) and 23.24 (excommunication and reconciliation). If sacred orders were lacking, an apostolic permission enabled one to preach outside the monastery (see *Dial.* 1.4, p. 31, 17–37.21, where Gregory shows himself undemanding in this regard). An abbot could excommunicate and reconcile his subjects (see above n. 27), among whom, for some reason unknown to us, there were indubitably the two nuns. In the case of these nuns, the power exercised by Benedict is explained by Gregory not in canonical but in spiritual terms (*Dial.* 2.23, p. 115,21–116,10). See *La Communauté et l'Abbé*, p. 137, n. 1 (E.T. p. 109; n. 80 on p. 151), as well as I. Hausherr, 'Paul Évergétinos a-t-il connu Syméon le Nouveau Théologien?', in OCP 23 (1957) pp. 74–9; *Évergétinos* 4.39 cites Gregory, *Dial.* 1.4 and 2.23 to prove the powers exercised by spiritual men who were not priests.

47. Gregory, *Dial.* 2.35. Afterwards he is called simply *diaconus* (p. 128,17 and 130,1).

48. Gregory, *Dial.* 1.1–2 (Honoratus and his successor); 1.3 (Fortunatus); 1.4 (Aequitius and Valention); 1.7 (the abbot of Soracte); 1.8 (Anastasius); 2 Prol. (Constantine, Valentian, Simplicius, Honoratus); 2.1 (Adeodatus); 2.3 (an anonymous and Benedict); 2.22 (the abbot of Terracina); 3.14 (Eleutherius and Isaac); 3.15 (Euthicius); 3.23 (abbot of Praeneste); 3.36 (Maximian); 4.20 (Stephen); 4.23 (Soranus); 4.48 (? anonymous); 4.57 (? Pretiosus). The

priest who led a sort of monastic life with his clerics (3.22) was not a true abbot, it seems. On the priest-abbot, see the Addendum following the Epilogue.

49. *Dial.* 1.4, p. 31,19–22.

50. Compare *Dial.* 3.36 (*mei monasterii patrem*) and 4.33 (*qui . . . meo monasterio praefuit*), with *Hom. Ev.* 34.18 (*patre monasterii mei atque presbytero*). Moreover, it is curious that the *Dialogues* do not mention a single monk-cleric in Benedict's communities, in spite of RB 60 and 62 (do not confuse, as Moricca does, the two men named Speciosus of *Dial.* 4.9 and 16). Secular clerics, however, are numerous in the Life of Benedict.

51. To the list of fifty-three names given by the Index of *MGH, Epist.* II, p. 514, we can add some anonymous abbots (*Ep.* 2.28; 8.34; 9.4; 10.11; 11.44) as well as the abbots Amandinus, the two abbots named Anastasius, Augustine, Barbatianus, Domitius, Gregory, Lupus, Saturninus, Trajan.

52. Anastasius (Jerusalem), Helias (Isauria), Lupus and Senator (Autun), perhaps Martin (Illyricum? Compare *Ep.* 7.17 and 18). Among the abbots without priesthood or diaconate, several also lived outside Italy: Stephen and Conon of Lérins, John of Sinai, the African Cumquodeus, to whom can be added Augustine and Mellitus, Romans sent on a mission.

53. *Ep.* 5.34: is the priest Saturninus an abbot? We can ask the same question for the priests Valentine of Spoleto (above, n. 27) and Paulinus (*Ep.* 1.24). The other Paulinus, a refugee bishop in Messina who was set over a monastery (*Ep.* 1.40–41) constitutes a separate case. There remains Domitius (*Ep.* 9.28 = *Reg.* 9.82; already a priest, cf. *Ep.* 11.48 = *Reg.* 9.20), Gregory, (*Ep.* 1.9 and 5.6), the priest Amandinus and the deacon Jovinus of Porto Venere (*Ep.* 5.3–4).

54. See above, no. 9. We can add *Ep.* 2.28.

55. See *Ep.* 4.18; 6.42 and 56; 9.92; 11.1–2,14,48,54; 12.48.

56. Gregory, *Ep.* 11.49 = *Reg.* 9.21, calls the superior of his monastery in Palermo simply *abbas*, although he was the priest Domitius, according to the preceding letter. As in the *Dialogues* (above, n. 50), he calls Maximus or Maximianus, the abbot of *Clivus Scauri*, simply *abbas* (*Reg.* 1.14a), although he was also a priest, according to the Homilies on the Gospel.

57. This is the case of Gregory, Saturninus, Jovinus and Amandinus (above, n. 53), as well as Martin (n. 52).

58. See our articles 'Le monastère, Église du Christ', in *Studia Anselmiana*, 42 (Rome, 1957) 40–42; 'Monachisme et Église dans la pensée de Cassien', in *Théologie de la vie monastique* (Paris, 1961) 223–5.

59. See *Les Vies coptes*, p. 96 (Bo 25 and parallels; cf. G¹ 27). Pachomius extols recourse to the diocesan clergy. In regard to clerics received in the community, he 'respects their rank', but does he have them celebrate Mass? Another uncertainty for Horsiesius (ibid., p. 393): are 'those who come to us' clerics who become monks, as I interpreted it in *La Communauté et l'Abbé*, p. 331, or are they those who came to celebrate Mass at the monastery (cf. p. 96, 8–9 and 10–22)?

60. See for example O. Rousseau, 'Sacerdoce et monachisme', in *Études sur le sacrement de l'ordre* (Paris, 1957) 215–31; J. Leclercq, 'Le sacerdoce des moines', in *Irénikon* 36 (1963) 5–40. We hold here to the viewpoint that priesthood was exercised *intra muros*. The priestly ministry exercised outside the cloister, as a service for the secular Church, is incompatible with the monastic life according to Gregory, *Ep.* 4.11; 5.1; 7.43; 8.15. The exegesis of these texts by R. Rudmann, *Mönchtum und kirchlicher Dienst in den Schriften Gregors des Grossen* (Rome, 1956) pp. 105–108, seems to us too restrictive.

Chapter XXI

FROM ORDER TO CHARITY

(RB 63-72)

ENEDICT had not finished his series of chapters on the admission of candidates when he began to deal with a subject close to his heart: the order in which the brothers are ranked within the community.[1] This question is treated by him later *ex professo* in a distinct chapter entitled 'On the Order of the Community', where it stands out more by being completely separated from the problem of abbatial succession, to which the Master had connected it.[2]

Although the theme of rank in community is considered in itself, it is not therefore shut off by itself. If it no longer relates to the election of the abbot, it opens out on another question, that of relations between the brothers. The second half of the chapter 'On the Order of the Community', which regulates these relations, is completely new by comparison to the Master. Benedict regulates there the respect which the monks should have for one another according to their rank, without excluding the abbot.[3] Although it deals chiefly with mutual 'honors', it also speaks of 'affection' and 'love'.

This charter of fraternal relations has more than one complement in the following chapters. Prepared for by the legislation on rank, it prepares in its turn for a new spate of recommendations, in which the note of charity finally dominates clearly.[4] In the chapter 'On Good Zeal', the real conclusion of the Rule, this theme of reciprocal love not only covers and encompasses the theme of respect, but even goes so far as to set aside the whole system of rank. Honors and obedience become simply 'mutual', without prerogatives of seniority being mentioned.[5]

This is the general line of these last ten chapters. Without repeating the detailed study which we have made elsewhere,[6] we would like to reflect briefly on Benedict's procedure in these pages, which are entirely his own.

The order of seniority is the foundation on which Benedict builds his rules for common life. In establishing it he departs from the Master, but rejoins the best cenobitic tradition. The jewish Therapeutae, according to Philo, took their rank not according to their natural age, but according to the date of their admission into the community.[7] The christian monks apparently did the same spontaneously. The existence of a fixed order, suggested by certain statements of Basil and Augustine,[8] is evinced for the pachomian congregation by a very clear affirmation of Jerome, confirmed by Pachomius' directives in his Rule.[9] According to Jerome, this order is determined by one's time of entry into the monastery, so that account is taken not of age, but of 'profession'. If certain later rules only mention 'order' without specifying the criteria,[10] other legislators, beginning with Benedict, reproduced the pachomian norm transmitted by Jerome, and even added a negative precision to it: not only is age not taken into consideration, but neither is social condition.[11]

This final feature is of great interest, for it reminds us of the famous text of the Epistle to the Galatians where Paul declares that former distinctions no longer exist after baptism: 'there is neither Jew nor pagan; there is neither slave nor free man; there is neither male nor female. For you are all one in Christ Jesus'.[12] Civil liberty counts no more than belonging to Judaism or to the stronger sex does. The Master and Benedict based on this sentence specifically their prohibition to the abbot to prefer the brothers of freeborn origin to former slaves.[13] In the same passage of the abbatial directory they again invoked the pauline principle which denies every privilege to social condition or to religious obedience: 'God is no respecter of persons'.[14]

These references in chapter two to Saint Paul concern us all the more because Benedict was obviously thinking of the question of rank when he copied them. We have here the scriptural roots of the chapter 'On the Order of the Community'. This chapter appeals to the example of Samuel and Daniel to reject the criteria of age.[15] In rejecting equally the criterion of 'dignity',[16] it bases itself implicitly on the Apostle's words cited in the second chapter.

The repudiation of distinctions based on nature or social law is, there-fore, a characteristic which monasticism borrows from the writings of the New Testament. Monastic profession has the same effects as baptism: it radically annuls previous qualifications and disqualifications. Like Chris-tians leaving the baptismal fonts, monks are new men, 'all one in Christ', with no traces of a past that no longer matters.

Yet monasticism advances much further along this way than does sim-ple christian practice. The abrogation of natural and social differences is only a mystical theme for Saint Paul, real in the eyes of God and the believer, but without tangible effect: man and woman, master and slave, Greek and barbarian remain what they were.[17] In practice the Apostle thought so little of denying these distinctions that he took them as the framework for his moral exhortations addressed to different categories of Christians.[18] Husbands and wives, parents and children, masters and slaves, all are to take seriously their respective condition and to live it in a holy way for Christ.

On the contrary, the monastery effectively abrogates the differences which distinguished the monks before their entry. It demands a complete renunciation of property, and therefore of the domination of master over slave and the superiority of the rich over the poor. In the cenobium the equality of all before God is expressed in a tangible way, and engenders a new social order. The privilege of age is itself annulled. There are no more parents and seniors according to nature than there are masters and superiors in virtue of fortune.

No doubt we should not exaggerate the extent of this revolution, and forget the wise measures taken here or there to account for the con-sequences of social condition[19] or the permanent reality of age.[20] It re-mains however true that in the common life as a whole, and notably in the matter of rank, the intention is to set aside these differences. This desire to express concretely the equality which exists in Christ clearly dif-ferentiates cenobitism from the Church. The Church surely exerts itself—remember the Epistle of James—not to respect persons in the arrange-ment of its assemblies.[21] But this rule, whether applied or not,[22] in any case only matters at the liturgy, without reaching the social reality outside the sacred precincts. Only in the cenobia does it extend to the whole of life.

Further back than the state of the Church reflected in the apostolic

writings, the model of the primitive community of Jerusalem described in
Acts is what the monasteries reproduce, a state of society in which the
members are no longer distinguished and ranked according to their
wealth, since everything has been pooled in common ownership. What
was only a fleeting moment for the Church becomes in monasticism an
enduring order, showing the world, by the total disappropriation of each
person, the invisible equality of the children of God.

But this visible projection of the christian mystery of unity is not the
only thing that differentiates the monastic community from the secular
Church. To the rejection of natural and social distinctions the cenobium
has added a positive trait: the establishment of a new order founded on
the spiritual principle of seniority in the religious life. This innovation is
still bolder than the preceding one, since Christians never seem to have
ranked themselves according to the date of their entry into the Church.[23]
If the monastery can claim an ecclesiastical model in this matter, it is the
clerical hierarchy which furnished it.[24] But nothing shows that the pachomian congregation, and the other monastic centres after it, were inspired
by this example. Instead, as the precedent of the Therapeutae suggests, it
was an order spontaneously adopted by groups strongly conscious of their
break with the world and of the incomparable value of the new way of life
they were leading.

Monastic profession thus has effects which baptism itself did not. It
determines rank in the community and sets an order of seniority. This
order, at least with Benedict, can be modified by recourse to another criterion, that of merit, but even then reference is still made to profession,
for the most meritorious monk is the one who does greater honor to his
commitments.

Once the former distinctions have been abolished, the brothers are not
thrown every which way into an undifferentiated mass therefore, but are
ranged according to new distinctions. For natural age is substituted monastic age, and for the advantages of birth and fortune that of recognized
worth.[25] The new order imitates the old while substituting its own
norms. The cenobium thus gives a visible organizing significance to the
spiritual principles by which it lives. Both in effectively abolishing the former order and in reconstituting its own system, it invests its values in the
concrete, and draws social applications from them.

Although founded on its own criteria, this fixed order of the monastic community may be considered a resurgence of the differences abolished in principle by baptism. The Master's attitude in this regard is interesting. Not only does he admit no fixed rank—the abbot should constantly 'change their ranks'[26]—but he also rejects positions that have been acquired in the name of past merits. If the 'second' [superior] of the monastery, chosen for his exemplary observance, should grow slack, the abbot is to deprive him of his rank; and to cite in this regard the pauline axiom already invoked in the abbatial directory, 'God is no respecter of persons'.[27] What is understood at the beginning of the Rule about social condition and birth is applied equally here to past worth. There are no acquired rights in monastic society any more than there are in the eyes of the Lord. Perpetual mobility of rank expresses that of free wills. Everything has to be begun over again, as in Origen's spiritual cosmos.

Nor does Benedict let himself be tied by intangible privileges. Like the Master, he foresees the dismissal of the 'second' [superior], as well as of deans[28] if they deserve it. Rank according to seniority is itself subject to revision according to merit.[29] Yet this rank does exist and possesses a certain fixity. Benedict even speaks of 'justice' in connection with it.[30] That is, he recognizes the right of each to keep his place. Returning to the pachomian tradition which had become common in his time, he established in his monastery a relatively stable order which annulled and replaced that of the world. This restoration of ranks, together with the charter of fraternal relations flowing from it, is one of the most notable modifications which our Rule brought to the Master's.

To begin with, mutual relationships according to rank are defined by a maxim that almost repeats two of the instruments of good works: 'The young shall honor their seniors, the seniors shall love their juniors'.[31] This way of differentiating the relationships by presenting 'love' as a movement from above in response to 'honor' corresponds closely to the analysis, made in the Captivity Epistles, of the relationship between husband and wife, therefore between Christ and the Church:[32] the love of one corresponds to the submission and respect of the other. We think also of the relationship between parents and children described by Saint Paul shortly afterwards: the submission of children is based on the precept of honoring father and mother, while they are invited to show kindness to their sons.[33]

However, this over-simple scheme is quickly nuanced. Honor is not shown only by the young to the old. The old, for their part, are obliged to show some regard to their juniors. The title, 'brothers', which they should give them is no doubt stamped with familiar affection, but it also expresses a religious respect which does not appear when one calls another simply by name. We can say then that the honors are 'mutual', according to St Paul's word, which Benedict cites in conclusion.[34]

Love, in its turn, is not reserved to the relationship of the old to the young. In speaking of the titles given to the abbot 'for the honor and love of Christ',[35] Benedict suggests that love accompany respect in the movement upwards. To tell the truth, love and honor are almost inseparable. Love is respectful, and respect, after all, always implies love.

Having said this, we must recognize that the words *honorare, honor, reverentia* occur twice as often as *diligere* and *amor*. Also, the chief emphasis is placed on the respect due superiority and seniority. This predominance of the movement up from below certainly weakens the 'reciprocal' character of the 'anticipations of honor' demanded by the Apostle.[36] The respect which is the major theme of this second part of the chapter is shown almost exclusively, in fact, by the juniors to their seniors, according to very precise rules. This unilateral and specific application of the pauline instruction contrasts with the indeterminate use made of it by Cassian, Augustine, and the Second Rule of the Fathers.[37]

Along with this pauline text and those we spoke of above, Benedict doubtless remembered the prescription of Leviticus: 'Stand up before the greyhaired man, and honor the person of the agéd', inasmuch as Cyprian had already drawn an argument from it to prescribe 'rising when the bishop or priest enters.'[38] The precept of honoring father and mother, which Augustine understood of respect due to the superior, can justify in turn the marks of honor given to the abbot and the *nonni*.[39]

However, these Old Testament references, which remain implicit, indeed uncertain, have less weight than the express citation of Paul's word to the Romans. This phrase 'with honor anticipating one another' should hold our attention the more, since Benedict seems to remember also the phrase which immediately precedes it in the sacred text: 'loving one another with the charity of brotherhood'.[40] Perhaps the pair honor-love, which opens the second part of Chapter 63, comes from there. In any case, the expression 'the charity of brotherhood' is found in Chapter 72, probably in dependence on this word of the Apostle, whose sequel is also represented.[41]

Benedict refers then chiefly to the primitive Church when he requires these marks of mutual respect and affection. The monastic community wishes to resemble the apostolic communities. The same model surely inspires, either directly or indirectly, the specific requirement to call each other 'brothers'. This monastic custom is the continuation or resurgence of a paleo-christian practice already well attested in the New Testament writings.[42] Actually, the New Testament does not indicate that the title brother preceded the name of each person addressed, as Benedict would have it.[43] This particular rule was not observed in the first monastic generations either,[44] it seems, but, as far as we know, first appeared with Benedict and his contemporary, Fulgentius.[45] At the end of the century Gregory seems to have been careful to conform to it, not only when he quoted monks speaking in his *Dialogues*, but also when he reported the conversations of clerics or pious laymen.[46] It seems then that the sixth century saw the development, in certain ecclesiastical circles, of an original effort to make this old christian title a true courtesy title normally preceding the proper name.

Even if Benedict and his epoch went somewhat beyond previous usage, it is indeed that usage which is perpetuated in the appellation 'brothers' given each other by the monks. From the Church of the first centuries come as well the two other signs indicated later: blessing one's neighbor,[47] and standing up when he passes.[48] Monasticism meant to collect and develop the fine testimonials of religious respect bequeathed it by the ancient Church.

This sense of respect, the dominant note of the present chapter, cannot but remind us of the 'fear of God' so strongly inculcated elsewhere by the Rule. The reverential attitude shown to the Lord, marks as well relationships with one's neighbor. In both cases the deep respect which the sacred person inspires is not opposed to love, but includes it.

By a series of complementary touches[49] scattered throughout chapters 64–71, Benedict leads his reader to the summit formed by the little treatise 'On Good Zeal'. In it is found not only the 'reciprocal honors' of chapter 63, but also the 'love for the abbot' of the second abbatial directory, and the 'mutual obedience' just treated.[50] More remotely, 'good zeal' recalls several of the instruments of good works.[51] With its eight maxims leading to eternal life, it is like a second list of good works, nine times shorter than the first. Its conciseness is matched by a far greater homogeneity than that of the great catalogue of chapter 4. This time the reader is not obliged to search for some thread to guide him through the disparate recommendations. The unity of theme is evident. From one end to the other, good zeal concerns the relations of the brothers among themselves and with their abbot, in a fervent love of God and Christ. This second 'spiritual art' is purely monastic, indeed conventual. Its maxims are no longer phrased in the singular, but in the plural; and 'all together' the monks hope, in return, to be introduced by Christ into eternity.

But the unity of this admirable section does not result from its dealing with mutual relationships alone. These take on a common character, that of charity. *Amor* and *caritas* each occur twice, and *diligere* is also added so that—unlike chapter 63—the vocabulary of love clearly here predominates over that of honor and fear. Moreover, several maxims which do not speak expressly of charity describe attitudes whose relationship with this virtue is clear: what are patience, obedience,[52] seeking another's good, preference for Christ, if not love?

Thus this little chapter picks up again that 'On the Order of the Community' and corrects it. Taking up where the other left off,[53] it advances further in the direction of love. Reverence and love still mingle, but the latter decidedly predominates. This triumph of charity at the end of the Rule makes us think of the finale of the great treatise on humility. As the ladder of humility rose from fear to love, so the last chapters of the Rule, starting from the order of the community and the rules of courtesy implied therein, rise to a general view of fraternal relations in which loving is almost the only activity. In each case charity is discovered at the end of the ascent, resulting from a pedagogy and crowning an order.

What is more, the chapter 'On good zeal' passes over in silence the specifications which limited the reciprocity of honors and obedience. Largely for the first, and entirely for the second, this had, in fact, been a matter of unilateral obligations, incumbent only on juniors.[54] The precise details given on this subject by chapters 63 and 71 are now missing. Apparently, honors and obedience are now 'mutual', without restriction. Surely the preceding legislation is not abrogated for all that, but the omission of the restrictive clauses is nonetheless a significant fact, suggesting a transcendence. If order and its laws exist, charity tends to surpass them. No precedence resists its demands.

Thus is completed the regulation of the mutual relationships whose first features appeared a dozen chapters earlier. It began with the establishment of an order. Then relations between the brothers were settled according to this order. Finally, these relations blossom, at least ideally, into a limitless charity which no longer recognizes an order. The initial organization exists, but the atmosphere enveloping it has been totally spiritualized.

At the end of this dialectic, the situation of the monastery makes us think of that of the Church evoked by Paul. 'Good zeal', like baptism, mystically effaces the degrees of a hierarchy which continues to set persons visibly apart. Cenobitism, starting from the pauline refusal of natural and social distinctions, claimed, in its first stage, to give this negation of the principle an effective execution. But it immediately substituted for the old distinctions its own, founded on the new criteria of profession and merit. And now, in their turn, these new distinctions disappear, not indeed in terms of an express affirmation declaring them outmoded, but in virtue of an indeterminate spiritual language which passes over them in silence. And this language is exactly that of Paul exhorting the Romans and Corinthians to fraternal charity, to mutual attention, and forgetfulness of self in securing another's interests.

Thus the inspiration of the New Testament tends a second time to blur distinctions of the established order. First it abrogated the effects of natural age and social rank, and now it surmounts those of monastic age and recognized merit. As the first distinction remained in effect in christian society and there defined reciprocal duties, so the second also continues to structure the monastic community and there determine mutual relations. But the importance of them both is made relative by a view of faith and a breath of love which transcends them.

Today the part of the Rule we have just studied has been greatly affected by the general shaking of institutions and manners. In many monasteries during these last few years community rank has vanished from some conventual gatherings. The titles 'Brother' and 'Father', the use of *Benedicite* before speaking, the gesture of standing up in the presence of seniors, the authority normally exercised by these latter—all this has often vanished or is tending to disappear.

This loss is not due solely to an egalitarian rejection of precedence and marks of respect, or to a spirit of simplicity and fraternity which makes fun of prestige, or to a youthfulness impatient of the yoke of old ways. It also springs from a tendency to secularization. Religious signs are no longer expressive, and monks are afraid that such signs will separate those who use them from the secular world. In order not to be shut into a ghetto, they will therefore do as everyone else does. The monks will use no other names or other signs than those used by their contemporaries in the world.

The disfavor into which rank has fallen nowadays might claim to go back to the pauline refusal of distinctions among Christians. But we cannot forget that for the Apostle this rejection remained in the mystical order, without destroying visible structures. These did crumble in monastic society, but were replaced with equivalents of a religious character. From its inception and almost constantly, cenobitism has used an organization based on rank. Benedict's wisdom was not to abolish it, as the Master invited him to do, but rather to surpass it, like Paul, with a current of faith and love. With him, charity flourishes within an order. It presupposes a right which is not voided by it, but transcended.

On the other hand, the refusal of traditional religious signs not only goes against the letter of the Rule, but is opposed to the very impulse which led monasticism to adopt the customs of the primitive Church, indeed to refine and develope the code of human relationships inherited from the Fathers. Without fearing the criticism of pagans, who were not slow to ridicule them on this point,[55] the first Christians resolutely called each other 'brothers'. This title expressed their conviction of being sons of God and brothers of Christ, and therefore in very truth one anothers' brothers. Their faith, and that of the monks after them, was supported by such signs. We can see here a permanent warning. Is a faith that does not express itself a living faith? The disappearance of the signs of faith risks entailing the disappearance of the faith itself.

The monks' fear of shutting themselves off in a closed society is scarcely more plausible. The courage to be oneself and different from other men was the salt of primitive Christianity. In the midst of a world that was theoretically christianized, monasticism was able to take this opprobrium upon itself.[56] We do not see how it could have rejected it without ceasing to exist.

What contemporary monasticism needs is to recover the meaning of ancient usages. The chief thing here is to restore the authentic form. The rule of *Benedicite* has too often been applied in exactly the wrong way.[57] The titles of 'father' and 'brother' have nothing to do with the division of communities into priests and non-priests, choir religious and laybrothers. With the disappearance of this distinction, each should call those who come after him 'brothers', and those who precede him 'fathers',[58] as the Rule enjoins.

Yet the application of these norms should be not only intelligent, but also spiritual. The names 'father' and 'brother' are appeals to charity. When this has been wounded, they should be understood as reproaches. What Benedict says to the abbot, is valid for everyone: the titles one takes are to be reflected on.[59] Such is indeed the pedagogy of monasticism. It goes from the outer to the inner, from practice to reflection, from observances to the spirit.

NOTES TO CHAPTER 21

1. See RB 60.4 and 6–8; 61.11–12; 62.5–6.
2. RB 63.1–9. Compare RM 92 and RB 64.2.
3. RB 63.10–19.
4. The vocabulary of charity (*amare* and *amor, caritas, diligere* and *dilectio* applied to persons) is remarkably frequent in RB 63–72. It occurs there fourteen times, as compared to twenty-two uses in the rest of the Rule.
5. See RB 72.
6. See *Le Communauté et l'Abbé*, pp. 438–503 (cf. pp. 367–87).
7. Philo, *De vita cont.* 67.
8. Augustine, *Praec.* 6.3 (*minoribus . . . subiectos*); Basil, *Reg.* 10 (*ordinem*) = *Long Rules* 21 (*taxin*).
9. Jerome, *Praef. ad Reg. Pach.* 3. Cf. Pachomius, *Praec.* 4 (*locum sedendi standique*); 20 (*sedentes sive stantes fratres suum ordinem non mutabunt iuxta domorum ordinem et hominum singulorum*); 59 (same expression; Greek: *kat' ordinon*); 49 (*in vescendi ordine*). We find *kata pordinon n̄n̄eï*, 'according to the order of the houses', in Horsiesius, *Règlements* (CSCO 159: p. 94,17 = CSCO 160: p. 94,13).
10. *Reg. IV Patrum* 2.10–15; *Reg. Patrum II* 17–21; *Reg. Orient.* 32; *Reg. Pauli et Stephani* 6.1–2 (cf. 22.2–4; 33.7, etc.).
11. RB 63.7–8 (*aetatis aut dignitatis*); Isidore, *Reg.* 4.3 (*nec aetas nec conditio*); Fructuosus, *Reg.* I. 23 (*generis dignitas . . . aetatis grandaevitas*). Ferrandus, *Vita Fulg.* 39, says simply: *tempus conversionis ordinemque.*
12. Gal 3:28. Cf. Rm 10:12 and Col 3:11. See also 1 Co 12:13.
13. RM 2.19 = RB 2.20 (beginning).

14. RM 2.19 = RB 2.20 (end). Allusion to Rm 2:11 (Jew and pagan); Eph 6:9 and Col 3:25 (master and slave); 1 Peter 1:17 (indefinite).

15. RB 63.6.

16. RB 63.8.

17. It is not even said that Jew and pagan keep nothing of their respective patrimonies.

18. See Eph 5:22–6:9; Col 3:18–4:1. Cf. 1 Peter 2:18–3:7 and 5:1–5 (this last passage, on the relations of *seniores* and *adolescentes*, makes us think of RB 63.10–19, but it really deals with the pastors of the Church, not simply with those advanced in years).

19. Augustine, *Praec.* 1.3–8 and 3.3–5; RB 34.1–5 and 55.20–22; Caesarius, *Reg. virg.* 21; *Reg. Tarn.* 14.3–19 and 16.3–14. Cf. Jerome, *Ep.* 108.20.

20. RB 63.9 and 18–19; 71.4. Cf. Fructuosus, *Reg.* II. 6.

21. James 2:1–9. Cf. 1 Co 11:21–22.

22. See *Ordo Rom.* I. 113 and 117 (the *senatorium* where one receives communion from the pope himself); 118 (the *partes mulierum*; cf. *Const. Apost.* 2.57). According to *Const. Apost.* 2.58 respect of persons was still avoided in the Church.

23. Still the date of baptism was not lost sight of by individuals. Cf. Gregory, *Dial.* 4.27 (268.4–15); *Sacram. Gelas.* I. 54.

24. Ferrandus, *Vita Fulg.* 60 (bishops); Gregory, *Dial.* 2.16 (clerics) and *Reg.* 2.38, p. 135, 14 (defenders). In this last case a *locus superior* is awarded by reason of merit.

25. In addition, the clerical state may advance a monk (RB 60.4 and 8).

26. RM 92.33, etc. The purpose was to stimulate rivalry.

27. RM 93.88, citing Rm 2:11 (cf. RM 2.19).

28. RB 21.5–7 and 65.18–20. The dismissal of deans is something new.

29. RB 63.6 (*praetulerit . . . degradaverit*). Cf. RB 2.18–19; 29.2

30. RB 63.2–3 (against promotions not based on merit).

31. RM 63.10. Cf. RB 4.70–71 (original maxims).

32. Eph 5:22–33; Col 3:18–19.

33. Eph 6:1–4; Col 3:20–21.

34. RB 63.17, citing Rm 12:10b. For a nuance of disrespect in the *purum nomen*: see Ferrandus, *Vita Fulg.* 53.

35. RB 63.13.

36. Rm 12:10b. However, the 'mutual submission' recommended by Eph 5:21 is followed by developments in which wives, children, and servants alone are invited to be submissive, while husbands, parents, and masters receive different recommendations. Does RM 12:10b deal with 'reciprocity' of this kind?

37. Cassian, *Conf.* 16.11.2; Augustine, *Praec.* 1.8; *Reg. Patrum II.* 4. All three refer previously to Ph 2:2 ('unanimity').

38. Lv 19:32 (*cano capite . . . senis*); Cyprian, *Test.* 3.85 (*senioris . . . presbyteri*).

39. Ex 20:12; Eph 6:1–2. See Augustine, *Praec.* 7.1; RB 63.12–13.

40. *Caritate fraternitatis invicem diligentes*, Rm 12:10a.

41. RB 72.4 (Rm 12:10b) and 8 (cf. Rm 12:10a, the more probable reference, given the preceding, than 1 Th 4:9; Heb 13:1; 1 Peter 1:22 where *caritas fraterna* occurs).

42. See H. Pétré, *Caritas* (Louvain, 1948) 103–40; L. Th. Lorié, *Spiritual Terminology in the Latin Translations of the Vita Antonii* (Nijmegen, 1955) 34–43; C. Mohrmann, *Etudes sur le Latin des chrétiens*, t. II (Rome, 1961) 335–6.

43. Christ says 'Lazarus' (Jn 11:43), 'Philip' (Jn 14:8), 'Simon' (Jn 21:15). In the rest of the New Testament, each one is usually designated by his name with no further addition. Cases such as *Sosthenes frater* (1 Co 1:1; cf. Ac 9:17 and 22:13; 2 Co 1:1) are exceptions.

44. When Pachomius, for example, addresses his disciple, he calls him simply 'Theodore',

whether in Coptic, Greek, or Latin. In Eugippius, *Vita Severini* 10 and 37, Severinus designates his monks by name with no further addition.

45. RB 63.11–12; Ferrandus, *Vita Fulgentii* 53. To tell the truth, Fulgentius does not seem to observe a rule, but to show singular condescension in not calling *puro nomine* any of the monks of whom he is the abbot.

46. Gregory, *Dial.* 1.10: *Frater Marcelle* (a bishop to a pious layman); 2.7: *Frater Maure* (Benedict, abbot, to one of his monks); 4.14: *Soror Benedicta* (one nun speaking to another). *Frater* alone, in the vocative case, is used not only when an abbot speaks to one of his monks (2.20), but also when a monk addresses a secular (1.3; 3.14; 4.40). See also Gregory, *Reg.* 2.38 (*fratre Cyriaco servo Dei . . . fratre autem Martiniano abbate*) and 3.3 (*frater Bonifatius*), but Gregory only exceptionally gives this title to monks in his correspondence. Barsanuphius and John regularly employ the titles *adelphos* and *abbas* before the monks' proper names.

47. According to Tertullian, *De testim. animae* 2.2 the formula *Benedicat te Deus*, current among pagans, was 'necessary' for Christians. The monks asked this benediction by saying *Benedicite* (RM 1.51, etc.) or *Benedic* (RM 27.8; RB 66.3), to which the other might be content to reply *Deus* (RM 13.46). See *La Règle du Maître*, t. I, p. 83 (E.T. pp. 35–6). Here as elsewhere (RB 53.24; 66.3) Benedict requires and refines the usage.

48. Cyprian, *Test.* 3.85. Similar custom in Ps.-Basil, *Serm. Ascet.* 8; PG 31:644a. New refinements occur in Benedict.

49. Besides the features noted below, cf. RB 66.4 (*cum omni mansuetudine timoris Dei . . . cum fervore caritatis*); 68.1–2 (*cum omni mansuetudine . . . patienter*) and 4 (*ex caritate*); 70.7 (golden rule).

50. RB 64.15 (*amari*); 71.1–4 (*omni caritate*). Cf. RB 72.6 and 10.

51. Compare RB 72.11 and 4.21; 72.4 and 4.70; 72.5 and 4.16,30. Cf. RB 72.6 and RM 3.76; RB 72.9 and RM 3.1.

52. Compare RB 72.6 and 71.4 (*omni caritate*).

53. RM 12:10b, cited by RB 63.17 and 72.4.

54. See *La Communauté et l'Abbé*, pp. 453–6.

55. See H. Pétré, *Caritas*, pp. 104 and 118.

56. Seculars made fun of the monks: see RM 24.20–21; 58.5; 95.21.

57. *Benedicite* should be said by the junior, *Deus* by the senior (above, n. 47).

58. On *nonni*, see *La Communauté et l'Abbé*, p. 443. On the apparent contradiction between the title 'father' and Mt 23:8–10, see *ibid.*, pp. 139–40 (E.T. p. 110).

59. RB 63.14.

Chapter XXII

A RECOMMENDATION OF THE RULE
(RB 73)

T HIS CONCLUSION is, as it should be, a glance back over the completed work, a reflexion on the Rule. Although without parallel in the Master, it makes us think of the end of Augustine's *Praeceptum*.[1] In the same way, Benedict presents the Rule as a whole and recommends observance of it. But while Augustine considers his directives without disfavor—he who observes them 'loves spiritual beauty, leads a good religious life, exhales the good odor of Christ'—, Benedict judges his with reservations, contrasting their 'initial', 'inchoative' character with the perfection and sublimity of the Fathers' writings.

That this humility in comparison to great ancestors is a commonplace in the sixth and seventh centuries[2] does not prevent Benedict from being sincere in expressing himself this way.[3] Moreover, it is quite simply true that his Rule does owe much to many ancient or recent authors—the Master, Cassian, and Augustine in particular—and it often does lack theoretical foundations and doctrinal clarifications which would give its precepts their full meaning. In addition—and this is what the author seems to have chiefly in mind—these prescriptions themselves are sometimes less demanding than the norms, real or ideal, of the preceding generations.

Benedict's modesty gives us a precious insight into the tradition to which he meant to belong. What strikes us most in this list of references is his deliberate Catholicism. In using this word, we think chiefly of the mention of the 'holy Catholic Fathers', with the notes of orthodoxy in faith, rectitude of conduct, and adherence to the unique and universal Church, which attach to this term.

But in addition, Benedict does not separate these 'Catholic Fathers' from the Fathers of the Desert and other monastic authors mentioned later. For him, monasticism is simply part of the Church of Christ. The legislators and heroes of the monastic life are members of the great senate of Fathers, and their teaching and examples are only the purest emanation of the spiritual teaching and life of the Church. Monasticism, connected by the patristic tradition to the 'divine authority' of Scripture, appears as a christian actuality without further qualification. For its self-realization, it needs 'the aid of Christ',[4] and that is the only help it invokes.

Thus Benedict formally points out in his epilogue the entire and exclusive attachment of monasticism to the christian tradition and to the Church which was already apparent when, in the light of the Master, we were studying the definition of the monastery at the end of the Prologue as 'the school of the Lord's service'. As we noted then, monastic life was not conceived by our authors as a universal religious phenomenon which received from the Gospel only some particular coloring, but purely and simply as a response to Christ's appeal. Now we see that this response was inspired only by the authorities of the divine Scripture and the Catholic tradition, without recourse to some secular method. And yet could not certain resources of ancient wisdom for the natural hygiene of the soul be compared to the resources offered in our day by Yoga and Zen?

These riches of secular culture are not, for all that, alien to monasticism, for its Fathers, as well as the Catholic Fathers, assumed an important part of them because they listened to the appeal of Christ in the men of their world and of their times.[5] But this assumption was a real assimilation of human values by a life of powerful faith.

If the monastic tradition was catholic in this sense, by joining to Christ the best of the secular heritage, it was so as well in virtue of its openness to different, sometimes opposing, currents, which witness as to its capacity for assimilation and to its vitality. In the same breath Benedict mentions the works of Cassian and Basil's *Rule*, whose opinions on eremitism are scarcely compatible, and his esteen for Cassian's *Conferences*, affirmed here and elsewhere,[6] does not prevent him from following Augustine in his doctrine of grace as well as in his presentation of the common life.

This admission of divergences, even on points which cannot be called secondary, remains, however, very far from the pluralism which has prevailed within the benedictine family in recent times. The different perspectives of which we have spoken converge on a kind of common life defined by a group of observances which are vigorous and undisputed. Fasts and vigils, separation from the world and silence, manual work and poverty, *lectio divina* prolonged by continual meditation on the Bible and frequent prayer—all that, and the rest, forms a well-defined *conversatio* in which one can point out, as Benedict in fact does point out, a beginning, progress, and perfection.[7] This specific program has nothing to do with a pluralism in which a residue of rites and a vague reference to the Rule covers every kind of activity and nonchalance.

Against such a mess, Benedict proposes in this epilogue the effective observance of his *regula*, with a view to approaching the fullness of the traditional doctrine and virtues. That this Rule is not in fact, and cannot be, exactly ours[8] does not prevent the appeal to observe it from being addressed to us as well. As the historical source of our concrete rules, the Benedictine Rule remains our ideal rule, the supreme norm which judges our behavior, orients our generosity, and calls forth our efforts. Its role in our regard is like the one which Benedict assigned, for the improvement of his own readers, to the Fathers' writings. Tending constantly to put it into practice, respecting what we have kept of it, seeking prudently to recover the rest: such fidelity, both generous and intelligent, constitutes our best chance of remaining or becoming monks.

By its means we shall approach not only the Fathers' teaching, but the Gospel. The rule was the 'abridgement of all the teaching of the Gospel'[9] for the monks of the sixth century, and it remains that for those whom God destines by nature and by grace to live according to the particular obedience to his word that constitutes monasticism. Benedict does not claim to lead his disciples to any 'summits' other than the Old and New Testament. And a monastic *regula*, something made by man, is not inappropriate to lead him there. For man, alone or in society, needs a rule, and the Gospel is not a rule, but the good news of the salvation wrought by God in Christ. Between this inexhaustible declaration and the transitory existence of those who hear it, there is room for a rule which tries to form a concrete humanity, here and now, according to the eternal requirements of the divine word.

Or to express it better while remaining closer to its original figure, the *regula* is the rigid and rectilinear support around which supplely entwines a Life which mounts upward.

NOTES TO CHAPTER 22

1. To Augustine's *Praec.* 8.1 (prayer for the 'observance of all that' by a good *conversatio*) and 2 (to read the Rule each week) corresponds, in inverse order, RB 66.8 (frequent reading of the Rule in community) and 73.1-2 (to observe it in order to show a beginning of *conversatio*). These passages probably followed each other originally (see t. IV, pp. 95-6).

2. See t. IV, pp. 103-106.

3. See t. IV, pp. 107-108 and 116-118 (cf. t. I, pp. 39-44).

4. RB 73.8-9.

5. On the Pythagorean sources of the ideal of 'spiritual beauty' proposed by Augustine, *Praec.* 8.1, see L. Verheijen, 'Éléments d'un commentaire de la Règle de saint Augustin', in *Augustiniana*, 22 (1972) 469-510. Cassian, to take another example, owes much to the philosophical tradition, especially through the channel of Evagrius and Origen.

6. RB 42.3 and 5.

7. Compare RB 73.1-2 (*initium . . . perfectionem*) and *Prol.* 49 (*processu*).

8. See our article '*Sub regula vel abbate*' in Coll. Cist. 33 (1971), pp. 209-41, especially p. 234-235 (E.T. in *Rule and Life*, ed. B. Pennington, [Spencer, Mass., 1971], p. 21-63, especially p. 53-5).

9. According to the word of Bossuet. See our article '*Per ducatum evangelii*', in *Coll. Cist.*, 35 (1973) 186-98, especially 186-7.

ADDENDUM

The union of the abbacy and priesthood[1] appears as a quasi-universal fact in the East according to the Acts of the Council of Constantinople in 536.[2] Of the more than sixty superiors of monasteries who signed it, only a certain Joseph calls himself simply *higumenos*;[3] he also signed 'by the hand of the priest Stephen, my assistant'. All the others are 'priest and archimandrite' or 'priest and *higumenos*'. It would obviously be imprudent to draw conclusions relative to Italy from this information on Constantinople and the East. At that very moment, however, Italy was entering into closer and closer relations with the East because of the byzantine reconquest. In the following century Anglo-Saxon monasticism, one of whose sources was roman, had numerous priest-abbots, according to the historical works of Bede.

NOTES TO ADDENDUM

1. See above, Chapter 20, nn. 31 ff.
2. Labbe, t. V:130–42 = Mansi, t. VIII: 985–96.
3. Labbe, p. 133; Mansi, p. 992.

ABBREVIATIONS
JOURNALS AND SOURCE COLLECTIONS

ASOSB	*Acta Sanctorum Ordinis Sancti Benedicti*, ed. Malsillon.
BM	*Benediktinische Monatschrift*. Beuron (also see EA).
CC	*Corpus Christianorum*. Steenbrugge.
Coll. Cist.	*Collectanea Cisterciensia*. Scourmont.
CS	*Cistercian Studies Series*. Kalamazoo.
CSCO	*Corpus Scriptorum Christianorum Orientalium*. Louvain-Washington.
CSEL	*Corpus Scriptorum Ecclesiasticorum Latinorum*. Vienna.
DACL	*Dictionnaire d'Archéologie Chrétienne et de Liturgie*. Paris.
EA	*Erbe und Auftrag*. Beuron (continuation of BM).
GCS	*Die griechischen christlichen Schriftsteller der ersten Jahrhunderte*. Leipzig.
IQS	The Manual of Discipline: The Rule of Qumran, *The Dead Sea Scrolls*. New Haven.
LQF	*Liturgiewissenschaftliche Quellen und Forschungen*. Münster.
MGH	*Monumenta Germaniae Historica*. Berlin.
NRT	*Nouvelle Revue Théologique*. Louvain.
OCA	*Orientalia Christiana Analecta*. Rome.
OCP	*Orientalia Christiana Periodica*. Rome.
PG	J.P. Migne, *Patrologia, Series Graeca*. Paris.
PL	J.P. Migne, *Patrologia, Series Latina*. Paris.
PLS	A. Hamman, *Patrologia, Series Latina, Supplementum*. Paris.
PO	*Patrologia Orientalis*. Paris.
Patr. Syr.	*Patrologia Syriaca*. Paris.
RAM	*Revue d'Ascétique et de Mystique*. Toulouse-Paris (also see RHS).

RBS	*Regulae Benedicti Studia. Annuarium Internationale.* Hildesheim.
REA	*Revue des Etudes Augustiniennes.* Paris.
Rev. Bén.	*Revue Bénédictine.* Maredsous.
RHE	*Revue d'Histoire Ecclésiastique.* Louvain.
RHS	*Revue d'Histoire de la Spiritualité.* Paris (continuation of RAM).
RSR	*Recherches de Science Religieuse.* Paris.
SC	*Sources Chrétiennes.* Paris.
SM	*Studia Monastica.* Montserrat.
SMGBO	*Studien und Mitteilungen zur Geschichte des Benediktiner-Ordens und seiner Zweige.* Munich-Ottobeuren.
TU	*Texte und Untersuchungen zur Geschichte der altchristlichen Literatur.* Berlin.
VS	*La Vie Spirituelle.* Paris.
VSS	*La Vie Spirituelle, Supplément.* Paris.

ABBREVIATIONS OF WORKS CITED AND SOURCES

General abbreviations

can.	*canon(es)*
ep.	*episotla(e)*
hom.	*homilia(e)*
serm.	*sermo(nes)*

WORKS BY AUTHOR/TITLE

Ambrose
In Luc. — Expositio evangelii secundum Lucam (*In Lucam*), ed. G. Tissot, SCh 45bis, 52 (1971, 1958); ed. H. Adriaen, CC 14; CSEL 32/4 (1902)

Aphraates
Dem. — Demonstrationes, Patrologia Syriaca 1 (Paris, 1894)

Apophthegmata patrum — PG 65 (E.T. *The Sayings of the Desert Fathers*, tr. Benedicta Ward; CS 59 [1975])

Aristeas
Letter to Philocrates — Lettre d'Aristée à Philocrate, ed. A. Pelletier, SCh 89 (1962)

Athanasius
De virg. — De virginitate, PG 28, ed. E. von der Goltz, Texte und Untersuchungen, 29 (Leipzig, 1905)

Augustine
De haer. — De haeresibus, PL 42, CC 46
De mor. eccl. — De moribus ecclesiae catholicae, PL 32
De op. mon. — De opere monachorum, PL 40, CSEL 41
De ord. — De ordine, PL 32, CC 29, CSEL 63
Enarr. in Ps. — Enarrationes in Psalmos, PL 36–7, CC 38–40
Ordo monasterii — La Règle de saint Augustin, ed. L. Verheijen, I (Paris, 1967) 148–52
Praec. — Praeceptum, Ibid., pp. 417–37

Aurelian (see *Regulae*)

Basil (see also, *Regulae*)
Hom.	*Homiliae de jejunio*, PG 31
In mart. Iul.	*In martyrem Iulittam*, PG 31
In Ps.	*In Psalmos*, PG 29
Mor.	*Moralia*, PG 31

Caesarius of Arles (see also, *Regulae*)
Serm.	*Sermones*, ed. G. Morin, CC 103–104 (1953), ed. M.J. Delage, SCh 175, 243, (1971, 1978)

Callinicos
Vita Hyp.	*Vita Hypatii*, ed. G.J.H. Bartelink, SCh 177 (1971)

Clement
Paedag.	*Paedagogus*, GCS 1, PG 8, edd. H.I. Marrou & M. Harl, SCh 70, 158 (1960, 1970)
Strom.	*Stromata*, GCS 2, PG 8, edd. C. Mondésert & M. Caster, SCh 30 (1951), 38 (1954)

Columban (see *Regulae*)

Const. Apost.	*Constitutiones Apostolicae*, PG 1, ed. F.X. Funk, *Didascalia et Constitutiones apostolorum* (Paderborn, 1905)

Cyprian
De dom. or.	*De dominica oratione*, PL 4, CSEL 3
De habitu virg.	*De habitu virginum*, PL 4, CSEL 3
De lapsis	*De lapsis*, PL 4, CSEL 3
De unit.	*De catholicae ecclesiae unitate*, PL 4, CSEL 3

Cyril of Scythopolis
Vita Abraam.	*Vita Abraamii*, ed. E. Schwartz, *Kyrillos von Skythopolis*, Texte und Untersuchungen, 49/2 (Leipzig, 1939)
V. Cyr.	*Vita Cyriaci*, ibid.
V. Euth.	*Vita Euthymii*, ibid.
V. Joh.	*Vita Johannis hesychastae*, ibid.
V. Sab.	*Vita Sabae*, ibid.
V. Theod.	*Vita Theodosii*, ibid.
V. Theog.	*Vita Theognii*, ibid.

Diadochus of Photike
    Cap.   *Cent chapitres gnostiques*, ed. E. des Places, SCh 5ter
                    (1966)
Didache   *Didache*, ed. F.X. Funk, *Patres Apostolici*, I
                    (Tübingen, 1907), W. Rordorf & A. Tuilier, SCh
                    248 (1978)

Donatus (see *Regulae*)

Dorotheos of Gaza
    Inst.   *Instructiones*, ed. L. Regnault & J. de Préville, SCh
                    92 (1963) (E.T. *Dorotheos of Gaza, Discourses and*
                    Sayings; CS 33)

Etheria
    Pereg.   *Peregrinatio*, CC 175; ed. H. Pétré, SCh 21 (1971)

Eugippius
    V. Sev.   *Vita Severini*, ed. H. Sauppe, MGH AA 1/2 (1877),
                    ed. R. Noll (Berlin, 1963)

Eusebius Gallicanus
    Hom.   *Homiliae*, CC 101, 101A, 101B

Evagrius Ponticus
    Pract.   *Praktikos*, edd. A.& C. Guillaumont, SCh 170–171
                    (1971) (E.T. *Evagrius Ponticus: Praktikos and*
                    Chapters on Prayer, CS 4)

Ferrandus
    Vita Fulg.   *Vita Fulgentii*, PL 65

Ferreolus (see *Regulae*)

Gregory the Great
    Dial.   *Dialogi*, edd. A. de Vogüé & P. Antin, SCh 251,
                    260, 265 (1978, 1979, 1980); ed. U. Morrica
                    Gregorii Magni Dialogi (Rome, 1924)
    Hom. Ev.   *Homiliae in Evangelium*, PL 76

| *Mor.* | *Moralia in Job*, PL 75–6, ed. R. Gillet & A. de Gaudemaris, SCh 32 bis (1975), A. Bocognano, SCh 212 (1974), 221 (1975), ed. M. Adriaen, CC 143, 143A |
| *Reg.* | *Registrum, MGH Epp.* I–II |

Gregory of of Tours
Lib. de glor.
  conf.   *Liber de gloria confessorum*, PL 71

Hippolytus of Rome
Trad. apost.   *Traditio apostolica*, ed. B. Botte, *Liturgiewissenschaftliche Quellen und Forschungen*, (Münster, 1966), (E.T. *The Apostolic Tradition*, tr. Gregory Dix [London, 1937])

Historia monachorum
Hist. mon.   *Historia monachorum in Aegypto*, Rufinus' Latin translation = PL 21 (E.T. *The Lives of the Desert Fathers*, tr. Norman Russell, CS 34 [1982])

Horsiesios
Liber   *Liber Orsiesii*, ed. A. Boon, *Pacomiana Latina* (Louvain, 1932) (E.T. in *Pachomian Koinonia*, III, tr. Armand Veilleux, CS 47 [1982])

Isaias
Log.   *Logoi (Asceticon)*, ed. R. Draguet, CSCO 293–94

Isidore of Seville
De eccl. off.   *De ecclesiastico officiis*, PL 83

Jerome
Adv. Iovin.   *Adversus Iouinianum*, PL 23
De obed.   *De obedientia*, CC 78
Ep.   *Epistolae*, CSEL 54–56, 58, PL 22
Vita Pauli   *Vita Pauli*, PL 23

John Cassian
Conf.   *Conferences (Conorlationes)*, ed. M. Petschenig, CSEL 13 (1886), ed. E. Pichery, SCh 42, 54, 64 (1966, 1971)
Inst.   *Institutes: De institutis cœnobiorum*, ed. M. Petschenig, CSEL 17 (1888); *Institutions cénobitiques*, ed. J.C. Guy, SCh 109 (1965)

John Chrysostom
  Hom.   *Homiliae*, PG 57–63
  Hom. Incompr. *Homiliae de Incomprehensibili*, SCh 28 bis
  Serm. de Anna *Sermones de Anna*, PG 53

John Damascene
  De haer.   *De haeresibus*, PG 94

Josephus
  Antiq. Jud.   *Antiquitates Judaicae*, ed. G. Dindorf (Paris, 1845)

Liber (see Horsiesios)
Macarius
  Hom.   *Homiliae*, PG 34, ed. H. Dörries, E. Klostermann,
                   M. Kroeger, (Berlin, 1964) (E.T. A.J. Mason,
                   [London, 1921])

Nicetas
  De psalm. bono *De psalmodiae bono*, PLS 3

Ordo monasterii (see Augustine)

Origen
  Contra Cels.   *Contra Celsum*, GCS 1–2, PG 11, ed. M. Borret,
                   SCh 132, 136, 147, 150 (1967–1969)
  De orat.   *De oratione*, GCS 2, PG 11
  In Gen. Hom.   *In Genesim homiliae*, PG 12, GCS 6, ed. H. de
                   Lubac & L. Doutreleau, SCh 7bis (1976)
  In Matt.   *In Matthaeum commentarii*, GCS 10, ed. R. Girod,
                   SCh 162 (1970)
  In Num.   *In Numeros homiliae*, PG 12, ed. J. Méhat, SCh 29
  In I. Reg.,   *In Librum I Regum homiliae*, PG 12, GCS 3
    Hom.
  In Ps.   *In Psalmos commentarii*, PG 12

Pachomius
  Praec.   *Praecepta*, ed. Boon, *Pachomiana Latina* (E.T.
                   Pachomian Koinonia, II, CS 46 [1981])

Palladius
  Hist. Laus. *Historia Lausiaca*, ed. G.J.M. Bartelink (Milan, 1974), C. Butler, Cambridge Texts and Studies, 6 (1888, 1904) (E.T. W.L.K. Clarke [London, 1918], R.T. Meyer, ACW 34 [1965])

Pelagius
  Ep. ad Celant. *Epistola ad Celantiam*, PL 22
  Ep. ad Demetr. *Epistola ad Demetriadem*, PL 30

Philo Judaeus
  De vita cont. *De vita contemplativa*, ed. F. Daumas & P. Miquel (Lyon, 1964)

Philoxenus of Mabbug,
  Letter to ed. R. Lavenant, *Patrologia Orientalis* 30
  Patricius

Regulae (Monastic Rules)
  Aurelian, *Regula ad monachos*, PL 68, ed. A. Schmidt, *Studia*
    Reg. mon. *Monastica*, 18 (1975) 237–56
  Basil
    Reg. *Regula* = Rufinus' Latin translation, PL 103
    Long Rules *Regulae fusius tractatae*, PG 31
    Short Rules *Regulae brevius tractatae*, PG 31
  Caesarius, *Regula Caesarii ad virgines*, ed. G. Morin, *Sancti*
    Reg. virg. *Caesarii Arelatensis Opera Omnia*, 2 (1942)
  Columban, *Regula Columbani coenobialis*, ed. G.S.M. Walker,
    Reg. coen. *Sancti Columbani Opera* (Dublin, 1957)
    Reg. mon. *Regula Columbani monachorum*, ibid.
  Eugippius, *Reg.* *Regula Eugippii*, edd. F. Villegas & A. de Vogüé, CSEL 87
  Ferreolus, *Reg.* *Regula Ferreoli*, PL 66
  Fructuosus, *Reg.* *Regula Fructuosi*, PL 87
  Isidore, *Reg.* *Regula Isidori*, PL 83
  RB *Regula Sancti Benedicti*, edd. A. de Vogüé & J. Neufville, SCh 181–182 (1972), ed. R. Hanslik, CSEL 75 (1977)
  RM *Regula Magistri*, ed. A. de Vogüé, SCh 105–107 (1964–1965) E.T. *The Rule of the Master*, CS 6 (1977).

Reg. cuiusdam Patris	*Regula cuiusdam Patris*, PL 66, ed. F. Villegas, *Revue d'Histoire de la Spiritualité*, 49 (1973) 3–35, 135–144.
Reg. Mac.	*Regula Macarii*, PL 103, PG 34, ed. H. Styblo, *Wiener Studien*, 76 (1963) 124–258
Reg. 'Largiente Domino'	ed. A. Amelli, *Annales Ordinis S. Benedicti*, 5 (1912) 169–193
Reg. Orient.	*Regula Orientalis*, PL 50, PL 103, PG 34, ed. A. de Vogüé, *Benedictina*, 13 (1976) 241–71 (E.T. in C.V. Franklin, I. Havener, J.A. Francis, *Early Monastic Rules* [Collegeville, 1982] 61–85)
Reg. IV Patrum	*Regula Serapionis, Macarii, Paphnutii, et alterius Macarii*, PL 103, PG 34, ed. J. Neufville, *Revue Bénédictine*, 77 (1967) 72–91 (E.T. *Early Monastic Rules*, 16–31)
Reg. Patr. II	*Regula Patrum Secunda*, PG 34, PL 103, ed. Neufville, *Revue Bénédictine* 77: 92–95 (E.T. *Early Monastic Rules*, 32–39)
Reg. Patr. III	*Regula Patrum Tertia*, PG 34, PL 103, (E.T. *Early Monastic Rules*, 52–59)
Reg. Pauli et Stephani	PL 66, ed. J. Vilanova, Scripta et Documenta, 11 (Montserrat, 1959)
Reg. Tarn.	*Regula Tarnatensis*, PL 66, ed. F. Villegas, *Revue Bénédictine*, 84 (1974) 7–65
Waldebert, *Reg.*	*Regula Waldeberti*, PL 88

Sulpicius Severus
    Dial.   *Dialogi*, PL 20, CSEL 1

Tertullian
    Ad uxor.   *Ad uxorem*, PL 1, CSEL 70, CC 1
    De orat.   *De oratione*, PL 1, CSEL 20, CC1
    De testim. animae   *De testimonio animae*, PL 1, CSEL 20, CC 1

Theodore of Petra
    V. Theod.   *Vita Theodosii Coenobiarchae*, ed. H. Usener, *Der heilige Theodosios* (Leipzig, 1890)

Theodoret
    Hist. Rel.   *Historia Religiosa*, PG 82, ed. P. Canivet & A. Leroy-Molinghen, SCh 234, 257 (1977, 1979)

VP	*Vitae Patrum*, PL 73
Vita Abraham	Anonymous, *Vita Abraham* PL 73
Vita Alexandri	Anonymous, *Vita Alexandri*, PO 6
Vita Patr. Jur.	*Vita Patrum Jurensium*, ed. F. Martine, SCh 142 (1968)
Vita Theod. Syk.	*Vita Theodori Sykeonis*, ed. A.J. Festugière, Subsidia Hagiographica, 48 (2 volumes) (Brussels, 1970) (E.T. *Three Byzantine Saints*, tr. Elizabeth Dawes and N.H. Baynes, 1948, 1977)
Vita Sequani	Anonymous, *Vita Sequani*, ed. Mabrillou, *ASOSB* I

Waldebert (see *Regulae*)

Psalms have been cited according to the Vulgate enumeration.

BIBLIOGRAPHY

For a complete bibliography on the Rule, see the 'Bibliographie Internationale de la Regula Benedicti', edited by B. Jaspert, in *RBS* 2 (1973) ff. Following are titles quoted in abridged form in this volume.

Achery, L. d', et Mabillon, J., *Acta Sanctorum Ordinis S. Benedicti*, I–IX. Paris, 1668–1701.

Audet, J.P., *La Didachè, Instructions des Apôtres*. Paris, 1958 (*Études Bibliques*).

Blaise, A., *Dictionnaire Latin-Français des auteurs chrétiens*. Strasbourg, 1954.

Bruns, Th., *Canones Apostolorum et Conciliorum*, t, II. Berlin, 1839.

Burrows, M., ed. *The Dead Sea Scrolls*. The Manual of Discipline: The Rule of Qumran, Vol II/2. New Haven: Yale, 1951.

La Communauté et l'Abbé: see Vogüé.

Évergétinos: see Paulos Euergètinos.

I. Hausherr, *Penthos. La doctrine de la componction dans l'Orient chrétien*, Rome 1944 (*OCA* 132).

_____ . E.T. *Penthos. The Doctrine of Compunction in the Christian East*. Kalamazoo, 1982.

_____ . *Noms du Christ et voies d'oraison*, Rome 1960 (*OCA* 157).

_____ . E.T. *The Name of Jesus*. Kalamazoo, 1978.

_____ . 'La prière perpétuelle du chrétien', dans *Laïcat et sainteté*. II. *Sainteté et vie dans le siècle*. Rome, 1965, p. 111–116.

_____ . *Hésychasme et prière*, (*OCA* 176). Rome, 1966.

R.J. Hesbert, *Corpus Antiphonalium Officii*, t. I–111, (*Rerum Ecclesiasticarum Documenta, Series Major*, Fontes, VII–IX). Rome, 1963–1968.

G. Holzherr, *Regula Ferioli. Ein Beitrag zur Entstehungsgeschichte und zur Sinndeutung der Benediktinerregel*. Einsiedeln, 1961.

Ph. Labbe and G. Cossart, *Sacrosancta Concilia ad regiam editionem exacta*, t. I–XVIII. Paris, 1671–1672.

L. Lèbe, *S. Basile, Les Règles monastiques*. Maredsous, 1969.

L. Th. Lefort, *Les Vies coptes de S. Pachôme et de ses premiers successeurs, Traduction française*, (*Bibliothèque du Muséon* 16). Louvain, 1943. [The *Lives* of Saint Pachomius have been translated into English by Armand Veilleux and published in *Pachomian Koinonia I*, (Cistercian Publications, 1980)].

Mabillon, J., *ASOSB*: see Achery.

Mohrmann, C., 'La langue de S. Benoît', in *Études sur le Latin des chrétiens*, t. II. Rome, 1961, pp. 325–45.

Euergètinos Paulos, *Sunagôgè tôn theophtoggôn rhèmatôn . . . tôn . . . hagiôn paterôn*, tt. I–IV. Athens, 1957–1966.

Pétré, H., *Caritas. Étude sur le vocabulaire latin de la charité chrétienne*, (*Spicilegium Sacrum Lovaniense* 22). Louvain, 1948.

La Règle du Maître (*RM*): see Vogüé.

La Règle de saint Benoît (*RB*): see Vogüé.

O. du Roy, *Moines aujourd'hui. Une expérience de réforme institutionnelle*. Paris, 1972.

F. Ruppert, *Das pachomianische Mönchtum und die Anfänge klösterlichen Gehorsams*, (*Münsterschwarzacher Studien* 20). Münsterschwarzach 1971.

Les Vies coptes de S. Pachôme: see Lefort.

A. Veilleux, *La Liturgie dans le cénobitisme pachômien au quatrième siècle*, (*Studia Anselmiana* 57). Rome, 1968.

——————— . 'La théologie de l'abbatiat et ses implications liturgiques', *VSS*, 86, (Sept. 1968), 351–93.

L. Verheijen, *La Règle de saint Augustin*, II. *Recherches historiques*. Paris, 1967.

——————— . 'Éléments d'un commentaire de la Règle de saint Augustin. VI. Par les *praecepta uiuendi* à la *spiritalis pulchritudo*. 'Pythagore', le *De ordine* de saint Augustin et sa Règle', *Augustiniana*, 22 (1972) 469–510.

A. de Vogüé, 'Le monastère, Église du Christ', *Commentationesin Regulam S. Benedicti*, (*Studia Anselmiana* 42), éd. B. Steidle. Rome, 1957, pp. 25–46.

——————— . *La Communauté et l'Abbé dans la Règle de saint Benoît*, (*Textes et Études théologiques*). Paris: Desclée De Brouwer, 1961.

——————— . *E.T. Community and Abbot in the Rule of St Benedict*, Charles Philippi, translator, Cistercian Studies Series: Number Five/One and/Two. Cistercian Publications, Kalamazoo, Michigan: 1979, 1983.

——————— . *La Règle du Maître*, t. 1–11, (*SCh* 105–106). [E.T. by Luke Eberle, *The Rule of The Master* (Cistercian Publications, 1977)]. Paris, 1964.

——————— . 'Le sens de l'office divin d'après la Règle de saint Benoît. I. Prière continuelle et prière des heures (*RB* 16)', *RAM*, 42 (1966) 389–404; II. 'Psalmodie et oraison (*RB* 19–20)', *RAM*, 43 (1967) 21–34.

_____ . 'Scholies sur la Règle du Maître', *RAM*, 44 (1968) 121–160 et 261–92.

_____ . '*Sub regula uel abbate*. Étude sur la signification théologique des règles monastiques anciennes', *Coll. Cist.*, 33 (1971) 209–41. E.T. '*Sub regula uel abbate*' in *Rule and Life. An Interdisciplinary Symposium*, M. Basil Pennington, ed., Cistercian Publications, Spencer, Massachusetts, 1971, pp. 21–63.

_____ . *La Règle de saint Benoît*, t. I–II, Introduction, texte, traduction, notes, concordance (in collaboration with J. Neufville), (SCh 181–82); Paris, 1972; t. IV–VI, Commentaire historique et critique, (SCh 184–86). Paris, 1971.

_____ . 'Les pièces latines du dossier pachômien. Remarques sur quelques publications récentes', *RHE*, 67 (1972) 26–67.

_____ . '*Per ducatum euangelii*. La Règle de saint Benoît et l'Évangile' *Coll. Cist.* 35 (1973) 186–98.

ANALYTICAL TABLE

INDEXES

I. SCRIPTURAL INDEX

The numbers refer to the pages of the Commentary. The exponent numbers are those of the notes at the back of each chapter.

II. INDEX OF ANCIENT AUTHORS
AND OF TEXT COLLECTIONS

347

III. INDEX OF PROPER NAMES

The sign IA designates the Index of Ancient Authors and of Text Collections.

IV. INDEX OF THE TWO RULES

1. CITATIONS OF THE RULE OF THE MASTER

When a chapter or a passage of RM is the object of a thorough commentary, we indicate the pages where this commentary is found, without giving the detail of the verses. Numbers in boldface type indicate the most important of these formal commentaries.

2. Citations of the Rule of Saint Benedict

Where Benedict reproduces the Master without notable variant, we have given only the reference to RM (see index 1) without furnishing the reference to RB here.

V. THEMATIC INDEX

1. Modern Terms

Abbot	19-20, 21, 23, 46-47, 48-50, 52,
See also: *Teacher, Hierarchy*	56, 59-60, 65-76, 210-211, 215,
	218-221, 293-295, 302, 305, 307,
	311
Aggiornamento	4-6, 148-149, 162-163, 176-178,
	185-186, 204-205, 235-236,
	247-248, 255, 277-278, 296,
	309-311, 317
Almsgiving	80, 204-205, 222, 240, 245 [41]
Angelism	234-235
Antiphony	145, 147, 148
Apostolate	265
Apostolic (life)	276
See also: Church, primitive	
Ascesis, bodily	83, 229-236, 241, 269-270
See also: Fasting	
Baptism	10-19, 37, 187, 284-285, 302-305,
	309
Buddhist Monasticism	
See Pagan	
Canons	132-134
Catholicism	315-316
Cell	181-182
Cellarer	198-200, 202-204
See also: Diaconate	
Charity	23, 31, 32, 34, 84-87, 106, 115,
See also: Love of God, Love of Neighbor	118, 119, 121-124, 255, 262-263,
	301, 308-309
Chastity	
See Sexuality	
Church	3, 19, 60, 70, 95-100, 103-105,
	134, 202, 276, 291-292, 293,
	295-296, 309, 316
Church, contemporary	5-6, 229-230, 282
Church, primitive	53, 203, 221-223, 304, 307
Clergy	27 [73], 137, 304
See also: Priesthood	
Commandments of God	31, 34, 77, 80, 84-87
See Holy Scripture, Gospel, Law	

2. Latin and Greek Terms

Only the words and expressions commented on are listed. Greek terms are preceded by an asterisk.

CISTERCIAN TEXTS

Bernard of Clairvaux

- Apologia to Abbot William
- Five Books on Consideration: Advice to a Pope
- Homilies in Praise of the Blessed Virgin Mary
- Letters of Bernard of Clairvaux / by B.S. James
- Life and Death of Saint Malachy the Irishman
- Love without Measure: Extracts from the Writings of St Bernard / by Paul Dimier
- On Grace and Free Choice
- On Loving God / Analysis by Emero Stiegman
- Parables and Sentences
- Sermons for the Summer Season
- Sermons on Conversion
- Sermons on the Song of Songs I–IV
- The Steps of Humility and Pride

William of Saint Thierry

- The Enigma of Faith
- Exposition on the Epistle to the Romans
- Exposition on the Song of Songs
- The Golden Epistle
- The Mirror of Faith
- The Nature and Dignity of Love
- On Contemplating God: Prayer & Meditations

Aelred of Rievaulx

- Dialogue on the Soul
- Liturgical Sermons, I
- The Mirror of Charity
- Spiritual Friendship
- Treatises I: On Jesus at the Age of Twelve, Rule for a Recluse, The Pastoral Prayer
- Walter Daniel: The Life of Aelred of Rievaulx

John of Ford

- Sermons on the Final Verses of the Songs of Songs I–VII

Gilbert of Hoyland

- Sermons on the Songs of Songs I–III
- Treatises, Sermons and Epistles

Other Early Cistercian Writers

- Adam of Perseigne, Letters of
- Alan of Lille: The Art of Preaching
- Amadeus of Lausanne: Homilies in Praise of Blessed Mary
- Baldwin of Ford: Spiritual Tractates I–II
- Geoffrey of Auxerre: On the Apocalypse
- Gertrud the Great: Spiritual Exercises
- Gertrud the Great: The Herald of God's Loving-Kindness (Books 1, 2)
- Gertrud the Great: The Herald of God's Loving-Kindness (Book 3)
- Guerric of Igny: Liturgical Sermons Vol. I & 2
- Helinand of Froidmont: Verses on Death
- Idung of Prüfening: Cistercians and Cluniacs: The Case for Cîteaux
- Isaac of Stella: Sermons on the Christian Year, I–[II]
- The Life of Beatrice of Nazareth
- The School of Love. An Anthology of Early Cistercian Texts
- Serlo of Wilton & Serlo of Savigny: Seven Unpublished Works
- Stephen of Lexington: Letters from Ireland
- Stephen of Sawley: Treatises

MONASTIC TEXTS

Eastern Monastic Tradition

- Besa: The Life of Shenoute
- Cyril of Scythopolis: Lives of the Monks of Palestine
- Dorotheos of Gaza: Discourses and Sayings
- Evagrius Ponticus: Praktikos and Chapters on Prayer
- Handmaids of the Lord: Lives of Holy Women in Late Antiquity & the Early Middle Ages / by Joan Petersen
- Harlots of the Desert / by Benedicta Ward
- John Moschos: The Spiritual Meadow
- Lives of the Desert Fathers
- Lives of Simeon Stylites / by Robert Doran
- Mena of Nikiou: Isaac of Alexandra & St Macrobius
- The Monastic Rule of Iosif Volotsky (Revised Edition) / by David Goldfrank
- Pachomian Koinonia I–III (Armand Veilleux)
- Paphnutius: Histories/Monks of Upper Egypt
- The Sayings of the Desert Fathers / by Benedicta Ward
- The Spiritually Beneficial Tales of Paul, Bishop of Monembasia / by John Wortley
- Symeon the New Theologian: The Theological and Practical Treatises & The Three Theological Discourses / by Paul McGuckin
- Theodoret of Cyrrhus: A History of the Monks of Syria
- The Syriac Fathers on Prayer and the Spiritual Life / by Sebastian Brock

Western Monastic Tradition

- Anselm of Canterbury: Letters I–III / by Walter Fröhlich
- Bede: Commentary…Acts of the Apostles

- Bede: Commentary…Seven Catholic Epistles
- Bede: Homilies on the Gospels I–II
- Bede: Excerpts from the Works of Saint Augustine on the Letters of the Blessed Apostle Paul
- The Celtic Monk / by U. Ó Maidín
- Life of the Jura Fathers
- Peter of Celle: Selected Works
- Letters of Rancé I–II
- Rule of the Master
- Rule of Saint Augustine

Christian Spirituality

- The Cloud of Witnesses: The Development of Christian Doctrine / by David N. Bell
- The Call of Wild Geese / by Matthew Kelty
- The Cistercian Way / by André Louf
- The Contemplative Path
- Drinking From the Hidden Fountain / by Thomas Spidlík
- Eros and Allegory: Medieval Exegesis of the Song of Songs / by Denys Turner
- Fathers Talking / by Aelred Squire
- Friendship and Community / by Brian McGuire
- Gregory the Great: Forty Gospel Homilies
- High King of Heaven / by Benedicta Word
- The Hermitage Within / by a Monk
- Life of St Mary Magdalene and of Her Sister St Martha / by David Mycoff
- A Life Pleasing to God / by Augustine Holmes
- The Luminous Eye / by Sebastian Brock
- Many Mansions / by David N. Bell
- Mercy in Weakness / by André Louf
- The Name of Jesus / by Irénée Hausherr
- No Moment Too Small / by Norvene Vest
- Penthos: The Doctrine of Compunction in the Christian East / by Irénée Hausherr
- Praying the Word / by Enzo Bianchi
- Rancé and the Trappist Legacy / by A. J. Krailsheimer
- Russian Mystics / by Sergius Bolshakoff
- Sermons in a Monastery / by Matthew Kelty
- Silent Herald of Unity: The Life of Maria Gabrielle Sagheddu / by Martha Driscoll
- Spiritual Direction in the Early Christian East / by Irénée Hausherr
- The Spirituality of the Christian East / by Thomas Spidlík
- The Spirituality of the Medieval West / by André Vauchez
- The Spiritual World of Isaac the Syrian / by Hilarion Alfeyev
- Tuning In To Grace / by André Louf
- Wholly Animals: A Book of Beastly Tales / by David N. Bell

MONASTIC STUDIES

- Community and Abbot in the Rule of St Benedict I–II / by Adalbert de Vogüé
- The Finances of the Cistercian Order in the Fourteenth Century / by Peter King
- Fountains Abbey and Its Benefactors / by Joan Wardrop
- The Hermit Monks of Grandmont / by Carole A. Hutchison
- In the Unity of the Holy Spirit / by Sighard Kleiner
- A Life Pleasing to God: Saint Basil's Monastic Rules / By Augustine Holmes
- The Joy of Learning & the Love of God: Essays in Honor of Jean Leclercq
- Monastic Odyssey / by Marie Kervingant
- Monastic Practices / by Charles Cummings
- The Occupation of Celtic Sites in Ireland / by Geraldine Carville
- Reading St Benedict / by Adalbert de Vogüé
- Rule of St Benedict: A Doctrinal and Spiritual Commentary / by Adalbert de Vogüé
- The Rule of St Benedict / by Br. Pinocchio
- The Spiritual World of Isaac the Syrian / by Hilarion Alfeyev
- St Hugh of Lincoln / by David H. Farmer
- The Venerable Bede / by Benedicta Ward
- Western Monasticism / by Peter King
- What Nuns Read / by David N. Bell
- With Greater Liberty: A Short History of Christian Monasticism & Religious Orders / by Karl Frank

CISTERCIAN STUDIES

- Aelred of Rievaulx: A Study / by Aelred Squire
- Athirst for God: Spiritual Desire in Bernard of Clairvaux's Sermons on the Song of Songs / by Michael Casey
- Beatrice of Nazareth in Her Context / by Roger De Ganck
- Bernard of Clairvaux: Man, Monk, Mystic / by Michael Casey [tapes and readings]
- Bernardus Magister...Nonacentenary
- Catalogue of Manuscripts in the Obrecht Collection of the Institute of Cistercian Studies / by Anna Kirkwood
- Christ the Way: The Christology of Guerric of Igny / by John Morson
- The Cistercians in Denmark / by Brian McGuire
- The Cistercians in Scandinavia / by James Fran
- A Difficult Saint / by Brian McGuire

- A Gathering of Friends: Learning & Spirituality in John of Ford / by Costello and Holdsworth
- Image and Likeness: Augustinian Spirituality of William of St Thierry / by David Bell
- Index of Authors & Works in Cistercian Libraries in Great Britain 1 / by David Bell
- Index of Cistercian Authors and Works in Medieval Library Catalogues in Great Britian / by David Bell
- The Mystical Theology of St Bernard / by Étienne Gilson
- The New Monastery: Texts & Studies on the Earliest Cistercians
- Nicolas Cotheret's Annals of Cîteaux / by Louis J. Lekai
- Pater Bernhardus: Martin Luther and Saint Bernard / by Franz Posset
- Pathway of Peace / by Charles Dumont
- A Second Look at Saint Bernard / by Jean Leclercq
- The Spiritual Teachings of St Bernard of Clairvaux / by John R. Sommerfeldt
- Studies in Medieval Cistercian History
- Studiosorum Speculum / by Louis J. Lekai
- Three Founders of Cîteaux / by Jean-Baptiste Van Damme
- Towards Unification with God (Beatrice of Nazareth in Her Context, 2)
- William, Abbot of St Thierry
- Women and St Bernard of Clairvaux / by Jean Leclercq

MEDIEVAL RELIGIOUS WOMEN

- Medieval Religious Women/edited by Lillian Thomas Shank and John A. Nichols
- Distant Echoes
- Hidden Springs: Cistercian Monastic Women (2 volumes)
- Peace Weavers

CARTHUSIAN TRADITION

- The Call of Silent Love / by A Carthusian
- The Freedom of Obedience / by A Carthusian
- From Advent to Pentecost / by A Carthusian
- Guigo II: The Ladder of Monks & Twelve Meditations / by E. Colledge & J. Walsh
- Halfway to Heaven / by R.B. Lockhart
- Interior Prayer / by A Carthusian
- Meditations of Guigo II / by A. Gordon Mursall
- The Prayer of Love and Silence / by A Carthusian
- Poor, Therefore Rich / by A Carthusian
- They Speak by Silences / by A Carthusian
- The Way of Silent Love (A Carthusian Miscellany)

- Where Silence is Praise / by A Carthusian
- The Wound of Love (A Carthusian Miscellany)

CISTERCIAN ART, ARCHITECTURE & MUSIC

- Cistercian Abbeys of Britain
- Cistercians in Medieval Art / by James France
- Studies in Medieval Art and Architecture / edited by Meredith Parsons Lillich (Volumes II–V are now available)
- Stones Laid Before the Lord / by Anselme Dimier
- Treasures Old and New: Nine Centuries of Cistercian Music (compact disc and cassette)

THOMAS MERTON

- The Climate of Monastic Prayer / by T. Merton
- Legacy of Thomas Merton / by P. Hart
- Message of Thomas Merton / by P. Hart
- Monastic Journey of Thomas Merton / by P. Hart
- Thomas Merton/Monk / by P. Hart
- Thomas Merton on St Bernard
- Toward an Integrated Humanity / edited by M. Basil Pennington

CISTERCIAN LITURGICAL DOCUMENTS SERIES

- Cistercian Liturgical Documents Series / edited by Chrysogonus Waddell, ocso
- Hymn Collection of the…Paraclete
- Institutiones nostrae: The Paraclete Statutes
- Molesme Summer-Season Breviary (4 vol.)
- Old French Ordinary & Breviary of the Abbey of the Paraclete (2 volumes)
- Twelfth-century Cistercian Hymnal (2 vol.)
- The Twelfth-century Cistercian Psalter
- Two Early Cistercian Libelli Missarum

STUDIA PATRISTICA

- Studia Patristica XVIII, Volumes 1, 2 and 3

Editorial Offices & Customer Service

- Cistercian Publications
  WMU Station, 1903 West Michigan Avenue
  Kalamazoo, Michigan 49008-5415   USA

  Telephone 616 387 8920
  Fax   616 387 8390
  e-mail   cistpub@wmich.edu

Canada

- Novalis
  49 Front Street East, Second Floor
  Toronto, Ontario M5E 1B3   CANADA

  Telephone 1 800 204 4140
  Fax   416 363 9409

U.K.

- Cistercian Publications UK
  Mount Saint Bernard Abbey
  Coalville, Leicestershire LE67 5UL   UK

- UK Customer Service & Book Orders
  Cistercian Publications
  97 Loughborough Road
  Thringstone, Coalville
  Leicestershire LE67 8LQ   UK

  Telephone 01530 45 27 24
  Fax   01530 45 02 10
  e-mail   MsbcistP@aol.com

Website & Warehouse

- www.spencerabbey.org/cistpub

- Book Returns (prior permission)
  Cistercian Publications
  Saint Joseph's Abbey
  167 North Spencer Road
  Spencer, Massachusetts 01562-1233   USA

  Telephone 508 885 8730
  Fax   508 885 4687
  e-mail   cistpub@spencerabbey.org

Trade Accounts & Credit Applications

- Cistercian Publications / Accounting
  6219 West Kistler Road
  Ludington, Michigan 49431   USA

  Fax   231 843 8919

Cistercian Publications is a non-profit corporation. Its publishing program is restricted to monastic texts in translation and books on the monastic tradition.
A complete catalogue of texts in translation and studies on early, medieval, and modern monasticism is available, free of charge, from any of the addresses above.